# UNSUNG DAVIDS:

## Ten Men Who Battled Goliath Without Glory

*To Barrackaid #1*

By
Ben Barrack

Cover Art by Osmar Schindler

ISBN: 978-0982567999

1st Edition

Printed in the United States

# TABLE OF CONTENTS

## Chapter Five

# ACKNOWLEDGMENTS

If anyone tells you that writing a book is a sacrifice, believe them! That sacrifice is made more by those closest to the writer than by the writer himself. The patient understanding of a family, who tolerates the perceived inanity of such an endeavor as it is unfolding, is beyond explanation. In that regard, I am blessed far more than most and far more than I deserve.

In September of 2010, when I first sat down to write this book, I had no idea how long it was going to take or in what form it would actually manifest itself. One year later, I completed writing but the work was nowhere near complete. If there is one thing I learned first-hand in writing my first book, it's that writing one is only half the battle. It takes a special talent to take it to the next level. Keith Davies of Walid Shoebat's organization has that talent in spades. At every turn, he was out in front, doing the work I didn't even know how to ask for. If not for him, this book wouldn't be in your hands right now.

As part of Keith's effort, he put my work in the hands of a woman who is beyond capable and goes far beyond the extra mile. Cheryl Taylor is a conscientious maven when it comes to detail. If you find a mistake in the ensuing pages, it is offset by the countless others she corrected. Even if you find one or two, she's still nearly super-human. The tirelessness and diligence with which she works is unmatched.

There is a former Marine whose efforts I'd like to acknowledge but he doesn't want me to. I begrudgingly honor his request out of respect for his wishes and for his humility. Perhaps you'll learn more about him as a result of his insistence that I not recognize him.

Jerry McGlothlin of Special Guests, Inc. most definitely deserves to be acknowledged. Special Guests has been on the cutting edge when it comes to representing strong conservative guests who are seeking to get on the air to communicate their message. McGlothlin has done an untold amount of good that far too many will never know. In fact,

Special Guests is responsible for making one of the Unsung Davids in this book, known to this author – David Conn.

In October of 2005, I met with the afternoon drive host on *KIXL* 970, Jim Wagner in Austin. Thanks to an e-mail I sent to a woman named Dorothy Erminger – who then forwarded it to Wagner – he agreed to meet with me at a Seattle's Best coffee shop in downtown Austin on Lamar Blvd. During the course of our conversation, he invited me to co-host his show with him the following day. It was a welcome surprise. I did so and he made a point of telling his producer to pull an air-check for me so I could use it to approach Program Directors. Ultimately, that air check is what got my foot in the door with *KTEM* 1400 in Temple, TX. I have little doubt that if the opening at *KTEM* hadn't happened, I'd still be working for the company I left in 2007 and this book wouldn't have been written.

As for the radio business, it's not often that a seasoned, professional talk show host is syndicated while broadcasting from a place like Temple, TX. Fortunately for me, Lynn Woolley is just such a guy. To say his career is storied would be an understatement. If you engage him in a discussion about radio history in Texas, you'll assuredly get an education. Perhaps most amazing is the effortlessness with which Lynn is able to do three hours of talk radio five days a week with virtually no time to prep while having other obligations as soon as the show is over. A true professional, Lynn can show up an hour or two before he goes on the air and give three hours of hard-hitting conservative talk five days a week. He's as good as there is or ever was. He also brought me on as executive producer of the Lynn Woolley show in January of 2009. His willingness to mentor – and turnover the microphone to a novice on occasion – has not gone unnoticed. When it comes to the broadcasting business, Lynn is the quintessential professional.

Thanks go to Mike Kasper of the *Able Danger* blog. He took a significant amount of his time to critique and contribute to Chapter 9. He did so willingly. I very much appreciate his help in making that chapter better.

Thanks to Marshall Jennings for manning the controls every Sunday morning.

Growing up, I could not have asked for better parents or brothers. We were a nuclear family. My respect and admiration for them continues to grow. Eventually, we all moved on but each of us took that idea with us and has applied it as best we could within our own families.

There is an old saying that behind every successful man is a woman. The degree to which I'm successful is up for debate but I will unequivocally state that there is a phenomenal woman behind me. A better wife and mother of my children I could not have found. Before I grew up, there was Mom. As I continue to grow up, there is my wife.

Without either, this book would not have been written.

# FOREWORD

There was once a time when many people had become cynical. Some, on the occasion of passing a mugging in progress, opted to look the other way and perhaps walk a little swifter. The operative phrase of the day was: "I didn't want to get involved."

How sad for our country when bad people do bad things. But how much sadder is it when good people know what bad people are doing – and yet choose to do nothing – not to "get involved." But what if it's more than just a simple mugging? What if there are crooked politicians, terrorists, cults, political parties, movements – yes, even the world!— that cry out to be exposed? What if nobody stepped up to the plate?

Here are ten instances where somebody did. In each case, one person, far less powerful than his adversary, stood up to power. He got involved.

What he didn't get was any type of tangible support. Not from the people around him, not from the "authorities," and certainly not from the Mainstream Media. These are people who fought the odds with little more than a slingshot while the powerful sat on their hands.

Their stories deserve to be told.

And that's where Ben Barrack comes in. If there's one thing I have learned about Ben in the few years I've known him and worked with him it's this: When Barrack makes up his mind that that's he's going to get something accomplished, stay out of his way. Because he will do it, and he will do it well.

Ben comes out of a former career in operations with a Fortune 500 company, having been inspired by events around him to do something – to make a difference. He managed to snag a lonely hour on Sunday morning on a radio station in a medium market. The audience numbers may have been meager, but Ben used the weekly show to hone his skills. Soon, he had a website and not long after that, he was writing columns that were strong enough to get carried on prominent websites. How did he do that?

I was impressed enough that I sought Ben out when I needed a producer for my own show, which runs weekdays on a few radio stations in Texas. He leapt into the job, savoring the daily routine of talk radio, trolling for breaking stories to put our show on the map, and becoming an accomplished guest host.

Did I say "our" show? I did, and it was no accident. No matter whether it's a slow news day or a day with more in the stack than I can possibly get to – Barrack will often find hidden jewels that are more interesting, more entertaining, and often more important than what I was about to cover. I've learned to turn on a dime.

Most of the men covered in this book – the "Davids," – have been discussed at some length or interviewed on our show. Sometimes I've said, "Barrack! We can't do another segment on this story." And Ben will invariably say, "But Lynn, this is huge. There's new information here that our audience needs to know."

So I complain (as hosts do to their producers) and go with it. And after the interview, I say to Barrack, "That wasn't bad. That was OK." Translation: that was one heck of a segment, but I'm not going to admit it!

So let me admit something now! A few months ago, Barrack told me he was writing this book and I was skeptical. Oh, I knew he could do it. But having written four books myself (plus one unpublished novel), I know what the commitment is. When you're writing a book, you give up your nights and your weekends. You do the research, you check facts, you plan the chapters, you write and you rewrite. It's not for the wishy-washy.

So when Barrack plopped the manuscript on my desk, I can't say that I was really surprised. And when I read it, enjoying it not only for the vast array of information he provides, but also for the excellence of style in which it is written – I decided not to be surprised anymore.

Just like the Davids in this book, Ben Barrack is not afraid to get involved. If this isn't the best book Ben will ever write, then I can't wait to see the next one. I know it will be good and I know it will be about something important.

Lynn Woolley
Radio Talk Show Host
August 27, 2011

# INTRODUCTION

The chapters in this book appear in an order completely different from the order in which they were written. Initially, it was anticipated the sequence wouldn't matter; each chapter was to be about a different man with a different battle against a different 'Goliath.' In essence, the plan was to write each chapter in no particular order and assemble the book into ten smaller books. Then something unexpected happened.

As I compiled the stories of ten separate men who had completely separate life experiences, I discovered that they shared much more in common than I had previously believed or imagined. In all cases the characteristics and tactics shared by their opponents were so eerily similar that they helped to comprise a single beast each of these men attempted to fight.

For example, the enemy Richard Landes identified and fought in chapter two is 'Pallywood.' It's a term used to describe techniques used by people who play for the cameras and the media in an effort to use victimhood to gain political sympathy when their actions are more deserving of handcuffs. In at least two other chapters, the heroes in this book had to deal with the same phenomenon. I therefore decided to put those chapters in a consecutive order. This is but one example and such instances are too numerous to chronicle in the introduction. In some cases, even though there were strong similarities found in the opponents of two separate men, I was not able to put those chapters in consecutive order because similarities elsewhere were stronger; you'll just have to read for yourself.

Whenever you see a certain chapter referenced inside one set of brackets [See Chapter X], it means that there is a similarity found to be so incredibly obvious in another chapter that it was too significant to ignore. In many ways, these similarities served to build much stronger cases against the opponents of the men featured in this book because two men who don't even know each other corroborate one another's story. Each chapter also concludes with its own "Battle Assessment" of the fight waged by that chapter's "Unsung David."

In the Bible, a shepherd boy named David slew Goliath. Though he gave all the glory to God for Goliath's defeat, he was still recognized for his achievement by his countrymen. He became King David and continued to give glory to God through song.

This book makes no attempt to elevate the ten men it features to such a level. Rather, it is intended to recognize them as men who were grossly overmatched in their battles with ominous and wicked opponents. In virtually each case, victory would have been all but assured if only others would have joined the fight. In the cases where victory is not as obvious as it could be, that did not happen. The reasons were always found to be similar.

While each man in this book was, to varying degrees, victorious against evil, each continues to remain unsung as of this writing.

In either 2003 or 2004, on my daily commute into Austin, I was listening to a re-broadcast of a radio interview between talk show host Mike Gallagher and the author of a book entitled *Tea with Terrorists* (TwT), Craig Winn. As I navigated my 1996 Isuzu Hombre – equipped with a 5-speed manual transmission – slowly through the start and stop traffic of I35, what I heard left enough of an impression on me to make a mental note to get the book one day. I don't remember much of what intrigued me about the interview but I finally read TwT in the spring of 2005; little did I know at the time that doing so would play a significant role in altering the course of my life.

When I finally decided to crack open TwT, I was admittedly disappointed when I learned that it was a novel, though it did consist of one chapter that was non-fiction. It didn't take long for me to become an even bigger proponent of the proverbial phrase, 'never judge a book by its cover' – in quite the literal sense.

While the book was a work of fiction, it was based on a possible course of American history after the September 11th attacks. Published in 2003, TwT portrayed a future in which the US war in Iraq would

become a quagmire that led to George W. Bush's electoral defeat in 2004 to a female candidate modeled after Hillary Clinton, who was clearly the one being depicted as the successor to Bush.

In TwT, the Hillary Clinton presidency was an unmitigated disaster. The United States suffered multiple Islamic terrorist attacks and the female president was portrayed as a power hungry political animal whose incompetence and inability to confront the truth led to the deaths of hundreds of thousands of Americans unnecessarily. The protagonist was a highly decorated military veteran who succeeded Clinton and was taught the power of Scripture by a woman who would eventually become his wife.

The novel did something else too; it caused me to re-examine my own Christian faith. Upon doing so, that faith was greatly strengthened and continues to be.

While I had always leaned politically conservative, I never really got into the weeds of political analysis or discourse. That also changed in the summer of 2005, as I began to read as much as I could about politics, Islam, and the importance of western civilization's support for Israel. With a great deal of naiveté about how the business of radio worked, I decided I wanted my own talk show. Who doesn't, right?

After contacting several program directors at different stations within driving distance, one left a door slightly open at KTEM in Temple, TX. With persistence, follow-up, and a lucky break courtesy of Program Director, Jamie Garrett, I had my first one hour radio show – every Sunday morning from 7am – 8am.

Prior to Barack Obama announcing his intention to run for president in early 2007, Hillary Clinton was widely viewed as the presumptive Democratic nominee in 2008 – and likely the president based on Bush's declining popularity, a fiscally irresponsible Republican congress, and a de-energized base.

I'd never followed the details of Hillary's trials, tribulations, or scandalous career but I was absolutely not a fan based on what I knew. In early 2007, the prospect of her becoming president of the United States – especially after reading TwT – troubled me more than a little bit. A novel would serve as the catalyst for my heightened interest in a very complicated lawsuit that involved the former first lady and a man named Peter Paul [See Chapter 1].

This book is about the fights of ten men who all shared something in common – dauntingly superior opponents who viewed them as threats. Each of the men in this book fought his Goliath valiantly and with varying degrees of success but one thing is certain. Each man delivered devastating blows; some continue to do so; others can declare outright victory. All have earned the respect, if not admiration, of their opponents.

Each one of these men has contributed greatly to the furtherance of justice and the defeat of various forms of corruption, power, injustice, and outright evil. They have each done so while operating in relative obscurity.

In doing the research necessary for this book, I have corresponded with all but two of these men – J.D. Cash and Roberto Micheletti.

# CHAPTER I

## PETER PAUL
### vs.
# HILLARY CLINTON

### ■ COOL HAND PAUL

Stories of heroes and villains, whether real or imagined, are always supposed to end with good defeating evil. Fights for justice are often protracted; victory is often elusive. Other times, victory is snatched from the jaws of defeat just when observers have given up hope, even when participants have not. At times, a superior force in battle moves on after believing its opponent has been sufficiently quarantined, defeated, or otherwise dealt with. A persistent will can itself serve as a weapon that can help the inferior force emerge victorious as long as there is no time limit. Other times, the hero is paradoxically victorious in defeat.

In the film *Cool Hand Luke* that starred Paul Newman, the hero dies in the end while smiling as the car he's in runs over the dark sunglasses that moments earlier hid the villain's eyes all could now see. As the result of ill-advised dealings with the Clintons, Peter Paul got close enough to remove the sunglasses from the faces of those whose only allegiance is to power and corruption. What is a valid penance for such a man? Should he be punished further with unjust punishment for damaging the powerful who attempted to keep him down? Does he not do a service for others by telling his story and carrying on the fight?

Those inclined to dismiss Paul's claims because he ingratiated himself to the Clintons in the first place missed a larger point; Paul had the goods on the Clintons. When the powerful are exposed, they use lies, deceit, and smears against those who expose them. Paul was no exception; the character assassination carried out against him only served to bolster his case.

Paul has done wrong; he does not deny that. It's a reality that almost singlehandedly puts him on ground much higher than that occupied by his opponents, whose smear merchants were hard at work, projecting their master's malevolent nature onto the opposition, thereby creating noise that was difficult to filter. As those villainous opponents continued to marginalize him, Paul just continued firing back with pinpoint accuracy in the form of evidence no one could deny. Unfortunately, it was evidence few wanted to acknowledge because of Paul's past. That past was exploited by apparatchiks within the Clinton machine.

The story of Peter Paul is not for those with faint hearts who want to believe justice is always served. It is, however, for those with a diehard belief that the truth always wins out when it is fought for until the bitter end.

## ■ PERSPECTIVE

It was on the dark night of July 4, 2007 when I looked out the window of the plane as it descended into Pittsburgh; I was struck by something I had never seen before – fireworks from above. In multiple spots – too many to count – the earth gave forth small, colorful eruptions that seemed to communicate why American ground was so precious.

The sight from above took me back to a scene from the film *Apollo 13* in which an astronaut was able to put his entire view of earth behind his own thumb. On balance, my experience paled in comparison but I felt that I could relate at some level, albeit at a significantly less significant one – I was putting my view of fireworks from below behind *my* thumb while seeing them from a completely new perspective.

The view during the descent took on an added sense of irony; only hours earlier I had spoken with someone on-air who should have had national media outlets beating a path to his door. Instead, they chose the path of least resistance. As a talk show host on KTEM 1400 in Temple, TX I had the opportunity to interview a man by the name of

Peter Paul. His story was beyond fascinating and his connection to the Clintons – as well as to a plethora of Hollywood celebrities – was indisputable. What he revealed to me and anyone who was listening that day was jaw-dropping. Personally, it was my first, firsthand look behind the curtain of a federal government that was home to leaders so corrupt that the sheer notion of justice was nothing more than an idea to be derided by far too many who had taken an oath to guarantee it [See Chapters 8 and 9].

In the 2006 movie *300*, the film's narrator used the phrase, "a heightened sense of things," to describe increased awareness. In hindsight, I can relate to that sentiment as well. On that July 4th morning, I pulled up to the KTEM studio with a friend of mine who accompanied me. Upon entering the building, he made an observation we both found humorous at the time.

For a few weeks prior, the back door that provided access to the studio had been making entry difficult. It had a combination code above the handle and although the correct combination disengaged the lock, the handle would not disengage the locking pin from the strike plate. The result was often a fight with the door.

Upon arriving just prior to 6am, my friend and I noticed a post-it note on the outside of the door that said, "Do not lock this door." Upon entering, we closed the door behind us – though not all the way, out of respect for the post-it note instructions – he noticed a sign on the inside of the door that had been posted for much longer. It said: "This Door Must Remain Locked at All Times."

The contradiction was a source of humor but the paradox reminded me of a couple Bible verses (Isaiah 22:22 and Revelation 3:7-8) at the time. The verses were about opening doors no one shall shut and shutting doors no one shall open. As a brand new talk show host, running into this kind of story and talking with the guy at the center of it definitely gave me a "heightened sense of things."

## ■ INTRODUCTION TO PETER PAUL

Prior to April of 2007, I had seen random headlines about a convicted felon named Peter Paul, a man who claimed to have been double crossed by the Clintons and could prove it. My attempts to read about the case were short-circuited by its complexity, coupled with the prospect of rooting for someone who had been a little too friendly with the Clintons.

However, the latter premise, which was likely shared by many who decided to take a pass on the story, did not allow for two very important factors – contrition and the truth. Beginning in 2001, Paul would be relegated to spending each waking moment of his life trying to clear his name despite having mountains of evidence that backed him up. Justice would be denied over and over as his case would remain virtually ignored by leaders of institutions and agencies whose duty it was to expose the details of Paul's charges to sunlight [See **Chapters 4, 8, and 9**].

An excerpt of a video tape was released on the internet on April 25, 2007. Billed as the 'Smoking Gun' video that purportedly caught Hillary Clinton in the commission of multiple felonies, the recording was from July of 2000 and greatly simplified a key aspect of the case for the public. Seen in the video is Stan Lee of Marvel Comics fame, who was part of a phone conversation that included Hillary on the other end – she can be heard on the speaker thanking Lee and Paul for helping with a Hollywood gala that was being sponsored by Paul.[1]

At the time, Hillary was a Senatorial candidate in the state of New York. The gala was ostensibly intended to be both a star-studded farewell to Bill Clinton, who was closing out his second term as President, and a fundraiser designed to help his wife get elected to the US Senate.

This time, the story truly caught my attention. I grew increasingly optimistic that as this case moved along Hillary would certainly have to answer for crimes caught on video. It was not just about Peter Paul. This was about justice being served to an Alinsky-inspired Democrat[2] with a severely checkered past who had her eye on the presidency – and had for some time.

A subsequent article about this video was published a short time later. In it, the entire five minutes of video from Paul's end of the phone conversation was made available to the public.[3] It showed that Hillary was directly involved in the coordination of the event. The charge was

that by coordinating an event that cost Paul over $1 million to under-write, Hillary's campaign effectively received a $1 million political contribution from Paul.

The story carried added significance because Paul had filed a civil fraud lawsuit against Hillary and her husband in response to how he had been treated by the former first couple.

I found myself growing increasingly outraged that this story had not been picked up by the mainstream media. Hillary Clinton had been caught on video ostensibly violating Federal Election Law (FEC) statutes and the media seemed disinterested.

I remember contacting as many people as I could to help draw attention to the story. Among them was the office of my US Congressman, John Carter (R) who is considered to be one of the more conservative Republicans in the House. After speaking with the director and informing him of the story, I received a call back later from Carter's Round Rock, TX office saying that they would not be able to do anything because they were a "government office."

Upon reaching the *K-EYE* news desk in Austin, TX (*CBS* affiliate) a woman there told me to "contact the FBI" after I explained that Hillary Clinton had been caught on tape in the possible commission of multiple felonies.

An Editor at the *Austin American Statesman* gave me a response that left me incredulous. I was told that such a story "would have to be run through our Washington Bureau." It provided yet another example of why newspapers all across the country had been losing readers in droves. The notion that newspaper editors would grant such power to an entity so far away from said newspaper but so close to the establishment in need of the most accountability was breathtaking to consider.

At one point, I contacted the Washington, D.C., the New York City, and the Los Angeles offices of the *Associated Press*. The D.C. office told me to send an email to a woman who had demonstrated a liberal bias on more than one occasion.[4] The New York office hadn't heard of the lawsuit and said the LA office should be contacted since that was where the suit was filed. Upon doing so, I was put in touch with someone named "Peter." He was unaware of the lawsuit and said no record of the case existed in the *LA Times* archives.

When I first emailed Paul to ask him for a radio interview, I was surprised to get a response within one hour; we scheduled the July 4th interview and after hanging up, I remember wondering why he was so available. Shouldn't he have been busy pushing big media tin, fending off interview requests from much larger venues? It was a lesson that would be learned and reinforced for several months. It seemed inexplicable at the time but could it be that the truth itself was too controversial for those charged with exposing it (the media) to do so? Had the media establishment been so thoroughly corrupted as to ignore a scandal so unbelievably huge? This was the quintessential example of a story that constituted journalism's bread and butter. Yet, the institution of journalism itself seemed more interested in nurturing its own attrition, unwilling to even make an attempt to reach for the breadbasket or a butter knife [**See Chapter 5**].

I was soon contacted by Doug Cogan, a prolific blogger on the *Free Republic* website at the time. Known as "Doug from Upland," Cogan had been following Paul's case for a couple of years and was assisting the small team that was putting the finishing touches on a documentary entitled, *Hillary Uncensored: Banned by the Media*. The nearly fourteen minute trailer ultimately became an internet sensation and garnered over 10 million views when factoring in *Google*, *YouTube*, *Live Leak*, and other video streaming sites.[5]

## ■ PAUL REACHES OUT TO BILL

In 1998, Peter Paul and Spider-Man creator Stan Lee started a company together called Stan Lee Media, Inc. (SLM) after Lee had been fired by Marvel. Paul was a man of many connections in both the world of politics and entertainment. Calling on that experience, he was able to reach out to Bill Clinton through an intermediary. The goal was to hire President Clinton as a rainmaker for (SLM) once he left office. The complicated web was in the beginning stages of being woven.

At some point thereafter, the Clinton camp must have realized that Paul's connections could work to their benefit as well. Bill Clinton friend

and former owner of a Chicago strip club, Jim Levin came up with the idea of getting Paul to put on a Hollywood gala for both Hillary and Bill in return for Bill's promise to work for SLM. Levin was Bill's intermediary with Paul.[6]

Paul agreed and Hillary Clinton spokesperson Kelly Craighead became involved as well, acting as the on-the-ground liaison between Hillary and Paul; Hillary also refers to Craighead on the 'smoking gun' video as the person to be communicated with by Paul's people.

A deal had been reached. Bill Clinton would honor his commitment to work for SLM in return for Paul's money along with his Hollywood connections – required to put on a gala/fundraiser for Hillary's senate campaign. This would have made Bill an agent for Hillary and as liable for the violation of Federal Election laws as his wife. The date for the gala was set and it would take place on August 12, 2000. It was barely five weeks after Levin had been established as Bill's liaison with Paul.

By all accounts, the gala exceeded expectations. Among the performers were Whoopi Goldberg, Toni Braxton, Cher, Sugar Ray, and Paul Anka. Attendees included John Travolta, Nicholas Cage, Brad Pitt, and Jennifer Aniston; in 2000, it was Hollywood's A-list. Though Paul had spent between $1.2 and $1.6 million, he was confident that the Clintons were more than satisfied and would certainly keep up their end of the bargain. After all, it was pulled off in less than two months.

He didn't know the Clintons.

Two days after the gala Paul received a call from then DNC Chairman Ed Rendell – who would later become Governor of Pennsylvania. Paul described Rendell's demeanor as panicked. During that call, Rendell told Paul that *Washington Post* reporter Lloyd Grove was doing a story on Paul's felony record from the 1970s which, ironically enough, involved a sting operation intended to defraud the Castro-led Cuban government.[7] Most American capitalists would view such a thing as an act of patriotism.

Rendell told Paul to tell Grove, when asked, that he contributed no money to the Clintons, to "play along" and that Bill would still honor his agreement to work with Stan Lee Media. Sure enough, Grove called Paul less than one hour later. This has been verified courtesy of call logs (**Appendix A**).[8] The revelation should have outraged the media establishment in general and the *Washington Post* in particular, when it later became known. If Paul was telling the truth, the media had been played and didn't seem to care [**See Chapter 5**]. Such a scenario bolstered the argument that there is a fine line between incompetence and corruption. Had the shunning of bread and butter become a systemic problem within the media establishment? After all, when a body rejects sustenance, the body eventually dies. Many would later argue that journalism did just that in 2008.

Perhaps one of Paul's biggest mistakes was following Rendell's advice on August 14, 2000. He did "play along" but in so doing, he lied to Grove. There is no telling how things may have turned out if Paul had been honest with Grove but his decision to "play along" was a flashpoint in this saga. While his motive was to protect his investment, a consequence was giving the Clintons another gift. The first gift was the gala itself and the second was an easy way for the Clintons to distance themselves from him. In true Clinton fashion, they seemed to waste little time in exploiting the opportunity afforded them by the second gift.

Another individual very important to understanding all of this was a man named Tendo Oto, a Japanese business partner of Paul at the time and CEO of Venture Soft Co. SLM was set to benefit greatly via an infusion from Venture Soft in the amount of $5 million.[9]

Sandwiched between the gala and the call from Rendell was an agreement reached between Oto and SLM (**Appendix B**).[10]

On August 15, 2000 Lloyd Grove's *Washington Post* article was published. In it, Hillary Clinton spokesman Howard Wolfson is quoted as saying that Hillary never took any money from Paul.[11] The gap between the cost of the gala and Wolfson's claim required a bridge too far.

That leads to the next Grove article, published on August 17th. As Hillary's spokesman, Wolfson claimed that the campaign actually had received a contribution from Peter Paul in the amount of $2000 and would promptly return it.[12] It would be beyond laughable to label the claim a mea culpa. Wolfson also conceded in the Grove article that the gala did in fact cost more than $1 million.[13] An obvious question the media and the authorities seemed disinterested in asking was one that involved the origin of that money. If Paul didn't pay for it, who did? It seemed like a logical follow-up question to Wolfson's claim. Why was there no journalistic curiosity on the part of Grove? Who was buttering the bread – and for whom?

What a deal! Hillary could secretly benefit from a fundraiser that cost well over $1 million while being seen as taking the high road by returning $2000 without attributing the cost of the gala to the person who actually paid for it. As an added bonus for the Clintons, the man responsible – Paul – was in the process of being publicly demonized as a felon the Clintons inadvertently and unknowingly associated with. It was an absurd premise. The side with the evidence was being successfully smeared by the side with blatant and glaring inconsistencies. The latter was given voice by a media willing to air its smears while that same media ignored the other side's facts – all in the name of balanced coverage.

A convicted felon was given access to the President and first lady as long as he was useful. As soon as he wasn't, he became a liability once both had received the benefit of his money. How was this possible with a free press? The answer involved another faulty premise that a free press existed; the veracity of such a charge was bolstered in a major way just a few short years later during the presidential campaign of 2008 when an incredibly biased and fawning press was revealed. Ironically, Hillary Clinton would become a casualty of that bias after having benefited from it in the past.

After the gala, the Clintons painted Paul as a pariah they barely knew; they feigned regret and begged for a public wrist slap they knew they would get. Subsequent to that, Peter Paul would become Peter Who?

Unfortunately for the Clintons, Paul had video recordings of several encounters he had with Bill and Hillary prior to the gala. He did so, in part, as insurance in case Bill reneged on the agreement to work for Stan Lee Media.

In many cases, Paul is seen within inches of the first lady and the President in the recordings. Even the most skeptical of Paul's critics should be struck by the notion that the Clintons distanced themselves from him – citing his felony record – only after the gala. Are we to believe that Paul wasn't vetted prior to gaining such intimate access to the Clintons? If he wasn't properly vetted, how come no one was fired or forced to resign? Even the Salahis – the White House party crashers during the Obama administration in November of 2009 – saw the resignation of White House social secretary Desiree Rogers over much less.[14]

The Salahis were not felons and only had brief access to President Barack Obama. Paul was a convicted felon and had repeated access to the Clintons. Yet, no one was forced out when Paul's background went public, courtesy of Lloyd Grove via an unlikely source. According to Paul, Fabio – a man whose career Paul takes credit for launching – tipped Grove off to Paul's past convictions.

Another vetting matter worthy of note involved Paul's business partner, Oto. As a Japanese citizen, Oto was not permitted to contribute to a federal fundraising event, though he was in attendance at the gala. In fact, he was seated directly behind the President.[15] Additionally, vetting of attendees necessarily includes a check of social security numbers. As a Japanese citizen, how did Oto get a seat directly behind the President and first lady? Again, no one was forced out. Was the Secret Service instructed by Hillary to stand down after raising these red flags?

## ■ THE UNRAVELING

On Sunday – the day after the gala – Barbra Streisand hosted a brunch for Clinton library donors. Paul was in attendance. Why? He didn't contribute to the Clinton library. In fact, according to Wolfson only days later, Paul contributed no more than the legal amount to Hillary's Senate campaign – $2000. Did he buy access to Streisand's mansion for a meager $2000 that, according to Wolfson, went toward a completely separate luncheon?

According to Paul's wife Andrea, Hillary personally introduced her to Streisand as the wife of the man "who funded last night's event."

Also taking place on the same day was the formal agreement between Stan Lee Media and Oto's Venture Soft.[16] It came with $5 million coupled with a promise of another $5 million in November. The latter half of that agreement was not ironclad. As Bill's intermediary between himself and Paul, Jim Levin was ostensibly responsible for vetting Clinton's future business partner, whose record the public was supposed to believe the Clintons knew nothing about. One of Levin's assignments was to befriend Oto – allegedly for vetting purposes. After all, if Bill was going to work with Stan Lee Media after leaving office, he would want to know about his Japanese business partner as well, right?

Paul, while skeptical, agreed to allow Levin access to Oto. As a consequence, Levin was able to lure Oto away from Paul. Video of Levin and Oto in Japan appears in the *Hillary Uncensored* documentary.

Posted on Paul's *HillaryTruth* blog is the following about Levin and Oto:

> In November, 2000, just days after Hillary's November 7, 2000 election to the Senate, the Clintons' admitted agent Jim Levin incorporated Venture Soft USA in Illinois November 13, 2000, secretly. Because of Levin's lack of any business experience (beyond selling fences for his parents' fence company and owning the Doll House strip club) it is clear he was selling his relationship with the Clintons and their "silent partnership" to Oto.[17]

Perhaps Hillary's brashest move with Paul occurred after Wolfson pledged that she would never take any money from Paul. On August 24th, Paul received a fax from Hillary's finance director – David Rosen – on Hillary Rodham Clinton for Senate letterhead **(Appendix C)**.[18] Amazingly, the second page of the fax directed Stan Lee Media to transfer $100,000 worth of stock to Hillary's Working Families Party (WFP) account.[19]

In light of what America has learned about the Association of Community Organizations for Reform Now (ACORN) since Barack Obama's election in 2008, the relationship between ACORN and WFP in

2000 should be viewed with renewed historical interest; it was very close. For example, Bertha Lewis, national director of ACORN at the time of Obama's inauguration, was executive director of ACORN New York in 2000 as well as co-chair of the Working Families Party.[20]

In addition to being on the Democrat party ticket in New York at the time, Hillary was also on the WFP ticket and was on the receiving end of some strong words from Lewis:

> "Candidates know that when they're on our line, they're committed to certain things," explains Bertha Lewis, who moonlights as WFP co-chair and New York ACORN executive director. Speaking days before Hillary won her Senate seat in 2000, Lewis noted, "Hillary knows that if she wins, we're going to be knockin' on her door. She won't be able to hide." (quoted in *The Village Voice*, November 1-7, 2000)[21] **[See Chapter 5, p. 142]**

In light of what has been learned about ACORN in the years since, it's interesting that the Clintons would go through so much effort to distance themselves from Peter Paul.

Lewis was obviously not shy about confronting Hillary's campaign over what she thought was owed in return for the continued support of ACORN and WFP. It really isn't all that much of a stretch to wonder if Lewis was applying this kind of pressure to Hillary's people in August of 2000. One is left to conclude that Rosen thought it more advantageous to reach out to Peter Paul after Hillary's spokesman publicly declared to never again accept money from him than to see WFP not get paid – whatever the reason.

Paul, still skittish about what was going on between Oto and Levin/Clinton, paid slightly more than half of the requested amount but only after Clinton agreed to meet with him. Paul can be seen in a photo with Bill Clinton on September 22, 2000 **(Appendix D)**. The reason for the photo, Paul contends, is that it was a condition he set before acting on Rosen's request to transfer funds to WFP. As a consequence of the meeting with Clinton, Paul transferred $55,000 of the $100,000 requested. The meeting took place on the tarmac of Los

Angeles International Airport.[22] Paul has a photo of the encounter in which he is seen within feet of the President, wearing sunglasses in the far left hand side of the photo (then California Governor Gray Davis is pictured in the far right of the photo).[23]

Any lapses on the part of the Secret Service prior to September 22, 2000 would have been rendered trivial by this one. Remember, Howard Wolfson was quoted little more than a month earlier as saying the Clinton campaign would accept no money from Peter Paul. The implication was clear; Paul was a felon and had no business being anywhere near – much less associated with – the President. The irony was that the alleged reason Paul sought this meeting was so the Clinton campaign could pay a group tied to ACORN. Yet, Paul was the individual they wanted to distance themselves from publicly while taking his money privately – in order to satiate a group headed by Bertha Lewis. It was like robbing Peter to pay Saul.

So how did Paul get by the Secret Service over one month later? Did he do so in a way similar to that of Tendo Oto at the gala? Paul maintains to this day that Bill Clinton told him while on the tarmac, that the deal he (Clinton) agreed to was still intact. This meeting allegedly prompted Paul to transfer the $55,000 to Hillary's Working Families Party.

The money promised to Stan Lee Media by Tendo Oto and Venture Soft never came in November. By December, SLM had collapsed. Paul attributes Oto not living up to his end of the bargain to the latter being wooed by Levin and Clinton. This was certainly made more believable when Venture Soft was incorporated in Chicago, Levin's hometown.

Following Paul's timeline, Levin's interference was quite fortuitous, especially if Clinton had no plans of following through on his agreement to work with Paul after leaving office in January of 2001. Thanks to Levin wresting Oto's interest in SLM and, more important, the money he had pledged, the collapse of Stan Lee Media ensured that Bill wouldn't need to break his promise to work for SLM. By the time he left office, SLM would no longer exist.

If Paul had decided to concede defeat there, his life would have gone in an entirely different direction. Instead, he chose to fight.

## ■ PETER PAUL – POLITICAL PRISONER

Upon learning that the Hillary Clinton campaign filed fraudulent FEC reports relative to the Hollywood gala, Paul filed a lawsuit against the Clintons, Jim Levin, and others on June 18, 2001 for fraud. At about that same time, Paul was in Brazil to aid in the efforts of one of his other companies.

*ABC*'s Brian Ross traveled to Brazil in 2001 to do a report on the relationship between Paul and the Clintons.[24] Paul insists that he named Hillary's Finance Director David Rosen in the interview as having directed him in the coordination of the gala. He also maintains that the claim was even in Ross's final report but that *Disney* had any and all references to Rosen edited out the day before it was set to air. This would become important a few years later during Rosen's trial in which the defendant pointed to the edited report that aired as evidence he was not directing Paul in the coordination of the gala.

During one of my discussions with Paul I asked him why he thought "*ABC* Brass" – as he termed it – went out of their way to edit out all references to David Rosen in the *20/20* piece. He responded with two reasons. 1.) Michael Eisner was a big Clinton supporter and 2.) Eisner disliked Paul for stealing employees to work for SLM. He insisted that even at that time, it was known that Rosen was the link to how much the Clintons knew about the gala's source of funding.

What happened next can only be described as the first in a chain of events that would lead to one of the most egregious miscarriages of justice in modern history, regardless of what one might believe about the merits of the case.

While in Brazil, Paul was arrested on August 3, 2001 for his role in the manipulation of the SLM stock price, a violation of SEC Reg. 10(b)5. Should he have paid a price? Yes. Was the price he paid equal to the crime? As of this writing, Paul is still paying a price that includes incarceration that isn't scheduled to end until 2014.

Instead of being extradited to the United States after his arrest, Paul served over two years in a Brazilian prison. Not only was he placed in a wing known as the "corridor of death" but he found himself housed with hardened criminals serving multiple life sentences for murder – for over two years. At one point, he confessed to me that he was placed in a cell with an alleged al-Qaeda terrorist from South America.

In September, 2003 Paul was finally extradited to the United States after more than two years in that Brazilian prison. In an article by John O. Edwards at *Newsmax*, Paul was quoted as saying the following just two days before leaving Brazil:

> "I can prove everything. It was the biggest Senate campaign contribution in history and she didn't declare it. The events I organized to raise money for her are demonstrated in my account statements from Merrill Lynch. I have letters from both Clintons thanking me for my help as well as a fax dated August 20 from David Rosen (National Finance Director for Hillary Clinton's campaign) asking Gordon (Vice President of Stan Lee Media) to transfer shares from the company to their campaign account."[25]

Upon arriving in the United States, Paul was incarcerated in the Metropolitan Detention Facility in Brooklyn, NY for almost one year. In August of 2004, the SEC filed charges against him relative to the manipulation of SLM stock and Paul was given an ankle bracelet along with house arrest in 2005 pending sentencing after serving 43 months behind bars.[26] That sentencing wouldn't come until June of 2009.

Paul wore that ankle bracelet for more than four years until he was sentenced in 2009 to ten years in prison near El Paso, TX.[27] Colette Wilson – his most loyal attorney throughout the entire ordeal – conveyed to me very strong suspicions that the Clintons were behind what happened to Paul, who was ordered to voluntarily surrender on September 30, 2009; he received the maximum sentence for the crime he pleaded guilty to in 2005.

However, when sentenced in 2009, Paul was informed that the more than four years he spent under house arrest would not count as time served despite a bail hearing transcript from late 2004 that indicates time under house arrest would count toward time served. Based on the plea deal he allegedly accepted, Paul served more than eight years after turning himself in, with more than two of them behind bars in a Brazilian prison; Wilson maintains that emails between Paul and his attorney at the time back up the claim that this was part of the plea deal.

If true, someone reneged on their deal with Paul; the Clintons certainly had a motive. By any sensible standard, Paul served his time – and then some. Yet, in the fall of 2009, he found himself faced with the prospect of serving five more years behind bars.

Was Peter Paul a political prisoner in America?

## ■ THE DAVID ROSEN TRIAL

Hillary's campaign finance director in 2000 was a man named David Rosen. In January of 2005, his 2003 indictment for submitting false FEC reports relative to the Hollywood gala was unsealed and he went to trial shortly thereafter. At the time, Paul had Judicial Watch working on his behalf and their case had benefited greatly from the documentation Paul had on Rosen. These things coupled with public pressure all contributed to Rosen's indictment.[28]

This entire trial was obviously a thorn in the side of the Clintons, who have quite the reputation for very long memories; keep in mind what happened at Paul's sentencing in 2009 as we review the Rosen trial.

*Newsmax* reported in May of 2005 that the prosecution, led by Bush prosecutor Peter Zeidenberg, seemed to be as concerned with protecting Hillary as it was with mounting a case against Rosen [**See Chapter 9, p. 261**].

> "You will hear no evidence that Hillary Clinton was involved [in Rosen's crimes] in any way, shape or form," Zeidenberg told a US District Court Judge A. Howard Matz on Wednesday.
>
> "In fact, it's just the opposite," the prosecutor insisted, in quotes picked up by the *Associated Press*. "The evidence will show that David Rosen was trying to keep this evidence from the campaign."[29]

In light of the 'smoking gun' video, which clearly shows Hillary knew about the event, Zeidenberg was putting forth an extremely

flawed premise. To suggest he didn't know that would simply not be believable. Was the fear of disbarment trumped by something else? If so, what was it?

On May 18, 2005 *Newsmax* reported that Zeidenberg (George W. Bush administration) announced that the prosecution would not even introduce its most damaging piece of evidence against Rosen – an audio recording of Rosen himself, admitting his involvement:

> "The government does not intend to introduce the tape or elicit any testimony from the witness about that conversation," Zeidenberg told Judge A. Howard Matz.[30]

According to the *Newsmax* article, the contents of the recording were chronicled in an FBI affidavit and that Rosen can be heard on it, admitting that Paul's gala cost over $1 million. Rosen's FEC report indicated the figure was closer to $400,000. Zeidenberg – remember, the guy in charge of prosecuting Rosen – identified the recording as "hearsay" and didn't even want the defense team to have access to it. Why would any prosecutor call for his own silver bullet to be removed from the chamber?

Believe it or not, there's more.

The judge presiding over the Rosen trial was Justice A. Howard Matz, a Clinton appointed federal judge in Los Angeles. Before the trial even began, he instructed the jury that Paul was "prone to criminality" and "a thoroughly discredited, corrupt individual."[31]

Shockingly, despite Paul being an integral part of the prosecution's case against Rosen, Zeidenberg remained silent. He did not object; he did not make any effort to request that Matz recuse himself after the Clinton appointed judge handed the defense a major victory on a silver platter; the silence from the prosecution after such claims by the judge was the equivalent of deafeningly tacit agreement **[See Chapter 8, p. 236]**.

Rosen was ultimately acquitted but documents and cold hard facts presented by Paul put the Clintons in an extremely contradictory and embarrassing position. Thanks to an FEC complaint filed by Paul relative

to the three false reports previously filed by Rosen, the Clinton senate campaign was found to have filed those false reports. Isn't that what the Rosen trial was supposed to be about? The short answer is, yes.

In December of 2005, a conciliation agreement was agreed to between the FEC and the Clinton campaign in which the campaign would be fined $35,000 for filing three false FEC reports relative to event #39 (the gala). Additionally, the filing of a fourth report would be required. All parties agreed that Hillary's campaign underreported Paul's contributions by over $700,000. Rosen, a recently acquitted defendant over these very kinds of allegations, couldn't possibly be the fall guy. Committee Treasurer Andrew Grossman took responsibility for the three prior reports as well as the promise to file a correct fourth – mandated by the agreement.[32]

It didn't take long for the fourth report to be called into question as well. Dated January 30, 2006 the report showed that Stan Lee contributed $225,000 to the gala.[33] However, in a sworn deposition on February 23, 2005 Lee testified that he never contributed any money to the gala, though he did confess that he and Peter Paul wrote each other $100,000 checks and switched them.[34] To accept the premise that the fourth report was accurate, one would have to believe that Lee lied under oath about switching checks and then proceeded to lie when he said he didn't contribute to the gala. What motivation would Lee have for admitting under oath to doing something illegal – switching checks – unless it were true?

On December 29, 2007 Paul's attorney, Colette Wilson, filed a new complaint with the FEC, asking them to re-open the case originally settled two years earlier based on factually inaccurate reporting on Hillary's fourth report.[35] The FEC never reopened the case nor resolved the discrepancy.

In a phone interview I conducted with Paul, he discussed the Rosen trial and brought up an extremely important point about the punishment Rosen was facing if convicted – 15 years in prison.

Said Paul, "If Rosen was facing 15 years in prison for keeping the cost of the gala hidden, how did Wolfson know it cost over $1 million three days after the event (reference to Lloyd Grove's August 17th

article)?" He points out that if Rosen's future was really on the line, why would he not call Wolfson to the stand to explain what he knew about the gala's expense?

Moreover, Paul insisted that in addition to the July 17, 2000 'smoking gun' video that he believed was erroneously released by the US Attorney's office in New York, another videotaped phone call – perhaps more damaging – was recorded six days earlier, on July 11th. Wolfson and Craighead, according to Paul, were on that call and both knew exactly how much the gala was going to cost. Again, why didn't Rosen's defense attorneys call these two individuals to testify?

Rosen also worked out of Paul's office during the coordination of the gala. That reality alone should more than demonstrate that Hillary's finance director knew exactly what was going on relative to the cost of the event.

## ■ THAT OTHER HILLARY MOVIE

As Cogan was helping to put the finishing touches on the *Hillary Uncensored* (HU) documentary, a group known as Citizens United was pro-ducing a film of its own about the former first lady. In *Hillary: The Movie* (HTM) Paul made an appearance that only served to bolster his case.

Citizens United had a significant-sized budget for production of its film. In fact, HTM was at the heart of the case known as *Citizens United vs. Federal Elections Commission*, in which the Supreme Court ruled in favor of the plaintiff by a vote of 5-4 in January, 2010.[36]

HTM was produced at much greater expense than HU; the Citizens United film would feature commentators like Ann Coulter, Dick Morris, Tony Blankley, Newt Gingrich, Robert Novak, Mark Levin, and many more.[37] Distribution of the film, however, was greatly hampered when the FEC ruled that Citizens United could not use corporate funds to produce a political film and then market it so close to an election. The producers of Paul's film didn't have this hurdle to overcome and flew under the radar – until the trailer went viral on the internet.

In August of 2007, Cogan relayed to me that Paul had just completed a lie detector test relative to his claims about Hillary

Clinton. It was administered by a postal expert for the Citizens United film. Paul was told that he passed the test "with flying colors." That test – and Paul's responses – made the final cut of HTM.

The Supreme Court decision spawned even more controversy when President Barack Obama, while speaking to a joint session of Congress in the days following the ruling, openly chastised the Court. Justice Samuel Alito could be seen shaking his head and mouthing words in obvious disagreement with the President's assessment.[38] Ironically, Obama also made a cameo appearance in HTM.

Arguments about the ruling can be debated elsewhere. The important things to note about the Citizens United film are two-fold. First, Paul's passing a lie detector test about his claims regarding Hillary Clinton is significant. Since the August 12, 2000 gala, it has been Paul who has demonstrated openness, honesty, and transparency. Passing a lie detector test on camera only serves to reinforce that. Conversely, Hillary Clinton has gone out of her way to avoid answering real questions about the event. The odds of her taking a lie detector test may actually be longer than the odds of her passing one.

Second, and in keeping with the theme of this book, there was an underdog component involving a head-to-head matchup between *Hillary Uncensored* and *Hillary: The Movie*. The latter had the money; it had talent name recognition; it had the production expenses; and it was the odds on favorite to do more damage to Hillary Clinton than was a low to no budget comparative project sporting a no-name cast, aside from the footage Paul had on home video in which several Hollywood celebrities appeared.

As Citizens United was preparing to do battle with the FEC, *Hillary Uncensored* was making great strides and, in the end, may have ultimately done more damage to Hillary's presidential aspirations, despite an extremely suspect chain of events involving *Google* video.

## ◼ GOOGLE PULLS THE RUG OUT

The viral origin of videos is often difficult to pin down but in the fall of 2007, Peter Paul was able to ascertain that his trailer of *Hillary*

*Uncensored* began getting viewed by thousands of people per day as a direct result of its being posted to the *Lucianne* blog in October.

According to Paul's blog post, the thirteen minute trailer that went viral was intended to be cut down to three minutes before receiving so much exposure. In hindsight, this may have prevented more sales of the final documentary. A clear upside, however, was that it did afford millions of people the opportunity to get a better understanding of the case than they otherwise would have without purchasing the entire documentary.

Throughout the month of October, the rough cut trailer skyrocketed to the top of *Google*'s video rankings. An added benefit to that distinction was the inclination of *Google* visitors to view *Google*'s top 100 videos – a page that the search giant included in its offerings. The viral nature of the video was feeding off of its own popularity.

The thirteen minute trailer was on fire. Throughout the month of October, results on *Google* showed that it was consistently the number one viewed video. More than 50,000 views per day was becoming the norm. Several days in a row, the *Hillary Uncensored* trailer made the #1 spot. It was getting noticed and that fact was indisputable.

Then, suddenly, the video had been pulled from *Google* for a short time. By the time it had been re-posted on November 3rd, HU was no longer listed as the #1 *Google* video. The #1 video was suddenly and inexplicably "Soulja Boy" and HU was no longer even listed as one of the top 100 videos.

The sudden removal from the top 100 *Google* videos greatly diminished the inertia of exponentially increasing viewership. This happened after the video had experienced several days in the number one spot.

Paul caught what he thought might be a break when he was scheduled to appear on the *Fox News Channel* on Sunday, November 4th with Eric Shawn. This appearance was at least partially attributable to the success of the trailer on the internet. Unfortunately for Paul, the interview on *Fox* didn't do him any favors. In fact, he may have been better served had he not appeared at all. He was interviewed via phone and *Fox* showed a picture of him in an orange jump suit when he spoke. Opposite Paul were two individuals who appeared to have successfully discredited him in the minds of viewers, with the help of the jump suit photo.

At one point, I had attempted to get a prominent Texas radio station to have Paul on as a guest to discuss the success of the video and the merits of the case. When I asked the man on the other end if he'd be interested, the response I got back was, "No. It's nothing more than a novelty." When I told Paul about the conversation, he laughed in disgusted amazement before blurting out, "A novelty is a snake that spits up a Hippo. This is no novelty…"

In email correspondence with Paul's attorney, Colette Wilson, she had the following to say about the effectiveness of the video:

> "In a sense, the viewing of the video by so many millions of Americans was the only time Peter's claims ever got in front of a jury of his peers. In every other instance, whether presenting his case to the FEC, the L.A. Superior Court, the California Court of Appeal, or the Senate Ethics Committee, the people charged with administering justice seemed more interested in looking the other way than in holding the Clintons accountable."

Wilson admitted to being frustrated by the lengths to which those in the establishment seemed willing to go in order to protect the Clintons [See Chapter 9, p. 261]. There was one instance in which Paul was successful at getting his message heard via the internet – and he was cut off at the knees just as his story was set to explode nationally.

## ■ PAUL'S MOST LOYAL ATTORNEY

In early 2006, Peter Paul's case was picked up by the United States Justice Foundation (USJF). A USJF employee at the time, Colette Wilson was initially assigned to the case as an associate but eventually became the face of Paul's legal representation.

Her history is an amazing testament to servitude. She became an attorney in 1986 but chose the much less monetarily lucrative life of a Christian missionary in 1990, defending Operation Rescue activists charged with trespassing in front of an abortion clinic. She even married one of those activists. Ironically, he was a carpenter at the time. She was also one of several attorneys who worked on the *NOW v. Scheidler* case and has spent countless hours "sidewalk counseling" expectant mothers not to make the horrible choice of abortion.

As Wilson, a convert to Catholicism, continued learning more about this very complex and multi-layered case, she ultimately became the most qualified attorney to litigate it, but such a course wasn't her strength – by her own admission:

> "...while I would be the first to admit that I'm anything but a top-gun lawyer, I don't think that's the main reason the L.A. civil litigation and the FEC complaint didn't ultimately go anywhere. I think it's because in both cases, the court and the compliance agency just refused to permit any action against the Clintons, the same way the prosecutor and the federal judge acted in the Rosen trial."

In fact, during one of my phone conversations with Doug Cogan he said, "This is David in the womb vs. Goliath." Wilson, like Paul, was facing a machine, not just a defendant **[See Chapter 9]**.

## ■ CASUALTIES OF INJUSTICE

Regardless of one's thoughts about the facts surrounding the Hollywood gala, there were several people involved. Yet, the only person to pay a price for all that went on was Peter Paul, though three people who had been involved in the production of the gala – Aaron Tonken, Jim Levin, and Ray Reggie were all found guilty of fraudulent activities in separate cases.[39] Still, the fact that Paul was the only person to pay a price – a steep one at that – with respect to the gala, should raise red flags. That is, if one accepts that Clinton and Paul had agreed to work together as a consequence of a successful gala.

Both Bill and Hillary were ultimately dismissed from Paul's lawsuit against them. Adding insult to injury, however, was Hillary being awarded $130,000 in legal fees against Paul in April of 2009.[40]

The Clinton for Senate campaign was found guilty of filing three false FEC reports, a very serious crime that no one paid any price for. Rosen faced 15 years but was acquitted while Hillary's Treasurer was allowed to accept responsibility only to file another false report. He paid no price either. Ed Rendell, Howard Wolfson, Kelly Craighead, Jim Levin, and the Clintons themselves not only escaped scrutiny but they all escaped being held to account while the man who had the evidence and the facts on his side was given more than the maximum sentence in 2009.

In fact, Paul takes that twist even further by making the charge from prison in Anthony, TX that not only did the government fail to live up to its obligation based on a plea deal that Paul would be given credit for house arrest but that the judge coerced Paul into accepting such a deal in the first place. He explained:

> "The judge sealed a bail hearing transcript which had him threatening me if I didn't plead guilty with various sanctions the most blatant was he said if I didn't plead guilty I wouldn't get credit for the 4 years I had been detained prior to trial (which he had no authority to do in any event) he also conspired with teh (sic) government to deny bail unless I pled guilty and as soon as I agreed to because I had no other way to save my family after 43 months of detention without a trial I was granted bail and held in home confinement for 5 years because they refused to sentence me this is all finally before the appeal court and the transcript speaks for itself."

According to Paul, the home confinement totaled 53 months on top of the 43 months of actual jail time. The government had agreed that the total of 96 months was sufficient for a sentence that would include time served. Instead, says Paul, the judge gave him the maximum sentence of ten years without credit for the time spent under house arrest and without explanation.

Paul argued further that the judge had no legal authority to grant or deny pre-sentence credit; that authority rests solely with the office of the Attorney General (Eric Holder at the time), which Paul claims credited him for 96 months of time served. The US Attorney in the case did not challenge the judge's sentencing, which contradicted what the US government had agreed to. Paul explained further that when the Bureau of Prisons indicated that it would do as the judge instructed, he challenged the action but to no avail:

"…the atty for the government opposed my motion to amend the sentence and without one case authority supporting his opposition, stated the judge was corrrect (sic) something not allowed by court rules in responsive pleadings not to cite any case law supporting the opposition I cited over 6 2nd circuit cases adn (sic) a supreme court case as binding authority why the judge could not deny me credit for home confinement."

Many on the right found it difficult to sympathize with Peter Paul because of his willingness to deal with the Clintons. In their view, he simply played with fire, got burned, and deserved to face the consequences. In the eyes of many, there were more noble fights to wage. Those on the left saw him as a threat to the Clintons and had no compunction about piling on by further assassinating his character. His past made him an easy target as well.

After all, he was nothing more than an ex-convict who simply got out-conned by Clintonista con-artists who were much more powerful than he was. At least that was the view of many who took the time to peel back a layer or two of the onion before moving on to something else. Justice demanded so much more than that; the onion should have had every one of its layers peeled back by: a responsible Fourth Estate that insisted on getting to the bottom of it; judges who wouldn't continually and blindly rule in favor of the Clintons, their associates or lackeys; a Department of Justice that would prosecute based on the letter of the law instead of on the politics of power [See Chapter 8, p. 243, 252]; a Federal Election Commission that would not administer wrist slaps in response to egregious election law violations; or a congress that had the courage to hold hearings consisting of dogs and ponies with teeth instead of a proclivity for entertaining the television cameras in search of a sound bite. Not one of these bodies or institutions did what should have been done.

Paul had the ability to lead the way – if only he had been listened to. Instead, he was marginalized and those who could have done the right thing chose to cover up the coverups [See Chapters 8 and 9].

At every turn, Paul has been open, transparent, and forthcoming about what he knows. He has produced countless documents, recordings, photographs, signatures, and faxes that back up his claims. He even passed a lie detector test for a documentary film at the heart of a Supreme Court case that ruled in favor of the group that produced the film. He looked on as the man charged with prosecuting Hillary Clinton's Finance Director, refused to put forth the most damning evidence that would take out the financial Rook stationed next to Queen Hillary, allegedly because of how badly it would expose the former first lady. Paul sat and listened to a Clinton-appointed Judge discredit him in front of the entire courtroom by calling him a "corrupt individual" before the trial even started.

For years, the left had smeared its opponents by invoking the name of Joe McCarthy, a Republican Senator from Wisconsin in the 1950s who attempted to call public attention to the large number of communists hard at work on American soil. McCarthy was demonized and portrayed as a demagogue who was bent on smearing innocent people unjustly. How tragically ironic is it that so many individuals within the Democrat establishment would go to such lengths to smear someone like Peter Paul who, unlike McCarthy's targets, could prove his case with cold hard facts?

When asked to clarify accounts or further explain them, Paul has always done so immediately, without having to concoct another story. He has lived this nightmare every day of his life since it began. The case has so many layers that Paul would have slipped up several times by now if he wasn't telling the truth. That may actually help to explain the silence of those he accuses. After all, the truth is the easiest thing to remember. Yet, he remains behind bars while the wicked perpetrators of the heinous acts and despicable behavior Paul appears to be able to

prove, go on with their lives while sticking their collective thumb in the eye of Lady Justice **[See Chapter 6, pp. 182-183]**.

Those not enraged are simply not informed.

Peter Paul became a political prisoner in the United States of America. That bears repeating. Peter Paul became a political prisoner in the United States of America. As of this writing, he has been incarcerated in some form or fashion for more than ten years. Yet, he is the one with the evidence no one will let him present. He is the one who has not only been humbled but beaten down incessantly by a system and by a machine that has shown total disregard for the rule of law and due process.

Paul is a man with mountains of evidence that implicate his oppressors. In return, he has been smeared and mistreated by those his mountains implicate. Yet, no one comes to his defense. Why? The smear merchants have no facts. They just have power – and they use it with impunity to save their own skins without regard for the skins of the innocent. For all the wrong Paul may have done, he's paid his debt while the system that incarcerates him is overdrawn as it continues to corruptly demand he pay more.

Other casualties in this war against one man, who simply wants justice, include his family, which consists of his wife Andrea and three children, one of whom is autistic. The years of imprisonment have not only taken a huge emotional toll but a financial one as well. Paul's loved ones are left virtually destitute while he sits in the La Tuna Federal Correctional Institution in Anthony, TX.

## ■ BATTLE ASSESSMENT

The confrontation between Peter Paul and Hillary Clinton began in August of 2000. In some ways, it is still playing out. As of this writing, Paul sits in prison and talk abounds that Hillary may run for President again, though she didn't even win the nomination in 2008. Did Paul's efforts play a role in her defeat?

In 2004, a young senator from Illinois burst onto the scene with a speech at the Democratic National Convention that foreshadowed what would become an overly-hyped, style over substance campaign in 2008. George Soros, the money man with virtual monetary control of the modern left, was expected to be Hillary's most powerful supporter when she ultimately ran for President.

In late 2006, it became obvious that George Soros was taking great interest in Barack Obama, meeting with him and other Democrat donors in Soros's New York office.[41] At the time, conventional wisdom was that Hillary would become President in 2008; the campaign and subsequent elections were supposed to be mere formalities along the yellow brick road to her coronation.

By January of 2007, Obama had announced an exploratory committee and by February, he announced that he was running for President.[42] From that moment on, Hillary was locked in a battle that she would ultimately lose by the narrowest of margins. Unbeknownst to her at the time, while she was in the middle of a contentious campaign with Barack Obama, a very persistent nemesis was hard at work, doing everything he could – while wearing an ankle bracelet and under house arrest – to derail her presidential aspirations.

After reviewing the facts, it may not be that much of a stretch to conclude that the 13 minute trailer for *Hillary Uncensored* played a significant role – if not the primary role – in Hillary losing the nomination. From October of 2007 through May of 2008, Paul's trailer received more than 8 million views on *Google* and *YouTube*. On his website, Paul makes the case that Hillary's nomination was torpedoed by this trailer.[43]

This may be a difficult reality to accept for those who witnessed the meteoric rise of candidate Obama in 2008. His campaign took on a life of its own. The argument against Paul's claims would likely be that nothing could have stopped Obama, that he won the nomination; Hillary didn't lose it.

That may be the inclination of most people but consider that Obama only won the popular vote by a mere 41,622 votes.[44] Paul's trailer was viewed 8.2 million times during the Democratic primaries, notwithstanding the coverage it got via interviews on radio shows in large markets like Boston, Pittsburgh, Des Moines, and several others. The margin of victory for Barack Obama when it came to the popular vote represented slightly more than one-half of one percent of the people who watched the trailer. If just three percent of those who viewed the *Hillary Uncensored* trailer changed their minds away from voting for Hillary to voting for Barack Obama, that number would represent a swing of 246,000 votes. Also consider that there was a huge swath of independents that were leaning away from the prospect of another Republican President. Many of them were looking for a reason to vote for or against Hillary or Obama. HU made a great case for voting against Hillary.

Some may argue that Rush Limbaugh's 'Operation Chaos' which was launched in February of 2008 to get Republicans to vote for Hillary in selected primaries in order to keep the Democrat primaries going, made the race closer than it otherwise would have been. It's worth considering that Limbaugh launched the operation several months after HU had gone viral. It's quite possible that the talk show giant wouldn't have engaged such a strategy had Hillary not taken such a hit on the internet.

Election campaigns are very fluid and perceptions play a huge role. Each side scratches and claws for every advantage it can get. If Hillary had been able to win a few more states early on than she did, perhaps she would have garnered more Super Delegates from politicians concerned about Clintonesque, political reprisals. Had she been able to declare a popular vote lead early on, she may have been able to build on the momentum.

The actions by *Google* in November of 2007 speak volumes. The fact that the *Hillary Uncensored* trailer was pulled from *Google*'s top 10 ranking indicated there was serious concern on the part of someone about it being *Google*'s #1 most watched video. If so, the potential for damage to Hillary was perceived to be real. Otherwise, why pull it?

For those inclined to believe that Hillary Clinton would have been a better president than Barack Obama, aside from there being little ideological difference between the two – both revered the teachings of Saul Alinsky for example – Hillary was much more politically seasoned than Obama and may have been more adept at suppressing the passionate opposition Obama garnered. There is also the case of Clinton's closest adviser, Huma Abedin [See Chapter 10, p. 328].

In the end, Peter Paul – a huge underdog with significantly limited resources – put up an extremely noteworthy fight against the Clintons. While not entirely quantifiable, he unequivocally contributed to the defeat of Hillary Clinton in 2008.

An incarcerated man who had been arrogantly cast aside by the Clinton machine may have actually played a significant role in derailing the campaign of Hillary Rodham Clinton. Wouldn't such a scenario be sufficient reason for him to be the victim of so much government suppression and oppression?

As these possibilities are considered, one can't help but wonder if Paul occasionally smiles while in prison. Perhaps he's riding in a car that's running over Hillary's sunglasses.

For more than ten years and counting, Peter Paul has felt as if he's been under the thumb of the Clintons with additional pressure added in response to how much damage he's done to them. Perhaps one day he will be able to put them behind his thumb, thereby rendering them insignificant in size.

At least the current system can't administer poetic justice.

# CHAPTER 2

## RICHARD LANDES
### vs.
# PALLYWOOD

### ■ THE SHOT SEEN ROUND THE WORLD

Historians may debate what started the 'Second Intifada' or 'Palestinian Uprising' of 2000. Few if any, however, will dispute that the equivalent of gasoline was poured onto the proverbial fire with the alleged death of a twelve year-old boy named Muhammad al-Dura on September 30th of that year at Netzarim Junction in the Gaza Strip.

Though bullets did fly that day, the shot that would drastically alter world history was not fired from a gun; it was captured by a news camera. As the young boy lay next to his father, who was sitting behind a concrete barrel, the sound of gunfire can be heard; the camera belonging to a man named Talal Abu Rahma recorded the raw footage of what would birth the raw outrage of an Islamic world already hungrily looking for any excuse to act on its hatred for the Jews. Jews were blamed for al-Dura's death as a matter of fact in the subsequent news report – produced from this raw footage.

The images from the scene – after they appeared in an edited news report – would ultimately be used as an excuse to kill *Wall Street Journal* reporter Daniel Pearl.[1] After all, little al-Dura's death had to be avenged. Suicide bombings increased dramatically; Muslim media outlets began popping up in greater numbers.[2] After the September 11th attacks on the United States, Osama bin Laden himself pointed to the death of the young boy as one of the reasons for those attacks.[3] The degree to which the al-Dura story enflamed the Islamic world cannot be overstated; it mobilized mountains of people in the Middle East.

The footage shot that day by Talal, a Palestinian, was used by a European news entity known as *France 2* (FR2). The reporter with FR2 – Charles Enderlin – was nowhere near the alleged shooting; he was in the West Bank at the time and relied on Talal's footage as well as his interpretation of what that footage depicted.[4] Both were virtually the only sources for Enderlin's news report.

Enderlin's reliance on Talal would not only prove destructive to the former's career but both men would one day have blood on their hands – lots of it.

## ■ RED FLAGS

As the Islamic world continued to ingest the propagandistic news reports of al-Dura's death, increased scrutiny became an undesired consequence. Eventually, there were two major bones of contention with respect to the collective work of Talal and Enderlin. First, the voluminous amount of raw footage or 'rushes' shot by Talal – compared to the finished product – was substantial. Second, the angle of the shots fired at the al-Duras was inconsistent with shots fired from the Israeli position.[5]

An investigation served to vindicate the Israeli military in the death of al-Dura. Based on where the IDF was stationed during the younger al-Dura's alleged shooting, there is no way that their bullets could have made the 'straight on' holes in the wall behind the al-Duras that were evident in the raw footage. Any bullets fired from the Israeli position would have hit the wall behind al-Dura and his father at a distinct angle; this was not the case. A thorough investigation was carried out by Joseph Doriel, an Industrial Engineer, former IDF sniper, and expert in Military Operations Research. He concluded that not only was it impossible for the Israeli military to have committed the murder but that if the boy was killed by a bullet, that bullet was fired by a Palestinian.[6] A diagram that appeared in Doriel's report clearly demonstrates this reality **(Appendix A)**.

Despite this thoroughly detailed evidence – if the murder of the young boy even took place, it had to have come at the hands of Palestinians – *CBS's 60 Minutes* ignored the work of Doriel and physicist Nahum Shahaf, deciding instead to air a story about the various incidents that happened at Netzarim Junction based solely on a manufactured, collective melodrama caught on tape in what would amount to a macabre form of theatrics in and around Netzarim Junction on September 30th. Doriel's report was rejected and *60 Minutes* filed a report of its own entitled, 'To be Continued,' which aired almost one month after the al-Dura shooting.[7]

In 2003, David Kupelian echoed the sentiment that the shooting of Muhammad al-Dura was not the result of Israeli fire. He boldly claimed that it was nothing more than acting:

> "Multiple, exhaustive investigations have shown Mohammed al-Dura was not shot by Israelis. In fact, as a new journalistic probe conducted in France shows, it was very likely all a charade. Worse, the news media were almost certainly complicit in the charade."[8]

Such a charge would be severely damaging if true. The best case scenario would be that Palestinians in the Gaza Strip staged the death of a young child in order to further an agenda that involved demonizing the Israelis **[See Chapter 10, p. 298]**. The worst case scenario was that the young child's life was snuffed out as a result of some twisted form of sacrificial martyrdom in the name of a much greater cause. Such a reality would be ends-justify-the-means thinking – on steroids.

Unfortunately, in the days after the alleged shooting, the Israeli army accepted responsibility for al-Dura's death.[9] It would prove to be a gross miscalculation; the admission was made far too early and allowed the Arab world leverage whenever the validity of the FR2 account was brought into question. Those who set out to climb the mountain of truth faced a steeper incline as a result.

# ■ UNCOVERING THE RUSHES

French-Jewish reporter Charles Enderlin worked for FR2 and often relied on the raw footage or 'rushes' shot by camera man and correspondent Talal Abu Rahma – a Palestinian. On September 30th, Talal was at Netzarim Junction and contacted Enderlin who, at the time, was in Ramallah. Talal provided the reporter with a narrative about what happened to al-Dura and promised explosive footage for a news report. It would later be claimed that the Israelis fired at the al-Duras for 45 minutes that day but Talal only provided Enderlin with about 60 seconds of footage from the alleged al-Dura shooting.

As mentioned previously, the IDF accepted responsibility shortly after al-Dura allegedly died. Enderlin played a significant role in their willingness to do so; he was simultaneously serving with the IDF in some capacity, which carried weight and he leveraged it. In addition to being an Israeli, Enderlin was also a member of the reserves.[10] As such, he was able to contact the spokesman for the IDF and convince the office for which he once worked that it would be best for them to publicly apologize for the shooting – and quickly **[See Chapter 1, p. 7]**.[11]

In light of historical events, listening to Enderlin would prove to be a significant mistake on the part of the IDF. The initial IDF investigation found culpability with the Israelis. This only served to enflame Arab predispositions while bolstering the report Enderlin was complicit in filing.

A history professor from Boston University named Dr. Richard Landes took renewed interest in the al-Dura case after reading an article by James Fallows that appeared in the *Atlantic Monthly* in 2003.[12] Landes explained the impact that article had on him:

> "It was Fallows's article that renewed my interest in the al-Dura affair. As a medievalist, I was already familiar with the blood-libel motif. It didn't seem to me that the Israelis would fire for forty-five minutes at a father and son behind a barrel, nor that, if they had, it would take that long to kill the boy. But until I read Fallows, I assumed that the boy was caught in crossfire and that the 'blood-libel' dimension came primarily

from the accusation of deliberate murder. I had no idea the whole thing might be fake."[13]

That article would serve as the catalyst for a battle Landes would engage in for years with dogged determination. Unbeknownst to him, he would uncover more than the truth about what happened at Netzarim Junction that day; he would also eventually provide western civilization with a significant portion of its enemy's playbook.

Though the renewed interest Landes acquired in the al-Dura shooting was a direct result of the *Atlantic Monthly* article, the can of worms he was soon to open inside the doors of FR2 would be his own doing.

As Landes continued digging, he would be introduced to Charles Enderlin by Elie Barnavi, the Israeli ambassador to France. At the FR2 offices, Landes was able to view the rushes from Talal with Enderlin. Landes believed that Enderlin was so transparent because the latter likely thought that Landes had been vetted:

> "Before this, Enderlin had only shown the tapes to people whom he thought would back him up. I was introduced to him as a professor of medieval history and I think, because I came recommended, he expected me to be on his side.
>
> On 31 October 2003, I sat down in the *France 2* studios in Jerusalem and watched the rushes with Charles Enderlin and his Israeli cameraman, who happened to have been in Ramallah with him on 30 September 2000. That was when the shingles fell from my eyes."[14]

Landes continued watching the rushes in amazement. At one point, he saw a 'scene' when a man who was allegedly shot in the leg, tried to get men to carry him to an ambulance. He walked away without a limp after only young boys showed up to help him. In an interview I conducted with Landes, he had this to say about a conversation that ensued between himself, Enderlin, and one of Enderlin's cameramen:

> "The guy who's sitting next to me, who is a cameraman working for *France 2* – I saw this at *France 2* studios – says

something like, 'it seems so fake,' I said, 'yeah, everything seems fake,' at which point Charles Enderlin says, 'Oh yeah, they do that all the time.' And that's when I realized how bad it was."[15]

With six words – 'they do that all the time' – Enderlin unwittingly exposed the underbelly of an extremely disgusting beast to a man who would insist on exposing it. Enderlin had worked with Talal for years and relied on the cameraman's rushes when producing news reports. Yet, Enderlin admitted to Landes that Palestinians intentionally faked scenes for news cameras that willingly film them and then feed those scenes – as news – to western journalists.

It was after that experience at FR2 that Landes coined the term 'Pallywood.' The realization hit him – and he would later crystallize it perfectly in a documentary – that Palestinians were using theatrics as propaganda to push a political agenda. Many had vaguely suspected such dishonest tactics but Landes – thanks in large part to his fortuitous entry into FR2 – would have the facts necessary to prove it.

Here is how he described the term he coined while walking out of the FR2 studios that day:

> "Walking out of his office that Friday afternoon, I was in a state of shock. 'Oh my God,' I thought, 'they do it all the time… and the Western journalists just use the most believable seconds to run as news. It's a national industry!' That's when the term Pallywood occurred to me: just as Bollywood refers to Bombay Hollywood, Pallywood refers to the national Palestinian film industry that produces staged news footage. It tells a story of how the Israeli Goliath is pummeling the Palestinian David and both the Muslim and the Western media lap it up."[16]

Talal had been a cameraman who fed Enderlin footage to incorporate into his news reports for approximately ten years. Not only was Landes fighting a battle with his own eyes – which were telling him that a credentialed news cameraman was passing staged scenes off as actual news – but the respected news reporter was openly admitting that it was part of standard operating procedure. How deep did it go?

The seemingly innocuous meetings and conversations that led to Landes being at the FR2 studios that day were incredibly catalytic when taken in context. The institutionalized culture and insidious nature of what came flooding into Landes's consciousness shook him as he left FR2, in large part because of the far-reaching implications. None of that would have taken place if not for a magazine article and the relatively innocent words of recommendation from Barnavi.

His battle, though, would be uphill in nature. The official position of the Israelis regarding the incident was that it was best left unexplored and un-revisited. Despite the fact that the Doriel investigation revealed a smoking gun that didn't belong to the IDF, the Israelis seemed to be more interested in a strategy of letting a rabid dog lie. The liberal Jewish newspaper *Ha'aretz* bemoaned any attempt to give Doriel's investigation credibility. Doing so would necessarily require accepting the premise that the Palestinians killed al-Dura.[17] Making such a claim publicly would only serve to stir the hornet's nest.

The truth was so much stranger than fiction that any attempt to entertain it would have been framed as even more outrageous by those who knew the truth but didn't want it revealed. As a consequence, the silence from Israel not only allowed for it to be the object of continued bullying, it made the case of one of its staunchest defenders more difficult to win.

## ■ FRANCE 2 SUES FOR DEFAMATION

In 2004, a man named Philippe Karsenty founded a media watchdog website called *Media-Ratings*, the purpose of which was to challenge an extremely biased media that included FR2. In an interview with *Front-Page Magazine*, Karsenty specified what kinds of things his website looked out for. They included anti-Americanism, anti-Capitalism, and anti-Semitism.

Karsenty explained how much his very young – and relatively small – website was despised by media and government establishments:

"The whole French elites are against *Media-Ratings*. We disturb them because we oppose them when they lie. French media outlets hate us because we are criticizing them all the time. The French government dislikes us because we are not accepting their lies, especially concerning foreign affairs."[18]

By 2005, Karsenty found himself on the wrong end of a defamation lawsuit brought by FR2 and Enderlin over an article posted to the *Media-Ratings* website in which the resignations of FR2 news director Arlette Chabot and Enderlin were called for over their handling of the al-Dura story. *Media-Ratings* asserted that the story was based on staged footage and that it was a fake.[19]

It had been five years since the al-Dura story wrought untold damage around the world based on what was proving to be falsified visual pabulum for those who wanted desperately for it to be true; it had the effect of stoking anti-Semitic rage. Karsenty's website was no real threat to FR2, a much larger entity; the former was in its infancy and considered to be almost insignificant by comparison. Nonetheless, FR2 would attempt to bully and intimidate *Media-Ratings* in a way not all that dissimilar from how the liberal media and the Arab world were treating the Israelis.

As if the deck wasn't stacked enough against Karsenty, he didn't just have the leftwing media to contend with; he also had to make his case without the help of the party with the biggest stake in winning it – Israel. In the run up to the trial, it was learned that Enderlin received a letter from the spokesman for Israeli Prime Minister Ehud Olmert in which the FR2 reporter was assured that Israel would not challenge the veracity of his story.[20] This was extremely damaging to Karsenty for two reasons. First, if the people Karsenty was defending didn't welcome his assistance, what was the point of defending them? Second, in the Doriel investigation, Karsenty had an incredible piece of evidence but it was diminished by the fact that it didn't have the support of the Israeli government.

In October of 2006, Karsenty was found guilty by the French Court of First Instance and had to pay a negligible yet very symbolic award to FR2, along with the much more substantial legal fees. Karsenty lost

the case despite the public prosecutor's recommendation that the ruling be in his favor.[21]

As both a witness for Karsenty and someone who was present at the trial, Landes aptly described the reasons for frustration at the decision on the part of the defendant and his supporters:

> "Despite a strong presentation (I was one of the witnesses), and no response from *France 2*'s lawyers neither Enderlin nor Chabot deigned to even show up and despite the recommendation of the Procureur de la République in Karsenty's favor, the lower court found Karsenty guilty of defamation on 19 October 2006. Karsenty's lawyers had asked to have the rushes shown in the court, but *France 2* refused to release them. The judge did not act on Karsenty's demand."[22] **[See Chapter 1, p. 17, Chapter 8, p. 243]**

The agony of defeat was compounded by what appeared to be palpable injustice on multiple fronts. That defeat, however, would prove to open the door to a much broader venue. After the lower court's ruling, FR2 no doubt basked in its victory over the nagging *Media-Ratings* mosquito that had no right challenging its integrity.

Ironically, the outcome of the first trial would only serve to cause further damage to FR2 and vindicate Karsenty, who appealed the decision. Had the court ruled in favor of Karsenty's right to criticize the liberal media, the story would likely not have had the impact it did as a consequence of the subsequent trial.

Ever since Landes was exposed to the rushes in the FR2 studios that day, he would do all he could to expose the truth. His work included documentaries that went viral. Those documentaries were so damaging that they substantially influenced public opinion, not just about the al-Dura story but about all of the news coming out of that region. Many, for the first time, would see that the conflict between the Israelis and the Palestinians was not about an Israeli government that oppresses Palestinians or even about two sides that inexplicably can't get along. It was about one side that uses propaganda to bully the other while arrogantly demanding victim status.

In the case of al-Dura, Israel itself was willing to tacitly accept blame for something it didn't do while European Jews in the liberal French media establishment were willing to help the Palestinians exploit that admission to further some twisted political agenda.

# ■ PALLYWOOD DOCUMENTARIES

While Karsenty was busy establishing a website designed to hold the French media accountable, Richard Landes was hard at work, piecing together the many puzzle pieces that didn't just tell the true story of what happened at Netzarim Junction that fateful day. As a result of his exposure to the rushes, Landes was able to establish – in documentary format – the degree to which staged scenes were being used as news. It was insidious. Fake news reports had become part of an entire culture that Landes's documentaries captured in much the same way that a still shot camera catches a bolt of lightning. Prior to the documentaries, people suspected something was amiss but no one captured it as effectively as Landes did. Unbeknownst to him, once people saw his films, the tactics of the actors in Pallywood were spotted in other parts of the world [See Chapter 3, p. 69, Chapter 4, p. 115, Chapter 5, p. 123]. He even captured the phenomenon's essence with one word, making it easy to understand.

## PALLYWOOD: ACCORDING TO PALESTINIAN SOURCES...

By the time Landes released his most successful film, "Pallywood, According to Palestinian Sources..." in 2005, Philippe Karsenty was in the process of being sued. Though this film did not focus on the Muhammad al-Dura shooting, it exposed the underbelly of an extremely disturbing creature and culture that birthed the fraudulent saga; it analyzed footage from various rushes at Netzarim Junction on that day. It showed without any doubt that cameramen like Talal Abu Rahma and an untold number of Palestinians they filmed were more interested in portraying victimhood through acting than reality through reporting.[23]

One of the most egregious examples that lent credence to the contention that the al-Dura shooting was staged involved a Palestinian man who was firing his weapon through a hole in the wall of a factory

behind the Israeli outpost at Netzarim Junction. As part of an edited news report, the viewer is left believing that the shooter was involved in a gun battle with Israelis. Such a premise only served to grant underdog status to the Palestinians; it was exactly what the Palestinians wanted [See Chapter 4, p. 115].

If that premise was accurate, the point could be argued and debated honestly. The problem was that the entire scene was staged. The rushes showed that the hole the man was firing into exposed an empty building. Beyond that, prior to filming the short 'site byte' that was to be incorporated into a news report, the man was being directed and the entire area resembled a movie set, replete with stage hands that scurried away when it was time for the cameras to roll.

Landes narrated the film with corresponding video thusly:

> "Earlier footage gives us a look inside the hole in the wall. The street fighter is conversing with his comrades inside the room he will soon be spraying with gunfire. A large crowd, mostly civilians, and a few men in military garb, mills around as Palestinian soldiers climb in and out of the hole in the wall. Note the civilians giving orders to a military man. Does this look like a war zone?
>
> Orders come to clear the area. Military men line up as if they're taking cover but from what? Not Israeli bullets. And now the street fighter runs up to the hole in the wall and fires…into the empty room."[24]

Further bolstering his case, Landes included footage from Jenin in 2002, captured by an Israeli satellite. The video shows Palestinians carrying a man on a funeral bier. The alleged corpse is seen falling off the bier twice before climbing back on all by itself. The second time he does so, onlookers are seen fleeing from what appears to be a man rising from the dead.

Though Landes did not have access to all of the rushes from Netzarim Junction, his point was made in spades. The Pallywood documentary went viral on the internet but its creation was the result of the stonewalling and disinterest Landes encountered when he pleaded with western media outlets to cover what he knew was a scandal of gigantic proportions [See Chapters 1 and 5].

"I tried to get the media itself interested – *ABC*, *PBS*, the *Boston Globe* – and got nowhere. Teenagers looking at the footage spotted the fakes in a second; professionals either claimed that 'we could argue about each frame' or, if they acknowledged the fake, explained that they couldn't 'just do a program on this, they'd have to balance it with something the Israelis staged.' 'And if you can't find a case of Israeli staging...?' 'Then we wouldn't do it.' As one person at *ABC* said, 'I don't know how much appetite there is for this.'"[25]

It is a common theme present in this book. Whenever some truths about entrenched paradigms or powerful people are brought forward, there is a clear and palpable attempt by those in the western media establishment to dismiss them.

## AL-DURA: ACCORDING TO PALESTINIAN SOURCES II... BIRTH OF AN ICON

Though not necessarily as successful as the first installment, this documentary served to blow the lid off the case against FR2 and Talal. The latter was caught in a bald-faced lie and in one instance when he told the truth, it only served to vindicate the Israelis and implicate the Palestinians with respect to al-Dura's alleged death.

A key component for Landes in this film was the appearance of Talal in a 2002 German documentary by Esther Schapira entitled, "Three Bullets and a Dead Child."[26] In light of the events that transpired since the production of Schapira's film, many of Talal's words were particularly damaging to the narrative that said the Israelis killed al-Dura. Landes highlighted these inconsistencies masterfully and he did so with the assistance of Schapira's film as well as newly acquired facts that gave birth to the Pallywood moniker; the pieces began to fall into place as the arguments of the opposition fell to pieces.[27]

For example, Talal maintained in Schapira's film that he fed six minutes of the shooting to FR2 and Charles Enderlin. Yet, less than one minute ever survived the trip from Netzarim to FR2. Another curious aspect to footage of the shooting involved Talal's claim that the Israelis shot at the al-Duras for 45 minutes. Why wasn't there more footage available? The young boy was allegedly killed on camera but to this day, no such footage has been revealed.

Talal Abu Rahma's words from the Schapira documentary, when placed in this context, only served to make the case against him.

Said Talal in the Schapira film:

> "I'm the journalist; I decide what's important. All of that (other footage), the throwing of stones. Why I give them the throwing of stones (when) I have shooting?"[28]

Using Talal's logic, he should have had much more than 59 seconds to feed to FR2, especially in light of his claim that the Israelis had been shooting at the al-Duras for 45 minutes. His argument was in defense of footage he claimed wasn't sent because it paled in comparison to footage from the shooting of al-Dura. If that was true, why did only 59 seconds of 45 minutes exist?

Amazingly, Landes included footage in his documentary that only served to compound FR2's problems. In addition to the absence of video from Talal, there is video evidence that both *Reuters* and the *Associated Press* had cameramen who weren't just on the scene during the shooting; they were directly behind the al-Duras, crouched inches to their rear. Landes included some of their footage in his documentary as well.

Based on the Doriel investigation that should have cleared the Israelis, the al-Duras were sufficiently protected from Israeli gunfire. Conversely, and as Landes points out, the *Reuters* and *AP* cameramen were completely exposed as their cameras rolled.[29] Yet, none of the footage they captured added to the 59 seconds of the shooting Talal fed to FR2.

Perhaps even more startling is footage of Palestinians running from where both al-Duras were crouched behind the concrete barrel. The al-Duras didn't move while everyone else fled the (movie) set. The question that begs to be asked is: why didn't the al-Duras join the others in fleeing danger when they had the opportunity to do so?

Landes then picked up on another Talal assertion presented in the Schapira film. To understand the significance, one has to understand where Talal was when he was filming the al-Duras. He, along with the Palestinians allegedly doing battle with the Israelis, was positioned in a spot known as the "pita," which was directly in front of the wall the al-Duras were pinned against.

Here is an excerpt from the Landes documentary that includes Talal's words to Schapira followed by Landes's narration:

**Talal:** In the first five minutes (of the al-Dura shooting) it was shooting all directions but after that, no. It was only that direction, the direction behind me.

**Landes:** The direction behind him? Behind Talal is a Palestinian position, not Israeli soldiers. Could the Palestinians have been shooting in the al-Dura's direction?

This was a find that was missed in the Schapira film but impossible without the benefit of it. In Schapira's film, Talal's words were taken on faith to mean the Israelis were directly behind him. With the passage of time and the uncovering of facts since that film was made, Talal implicated the Palestinians with a hand motion. Based on his position, he made the case that bullets were coming from the Palestinian position. Further implicating himself, Talal can be heard on camera shouting, 'The boy is dead!' well before al-Dura was allegedly killed.[30]

Amazingly, evidence that the al-Duras were in more danger of being shot by Palestinians than by Israelis was captured on the 59 seconds filmed by Talal. Two bullets can be seen hitting the wall just above where the al-Duras were sitting. The plumes of smoke caused by the bullets indicated frontal shots, which would have meant they came from the Palestinian position. Additionally, the bullet holes were circular and not elliptical; oval-shaped holes would have been consistent with Israeli shots but there was an inconvenient problem for those who wanted to blame the Israelis; such holes didn't exist.

These facts seemed to back up Talal's contention that bullets were coming from behind him. Further torpedoing the case that the shooting went on for 45 minutes was the scarce number of overall bullet holes in the wall. The actual number was grossly inconsistent with the narrative.

Perhaps the most damaging footage came from a camera that filmed Talal for Schapira's interview. The FR2 cameraman was caught in an unequivocal lie and feebly attempted to cover it up. By itself, the lie would pique curiosity from viewers but when coupled with the overwhelming preponderance of evidence Landes presented, it destroys any shred of credibility Talal would hope to have. Keep in mind that none of the bullets from the scene were available; no autopsy of al-Dura was done; and no bullets were presented as having been recovered from the body of al-Dura or his father. The importance of this was the weaponry used by the Israelis and Palestinians respectively. The Israelis used M-16's and the Palestinians used the Russian Kalishnikovs. The reason given for why no bullets were retrieved from the elder al-Dura's body was that they fragmented. Yet, no fragments were recovered either.[31]

All of Landes's findings in 2005 seemed to make the case that al-Dura was shot by Palestinian gunfire – if he was indeed shot that day. A crucial piece of evidence to support his work had been uncovered by Schapira years earlier. An exchange that appeared in Schapira's film in which Talal is caught in a lie carried much greater importance in light of Landes's findings later.

This interview excerpt with Talal is another smoking gun:

**Talal:** We have evidence, the kind of the bullet. I filmed it. The kind of the bullet. We picked up the bullets from the wall.

**Schapira:** What bullet was it? What would you say? How long was it?

**Talal:** I don't know. (If) you interviewed one of the General(s), he could tell you.

**Schapira (narration):** But the general claimed that no investigation took place.

**Talal:** *France 2* collected… We have some secrets you know, for ourselves. We cannot give anything, just everything.[32]

In his film, Landes points out that Talal was the only representative from FR2 at Netzarim Junction that day. This necessarily meant that if FR2 collected the bullets, Talal himself had to have been the one to do it. Yet, he knew nothing about what kind of bullets they were. Talal implicated himself in the act of tampering with evidence at a murder scene.

## ACCORDING TO PALESTINIAN SOURCES III...ICON OF HATRED

In his third film, Landes demonstrated just how destructive the lies of Talal and Enderlin were. Jihadists the world over used the al-Dura murder to inspire Jihad and as an excuse to carry out despicably heinous acts. Osama bin Laden exploited the al-Dura story and used it to justify the September 11th attacks; the video of *Wall Street Journal* reporter Daniel Pearl's murder was juxtaposed with images of al-Dura. The Israelis were being blamed for acts of murder they didn't commit – beyond that of al-Dura.

Perhaps the most gruesome act – if not in scope, then in sheer barbarism – occurred in Ramallah, the unofficial capital of the Palestinians less than two weeks after the alleged al-Dura shooting. In the name of avenging the boy's death, which was staged at best and a blood-libel through some twisted form of sacrificial martyrdom at worst, a mob of Palestinians committed one of the most barbaric acts in modern history when they stormed a Palestinian police station that housed two detained non-combatant Israeli reservists who had inadvertently entered Ramallah after getting past a roadblock; they were arrested by Palestinian authorities.[33]

Yossi Avrahami was 38 years-old and a father of three children. Vadim Norjitz was 33 years old and recently married. Avrahami's wife called her husband's mobile phone but one of the Palestinians who murdered him answered it and said, "I just killed your husband."[34]

A lynch mob of approximately 1000 Palestinians descended on the Police station – which was under the charge of Yasser Arafat – after rumors circulated that there were two Israelis inside. The Israeli government blamed Arafat specifically when it was learned that the

Arab police officers encouraged the mob to participate in the lynching [See Chapter 6, p. 166]. In some cases, the Palestinian police reportedly participated in acts of barbarism and animalistic behavior that would turn a cast iron stomach.[35]

Landes highlights the words of a British photographer, who happened to be the only witness to the brutal murders of Avrahami and Norjitz. Mark Seager wrote about what he saw that day in an article entitled, "I'll have nightmares for the rest of my life." This is his account of what he saw when he noticed a crowd of Palestinians shouting as they were running toward him from the police station:

> "I got out of the car to see what was happening and saw that they were dragging something behind them. Within moments they were in front of me and, to my horror, I saw that it was a body, a man they were dragging by the feet. The lower part of his body was on fire and the upper part had been shot at, and the head beaten so badly that it was a pulp, like red jelly.
>
> I thought he was a soldier because I could see the remains of khaki trousers and boots. My God, I thought, they've killed this guy. He was dead, he must have been dead, but they were still beating him, madly, kicking his head. They were like animals."[36]

Something happened next that makes for a disturbing juxtaposition. When the al-Duras were being shot at, the cameras rolled. In the wake of the savage murders of the two Israelis in Ramallah, Seager feared for his life while the mob insisted no record exist on film. Seager explained:

> "Instinctively, I reached for my camera. I was composing the picture when I was punched in the face by a Palestinian. Another Palestinian pointed right at me shouting 'no picture, no picture!' while another guy hit me in the face and said 'give me your film!'"[37]

Seager narrowly escaped with his life but the reaction of the mob to being photographed as its members mutilated two human beings tells another story, especially when contrasted with what took place at Netzarim Junction less than two weeks earlier.

Israeli soldiers stationed at the Junction outpost were already prepared for Palestinian activity and anticipated that the intifada would show itself in the form of angry Palestinians very close to where they were stationed. Their state of alert was heightened not when Palestinians with rocks or Molotov cocktails showed up but when men with cameras did. In fact, in the Schapira film, an Israeli soldier who was there that day remembered a large number of cameras showing up before the protesters did:

> **Soldier:** The first people that come to the junction are the cameramen. Afterwards, all the people come. We know that when cameramen turn up, then something is going to happen. That day, we realized immediately that something big was going down as there was a lot of TV crews.[38]

One may be inclined to argue that the Palestinians at Netzarim Junction had no relationship with those outside the Ramallah police station less than two weeks later. It was entirely possible – even likely – that no one was present for both. That doesn't mean the savages in Ramallah were not inspired by the actors, directors, cameramen, and reporters in Gaza.

In Icon of Hatred, Landes explains what transpired in Ramallah moments after two Israelis were bludgeoned, kicked, tortured, and disemboweled in the streets:

> "The mob savagely killed the two men with their bare hands, tore their bodies to pieces, and dragged parts through the street, and all the while they shouted, 'Revenge for the blood of Muhammad al-Dura.'"[39]

That wasn't all the crazed, animalistic mob shouted either, according to Seager:

...the crowd was getting angrier and angrier, shouting 'Allah akbar' – God is great. There was such hatred, such unbelievable hatred and anger distorting their faces.[40]

While the facts about the despicable actions of Talal Abu Rahma and FR2's Charles Enderlin relative to the al-Dura shooting are incredibly damaging to both men, the consequences of those actions still may not be fully known. Innocent men, women, and children were killed as a direct result of the blood-libel in a television news report.

Amazingly, it was FR2 that sued Karsenty despite evidence that Talal staged scenes and passed them off as news; lied under oath in the form of a sworn statement; lied on camera; and likely tampered with evidence at a crime scene. Enderlin accepted Talal's story and footage without questioning either; he persuaded the IDF to accept responsibility before an investigation had been completed; and he admitted to Landes that staged scenes 'happen all the time.' Stranger still was the fact that Enderlin himself was a Jew and chose to libel his own people. Beyond that, innocent people were dead as a result of the false narrative and images manufactured by both men.

As if that weren't enough, Karsenty was a defendant on the losing end of a libel lawsuit. It was an injustice that defied the basic tenets of a rational world.

He would appeal the decision.

## ■ KARSENTY'S APPEAL

Almost one year after Philippe Karsenty was found guilty of defamation, the French Court of Appeals began the second trial in the fall of 2007. One of the main objectives on the part of Karsenty was to have the rushes shown in this trial; they were not shown in the first trial despite the testimony of Landes, who testified that he had seen the rushes three times and had already produced two documentaries which cast tremendous suspicion on the claims of FR2.[41] The second documentary – as noted earlier – was particularly damaging to FR2. Nonetheless, the court's decision against Karsenty in 2006 did not even mention Landes's testimony.[42]

In the earlier decision, the source of controversy surrounding the rushes centered around the fact that they were not played for the court. In the second trial, a controversy surrounding the rushes would arise as well but not because they weren't played for the court; the new controversy would be about how much was left out.

Ever since first walking into FR2's studios to view the rushes – which he later did two more times – Landes maintained that the length of those rushes was at least twenty-one minutes. Shortly after the FR2 news report in 2000, none other than Talal Abu Rahma signed a sworn statement that said he filmed the al-Dura shooting for twenty-seven minutes of the forty-five minutes that it allegedly lasted.[43]

The disparity between what Landes claimed to have viewed and what Talal swore he recorded was significant. Three times, Landes viewed approximately twenty-one minutes of rushes that consisted primarily of footage that did not include al-Dura; Talal swore he recorded twenty-seven minutes of the Israelis shooting at the al-Duras. Someone was lying and Talal's track record pointed directly to him as the primary suspect.

In 2004, a journalist by the name of Luc Rosenzweig was given access to the rushes. After watching the 27 minutes, Rosenzweig said there was no additional footage of the al-Dura shooting, which meant the only footage that existed from the 45 minutes in which the al-Duras were under fire was one minute that did not include the fatal shot.[44] Did this not implicate Talal in the commission of perjury in light of his sworn statement? This is to say nothing of Enderlin, who for years insisted that he was the one who edited out the murder from his report because of how gruesome it was. Yet, not even the raw footage contained what Enderlin said he left out.[45]

Earlier in this chapter, Talal was quoted in the Schapira film as saying the following:

> "I'm the journalist; I decide what's important. All of that (other footage), the throwing of stones. Why I give them the throwing of stones (when) I have shooting?"[46]

Using Talal's rationale for feeding Enderlin footage of the al-Dura shooting, the former should have shot far more than one minute of it. Either Talal was derelict in following his own reasoning and then lied about it or the shooting was staged and he tried to cover it up. If either scenario was correct, Talal perjured himself in his sworn statement.

## RUSHES AIRED IN COURT

Karsenty got a big break – or so he thought – when the presiding Judge at the trial ordered FR2 to produce the 27 minutes of rushes that Talal Abu Rahma swore under oath that he shot at Netzarim Junction. The rushes were to be presented to the court and subsequently viewed at a public hearing on November 14, 2007.

Astoundingly, Enderlin was quoted by the *Jerusalem Post* shortly before that hearing in an apparent attempt to soften the blow of tough questions about the length of the footage he submitted to the court. Enderlin, unwittingly or not, again implicated Talal in the commission of perjury. Said Enderlin:

> "I do not know where this 27 minutes comes from. In all, there were only 18 minutes of footage shot in Gaza."[47]

One person in the courtroom who knew otherwise was Landes; he had seen the rushes three times and could attest that they totaled more than 18 minutes. In an interview I conducted with Landes less than two weeks after the hearing, he explained the blatant discrepancy between what Enderlin presented at the hearing and what Landes saw in the FR2 studios:

> "Already we were suspicious because Enderlin was showing 18 minutes whereas I know I saw 21 minutes because I checked the time code at the end… They show the rushes and lo and behold, they actually cut some of the most obvious scenes of faking from the rushes."[48]

One of the more disappointing moments for Landes came after the rushes were shown to the court. Feeling confident that he would be asked by the judge to verify that everything he saw at the FR2 studios had been shown to the court, Landes anticipated the opportunity to tell the court that scenes had definitely been cut. That opportunity didn't come and the hearing was adjourned.[49]

In a story published one day before the hearing the *BBC* reported that FR2 and Enderlin said they were fighting a smear campaign levied against them by conspiracy theorists.[50] If Enderlin tampered with evidence, it was he who was smearing through an act of omission and criminal behavior. The lies told by Enderlin and Talal were being racked up; credibility was shattered. On issues in which Landes and FR2 disagreed, deference to the former was becoming increasingly warranted.

In fact, some could argue that Landes was honest to a fault. While the length of the rushes was widely accepted as being 27 minutes by those who wanted to see Karsenty victorious – Talal signed a statement under oath stating as much – Landes simply could not adopt that narrative, as tempting as it might have been. He viewed the rushes three times and only remembered the time code going as high as 21 minutes; his conscience would not let him state otherwise.[51]

## THE TRIAL

Despite increased public interest in the trial – attributable in large part to the judge's decision to include the rushes – media coverage was scant. It was as if the French media didn't want to draw attention to something that was certain to leave an indelible stain upon it. One reporter who witnessed the near seven hour marathon of arguments on February 27, 2008 was journalist, Nidra Poller.

If there was any doubt that FR2 was taking the new trial seriously, it quickly dissipated when they retained Maître François Szpiner, the former personal counsel for French President Jacques Chirac. Poller reported on Szpiner's tactics, saying that all he could do was smear the credibility of Karsenty because he couldn't beat him on the facts. Szpiner attempted to portray Karsenty's fight with Enderlin as being personal; Enderlin was painted as the level-headed, innocent, objective reporter and Karsenty as the rabid ideologue who couldn't see past the furtherance of his own agenda.[52] It's one of the first rules in litigating; when the facts aren't on your side, demonize the opposition.

How ironic. FR2's attorney was engaging in the precise tactics FR2 had sued Karsenty for using against them. FR2 was allegedly complicit in a blood-libel and was slandering the man who called them on it. Landes said Szpiner compared Karsenty to a known Holocaust denier and someone else who endorsed the idea that the September 11th attacks were perpetrated by the US government.[53]

According to another interview I did with Landes, the presentation given by Karsenty caused the lead judge to take notice. In particular, the footage taken from Landes's Pallywood film of the Palestinian man shooting a gun into an empty building prompted the judge to ask Enderlin to explain why the scene was incorporated into a news report. Landes explained:

> "Enderlin immediately took refuge in...these Palestinian cameramen are used by all the news stations. It was as if because everybody does it, there isn't anything wrong with it and the judge wasn't particularly impressed with Enderlin's argument."[54]

Poller reported that during a recess, FR2 News Director Arlette Chabot seemed to lose her cool over the unenviable situation her organization was in as a result of the scandal as well as the trial. Poller quoted Chabot during that recess:

> "I just want this sh***y affair over and done with. I want Karsenty to lose! This nutty case has been bugging me since day one."[55]

According to Poller, Chabot seemed to be asserting FR2's innocence and declared that she would investigate anyone or anything, follow every lead if it meant absolving her organization of any wrongdoing. Chabot's words rang hollow almost instantly when she then responded to a question from a man who gave her one of those leads. After laying out a discrepancy between the time Muhammad al-Dura was allegedly brought into the hospital (between Noon – 1pm) and the time when the shooting actually took place (approximately 3pm), Chabot became an apologist for Enderlin's story and placed the blame on some non-existent Palestinian time change (insert *Twilight Zone* music here).[56]

Landes expressed amazement in another regard and it involved a scene from the rushes which appeared in his initial Pallywood film. In the film, there was a man identified by Landes as the 'Molotov Cocktail Kid,' who was seen faking an injury while displaying no real sign of being injured except for a red splotch of something on his forehead. The man was immediately surrounded by several people who carried him rather disjointedly to an ambulance. As they approached the ambulance, they carried the allegedly injured man along the side of the ambulance that was exposed to the Israeli position, from which it was to be presumed he had been shot. To Landes's surprise, Enderlin presented that scene in the trial as actual footage.

"We got to see Talal's footage but used as if it were real events. It was fascinating to see how even when they're on notice that they've been using staged footage, they turn around and used staged footage, which suggests, among other things, that this goes really deep."[57]

After the seven hour trial ended, all parties had to wait nearly three months for the decision. The rushes were clearly the most integral part of the case. The question that would dog Karsenty's side as they waited for the decision involved the scenes edited out of the rushes. Would their absence help FR2 and Charles Enderlin or would the footage made available be enough to do the job?

After the hearing, when the missing footage was discovered, Landes saw a distinct parallel to the missing 18.5 minutes of the Nixon tapes in which Rose Mary Woods tampered with evidence and edited out the most damaging portions. What was left was damaging enough.

Landes hoped this parallel between both cases would continue on through the decision.[58]

## THE DECISION

Often, in judicial rulings, total victory cannot be declared by either side. Sometimes, the ruling may be black and white but the arguments fall

short of the victor's expectations. In still other cases, you just take the win and go home. That was the case with respect to the judgment rendered in this case. Presiding judge Madame Laurence Trébucq and her court ruled in favor of Philippe Karsenty.[59]

While the court did not rule that Karsenty had proven FR2 knowingly used staged scenes and thus committed fraud, it had ruled, based in large part on the video evidence, there was significant suspicion that the charge had merit, especially in light of the fact that Enderlin and FR2 were in the news business; they were public figures and could not expect their work to be above criticism. The court also ruled that Karsenty's charges were made in good faith.

The written decision even quoted Landes's assertion that the likelihood FR2 aired a report based on a staged death was "greater than 95 percent."[60] Think about that. If there was a 95 percent chance that al-Dura's death was staged, there was a 95 percent chance that subsequent murders took place in order to avenge a death that did not occur. There was more than a 95 percent chance that Israel was blood-libeled and virtually no one, not even Israel itself, came to Israel's defense.

In an interview I conducted with Landes four days after the decision, he interpreted the ruling thusly:

> "They (the court) said the evidence allows him (Karsenty) to make these accusations against FR2 even though they're very serious accusations and constitute an attack on FR2's honor and reputation."[61]

Karsenty wrote an article on the day of the decision and declared victory in the case, saying that the French appellate court found him innocent of defamation. In it, he illustrated his point with absurdity by equating the position of FR2 with that of someone who believes dead people can move:

> "It is ironic that I, a private individual, had to lecture one of France's most influential TV stations in order to demonstrate that a child cannot move; lift his head, arm, and leg; stare at the camera; and still be considered 'dead' a good 10 seconds after the newscaster tells us 'the child is dead.' One

need only look at *France 2*'s own footage to realize that the 'death' scene was faked."[62]

This ruling was the equivalent of a nuclear bomb in the world of western journalism but it got scant coverage in the international media. Conversely, when Enderlin's initial report that al-Dura had been killed was released, that same international media reported it en masse and helped to fuel the fire of outrage against the Israelis while doing so.[63] Not even FR2's rival media establishments seemed interested in damaging the credibility of their opponent, which had just been on the receiving end of a devastating blow. Its blood was in the media waters. Yet, its competitors seemed disinterested in going in for the kill.

After witnessing the November 14th hearing, Landes reported the media had no interest in that either. He told me there were no French media present at that hearing. He further explained that during Karsenty's first trial, attempts were made by Landes and others connected with Karsenty, to get the French press interested. Those attempts were unsuccessful. Then, when the initial decision in favor of Enderlin came down, the media took great interest.[64] In an article for the *Wall Street Journal*, Nidra Poller echoed similar sentiment, saying:

> An honest reading of the ruling calls into question the al-Dura myth. French media didn't bother to come to the funeral. Were they confident that Charles Enderlin would be vindicated? Did they think Philippe Karsenty, whose honor they had sullied by likening him to Holocaust deniers and 9/11 conspiracy nuts, was already dead and buried?
>
> Mr. Karsenty's defamation conviction in the court of first resort had been celebrated as proof that the al-Durra death scene was authentic. Reactions to his acquittal, which can be counted on the fingers of one bony hand, reassert that impression.[65]

Based on the media's lack of interest in the case – until Enderlin won the initial trial – coupled with its disinterest in the appellate court's decision, which was much more significant and in favor of

Karsenty, its actions spoke louder than any words any of its reporters would have chosen to describe the proceedings.

It cannot be underscored enough that the appellate court's decision in favor of Karsenty wasn't just about saying he had the right to criticize FR2. A lower court had already ruled in favor of Enderlin and FR2. Karsenty faced a heavier burden. He had to prove that there was sufficient reason for his criticism; the court ruled he did just that. The implication was monumentally clear. By showing interest in the case when Enderlin won and disinterest when he lost, any such media establishment expressed no interest in purging individuals and entities that defile the profession. Any such establishment was more interested in either showing tacit support or closing ranks to protect its own; both are equally despicable.

The manifestation of this reality came after the trial itself, in which 300 journalists signed onto a petition showing support for Enderlin. In an article by Anne-Elisabeth Moutet that appeared in the *Weekly Standard*, she interviewed several journalists who signed on. The range of responses, though diverse, pointed to excuse-making and loyalty to Enderlin being more important than journalistic integrity and facts.[66]

Ironically, it is those individuals who are much closer to being holocaust deniers than people like Karsenty will ever be.

## ■ SARKOZY HONORS ENDERLIN

If there was a journalist who emerged from the al-Dura incident, it was Philippe Karsenty. He exposed an individual who was complicit in the use of staged scenes repackaged as news. The public was lied to and much of the Arab world used that lie as an excuse to act on its hatred; deaths resulted from that manufactured outrage.

It was Karsenty who deserved recognition. His case was part of a movement that had the potential of bringing honor to France. If French President Nicolas Sarkozy had recognized Karsenty for his work, the ground could have shifted beneath the feet of the European media establishment. The absence of coverage relative to Karsenty's victory would have been rendered insignificant, even brought under a tremendously brighter spotlight and stronger microscope; the media establishment that shielded FR2 would have been exposed.

With respect to Sarkozy's involvement, the opposite happened little more than one year after the appellate court's decision.

In August of 2009, the French consul general in Jerusalem awarded none other than Charles Enderlin the Legion d'honneur, one of France's highest accolades, on behalf of President Sarkozy.[67] The *Tom Gross Mideast Media Analysis* website explained some curious realities. First, Enderlin received it from France's Foreign Affairs Ministry when it's usually awarded by the Ministry of Culture. Further, there were several indications that the award was presented in ways that would circumvent opportunities for controversy.

For example, the Legion d'honneur is reportedly never awarded in August but it was here, when people were on vacation in greater numbers; the award is typically given in Paris and not at a foreign consulate as in this case; no formal announcement prior to Enderlin's receipt of the award had been made.[68] It was as if those involved in the decision to honor Enderlin intentionally avoided those who would hold Sarkozy accountable to the disgraceful decision to honor a fraud.

## ■ BATTLE ASSESSMENT

Some may be inclined to ask why Philippe Karsenty's name is not in this chapter's title. It's a fair question. After all, he was the defendant against a much larger entity that used a former French President's personal legal counsel. The answer is that what Karsenty did was very much in the spirit of this book but in addition to Landes playing a critical role in Karsenty's legal victory, the latter did something else that carries far greater ramifications. He discovered and very accurately identified a key stratagem of war being used against western civilization; he gave it one word – Pallywood.

Sun Tzu, an ancient Chinese warrior whose principles are still required reading for many militaries across the world, wrote in *The Art of War*:

Know yourself and know your enemy.
You will be safe in every battle.
You may know yourself but not know the enemy.
You will then lose one battle for every one you win.
You may not know yourself or the enemy.
You will then lose every battle.[69]

Another precept in Sun Tzu's teachings is that war is deception. The FR2 case served as both a microcosm of a much larger problem and a vehicle through which Landes was able to uncover something far more insidious and pervasive. Through intimidation, Palestinians have been allowed to dictate how their 'plight' should be portrayed. Palestinian areas have become the lion's den most western journalists choose to avoid. In the case of al-Dura, a western journalist had to rely on a stringer with extremely questionable loyalties to provide him footage with a storyline if he wanted to report on the story at all. After a review of the evidence, it's clear that Charles Enderlin traded journalistic integrity for a dramatic news report. The consequences of that decision helped to change the world – for the worse.

The premise of Pallywood is so outlandish that short of smoking gun proof to the contrary, anything that comes out of it necessitates rejection. Those who deny Pallywood exists point to its conspiratorial nature but what Landes exposed through his work is a very real conspiratorial culture that has fed itself on denials like a fire feeds on oxygen. It's a culture replete with melodrama that western journalists eat up like candy.

Pallywood's set directors have even learned how to exploit their enemies for their own advantage. Remember, the primary goal of Pallywood is to demonize Israel and victimize Palestinians. Western media establishments that fail to acknowledge this while following the Pallywood narrative only further that effort. Israel is the eastern front in a war between civilizations. Western civilization in general and media establishments in particular betray that front to varying degrees based on the extent to which it and they are complicit in greasing the skids of the Palestinian propaganda machine.

Exposing Pallywood is only half the battle. The other half is getting people to believe their own eyes after having been so grossly fooled. Pride, an extremely destructive human emotion, played a key role in many not coming to this realization. To this day, Enderlin – Jewish by birth – has become a martyr for his own work. That work has been championed by those who would cast him aside once he was of no further use. Being a martyr for the opposition is a vexing notion but it's the only explanation in this case, whether intentional or unwitting.

In a phone conversation with Landes during the writing of this book, I asked him where Enderlin is today. He told me that while Enderlin is still at FR2, his career has come to a virtual standstill. After the decision against him in 2008, Enderlin vowed an appeal. It still has not materialized and the odds of such a thing grow longer with each passing day. Enderlin and FR2 were dealt an incredibly damaging blow but there was good to come out of it – Pallywood was exposed.

Enderlin became almost tacitly toxic within an establishment that is on record as having publicly supported him. Yet, he continued to double down rather than come to terms with what he'd done.

In 2010, Enderlin penned a book titled *Un enfant est mort* or *A Child is Dead*. During an interview with *France 24* to promote the book, Enderlin argued in support of Talal's credibility by saying that there was no evidence the camera man belonged to any organization that showed political bias against the Israelis or in support of the Palestinians.[70] This argument is refuted by what was exposed – the Pallywood culture.

There is something else the Palestinian side has proven adept at exploiting – the premise in western journalism that objectivity is the highest standard, regardless of the integrity of either side. Fighting dirty is permissible if it still garners a fair shake in the media. The argument for objectivity in journalism is short-circuited when one side isn't interested in an amicable solution. In any conflict, when one side wants peace and the other wants the extinction of its opposition, a journalist willing to operate from the premise of objectivity is only valued by one side – as a pawn **[See Chapter 10, p. 300]**.

Enderlin explained it differently to *France 24*:

"I had no problem on the Palestinian side, not with Hamas, not with Jihad, not with Fatah, not with any organization. The minute you behave not as belonging to one community or nationality... When you behave as citizenship journalist, it's different and it works for me... I am welcomed everywhere."[71]

Whether Enderlin wanted to admit it or not, he was only welcomed by one side so he could be exploited; he was tolerated by the other as a necessary evil. Again, the irony is that in trying to be accepted by all, he was respected by none. Trying to be liked by everyone is a recipe for disaster Enderlin should have learned in his childhood.

Landes didn't just identify the tactics used by the Palestinians; he also identified the insidious nature of Pallywood. It's far more prevalent than most realize. In the summer of 2006, *Reuters* had to admit that one of its photographers doctored a photo to make an Israeli air strike on Beirut look worse than it was.[72] Was it Pallywood in Lebanon? Recall that a *Reuters* cameraman was positioned immediately behind the al-Duras during the shooting.

In 2006, US Congressman and former Marine John Murtha (D-PA) accused US Marines of murdering innocent Iraqi civilians 'in cold blood' over an incident in Haditha, Iraq in 2005. Murtha took the side of the Iraqi accusers before any investigation had been completed.[73] Many of the allegations regarding US troops came from local Iraqis who said the Marines killed 24 innocent people. Murtha echoed the narrative of the liberal western media. Eight Marines were charged in the case. Seven were either acquitted or had charges dropped. The eighth Marine – Staff Sgt. Frank Wuterich – was ultimately exonerated of manslaughter charges after accepting a plea deal that involved no jail time.[74]

Based on the acquittals, the Haditha case mirrors the al-Dura case in at least one respect; those responsible for criminal behavior were shown not to have engaged in any. The western media in this case, acted very similarly to how Enderlin and FR2 acted after receiving footage from Talal. While Iraqis did die in Haditha, the narrative was owned not by those who were acquitted; it was owned by those who wanted the innocent condemned. Was it Pallywood in Iraq?

In 2005, *Newsweek* had to apologize for a story it ran about how American interrogators at Guantanamo Bay, Cuba flushed a Qur'an down a toilet after the story was proved to be demonstrably false.[75] *Newsweek* had used an anonymous source and the story spawned violence in Pakistan and Afghanistan. Was it Pallywood in Cuba?

Pallywood also reared its head in Honduras in 2009 when a protester there was caught wiping blood on his shirt before seeking out news cameras to tell them that a boy died in his arms **[See Chapter 3, p. 69]**. Was it Pallywood in Central America?

Pallywood is everywhere but it operated in the shadows until Richard Landes caught it on film and identified it for what it was. Pallywood is a stratagem of war that is being used against western civilization and has far too many willing accomplices in the liberal media. It is traitorous and fraudulent behavior that will continue as long as the righteous stand idly by and allow the tactic to work.

People do not like being lied to but until they realize it, the lies remain effective.

Landes has done his part; he has pulled back the curtain and revealed the lie that is Pallywood.

# CHAPTER 3

## ROBERTO MICHELETTI (HONDURAS)
## vs.
# THE WORLD

### ■ LONG, LONG ODDS

The power of Nationalism can be demonstrated in many ways but it was perhaps best exemplified by a tiny country in Central America during the seven month presidency of Roberto Micheletti in Honduras. He did not desire the job; he was thrust into it as the result of a Constitutional crisis. From the moment he took office, he refused to take the path of least resistance even when the pressure to do so would have broken most men who even consider avoiding it.

Micheletti consistently exhibited unyielding leadership in the face of unified world and hemispheric bodies that applied intense diplomatic pressure specifically intended to make him buckle. He seemed to strengthen as pressure increased, not giving an inch when even the staunchest of his supporters would have understood if he had backed down; he never did.

The government of Honduras during the Micheletti presidency is a testament to what can be accomplished when principles are not compromised. His story is partially reminiscent of a song by the *Wood Brothers* called "Luckiest Man." The song assures men who fight the good fight that even though they are destined to lose because of how outnumbered they are, they still have more valor than their arrogant opponents.

The chorus goes like this:

Running is useless and fighting is foolish
You're not gonna win but still you're the luckiest man
you're up against
too many horses and mysterious forces
What you don't know is you are the luckiest man
You're the luckiest man

That's only part of Micheletti's story; he defied the premise and thereby the defeatist attitude that can creep into the minds of those who feel too outnumbered to prevail. His firewall would prove impervious to such attitudes.

Micheletti demonstrated unequivocally that fighting is not foolish and there is no such thing as having too many horses or mysterious forces aligned against you if they meet the right level of determination. He stood against nations run by dictators who accused him of leading a coup d'état when, in reality, he was doing all he could to prevent one by a sitting President bent on usurping power not granted. Within his own borders, Micheletti had to deal with raucous agitators who shared the goals of those dictators. He fought valiantly and proved yet again that the best leaders are often the ones who lead reluctantly and without a thirst for power.

## ■ CONSTITUTION DEFENDED

In the early morning hours of June 28, 2009 sitting President of Honduras Manuel Zelaya – while still in his pajamas – was awakened and removed from his home by the Honduran military. The presidential palace had been seized and Zelaya put on a plane, flown to Costa Rica against his will.

The *Associated Press* reported that a military coup had taken place.[1] United States President Barack Obama likewise declared the removal of Zelaya a "coup" that was "not legal," adding that:

"It would be a terrible precedent if we start moving backwards into the era in which we are seeing military coups as a means of political transition rather than democratic elections."[2]

It didn't take long for the narrative that Zelaya was the victim of a coup to be seriously questioned. It was only a few weeks later that Obama would jump to another conclusion when the American President's friend, Henry Louis Gates was arrested; Obama declared at the end of a press conference on July 22, 2009 that the Cambridge police "acted stupidly" in arresting Gates.[3] The conclusion he jumped to in defense of his friend was reminiscent of the conclusion he had jumped to in defense of the Honduran dictator weeks earlier.

As the situation in Honduras played out, it became apparent that Obama was prepared to stay the course and not give in to the opposition. He learned such rigidity from his ideological hero, Saul Alinsky. Besides, he likely suspected that he could consolidate power in the form of significant international pressure to have Zelaya reinstated – that strategy was indeed tested as time went on. Zelaya was his guy and Obama was going to stick with him – until such time as it was deemed appropriate to throw him under the bus; more on that later.

In the days that followed, the ousted Honduran President Zelaya went on a Central American tour and attempted to persuade other heads of state that he had been the victim of an illegal coup. The Organization of American States (OAS), a hemispheric body of 35 member states belonging to the Americas would publicly align against the removal of Zelaya; they united in a call to have him put back in power.

The problem with the position that Zelaya was unconstitutionally removed was that the Honduran constitution was followed to the letter by each branch within the government that removed him. It would later be learned that the only error made during his removal was flying him out of the country instead of arresting him for treason. Perhaps this was an attempt to peacefully separate instead of going to the mat over the issue.

The controversy stemmed from a portion of the Honduras constitution which states that no sitting President can seek reelection. Zelaya, a known ally of the tyrannical Venezuelan President Hugo Chavez, was found to be in violation of his constitution by holding a referendum – he called it a "survey" – that would ostensibly allow him to remain in office as President. Since even the proposal of such a change was outlawed, Zelaya was found to be in violation of the constitution and a warrant for his arrest was issued two days prior to his removal.

Moreover, Zelaya attempted to fire the head of the military for refusing to oversee the referendum.[4] The court ordered the firing illegal and demanded the general's reinstatement. This only served to bolster the case of those who sought Zelaya's removal.

Under the Honduras constitution, any president found attempting to remain in office beyond his term is in violation of a very serious offense. In the case of Zelaya, the Supreme Court ruled that the military should forcibly remove him from office. The vote was unanimous. Once Zelaya's removal was complete, the constitution called for the head of the legislature to replace him. That man's name was Roberto Micheletti. All of this appeared to have been constitutional.

Miguel Estrada, one time George W. Bush nominee to the US Court of Appeals for the District of Columbia is not only an attorney but a native of Honduras, born in that nation's capital, Tegucigalpa. In the days after Zelaya's removal, upon reviewing that country's constitution, Estrada also determined that the action was justified.[5]

Based on Honduran law, Manuel Zelaya was guilty of treason for attempting to fundamentally alter its basic tenets. According to Estrada's interpretation, the rule that says a president cannot be re-elected is not even subject to change via the amendment process. Any attempt to do so would constitute a fundamental change to the Honduran form of government. When Zelaya attempted to use the formula of his friend, Hugo Chavez, to permanently install himself as president, the Supreme Court, the military, and the Congress all stood up against it.

Interestingly, Micheletti belonged to the same liberal party that Zelaya did. As head of congress, he was sworn in as President because Zelaya's Vice President had resigned earlier in order to run for president in the coming November elections. In the months that followed, Micheletti demonstrated tremendous courage and truly unyielding leadership. What's more is that as president from June thru November,

he would also be ineligible for reelection after serving less than a year, let alone a full term.

## ■ HONDURAS, CHAVEZ, AND THE OAS

The Organization of American States (OAS) is best described as the Western hemisphere's version of the United Nations. Prior to Zelaya's removal from office, Honduras had been a member state. On July 3, 2009 Honduras, under Micheletti's leadership, withdrew from the OAS. It did so, on its own terms and on its home turf, in the presence of OAS chief Jose Miguel Insulza, when a letter was recited aloud by Honduras' Vice Minister of International Relations with Micheletti present.[6]

This withdrawal from the OAS came at great expense to Honduras in the form of frozen loans, banned international help, and suspended donations; Micheletti could not be faulted for standing on principle. It was quintessential political courage. It was the equivalent of an American President announcing that his country was pulling out of the United Nations.

Then on July 5th, the OAS unanimously voted to suspend Honduras from participation in the "hemispheric body" known as the OAS. In fact, for nearly two years, the OAS website had a footnote on Honduras' suspension being the result of a "coup d'état." Aside from that claim being factually inaccurate, member states that never lost their membership status include Venezuela and Nicaragua, home to Hugo Chavez and Daniel Ortega respectively. Moreover, the footnote attributed to Cuba on the OAS website – unlike the one for Honduras – identifies that communist nation as being considered for entry. Formal procedures are apparently all that stand in the way of the Castro brothers joining the fraternity.[7]

Any international or hemispheric body that accepts nation states led by tyrants while rejecting nation states whose leaders reject tyranny, should be held accountable by its member states. If member states fail to do so, it's likely because the body itself is afflicted with the spirit of tyranny to some degree.

The political battle lines were being drawn in early July of 2009. Micheletti, in declaring that Honduras would exit the OAS, necessarily put his nation in opposition to the body. The OAS membership also includes the United States, Mexico, and Canada. Honduras had won a significant and principled battle but would Micheletti be able to withstand the pressure that was certain to be brought to bear as a result of his stand?

The circumstances surrounding Manuel Zelaya's attempt to usurp his country's constitution included the handiwork of Venezuelan dictator Hugo Chavez, a staunch supporter of Zelaya. No one was more noticeably upset at Zelaya's ouster than was Chavez. No clear-thinking American could rationally come to grips with the reality that the President of the United States and Hugo Chavez were on the same side in this case. Both were insistent that Zelaya be reinstated.

Based on how Chavez took power in Venezuela, it was obvious that his Honduran stooge (Zelaya) was being coached on how to do the same thing. As the events of June 28th demonstrated, Zelaya didn't have the luck that Chavez had. The sanctuary of an OAS gavel proved to be a mirage as well but only because of Micheletti's backbone.

In Venezuela, Hugo Chavez was able to intimidate the OAS, which sent a representative to oversee the elections that ultimately put Chavez in power. Jimmy Carter also made an appearance. Appeasement on the part of the OAS and the United States was the course of action chosen when election results could not be verified. As a consequence, Chavez became the leader of Venezuela and secured much more power within the OAS.[8]

## ■ PALLYWOOD IN HONDURAS

As it became more apparent that Honduras, led by Micheletti, was not going to back down, Zelaya's supporters needed new tactics to defeat him in the court of public opinion while they had a world stage. Those tactics involved a typical left wing propaganda campaign designed to portray Honduras' Zelaya supporters as victims, in the media.

In 2006, Boston University professor Richard Landes produced a ground-breaking documentary entitled, Pallywood: According to

Palestinian Sources [See **Chapter 2, p. 40**]. In it, a *CBS 60 Minutes* segment about the Israeli/Palestinian crisis was analyzed using raw footage shot for the story, along with other footage shot by *France 2* cameras. The film unequivocally proved that staged scenes were being shot as actual news and incorporated into completed news reports for public consumption.[9]

When factoring in the mutual affinity that exists between Iran's Mahmoud Ahmadinejad and Venezuela's Chavez, it's really not that much of a stretch to consider that some of the melodramatic tactics used by Palestinians to further an agenda could be implemented in Central America for the same purpose. Iran has been known to be a source of funding for both Hamas and Hezbollah as well.[10]

That leads to an incident that happened in Tegucigalpa, Honduras on July 5, 2009. A man named Juan Angel Atunez, a Zelaya supporter, was photographed by *Reuters* and interviewed by *CNN* during a protest in support of Zelaya. Atunez stuck out in the crowd because he was donning a white shirt that was covered with blood. The caption of the *Reuters* photo simply described him as a man with a "shirt covered in blood" while *CNN* went even further.

In a news report, *CNN* [See **Chapter 10, p. 330**] seemed to interview Atunez based solely on the fact that he had blood smeared all over the front of his white shirt. Atunez was quoted as saying that the blood came from a dying child he picked up and held in his arms. Through a translator, Atunez was quoted as saying, "I ran over beside the boy to try and help him because I didn't want him to die but he died."[11]

If that story were true, it would be accurate reporting. If untrue, it'd be the stuff of Pallywood. That's exactly what this incident appeared to be thanks to a blogger who decided to travel to Honduras and witnessed the incident first hand.

A site known as *Legal Insurrection* posted a story about a blogger named Hunter, who traveled to Honduras to see what he could uncover. While Hunter was away, he phoned in his reports so they could be posted to his blog. Amazingly, he seemed to witness how the blood got on Atunez's shirt.

He did see an older man in a white shirt reach down into the blood pool and cover his hands. He then wiped them on his shirt to make it look like his blood or that he had been involved. Hunter saw what he thought was an *AP* photographer take the man's picture. Hunter said if you see it on the web, don't believe it. It was faked.[12]

In watching the *CNN* news report, viewers were able to see 'Pallywood' influence beyond the allegedly staged, blood-stained shirt. When viewing the *CNN* interview of Atunez, you can see a man on the left-hand side of the screen wearing a face covering eerily reminiscent of Palestinian garb. Another similarity is the number of rioters at the beginning of the *CNN* report who are hurling rocks at authorities.

Remember, those protesters supported Zelaya; Zelaya was supported by Hugo Chavez; and Ahmadinejad is quite cozy with Chavez. In light of these events, Micheletti had a Palestinian style propaganda campaign he had to deal with in addition to the demands and pressure from the OAS.

*CNN* and *Reuters* running with a graphic visual without checking the facts may have been the most egregious example of media bias against Micheletti – who was already up against political pressure no one could imagine – but it wasn't the lone example.

The *Washington Post* ran a story by Juan Forero on July 9, 2009 with a deceptive headline in light of the facts on the ground. It read, "In Honduras, One-Sided News of Crisis." The article focused on Micheletti's supposed effort to shut down media outlets in opposition to the new provisional government.[13]

Instead of Forero doing a story on the biased coverage of *CNN* or *Reuters*, he piled on by painting the Micheletti-led government as oppressive and intolerant of dissent, wielding a heavy hand against the opposition. Apparently lost on Forero was the alienation of Honduras by 35 other nations, including Cuba, Venezuela, Nicaragua, and unfortunately, the United States.

In particular, Forero portrayed *Radio Globo* as a victim of oppression at the hands of Micheletti's government. *Radio Globo* was a staunch supporter of Zelaya. Daniel Greenfield of the *Canada Free Press* identified David Romero Ellner – head of *Radio Globo* – as Zelaya's "chief propagandist."[14]

According to Greenfield, not only was Ellner a known communist but he was heard on *Radio Globo* in the weeks after Zelaya's removal, saying of the Jewish holocaust that it would have been "...fair and valid to let Hitler finish his historic vision..." It is true that in a free society, a free press is paramount. However, in the context of what was going on in Honduras, the stance of the interim government led by Micheletti – with the near unanimous consent of all other branches – was that Zelaya was removed constitutionally. The state of affairs was tenuous, especially in the context of so many nations aligning against Honduras for defending its own constitution.

Honduras was in the midst of a constitutional crisis, fighting biased news reports from prominent foreign media sources.

Moreover, while Forero was reporting tales of woe relative to *Radio Globo*, CFP's Greenfield was citing the quotes of Ellner's daughter, describing in very graphic detail, how her father raped her on his birthday. Greenfield also reported that in his earlier days, Ellner – as a member of the Communist People's Revolutionary Union (PRU) – took part in the seizure of radio stations. Ironic, isn't it? Why would the *Washington Post* portray such a man so favorably?

In addition to fighting the OAS, Micheletti also had to fight a full-fledged propaganda campaign that incorporated the help of prominent, supposedly objective, media outlets like the *Washington Post*. Favorable coverage was being given to a communist whose "chief propagandist" expressed views sympathetic to Hitler – a man of history who mastered the art of deceptive propaganda; perhaps Forero should have connected those dots before writing his story.

Ellner's credibility did not warrant the level of trust or support he received from Forero, who should have questioned the very notion that Micheletti's government raided the radio station at all.

That's what we call Pallywood in Honduras.

## ■ UNITED NATIONS SUPPORT FOR ZELAYA

In addition to being isolated by the OAS, which included the United States, Mexico, and Canada, Honduras also found itself in opposition to the United Nations with respect to reinstating Manuel Zelaya as President. Two days after Zelaya's removal, the UN condemned it and demanded the "Immediate, Unconditional Restoration of President."[15]

At one point, UN Secretary General Ban Ki Moon actually chastised the OAS for not dealing effectively with Honduras, which meant giving Zelaya his job back. This embarrassment on the part of the UN and the OAS was made possible by the unyielding resolve of the Micheletti-led government which simply would not back down; it wouldn't even compromise to save face. Ironically, Ban's support for Zelaya included the statement that "constitutional order" needed to be "restored."[16] Lost on him was that constitutional order was restored with Zelaya's removal.

With 192 member states, the United Nations was another huge source of undeniable political pressure brought to bear against a small country in Central America; Micheletti had to deal with the pressure from the OAS, notwithstanding the fact that several OAS member states also belonged to the UN. In early July, nations all over the world were lining up against Honduras. Predictions that Micheletti would cave were in abundance.[17] At one point, the new government appeared to have the support of only Israel and Taiwan.[18]

As mentioned earlier, if there was one area in which the newly installed Honduran government erred with respect to enforcing its constitutional mandate to remove any sitting president who attempts to keep power, it was in not arresting Zelaya. Instead, by exiling him, Micheletti – at least initially – seemed to make matters worse for himself. As nations aligned in calling for Zelaya's reinstatement, the former President grew more and more brash, traveling from country to country, constantly lobbying for support.

Paradoxically, the decision by Honduras not to arrest him may have worked to the long term advantage of the new government; as

the days and weeks went by, Zelaya was proving to be perhaps, the biggest liability for his own cause.

## ■ ZELAYA THE LIABILITY

In the early days of his ouster, Zelaya had to feel supremely confident that he would get his job back. He had widespread international support. However, as the days and weeks went on, he began to reveal himself as reckless, impatient, sloppy, paranoid, and even extremely unstable. Had he been sitting in a Tegucigalpa jail since June 28th, there's no way he would have been able to short circuit the efforts of world bodies and nation states that were doing their best to put him back in power. He would likely have been able to garner more sympathy.

Another consequence of his behavior was that the world was able to see a stark contrast between the old President and the new one.

For example, as Micheletti was writing an editorial that appeared in the *Wall Street Journal* on July 27th, Zelaya was being deliberately provocative, literally walking into Honduras from Nicaragua to make a very dangerous political point. It was extremely reckless with potentially disastrous consequences for the region.

Reports were that Zelaya took a few steps into Honduras and began talking to his former military officials on his mobile phone. With supporters in tow – it would later be learned that the Fuerzas Armadas Revolucionarias de Colombia (FARC) was involved in funding them – Zelaya boasted that despite the colonel on the other end of the phone telling him he would not be allowed into the country, the "Welcome to Honduras" sign was behind him; Zelaya remained a few feet inside the Honduran border for thirty minutes before returning to Nicaragua. His reason for not staying longer or venturing deeper into Honduras was that he didn't want to be the cause of an international incident.[19] That statement was ridiculous on its face since Zelaya's actions were directly responsible for the potentially volatile situation he claimed to want to avoid.

Another aspect to the incident not becoming even more dangerous was the discretion exercised by Micheletti's forces, who didn't take the bait. The stunt was clearly an attempt by an increasingly frustrated Zelaya to make something happen. Discretion proved the better part of valor for Micheletti, who rightfully derided Zelaya's actions publicly. In fact, Zelaya's behavior was so egregious that US Secretary of State Hillary Clinton had to publicly denounce it, calling it "reckless."[20]

Moreover, thanks to *Fausta's Blog*, a news report was translated that showed Honduras officials – under Micheletti – had determined that the protesters who accompanied Zelaya to the Nicaraguan border were financed by FARC, the militant wing of the Columbian Communist Party with a less than stellar history.[21] It was Community Organizing on steroids. Providing further irony was the fact that Columbia – FARC's parent nation – was a member of the OAS, which was supporting FARC, if not overtly, then tacitly, through its support of Zelaya.

*Fausta's* translation of *Libertad Digital's* report was as follows:

> The article goes on to say that police seized a notebook and receipts showing that "Zelaya's government officials and supporters, leftist leaders, farmers, union members, and at least one mayor and one governor" were paid between $2,500 and $100,000 for the transportation of people and supplies" to the border region.
>
> The information was gathered from a computer seized from a FARC leader. No money was seized since the funds had already been distributed.[22]

As Zelaya was engaged in childish political stunts with nefarious intentions, in the form of FARC-style Community Organizing, Micheletti was making his case by enumerating the legal reasons for Zelaya's removal in an op-ed piece for the *Wall Street Journal*.[23] They were as follows:

- The Supreme Court, by a 15-0 vote, found that Mr. Zelaya had acted illegally by proceeding with an unconstitutional "referendum," and it ordered the Armed Forces to arrest him. The military executed the arrest order of the Supreme Court because it was the appropriate agency to do so under Honduran law.

- Eight of the 15 votes on the Supreme Court were cast by members of Mr. Zelaya's own Liberal Party. Strange that the pro-Zelaya propagandists who talk about the rule of law forget to mention the unanimous Supreme Court decision with a majority from Mr. Zelaya's own party. Thus, Mr. Zelaya's arrest was at the instigation of Honduran's constitutional and civilian authorities—not the military.
- The Honduran Congress voted overwhelmingly in support of removing Mr. Zelaya. The vote included a majority of members of Mr. Zelaya's Liberal Party.
- Independent government and religious leaders and institutions – including the Supreme Electoral Tribunal, the Administrative Law Tribunal, the independent Human Rights Ombudsman, four-out-of-five political parties, the two major Presidential candidates of the Liberal and National Parties, and Honduras's Catholic Cardinal – all agreed that Mr. Zelaya had acted illegally.
- The constitution expressly states in Article 239 that any president who seeks to amend the constitution and extend his term is automatically disqualified and is no longer president. There is no express provision for an impeachment process in the Honduran constitution. But the Supreme Court's unanimous decision affirmed that Mr. Zelaya was attempting to extend his term with his illegal referendum. Thus, at the time of his arrest he was no longer – as a matter of law, as far as the Supreme Court was concerned – President of Honduras.
- Days before his arrest, Mr. Zelaya had his chief of staff illegally withdraw millions of dollars in cash from the Central Bank of Honduras.
- A day or so before his arrest, Mr. Zelaya led a violent mob to overrun an Air Force base to seize referendum ballots that had been shipped into Honduras by Hugo Chávez's Venezuelan government.
- I succeeded Mr. Zelaya under the Honduran constitution's order of succession (our Vice President had resigned before all of this began so that he could run for President). This is and has always been an entirely civilian government. The military was ordered by an entirely civilian Supreme Court to arrest Mr. Zelaya. His removal

was ordered by an entirely civilian and elected Congress. To suggest that Mr. Zelaya was ousted by means of a military coup is demonstrably false.

The claim by Micheletti that Zelaya had millions of dollars illegally withdrawn from the Central Bank of Honduras was more than sufficiently substantiated. The *Washington Times* had reported on the story only days earlier. Not only did they have video of the money being wheeled away by agents of Zelaya but the surveillance camera that captured it was date stamped.

Additionally, the *Times* reported that this account was corroborated by multiple witnesses who testified under oath that the money was withdrawn to help Zelaya administer the illegal June 28th referendum. The money, according to witness testimony, was driven to the office of Enrique Flores Lanza, Zelaya's chief of staff.[24]

Regardless of what was acknowledged publicly by Zelaya's supporters – including Hugo Chavez, the Castro brothers, Daniel Ortega, and Barack Obama – the world stage on which Honduras' ousted President stood was being further defiled by inarguable facts about his character.

The radioactive fallout was damaging his supporters, regardless of how they tried to diminish that damage by feigning ignorance. Micheletti was the beneficiary and seemed to understand that if he stood his political ground, he could gain more if the former President continued showing his true colors. Did Micheletti know that Zelaya would unmask himself? Is this why Zelaya was exiled and not detained on June 28th?

If it wasn't the intention, events – as they played out – almost seemed to back up such a notion as being the best course of action given the circumstances. Zelaya's antics were not in short supply. His best – or worst – was yet to come.

Two months after Zelaya walked into Honduras from Nicaragua just to give Micheletti a raspberry, he doubled down hard on the behavior. On September 21st, the former Honduran President had returned to Honduras under cover of darkness, surfacing inside the Brazilian

embassy. The US State Department was almost immediately put in the unenviable position of having to answer questions about what it knew regarding the details of the situation. *Reuters* almost seemed to report the news as a counter-coup against Micheletti, stating that Zelaya's appearance had put increased pressure on the new government.[25]

Early on, this seemed like a victory for Zelaya, who demonstrated that he successfully navigated surreptitiously through his former country and reached a safe base from which to carry out some sort of a propaganda operation. As the days went on, that perceived success quickly devolved into an unmitigated disaster for the former President.

Exhibiting true leadership, Micheletti once again refused to take the bait. In much the same way Zelaya was allowed get away with stepping onto Honduran soil without incident – due more to the restraint of Micheletti's men than anything else – Honduras' new President took the high ground and summed up his position in very few words with respect to this grossly more reckless act on the part of Zelaya.

In an attempt to reassure Brazil that the Honduran military would not storm the embassy to arrest Zelaya, Micheletti said of Zelaya's presence at the embassy: he "can stay five to ten years" if he wants to.[26]

Throughout the ordeal, Micheletti's hard line on negotiations seemed to flummox Zelaya – and the world, for that matter – to the point that Zelaya's subsequent actions continued to do him increasingly more harm than good. An example of Micheletti's resolve was found in the closure of all Honduran airports, partially in response to the plans of Miguel Insulza, the secretary-general of the Organization of American States, who was planning to travel to Tegucigalpa to mediate an agreement.

Additionally, another man tasked with mediating between the two parties, Oscar Arias of Costa Rica, was basically dismissed by Micheletti when Arias would not deviate from his plan, which included re-installing Zelaya as President. Micheletti continued to insist that if Zelaya returned, he would be arrested and charged with treason.[27]

In the days after arriving at the Brazilian embassy, it became apparent that the initial elation Zelaya felt after making it to the embassy was wearing off. One of the reasons may have been the delayed realization that he was not a free man. Getting into the embassy would be much easier than getting out of it, especially in light of Micheletti's willingness to play hard ball.

Aside from the obvious reality that the Brazilian embassy served more as the Honduran version of 'Hotel California' than as an effective location for a strategic political platform, amenities were in short supply; rioting and looting was taking place outside as a result of Zelaya's presence. He demonstrated once again that he was willing to place himself over the interests of his former country and it was on display for the world to see. The *Miami Herald* reported on the conditions inside the embassy; Zelaya was relegated to sleeping on chairs and at one point had no change of clothes or toothpaste.[28]

Perhaps the most bizarre storyline of the entire saga involved the claims made by Zelaya about what was being done to him – and by whom – as he was holed up in the embassy. He insisted that his throat was sore thanks to "Israeli mercenaries" that were torturing him with high frequency radiation and toxic gases. As Micheletti exercised calm and reasoned political decision making in the face of unbelievable international pressure, the former President was having delusions of persecution, at one point saying that those Israeli mercenaries would attempt to storm the embassy and assassinate him.[29]

This irrational fear of Jews on the part of Zelaya added teeth to the claims that David Romero Ellner, head of *Radio Globo*, was in fact Zelaya's "chief propagandist." As reported earlier in this chapter, Ellner made claims that demonstrated he supported Hitler's solution.

In the months prior to holing himself up in the Brazilian embassy, Zelaya had developed an interesting relationship with the US State Department.

## ■ THE US STATE DEPARTMENT

On July 24, 2009 Secretary of State Hillary Clinton made a very public statement about Manuel Zelaya's ill-advised, childish, and FARC-funded entry into Honduras. She called it "reckless" while also endorsing the Oscar Arias plan for resolution. Arias' plan included the reinstatement of Zelaya as President; it also granted amnesty to those who removed him – constitutionally – from power.[30] Predictably, no mention of FARC was made. Are we to believe that the US State Department knew nothing of that connection?

The State Department had just been presented with an example of Zelaya's "reckless" behavior that it begrudgingly had to acknowledge. Instead of using this example as cause to re-examine the claims of the Micheletti-led government about Zelaya, it doubled down; Hillary Clinton acknowledged Zelaya's "reckless" behavior but continued to stand by him as the lawful President of his former nation despite the facts and the newly revealed character flaw – recklessness.

An example of the State Department's continued support for Zelaya came in the form of revoked visas days after Hillary's public statement about Zelaya's behavior. On July 28th, State Department spokesman Ian Kelly announced that the visas of four Honduran officials within the Micheletti government had been revoked. At the time, Kelly did not name the four but he did say that the revocations had to do with the stated position of the United States that the new Honduran government would not be recognized as legitimate.[31]

Perhaps even more telling was an exchange between a reporter and Kelly at the State Department press conference that same day. As a backdrop, the United States had suspended millions of dollars in aid to Honduras in response to Zelaya's removal.[32] During the press conference with Kelly, a reporter sought clarification on the stated policy within the State Department. That policy was ostensibly that the Legal Adviser's Office was in the process of determining whether Zelaya's removal was in fact constitutional. The presumption was that if it was determined to be unconstitutional, aid to Honduras would be suspended. The reporter caught Kelly in a position from which the latter could not successfully extricate himself.[33]

Here is the relevant portion of the transcript between the reporter and Ian Kelly:

QUESTION: And one – one other on Honduras. I'm well aware that the Legal Adviser's Office was examining whether the events in Honduras technically met their definition of a coup and therefore would trigger the cutoff in aid that I realize you have already suspended.

**MR. KELLY:** Yes.

**QUESTION:** Have you yet reached a determination on that question?

**MR. KELLY:** I'll have to get you an update on that.

The success of Micheletti's resolve cannot be overstated. In refusing to back down to the demands of the US State Department, he put them in a box. Was aid to Honduras suspended prior to determining if Zelaya's removal was constitutional because the Clinton-led State Department had no intention of exploring that possibility? Had Clinton's State Department failed to anticipate Micheletti's resolve? Micheletti's refusal to budge on the constitutionality of Zelaya's removal certainly raised those questions. Those possibilities were given viability when Kelly could not answer a very simple question about the State Department's position.

*The Hill* reported on July 29th that the revoked visas of Honduran officials may have been prompted by a letter the Obama administration received from Manuel Zelaya directly in which that request was made, along with a request to freeze select bank accounts of officials with the Micheletti government.[34] In light of the exchange between Ian Kelly and reporters at the State Department press briefing only a day earlier, it was a substantially newsworthy claim.

In the letter, Zelaya reportedly named names of people he wanted the Obama administration to target. One of them was said to be that of General Romeo Vasquez Velasquez, the military official Zelaya fired for not carrying out his orders with respect to the referendum. Another individual reportedly named in the letter was Judge Jose Tomas Arita Valle, the head of the Supreme Court responsible for giving the final sign-off to have Zelaya arrested. This was according to the deputy foreign minister of Micheletti's government.[35]

In the case of Arita Valle, a Honduran newspaper posted a copy of the letter he received, which stated his US visa had been revoked. Did the letter sent to Obama by Zelaya actually prompt this revocation? If so, did it prompt the other three? Additionally, a Spanish language newspaper named *Noticias 24* was translated by *Fausta* and reported that Zelaya stated Obama acted on his letters to revoke visas but that he expected more. Here is the relevant portion of the translation:

From Nicaragua, where he remains and is organizing a "resistance" movement for returning to Honduras, Zelaya acknowledged to the media that Pres. Obama's decision to revoke the visas of four Micheletti administration's officials is "a signal that it does not accept the coup d'etat."

However, he demanded that Obama "continue to squeeze them by seizing their [US bank] accounts, their money."[36]

US Senator from South Carolina Jim DeMint (R) threatened to delay the nomination of Arturo Valenzuela, who was picked to be assistant secretary of state for western hemisphere affairs.[37] This was a sign that the Obama administration could not take such a radical position in central America without feeling repercussions at home. DeMint would later find himself in a political battle with Massachusetts Senator John Kerry over US policy toward Honduras.

As chairman of the Senate foreign relations committee, Kerry attempted to prevent DeMint and three other Republican members of Congress from traveling to Honduras on a fact-finding mission. Though not successful, Kerry showed how much he was in agreement with the policy of Obama and the State Department when it came to Honduras. DeMint countered Kerry by reminding the Democratic Senator from Massachusetts that Zelaya was an ally of Hugo Chavez and that he was removed constitutionally. Kerry eventually relented and DeMint did indeed travel to Honduras.[38]

Upon DeMint's return from Honduras, it became apparent why Kerry didn't want him to travel there in the first place. The Republican Senator would find the supposed chaos that was the result of an alleged coup was non-existent and that constitutional order had been restored to that country. On October 10th, an editorial by DeMint appeared in the *Wall Street Journal* in which he discussed his findings. DeMint wrote:

While in Honduras, I spoke to dozens of Hondurans, from nonpartisan members of civil society to former Zelaya political allies, from Supreme Court judges to Presidential candidates and even personal friends of Mr. Zelaya. Each relayed stories of a man changed and corrupted by power. The evidence of Mr. Zelaya's abuses of presidential power—and his illegal attempts to rewrite the Honduran Constitution, ála Hugo Chávez – is not only overwhelming but uncontroverted.[39]

Additionally, DeMint claimed that in a day full of meetings in Tegucigalpa, he only found one person who supported the reinstatement of Zelaya as President. Ironically, that individual wasn't even a member of the Honduran government or its citizenry. Rather, it was Hugo Llorens, US ambassador to the country. When DeMint asked Llorens to provide legal justification for the ambassador's position, Llorens referred him to the legal opinion of the State Department's lead attorney, Harold Koh. That opinion was not made available to DeMint.[40]

The State Department's stand against Micheletti began to crack in early August when a letter was sent to Senators Richard Lugar (R) from Indiana and DeMint. The letter showed signs of equivocation. The letter to Lugar and DeMint from Richard Verma, assistant secretary for legislative affairs, was heavy on nuance. The wording seemed to indicate the State Department wanted to be seen as having no loyalty to Zelaya while supporting his reinstatement after he was constitutionally removed.

"Our policy and strategy for engagement is not based on supporting any particular politician or individual. Rather, it is based on finding a resolution that best serves the Honduran people and their democratic aspirations."[41]

The absurdity was palpable. The State Department wanted to distance itself from Zelaya while ruling in his favor without having all the facts. The Obama administration had been standing by Zelaya since June 28th. Micheletti achieved a small victory with that letter. The decision to stand up for his country was beginning to pay off; the State Department was blinking first.

When one factors in the stance of the State Department, that Zelaya was removed courtesy of a "coup" that was "not legal" – Obama's words – how could the letter be a sign of anything other than defeat? The Obama administration was seeking a diplomatic solution with or without Zelaya as a key piece of the puzzle. Micheletti was winning.

## ■ HONDURAN PATRIOT REVEALED

By late August of 2009, it became apparent that Micheletti had the edge, which is what made an offer he extended to Zelaya all the more telling. With the high ground firmly in hand and victory within his grasp, Micheletti offered to allow Zelaya's return to Honduras on the condition that both men renounce their respective claims to the presidency.[42] If Micheletti had been more concerned with consolidating power and seizing control than in preventing Zelaya from acquiring it, this offer never would have been made; it demonstrated deference to country.

Moreover, Micheletti demonstrated openly that he was not fixated on power. Based on the constitution he referred to for Zelaya's ouster, Micheletti would not even be able to run for reelection only a few months later. Micheletti was leading by example; he was demonstrating to Zelaya exactly what that meant.

Even former Clinton White House legal counsel Lanny Davis recognized this for what it was.

> "...Mr. Micheletti is not concerned about power – he is offering to resign entirely from public life... The question is, does Mr. Zelaya acknowledge that no one, even the President, is above the law?"[43]

The Honduran constitution would forbid not only Zelaya from being on the ballot for the November 29th election but also Micheletti. The former was seeking ways to get around that part of his country's constitution while the latter appeared determined to honor it. By all accounts, the man in power didn't really appear to want it all that much; it was a rare but welcome sight to those who value patriotism being placed above self-interest.

## ■ MURDER AND KIDNAPPING

By late October, it was becoming apparent that Micheletti would not back down. If he could hold out just a bit longer, he would be able to step down as President and watch a newly elected replacement fill the vacancy. The elections were little more than one month away when the *BBC* reported that Micheletti's nephew, Enzo Micheletti, had been murdered execution style; his hands were tied behind his back and he had been shot multiple times, several miles north of Tegucigalpa.[44]

In addition to Enzo Micheletti's murder – his body was discovered on Sunday, October 25th – a military officer was gunned down later that evening outside his Tegucigalpa home; he died later of his injuries. The incidents were reported to have been separate as Enzo's body was found two days after he had been killed and much farther north of Tegucigalpa than where Col. Concepcion Jimenez had been shot.[45]

The misfortunes of people having varying degrees of separation from Micheletti continued days later as the father of the acting deputy defense minister Gabo Jalil was kidnapped. The wife of Alfredo Jalil was reportedly convinced that Zelaya was behind the kidnapping.[46]

These three tragic incidents collectively represented the third time the mettle of Honduran President Micheletti was tested. The first was when Zelaya walked into Honduras from Nicaragua to provoke an incident; the second was when Zelaya popped up in the Brazilian embassy in Tegucigalpa for the same reason; this third test was even more difficult for Micheletti to pass because it called for restraint in the face of murder and kidnapping of family and soldiers. He would exercise a level of restraint many lesser men would not have been able to muster.

If one or more of these incidents had been tied back to Zelaya, Micheletti could have almost been excused for not exercising restraint. The three coincidences of murder and kidnapping, which all transpired in less than one week of each other, certainly would have raised suspicions at a time when stress levels were already off the charts. Micheletti's leadership had reached an unimpeachable level. Had he cracked down, he could have given the international community an

excuse to intervene militarily; he inherently must have known this and continued to stay the course.

Prior to the aforementioned events, *Reuters* published a news report on October 12th that highlighted the supposed lawlessness at the hands of the Micheletti government that was taking place in Honduras in the aftermath of Zelaya's removal. The reporting was in stark contrast to what Republican Senator Jim DeMint reported in his *Wall Street Journal* Op-ed two days earlier. It also painted a picture that would prove to be in direct opposition to the restraint Micheletti would soon demonstrate in the face of the murder of a nephew, a colonel, and the kidnapping of the father of his deputy defense minister.

The *Reuters* article was actually critical of the new government for confronting protesters who arrived outside the Brazilian embassy once they learned Zelaya had secretly entered the compound. Instead of identifying Zelaya as the lawbreaker, *Reuters* focused on how the protesters were the victims **[See Chapter 2, p. 33]**, while absolving the ousted President of any responsibility for stirring up lawlessness.[47] An important point to remember is that FARC had been implicated in the organizing of earlier Zelaya protesters when the former President stepped into Honduras from Nicaragua.

## ■ THE ELECTION

Turnout for the November 29th elections was significant. That didn't bode well for Zelaya, who had publicly called for a boycott of the election. When the votes were counted, the conservative candidate Porfirio Lobo – a rancher – had garnered 56 percent of the vote compared with 38 percent received by his liberal opponent.[48]

As the votes were counted, the US was forced to acknowledge the winner as the new President of Honduras. The election and vote count transpired as Zelaya remained holed up inside the Brazilian embassy. His fate subsequent to the election would prove interesting.

While the US State Department acknowledged Lobo's victory, it also seemed to hedge its bets. Simply accepting the election results without condition would signal surrender. Nuance was needed so the

State Department's official stance was that it would honor the election results but not accept them as the best solution for ending the crisis that started on June 28th.[49]

As Micheletti was breathing a sigh of relief, preparing to withdraw into obscurity and Lobo was excitedly looking forward to leading a new era in Honduras, the US State Department was crafting a strategy designed to save face while barking all along the way. Assistant Secretary of State for Western Hemisphere Affairs, Arturo Valenzuela told Honduras on November 30th what it must do in order to find itself back in the good graces of the OAS:

> "For the countries of the Hemisphere and for the United States, to work towards the restoration of Honduras to the Organization of American States [OAS] later on, Honduras must do more than just this election."[50]

Apparently lost on Valenzuela was the fact that Honduras had just defeated the entire world. They weren't even given a full day to celebrate. The last thing the newly elected Honduran government was thinking about was how to find its way back into the good graces of a hemispheric body that had aligned against it in a show of intimidation.

On January 27th, 2010 Lobo was sworn in as President of Honduras. Somewhere, Micheletti was likely breathing a sigh of relief; his job was done. Zelaya was still holed up in the Brazilian embassy but one of Lobo's first acts as President was to ensure Zelaya's safe passage outside of Honduras.[51]

Zelaya appeared to at least tacitly concede defeat when he requested that he be allowed to leave Honduras for the Dominican Republic. Lobo not only granted this request but dropped the charges of treason.[52]

The former Honduran President would continue living in the Dominican Republic until Lobo signed an agreement with him in 2011 that allowed the former President to return. It was a sign that Lobo didn't quite measure up to Micheletti. US Rep. Ileana Ros-Lehtinen, chairman of the House Foreign Affairs Committee insisted that Hugo

Chavez was involved in the deal and warned of Zelaya's intentions while Secretary of State Clinton lauded the agreement.[53]

## ◼ WIKILEAKS REVELATIONS

When it came to the battle between Manuel Zelaya and Roberto Micheletti, one thing is certain. The United States, under the Obama administration, aggressively supported the reinstatement of Zelaya. Could that support have been motivated by a desire to win favor with Hugo Chavez?

In late 2010, an organization known as *WikiLeaks* released hundreds of thousands of diplomatic cables that were incredibly damaging to governments across the globe. Julian Assange, editor in chief of the group, arguably caused great harm to American national security but in the case of Honduras, two cables proved what many suspected – the Obama administration's position had not been adequately communicated to the public. The document population that was released included cables from the US embassy in Tegucigalpa which provided insight into the mindset of the Obama administration during the crisis.

In Central America, Venezuela's Hugo Chavez was the bully on the block. His guy in Honduras was Zelaya. The public stance from the Obama administration was that Zelaya had been removed via coup. Conspicuously absent from that public stance was a response to the claims that Zelaya's removal was constitutional. The administration went out of its way to avoid addressing that issue.

According to two cables, the private stance seemed to involve a concession that Micheletti's claims had merit, which would explain why the administration publicly avoided the issue.

In one of the cables, Obama's Ambassador to Honduras – Llorens – conceded that the case against Zelaya was warranted but subsequently argued that his removal was still the result of a conspiracy.[54] Questions about why the Obama administration would so vigorously support such a strong ally of Hugo Chavez in Zelaya may not have been answered but questions about how biased it was in that support were.

Courtesy of *WikiLeaks*, it's no longer a secret that Obama was informed by his ambassador to Honduras that Micheletti had a case.

In standing his ground, Micheletti unwittingly reinforced perceptions that Obama was indeed an ideologue who didn't have the courage to state publicly what he believed privately.

Micheletti didn't have that problem.

## ■ BATTLE ASSESSMENT

When viewed objectively, the nation of Honduras was in the midst of a Constitutional crisis after removing its President from office on June 28, 2009. While the removal of Manuel Zelaya was indeed constitutional, the entire world – save for a few countries, including Taiwan and Israel – collectively sided with the ousted, would-be dictator in Zelaya.

Consider that a small nation in Central America stood up against the Organization of American States (OAS) – which included the United States, Mexico, and Canada – as well as the United Nations. Leaders of nations that opposed Micheletti were Barack Obama, Hillary Clinton, the Castro brothers, Daniel Ortega, and Hugo Chavez.

Every authoritative analysis that was done on Zelaya's removal showed that the Honduran government acted properly and legally. In fact, that government would have been derelict had it not acted. Yet, the world continued to push the lie that Zelaya was the victim of a coup d'état. The liberal media actively picked up that narrative, which made Micheletti's odds of success even longer.

At multiple points during the saga that played out from June 28, 2009 through early 2010, interim President Micheletti could have compromised in some form or fashion, saving face, while getting more than what he otherwise would have, had Zelaya not been forcibly removed. Instead, Micheletti refused to back down. He did not compromise. He did not waver. He had the law and the truth on his side and he used them masterfully as two very powerful weapons. He didn't sheath them or attempt to soften their blows. He fought with them hard – and won.

Paradoxically, the Honduran President that replaced Zelaya did not embrace power for power's sake. His actions communicated that he embraced accountability and love of country first and foremost. While Zelaya thirsted for power, Micheletti visibly wanted to cede it, though lawfully, and only after the November 29th election and the swearing in of Lobo on January 27th. Amazingly, Zelaya would not regain that power before Micheletti handed it over voluntarily to someone his fellow countrymen overwhelmingly elected.

Micheletti's actions were reminiscent of those of George Washington in some respects. He demonstrated a willingness to serve his country admirably – unlike Zelaya, whose actions demonstrated a desire to secure power indefinitely.

Had the world community sided with Micheletti – as it should have – this crisis would have been much more easily managed and it would have ended much sooner. Had the interim leader of Honduras been someone other than Micheletti, Zelaya may be President and dictator of Honduras today, not because he deserved it but because any other adversary would likely have chosen the path of least resistance.

Micheletti also exhibited extremely admirable levels of discretion throughout his brief tenure. Zelaya attempted to bait him on multiple occasions but Micheletti did not bite – also characteristics of true leadership.

In January of 2010, Roberto Micheletti was victorious. Again, paradoxically, that victory wasn't complete until he handed power over to another man – Porfirio Lobo.

# CHAPTER 4

## LARRY GRATHWOHL
### vs.
# WEATHER UNDERGROUND

### ■ UNEXPECTED CALL TO SERVE

A young Larry Grathwohl had already served his country. He enlisted in the Army and joined the 101st Airborne before being sent to Vietnam in 1965. He then extended his tour as a drill instructor. Unbeknownst to him, while standing on a Cincinnati street corner in 1969, he would soon feel called upon to serve his country once again.

As a student at the University of Cincinnati at the time, he was talking with some friends when two members of an extreme leftwing militant group known as the Weathermen – which would eventually become known as the Weather Underground – approached them. Grathwohl didn't like what they were selling – newspapers and radicalism. Subsequently, through a seemingly innocuous chain of events, his resolve took root and he would soon begin another tour of duty, only this time with an extremely unique distinction; he would become the only man to successfully infiltrate the Weather Underground for the FBI.[1]

For approximately six months, Grathwohl put his life in danger on American soil while simultaneously moving up through the ranks of a group whose leaders would become household names years later in 2008 – during the presidential campaign of Barack Obama. Bill Ayers and his wife Bernadine Dohrn were at the top of the list; Grathwohl came to know them both as an Informer.

Grathwohl's cover was blown not because of a mistake on his part but because the FBI was eager for an arrest after three Weathermen were killed in a bomb explosion in New York City.[2] The orders came down from Washington and Grathwohl wasn't happy. Rather than arrest several of the top leaders when the time was right, the FBI would only get Linda Evans. In exchange, they were willing to risk revealing Grathwohl's true identity to the group – and that is exactly what happened.[3]

Although his time underground had ended, Grathwohl would garner interest again almost thirty years later when questions arose about Obama's ties to Ayers.

In the years between, Grathwohl would write a book and live a humble life. Conversely, Bill Ayers would handle millions of dollars with the Chicago Annenberg Challenge and other organizations. In 2008, Grathwohl was doing all he could to get by while Ayers was living a lavish lifestyle. Injustice couldn't have been more obvious.

Lies were rewarded with acclaim and the truth assailed with silence.

## ■ TWO MINUTES IN 1982

In 1982, Grathwohl appeared in a documentary entitled, *No Place to Hide*. Thanks to the technology that is *YouTube*, coupled with public interest in the background of the man who would become the 44th President of the United States, Grathwohl's story resurfaced, though certainly not to the extent it should have. The relevant excerpt of the film went semi-viral in October of 2008, weeks before the election; the explosive portion of that appearance was barely two minutes in length. In it, Grathwohl explained his interactions with the group's leadership – which included Ayers – during meetings:

> "I brought up the subject of what's going to happen after we take over the government. You know, we, we become responsible then for administrating you know, 250 million people. And there was no answers. No one had given any thought to economics – how are you going to clothe and feed these people?
>
> The only thing that I could get was that they expected that the Cubans and the North Vietnamese and the Chinese and

the Russians would all want to occupy different portions of the United States. They also believed that their immediate responsibility would be to protect against what they called the counter-revolution. They felt that this counter-revolution could best be guarded against by creating and establishing re-education centers in the southwest, where we would take all the people who needed to re-educated into the new way of thinking and teach them how things were going to be.

I asked, 'Well what is going to happen to those people that we can't re-educate, that are die-hard capitalists?' The reply was that they'd have to be eliminated. When I pursued this further, they estimated that they would have to eliminate 25 million people in these re-education centers and when I say 'eliminate' I mean 'kill' – 25 million people.

I want you to imagine sitting in a room with 25 people, most of which have graduate degrees from Columbia and other well known educational centers and hear them figuring out the logistics for the elimination of 25 million people, and they were dead serious."[4]

Such claims were extremely alarming in light of the allegedly close relationship between the Democratic nominee for President – Barack Obama – and the Weather Underground's Bill Ayers.

Had Obama been vetted, his affiliation with Ayers alone would have prevented him from even dreaming of the presidency. Instead, he was given an ogling pass by the liberal media establishment.

## ■ THE OBAMA/AYERS RELATIONSHIP

Though the mainstream media refused to investigate or report anything that might harm the Obama campaign in 2008, some facts did manage to surface; nothing seemed to trump the overwhelming public intoxication for Obama's candidacy, however. The media – as well as its subjects – had drunk the kool-aid. Among the most egregiously under-reported stories was Obama's relationship with Bill Ayers. Obama's political career was launched in the home of Ayers and

Dohrn in 1995. The future President also served as chairman of the Chicago Annenberg Challenge (CAC), a group Ayers helped found.[5] Logic must necessarily lead to the extremely likely conclusion that Ayers had a hand in Obama getting that job.

Raising even more red flags with respect to the relationship between Obama and Ayers were some documents and photos posted to the *Verum Serum* blog on October 16, 2008. During Obama's tenure as CAC chairman, he oversaw grants totaling more than $1 million to another Bill Ayers group known as the Small Schools Workshop (SSW). The facts are that Ayers helped found the CAC; he ostensibly helped make Obama chairman; his organization then received over $1 million from the CAC under Obama's leadership. Does that not scream conflict of interest to even the least of the intoxicated?[6]

Perhaps even more shocking were the implications of the documents and photos posted by *Verum Serum*. Thanks to tax returns, letters, and various other paper trails, it was proven that Barack Obama and Bill Ayers shared a business address for at least three years from 1995 – 1998 at 115 South Sangamon Street, 3rd floor in Chicago **(Appendix A)**.[7]

Moreover, that same office was shared with a Chinese Maoist named Mike Klonsky for some time as well **(Appendix B)**. The Obama administration would later become known for housing individuals with expressed affinities for Mao. Anita Dunn, Ron Bloom, and Van Jones were among them.

In an April, 2008 primary debate between Obama and Hillary Clinton, *ABC* moderator George Stephanopoulos surprisingly asked Obama about his relationship with Ayers. The future President dismissed any such concern, saying he was eight years-old when Ayers was committing his "detestable acts" and that the two shared little more in common than the same neighborhood at the time of the debate. The implication was that no relationship of consequence existed and that Obama should be absolved of any and all guilt by association.

Clinton attempted to keep the issue alive by pointing to Obama's time on a board with Ayers at the Woods Foundation but was effectively shut down when Obama pointed to the fact that her husband

Bill commuted the sentences of two members of the Weather Underground before he left office.[8] Those two members were Linda Evans and Susan Rosenberg. Interestingly, it was Evans who Grathwohl was with when the former was arrested and the latter's cover was blown.[9]

Prior to October of 2008, I had never heard the name Larry Grathwohl and was introduced to him courtesy of the internet. Upon reading an article on the *Pajamas Media* website by Bob Owens entitled, "Eyewitness to the Ayers Revolution,"[10] I sought Grathwohl out and had the opportunity to talk with him.

On October 29th, Grathwohl appeared on the number one cable news show in America at the time. "O'Reilly Factor," host Bill O'Reilly interviewed Grathwohl on the *Fox News Channel*. It was with great anticipation that I tuned in, thinking that the bombshell about the intentions of the Weather Underground would be dropped; the interview was a disappointment in that regard as the most explosive claims made by Grathwohl about the Weather Underground's plans, which involved the mass extermination of millions of people, were not discussed.

It was a missed opportunity for the media to provide a much needed shock to Americans days before the election of Barack Obama as President.[11]

On November 2nd, two days before the election, Grathwohl appeared on my radio show. The more I thought about the implications of his claims, the more concerned I became for my country's future. That realization hit me like a ton of bricks on my way to the studio that day. I was hit with a flood of emotion coupled with an acute realization that the Obama presidency would be very bad for our nation. I will never forget that day.

If Grathwohl was right, America was going to elect a man to the highest office in the land who had a very close relationship with someone who had aspirations of topping Hitler's genocidal devastation. During that interview, he wasted no time talking about the objectives of the Weather Underground. "The Weather Underground's sole purpose was to overthrow the government of the United States," he said. "They intended to do this through...bombings."

Moreover, Ayers developed a reputation for being an unrepentant terrorist during the 2008 campaign because he never expressed any remorse for what he or his group had done. The now infamous quote of his, printed in a 2001 *New York Times* article was repeated in the conservative media during the campaign: "I don't regret setting bombs…I feel we didn't do enough." [12]

Another narrative that Ayers consistently repeated was that while his group did set off bombs, they killed no one. In that same *New York Times* article, he was quoted as saying, "I didn't kill innocent people." [13] It was a claim that Grathwohl vehemently denied. Unlike Ayers, Grathwohl made his claims under penalty of perjury. In *Bringing Down America*, Grathwohl's book, he relayed what Ayers said at one of the Weather Underground's meetings after a recent bombing:

> "It was a success," he said, "but it's a shame when someone like Bernadine (Dohrn) has to make all the plans, make the bomb, and then place it herself. She should have to do only the planning." [14]

A police officer named Brian V. McDonnell was killed as a result of that bombing at San Francisco's Park Police Station on February 16, 1970. Ayers' admission – as relayed by Grathwohl – would not only make his wife a murderer but also the murderer of a police officer. As of this writing, Grathwohl has been working very closely with others to re-open this case; he correctly points out that there is no statute of limitation on murder.

Even if one could somehow inexplicably dismiss the murder of McDonnell as completely accidental, further comments by Ayers relayed to Grathwohl would indicate that the former had absolutely no compunction about the loss of innocent life in the furtherance of his group's revolution.

One of Grathwohl's assignments while with the Underground was to help bomb the Detroit Police Officers Association (DPOA) building. He protested that the placement of the bomb should be in the rear of the building instead of on the side; His rationale was that innocent people in the Red Barn restaurant next door could be killed by the fence staples packed into the bomb. Ayers then told him, "We can't protect all the innocent people in the world. Some will get killed. Some of us will get killed. We have to accept that fact. The bomb is going to be placed on the side of the building."

Grathwohl even wrote about objecting at a later date. Ayers said again, "Stop worrying about those people in that restaurant. That's not your concern. You can't build a revolution worrying about a handful of people."[15]

To give Ayers the benefit of the doubt to this point would involve granting him lack of intent with respect to McDonnell's murder and the acceptance of collateral damage in the form of prospective innocents being killed in Detroit. How about Ayers giving his nod of approval to the assassination of Vice President Spiro Agnew and Detroit's Mayor respectively? The only reasons for the suggestions being dismissed involved practicality, not desire.[16]

Ayers clearly hated the police and sympathized with criminals. That too was reflected in 2008 as a *Chicago Tribune* article reported that Ayers' office door was adorned with photos of convicted cop killer Mumia Abu-Jamal.[17] Shockingly, a man who would become a member of the Barack Obama administration as the Special Advisor for Green Jobs, Van Jones had a past that included support for Abu-Jamal as well.

Once again, thanks to the *Verum Serum* blog, it was learned that a record label funded by the Ella Baker Center, an organization that Van Jones founded, featured Abu-Jamal as a narrator on an album entitled, *War Times: Reports from the Opposition*. The lyrics were explicit and seemed to echo the sentiments of Ayers' Weather Underground in the 60s. Not only was Jones the Executive Director of the Ella Baker Center, which funded the album's production but he personally appeared on it as well.[18]

Another revelation that dogged Jones was his signature on a 9/11 Truth document that alleged US government involvement in the September 11th attacks [See Chapter 9, p. 257]. Shockingly, the White House insisted that Jones was not fired; he resigned of his own volition. If ever there was an example of a statement that needed to be made by a White House administration in the form of a firing, it was in this instance. Yet, the official stance was that the decision to leave belonged solely to Jones. The White House punted on an issue it absolutely shouldn't have, if it was even remotely interested in debunking accusations that it was sympathetic to Socialist, Communist, or Marxist ideologies.[19]

Less than two months earlier, Obama displayed bias against the Cambridge Police Department during a press conference about the arrest of his friend, Henry Louis Gates. Obama – after being asked about the incident in which Gates was arrested at his home and charged with disorderly conduct – conceded that he didn't have all the "facts" but proceeded to assert that the police had "acted stupidly."[20]

As the facts did come out, Obama's comments proved to be a public relations disaster and led to what became infamously known as the White House beer summit; it was a tacit admission on the part of the administration that the episode was a major *faux pas*. Nonetheless, the incident proved that Obama was indeed capable of jumping to conclusions if those conclusions painted police officers in a negative light. Ayers would almost certainly have approved; he liked to refer to all law enforcement as "Pigs."

In an August 13, 2009 article written by Aaron Klein, it was revealed that another founder of the Weather Underground – Jeff Jones – served on a board with Green Jobs Czar Van Jones. The Apollo Alliance was instrumental in writing the infamous stimulus bill that Barack Obama fought for shortly after assuming office in 2009. This reality not only connected Barack Obama to a very close colleague of Bill Ayers but to someone who co-founded the Weather Underground with Ayers.[21]

Another scandal that dogged the Obama administration began on Election Day, 2008, at a Philadelphia polling station when two members of the New Black Panther Party (NBPP) were caught on video intimidating voters. One man was holding a night stick. Charges were brought against the two men, their group's leader, and the group itself by Justice Department Attorneys under the outgoing George W. Bush administration. After winning a default judgment, attorneys in Obama's Justice Department, headed by Attorney General Eric Holder, inexplicably dropped the case [See Chapter 6, p. 162].

The circumstances surrounding the decision were so suspect that the scandal would not go away. One DOJ attorney resigned in order to testify in front of the US Commission on Civil Rights and another defied DOJ orders not to testify and did so anyway. As the matter played out, it became more and more apparent that the culture within the Justice Department – when it came to equal enforcement of the law in a race-neutral manner – was deplorable.[22]

The case will not be analyzed here. There is plenty about it elsewhere. What is important is how it fits into the larger context of how Bill Ayers and Barack Obama view the world. The decision to drop the case had increasingly been shown to have involved members very high in Obama's Justice Department. The closer that decision got to Obama, the more it became a reflection of his own belief system; it would also demonstrate a racial bias he was supposed to help get America past.

In the 1960s and 70s, the Weather Underground allied with the Black Panthers and the Black Liberation Army (BLA); Ayers viewed them as comrades against US imperialism. In 2008, the New Black Panther Party – though adamant it had no affiliation with its earlier namesake – shared many of the same goals, tactics, and traits. The premise that the groups were not affiliated begs a question. Why would a group that doesn't want to be seen as affiliated with another group, adopt the same name? As a member of the Weather Underground, Ayers and the Black Panthers had shared goals. Members of the Underground fought alongside the members of the BLA. As President of the United States, Obama's Justice Department seemed to go out of its way to defend the New Black Panther Party (NBPP).

Obama and Ayers shared another common experience – exposure to bizarre, destructive, and dysfunctional sexual behaviors, cultures and ideals. As Grathwohl discovered while with the Weathermen, the revolution trumped relationships. Monogamy was vehemently rejected inside the group. It was viewed as a threat to the overall movement.[23]

Ayers also rejected monogamy to the point of engaging in at least one homosexual relationship. This, according to an article in the *New York Times*:

He (Ayers) also writes about the Weathermen's sexual experimentation as they tried to "smash monogamy." The Weathermen were "an army of lovers," he says, and describes having had different sexual partners, including his best male friend.[24]

Whether he realized it or not, Ayers' comments about monogamy served to corroborate Grathwohl's claims about his experiences with one of the women in the group, Naomi Jaffee; she was Grathwohl's girlfriend for a time and rejected monogamy herself.

Conversely, when Obama was ten years old, he was introduced to a black man named Frank Marshall Davis by his maternal grandfather. Obama wrote about Davis in his book, *Dreams From My Father*, referring to him only as 'Frank.' As an added touch of irony, writer Jack Cashill made the argument that Ayers was likely the author of that book.[25]

In addition to being a communist who had accumulated a 600 page FBI file, Davis was also a sexual pervert, an admitted bi-sexual who wrote about sex acts with a 13 year-old girl in a self-described autobiographical novel entitled *Sex Rebel*. The editor of the book – John Edgar Tidwell – attempted to qualify the content by saying it was only "semi-autobiographical."[26]

Notwithstanding the extension of such seemingly unwarranted and gracious courtesy, the fact remains that Davis was a sexual pervert who had influence over a very young Barack Obama.

In a *UK Telegraph* article written by Toby Harnden a few short months before the 2008 election, the words attributed to Davis himself seem to make the case that there was nothing "semi" autobiographical about the book:

> "I could not then truthfully deny that this book, which came out in 1968 as a Greenleaf Classic, was mine." In the introduction to *Sex Rebel*, Mr Davis (writing as Greene) explains that although he has "changed names and identities…all incidents I have described have been taken from actual experiences."[27]

In addition to the likes of Frank Marshall Davis being a part of Obama's early life, prior to that – and possibly after being introduced to Davis initially – Obama spent approximately four years in Indonesia living with an openly gay male transvestite as his nanny, according to an article in the *New York Times* that featured Obama's November 2010 trip to the country where he once lived.

His nanny was an openly gay man who, in keeping with Indonesia's relaxed attitudes toward homosexuality, carried on an affair with a local butcher, longtime residents said. The nanny later joined a group of transvestites called Fantastic Dolls, who, like the many transvestites who remain fixtures of Jakarta's streetscape, entertained people by dancing and playing volleyball.[28]

After a very young Obama had lived with a gay male transvestite, he was mentored by a sex pervert (Davis) with ties to the Communist Party USA. Years later, Obama would be introduced to a man – Ayers – who admitted to having had at least one homosexual relationship, with his best male friend, while belonging to a group that rejected monogamy.

Is the American public to believe that the relationship between Ayers and Obama did not involve any discussion whatsoever of these personal experiences after the two worked with millions of dollars together and shared an office building for at least three years?

Obama and Ayers shared something in common beyond a business address – exposure to bizarre sexual cultures. Obama's early exposure to that culture was not his fault. Nonetheless, that exposure was something that Bill Ayers could have exploited had he chosen to do so. Taking the tactic of exploitation off the table when talking about Ayers would not be wise. The similarities between Ayers and Davis cannot be dismissed either. Both were introduced to a younger Obama; both had aspirations of a leftwing ideology supplanting the United States Constitution; and both had backgrounds that showed exposure to perverse sexual cultures.

Consequently, a relationship between Barack Obama and Bill Ayers was likely much closer than what the liberal media was willing to report in 2008.

## ■ A MURDERED POLICE OFFICER

At 10:45pm on February 16th, 1970 a police officer by the name of Brian V. McDonnell was standing at the Teletype machine inside the Park Police station in San Francisco, CA. A co-worker named Frank Rath was seated nearby. As Rath leaned back in his chair to relax, a bomb loaded with inch-long fence staples on a nearby ledge outside exploded right in front of McDonnell. Rath escaped death by coincidentally leaning backward moments before the blast but McDonnell wasn't so lucky. Staples severed his jugular and lodged in his brain. He died two days later.

That is what retired San Francisco police officer James Pera relayed to me in a radio interview I conducted with both he and Grathwohl in 2009. The interview was prompted by an article written by Peter Jamison that appeared in *San Francisco Weekly* two days earlier.[29] Both Grathwohl and Pera were very pleased with the article because of the degree to which it validated Grathwohl's story.

After the explosion, Pera was one of the first on the scene. He was 24 years old at the time and revered McDonnell as a personal "mentor" of his and a "highly respected" officer.

When I asked Pera how convinced he was the explosion that killed officer McDonnell was the work of the Weather Underground and Bernadine Dohrn, he said without hesitating, "I'm totally convinced." He then proceeded to relay an example of exactly why he was so sure.

Pera said that about one year prior to the interview (fall of 2008), he was reading about Grathwohl in the form of articles that contained some of Grathwohl's recorded testimony. As a police officer who was there, Pera had saved something from the murder scene that played a part in convincing him of the Weather Underground's involvement when he read Grathwohl's testimony from years earlier:

> "Larry was describing how the Weather Underground was making bombs and planting them…What really drew my

attention to him was the fact that he described what the bomb was made out of.... Some of the materials that he described that were put into the bomb were barbed wire fence post staples...It just so happens that I have a barbed wire fence post staple that was used in the bomb to blow up Park Station. I said, 'this guy's right on the money.' He knows exactly what was in these bombs."

Pera continued...

"Larry was describing the guts of the bombs that the Weather Underground was using. Nobody could know that unless they were around the people that were doing it because I had this piece of shrapnel for thirty-nine years, at home in a scrap book and this was the first time that I'd ever heard anyone mention that barbed wire fence post staples were used in the bomb. So I knew he was genuine."

Conversely, the people Grathwohl had for years maintained were responsible for several bombings – to include the one that killed McDonnell – did what the guilty often do; they attempted to smear and discredit their accuser with ridicule instead of with facts.

"Through the years, Bill Ayers, Bernadine Dohrn, and others have called me a liar; they've called me a dishonest paid FBI informant and a pig.... The slurs have been tremendous and basically, now we're finding out that two other people, one of whom I knew barely and one that I didn't know at all have substantiated everything I said."[30]

The two other people Grathwohl was referring to were former Weather Underground member Karen Latimer and a man who once wrote for an underground (socialist) newspaper known as the *Berkeley Tribe*; his name was Matthew Landy Steen. The content of the Jamison article consisted largely of information brought forth by two retired FBI agents – Willie Reagan and Max Noel – who were able to provide facts about the Park Police station bombing that even further vindicated Grathwohl; that information involved the testimony of both

Latimer and Steen. Their testimony pointed directly to Dohrn as well as another Weather Underground member named Howard Machtinger being directly tied to the bombing – a charge Grathwohl had long maintained.[31]

Interestingly, Grathwohl also identified Machtinger in his book as someone who had jumped bail after being arrested in September of 1973 for his role in the Days of Rage in Chicago.[32]

According to Jamison, Steen had informed FBI agents in 1972 that he was present at a January 1970 meeting with the Weather Underground in the San Francisco Bay Area. Among the topics discussed was the bombing of the Park Police station that would ultimately take place the following month. Two of the people Steen identified as having been present at that meeting were Dohrn and Machtinger.

It helps to bolster Steen's credibility a bit here as well. That can be done with Grathwohl's account in *Bringing Down America*. A recurring theme in his book involved his observations of the living quarters for members of the Weather Underground; he often commented on the lack of furniture and the presence of newspapers and other leftist literature. Among the newspapers he routinely saw scattered about was the *Berkeley Tribe*, the paper that Steen once wrote for.[33]

The more compelling testimony came from former Weather Underground member Karen Latimer who, like Steen, also claimed to have been present during a meeting to discuss the Park Police station bombing in which both Dohrn and Machtinger were present. Latimer would approach the FBI years after Steen did but their stories each independently corroborated the implied conclusions of the other.[34]

After deciding to go to the FBI to tell them what she knew, Latimer added substantial credibility to the claims of both Steen and Grathwohl; she not only admitted to having personally cased the Park Police station before the bombing but accurately described the bomb as well as the package it was in when it detonated.

Latimer never did testify; her request for immunity was turned down thanks to San Francisco District Attorney John Jay Ferdon, who was concerned that she would take credit for the bombing and let everyone – herself included – off.

In hindsight, such a concern was likely borne of unjustified paranoia because years later in 2000, Reagan re-connected with Latimer. At that time, Latimer expressed frustration about her testimony not being used.[35]

During the 2009 interview, Grathwohl informed me that Latimer had since died and that the death was ruled a suicide by overdose.

Jamison made another astute observation about the Weathermen's period of heightened violence which lasted from late 1969 until early March of the following year, coming to a halt after the deaths of the three Weathermen mentioned earlier who died in an explosion in Greenwich Village when a bomb they were working on inadvertently exploded. The Park Police station was bombed during the time frame when the Weathermen were the most violent.[36] This was another small fact that bolstered the case against Dohrn in McDonnell's murder.

The bomb that exploded in Greenwich Village was intended to inflict massive casualties at the Fort Dix, NJ Army base during a dance. It's important to put that explosion – which killed three Weathermen – in the proper context in light of words spoken by Bill Ayers during a December 2010 radio interview. While appearing on *Citizen Radio*, a demonstrably leftwing venue, with Jamie Kilstein and Allison Kilkenny on December 1, 2010 Ayers took umbrage at how he was introduced after the host said he "always had to open up by denouncing the violence inflicted by the Weather Underground" when talking to the media.

> **Ayers:** "Did you just say I've always denounced the violence of the Weather Underground?"
>
> **Kilstein:** "Well, yeah. It seemed like...."
>
> **Ayers:** "I don't remember that."
>
> **Kilstein:** "It seemed like you always had to open up by being like, 'it was very you know, regrettable and so forth."
>
> **Ayers:** "I don't believe I've ever said it was regrettable."[37]

It cannot be understated that in refusing to express regret, Ayers was not only endorsing the intended actions of Underground members who were killed but also their intended targets – American troops and their spouses, during war time.

Two retired FBI agents in Reagan and Noel; one retired San Francisco police officer in Pera; and an FBI Informer in Grathwohl were convinced that Bernadine Dohrn planted the bomb that killed officer McDonnell. Three members of the Weather Underground were killed on March 6, 1970 when a bomb they were building exploded in their townhouse before they could use it to kill US officers and their spouses; Grathwohl testified that Ayers once told him that "innocent people" sometimes have to die in a revolution when Grathwohl expressed concern that a bomb he was instructed to plant next to the Detroit Police Officers Association building might kill innocent restaurant patrons as well.

In that *Citizen Radio* interview, Ayers adamantly rejected the notion that he had denounced the actions of his group. If he was telling the truth and if the others are correct, it necessarily means that Ayers refused to denounce acts of murder, including the alleged murder committed by his wife, of officer McDonnell.

To underscore the point regarding who was telling the truth about the Park Police station bombing, Grathwohl said the following in an interview with Cliff Kincaid of *USA Survival* on September 11, 2010 in the city where McDonnell was killed:

> "He (Ayers) calls me a liar. But again I would emphasize the fact that I've testified before three grand juries, federal grand juries, and one Senate sub-committee under oath. Bill Ayers hasn't."[38]

Grathwohl went on to explain the reaction of Dohrn to his charges:

> "When she was asked about my testimony and the accusation that she placed the bomb at the Park Police station, she wouldn't even respond to it. She just basically said 'Larry Grathwohl is a pig infiltrator' and that's all she would say. She wouldn't deny she had placed the bomb or admit she had placed the bomb."

In an ironic illustration of the absurdity, the Weather Underground actually circulated a "WANTED" poster of Grathwohl "for crimes against the people" after his cover had been blown. The poster appeared in his book.[39]

## POLICE OFFICERS MUZZLED

On March 12, 2009, The *San Francisco Chronicle* reported that an organization known as the San Francisco Police Officers Association (SFPOA) signed a letter accusing both Ayers and Dohrn of being responsible for officer McDonnell's murder. In it, they cited the testimony and claims of Grathwohl.

SFPOA Vice President Kevin Martin was credited with authoring the letter and was quoted by the *Chronicle* explaining why the group was coming forward with such strong allegations. "It's coming directly from a person (Grathwohl) who had close, confidential conversations with Ayers and members of the Weather Underground. We have no reason to doubt his assertions."[40]

Six days later, on March 18th, the *Chronicle* reported that the SFPOA had captured the interest of the Eric Holder led Department of Justice when it received phone calls from both the Feds and the police chief, Heather Fong. According to SFPOA president Gary Delagnes, his group was told to back off because the McDonnell case was still open.[41]

The irony was palpable. After expressing its views on a case that hadn't been solved in forty years, the SFPOA was told to cease and desist after only six days. Eric Holder's involvement was important because as Deputy Attorney General at the end of the Clinton administration, he presided over the commutation of the sentences of Weather Underground members Linda Evans and Susan Rosenberg; Holder helped set free members of a group that Grathwohl insisted killed a police officer.[42]

It certainly goes to show that when government institutions want to stonewall, they can. It also shows they can act quickly when doing so is in the interest of those institutions.

## ■ FBI THEN AND NOW

In 1969, the FBI embraced Larry Grathwohl as an invaluable resource in their fight to put the Weather Underground out of commission. His contact there was a man named Special Agent Clark Murrish. In 2005, that same FBI embraced a Weather Underground founder – Mark Rudd – as someone it chose to invite to its academy to provide "conflict resolution" training to its agents. Rudd himself wrote about how shocked he was to receive an email invitation from Special Agent Andrew Bringuel.

Rudd reported on his blog that after the training session, he received an email from Bringuel that said, "We spoke for about 30 minutes about your visit and the class unanimously said you should come back to future classes." Rudd then ended that blog entry by writing that if he were ever to get a paying job conducting training lectures for the FBI, he would "donate the first half million dollars I make to Leonard Peltier."[43]

Retired FBI Agent Max Noel (mentioned earlier) worked Weather Underground cases in San Francisco. Noel explained why Rudd's reference to Peltier was so significant:

> "If you want to get under the skin of former FBI Agents, you start talking about a fund to free Leonard Peltier... Peltier murdered two FBI Agents on the reservation at Wounded Knee [See Chapter 5, p. 144] back in the early 1970's."[44]

What had changed? Rudd, like Ayers, was not repentant and Grathwohl's story remained the same. That left the FBI as the only entity that could have morphed so drastically in less than forty years. Rudd had become the resource and Grathwohl had essentially become irrelevant in the eyes of the FBI establishment.

*Woe to those who call evil good and good evil, who put darkness for light and light for darkness, who put bitter for sweet and sweet for bitter! – Isaiah 5:20*

Though there are still very good agents within the FBI, as an institution, it once viewed Rudd as evil but without Rudd changing his stripes, the FBI had experienced a change in its culture. To a greater

degree, the FBI now fostered an environment in which evil was allowed to be called good.

## BERNADINE DOHRN, MARK RUDD, AND THE PINE STREET BOMB FACTORY

Members of the Weather Underground would have the public believe that the only people who died at their hands were three of their own – Dianne Oughton, Ted Gold, and Terry Robbins – who were killed in the Greenwich Village townhome explosion on March 6, 1970. That townhome doubled as a bomb factory and those three individuals died when the bomb went off prematurely. Not only did Mark Rudd have prior knowledge of why the bomb was being constructed but as a leader of the Weather Underground, he had approved the operation.[45]

Aside from having the blood of Oughton, Gold, and Robbins on his hands, Rudd would have had the blood of countless soldiers and their wives on his hands as well if the bomb had reached its intended target – a dance at the Fort Dix army base in New Jersey for officers and their spouses. Rudd admitted in his book that he approved the planting of that bomb.[46] In a sane world, Rudd – at the very least – would have been indicted, tried and convicted of attempted murder; he would have been held responsible for the deaths of his comrades, who were killed in the commission of a felony.

Another indicator of how close Rudd was to the bomb that killed three Weathermen can be found in Grathwohl's book. While sitting with other members of the group at a restaurant, news broke of the Greenwich Village explosion. One of the rumors communicated to Grathwohl and the members he was with was that Mark Rudd was among the dead. The believability of such a rumor was understandable since Rudd had approved of the mission.[47] This added even additional credibility to Grathwohl – as if he needed it.

A little more than one year after the death of Brian V. McDonnell – in April 1971 – the landlord of an apartment on 1038A Pine Street in San Francisco contacted the FBI upon entering the apartment to find Marxist-Leninist literature, bomb-making paraphernalia, rubber gloves, and other highly suspicious items [**See Chapter 5, p. 149**].

In addition to the apartment being used as a bomb factory – similar to Greenwich Village one year earlier – it was located a very short distance from the Park Police station where McDonnell had been killed. The FBI subsequently released a document that listed the names of people whose fingerprints had been found at the Pine Street bomb factory. Mark Rudd was among them, along with Bill Ayers and Howard Machtinger (**Appendix C**).

Rudd's presence there is important, especially in light of the fact that he was tied to the Greenwich Village bomb factory. Machtinger's prints were important because Peter Jamison's article – referenced earlier – reported that former Weather Underground member Karen Latimer and underground writer Matthew Landy Steen independently implicated Machtinger as having assisted Dohrn in coordinating the Park Police station bombing.[48] Ayers being placed at the Pine Street bomb factory, which was a short distance from the Park Police station, proved that he was familiar with the general location. Remember, Grathwohl testified that Ayers told him Dohrn placed the bomb that killed McDonnell. As for Dohrn, the Jamison article pointed to her living on a house boat in Sausalito at the time of the McDonnell murder. Sausalito is less than ten miles from San Francisco.[49]

Notably, Dohrn's fingerprints were not found in the Pine Street bomb factory. If she was indeed the one responsible for McDonnell's murder a very short distance away, wouldn't she have a motive for being as far removed from that bomb factory as possible? It would seem so, especially in light of a *TIME* magazine article dated October 6, 1975 in which Grathwohl was interviewed about his experience with the Underground:

> "We were all paranoid as hell. We never parked cars closer than two blocks from where we were staying. We never left or came back in groups. If we had the slightest idea that we were being followed, we spent hours losing the tail by riding buses endlessly or dodging through big stores."[50]

Lending additional credence to the claim that Dohrn was the one responsible for the murder of Police Officer McDonnell was something else in that *TIME* article, which reported that groups like the Weather Underground are often led by women and that Dohrn was considered a heroine. The article also quoted what Dohrn wrote in the Underground's manifesto, *Prairie Fire*: "Women fighters are frightening apparitions to the enemy and an example for us."[51]

Not to be given short shrift is another story relayed by Grathwohl about what he saw and heard from Dohrn at a strategy session in Flint, MI in which she discussed the Charles Manson murders:

"Not only did they kill those pigs, they shoved a fork in [Sharon] Tate's stomach and then sat down and ate dinner there."[52]

It should be noted that it wasn't Tate whose stomach had been stabbed with a fork; it was another victim in the murders but the sentiment was obvious. Grathwohl went on to relay that for the rest of their time in Flint, members walked around, holding out three fingers to represent a fork in a macabre salute. The detail from Grathwohl was graphic and Dohrn's only real way of responding to the claims has been to attempt to smear him. Again, it is not a leap to view the callousness of such an individual as yet another indicator of someone who would maliciously take innocent life.

One of the more bizarre practices of the Weathermen that Grathwohl witnessed firsthand was what they called "criticism sessions" where members of the group would single out someone else in the group. They would then collectively attempt to ridicule and intimidate the person by yelling and screaming at them **[See Chapter 5, p. 130]**. The goal was to break the person's will and to bend it toward that of the group. Grathwohl explained how the group would take LSD before engaging in this behavior.[53]

In 2005, Mark Rudd was given the red carpet treatment by the FBI. A few years later, he was given a cash advance by Rupert Murdoch – the Chairman of *Newscorp* – to write his book. That would be the same *Newscorp* that is the parent company of *Fox News*, which has consistently been demonized by the left as a mouthpiece for the Republican agenda. Rudd claimed that 15 percent of the $50,000 he received went to his agent and the balance went to cocaine.[54] While any true conservative would find the actions of Murdoch in this instance disgraceful, he would not have funded the publication of Mark Rudd's book if he was a Republican Party mouthpiece.[55]

Having already written a book in 1976, Grathwohl was looking for a publisher to re-release *Bringing Down America* in 2008. Instead, the man who was the face of the alleged conservative media – Rupert Murdoch – would promote a book penned by a leader of the group Grathwohl infiltrated at great personal risk. Murdoch's *Newscorp* treated Rudd the same way the FBI did. The same can be said for how both he and the FBI treated Grathwohl. Once again, the hero had been ignored and the villain had been lionized. After serving in Vietnam and then with the FBI as an informant, Grathwohl was still fighting the Weathermen in 2009 despite the gross mistreatment from those who could actually make a difference. He remained committed, not bitter.

During the Rudd book tour of 2009, a University professor could be added to the list of high profile entities that elevated Rudd while ignoring Grathwhol. His name was Henry Reichman of Cal State in Hayward, CA. Reichman shared a past with Rudd and welcomed him with open arms in April of 2009 to give a speech and promote his book.

Grathwohl was part of the audience and challenged the former member of the Weathermen. The FBI Informer bolstered his own credibility while further discrediting Rudd's. For example, Rudd wrote in his book that he never met Grathwohl. After Grathwohl challenged him on this, Rudd conceded that his memory could have failed him.[56] The lionized villain had been exposed while the ignored hero remained anonymous.

## ■ GRATHWOHL APPEARS ON GLENN BECK (SORT OF)

Glenn Beck became an invaluable asset to the Tea Party and conservative movements in America during the Obama administration. He catapulted to the top of the White House target list faster than anyone had previously; he had suddenly become to cable television news what Rush

Limbaugh had long been to talk radio. However, in the summer of 2010, Beck almost took it a step further.

It was late and after driving for hours on a family trip from Austin, TX to Augusta, GA, I was longing for sleep; my will to make good time was giving way to better judgment. A cheap hotel was in my immediate future – or so I thought. In the early morning hours of June 11, 2010 I tuned in to the *Fox News* Channel's re-broadcast of the Glenn Beck show on *Sirius Satellite* radio and was rejuvenated as I heard Glenn Beck talking about the Weather Underground and Larry Grathwohl.

Before long, Beck was playing the two minute clip from 1982 mentioned earlier in this chapter. I was not only wide awake but I was now pumping my fist. For some reason, I remembered Bruce Willis' character – John McLane – in the original Die Hard movie, when he finally got the attention of a police officer after no one would believe him that the building he was in was under siege. In October, 2008, The O'Reilly Factor had been given the two minute clip of Grathwohl from 1982 but chose not to show it. Here was Glenn Beck, nearly two years later playing the clip that went semi-viral before Obama was elected.

I called Grathwohl upon reaching Augusta early the next afternoon. He said he had seen the segment on Glenn Beck but said he hadn't been contacted by anyone from Beck's show and didn't know how the talk show host had ultimately come across the video, though he suspected a conservative Tea Party group he had established a relationship with may have made contact with Beck's producers. Grathwohl told me that he emailed one of Beck's producers and did get a reply. We held out hope that a live appearance on Beck might be in Grathwohl's future. This expectation increased as it was learned that Beck was going to do a three part series on the Weather Underground in the coming weeks.

Grathwohl appeared on my Sunday, June 20th show to discuss Beck's showing of his 1982 appearance in the *No Place to Hide* documentary. Again, he reiterated that he hadn't been contacted beforehand by anyone from Beck's show and explained how he learned of his appearance on the June 10th program:

"My daughter from California called me and said, 'Hey Dad, you gotta turn Glenn Beck on. You're on his program.' That's how I found out about it."[57]

Later in the interview, I asked Grathwohl if he knew of any plans on the part of Beck's producers to get him on the show. He told me he was expecting a call the next day – June 21st – to set something up. An appearance on Beck's television show would be huge. Not only would it put Grathwohl on a national stage but Beck's ability to drive book sales would likely entice a publisher to re-release Grathwohl's 1976 book if Beck promoted it.

That phone call Grathwohl was expecting never came. An opportunity to introduce America to a true patriot was missed again. Unlike Ayers, Grathwohl is far from wealthy but he has a wealth of knowledge, information and experience to offer America. He is a humble man who should be revered, not ignored. Conversely, it is the leaders of the group he tried to protect America from, who get the attention. His absence – and his silent phone – made no sense.

Beginning on July 27, 2010 Glenn Beck would air a three part series on the Weather Underground. A central them of the series was the group's Manifesto: "You Don't Need A Weatherman To Know Which Way The Wind Blows."

Though the series was interesting, not one mention of Grathwohl was made by Beck, who had presented Grathwohl to his viewers less than two months earlier as the only man to successfully infiltrate the group. Why was there no effort made on the host's part to incorporate Grathwohl into the series, even after Beck had demonstrated that he knew the importance of Grathwohl's contribution?

On July 28th, I contacted Grathwohl during the second Beck episode in which the latter focused on the Weather Underground. I wanted to know if there had been any contact. Grathwohl informed me that he had heard from no one. As for the Weather Underground Manifesto at the center of Beck's series on the group, no one knew it better than Grathwohl, whom Beck's producers decided to let sit at home.

He would watch part three of the Beck series on the Weather Underground on July 29th. Grathwohl watched as it ended without his name being mentioned. The man who knew the Weathermen better than anyone else had been ignored on a national stage. Yet, bitterness never set in – only resolve.

The fight would continue.

## ■ PALLYWOOD PRECURSOR

The seeds for a dynamic known as 'Pallywood' **[See Chapter 2, p. 41]**, at least to some degree, in the Muslim world may have been sown by the Weathermen. They at least used similar tactics.

The premise of Pallywood is to exploit the existence of news cameras in order to portray victimhood. In essence, one side behaves as actors to garner sympathy for their cause. This allows viewers to see the rabble rousers as victims and law enforcement as oppressors. During Grathwohl's time with the Weathermen, he was given clear instructions in this regard. Members were not supposed to engage the police unless there were cameras around to record the incidents. Under such a scenario, the Weathermen always looked like underdogs and they knew it was to their advantage to exploit such situations.[58]

In the days before Grathwohl's cover was blown at the behest of FBI leadership, which included James Edgar Hoover at the time, they introduced him to a man named Ali Baba. The only meeting between the two men occurred in a shack on Lake Erie. Grathwohl did not know – and would not learn – the significance of Baba aside from being informed that he was an Arab guerilla.

One could infer from the encounter that there was a connection between the Weathermen and the Palestinians, and that the FBI was interested. However, due to the decision to blow Grathwohl's cover – a decision that went all the way to the top – in order to arrest some low level operatives for political reasons, that connection was never revealed to Grathwohl.[59]

One thing was made clear years later; the Weather Underground leadership of Ayers and Dohrn supported the Palestinian cause against Israel. In fact, Ayers and Dohrn both supported the Free Gaza Movement, which was an integral part of the 2010 effort to break the Israeli naval blockade of Gaza.[60]

The narrative was quite reminiscent of what Grathwohl revealed with respect to the Weathermen behaving as underdogs in front of the cameras. Only in the case of the Free Gaza Movement as one example, they had taken their show on the international road and played it on a world stage.

## ■ BATTLE ASSESSMENT

When the Weather Underground disbanded, those who knew Larry Grathwohl's story would have understandably concluded that his contribution to American history was complete. They would have been wrong; it was not.

Grathwohl cemented his extremely unique legacy as an American patriot when he risked his life by infiltrating a domestic terrorist group shortly after serving honorably in Vietnam. The asterisk next to his name relative to his time with the Weather Underground was supposed to represent his being the FBI's only successful informant in the group. Years later, it would represent much more.

His story became relevant again in 2008, not because of anything he had done in the years since he had accepted a life of relative obscurity after serving his country but because of what his story revealed. Whether the American media would admit it or not, what Grathwohl knew about William Ayers shone a spotlight on the man who would become the 44th President of the United States – Barack Obama.

There was no direct connection between Obama and Grathwohl but there was a very quantifiable relationship between Obama and Ayers – someone whom Grathwohl had exposed years earlier in 1976 and then again in a stark 1982 documentary.

Eric Holder's name comes up multiple times in this book [See Chapter 6, p. 253]. As Deputy Attorney General at the end of the Clinton administration, he presided over the release of two members of the Weather Underground. In 2009, as Attorney General, Holder's Department of Justice quashed the actions of the San Francisco Police Officers Association (SFPOA), which aggressively called for a renewed investigation into the murder of one of its police officers in 1970.

Without Grathwohl's testimony, the SFPOA would not have been as bold as it was in so publicly and forthrightly pursuing justice for McDonnell. Despite that testimony, the Obama Justice Department appeared more interested in suppressing the truth than in allowing it to come out. When seeking a motive for this behavior, it is not a leap to conclude that Obama's relationship with Ayers had something to do with the Justice Department's forceful suppression of the SFPOA, which was making bold claims about the involvement of Ayers' wife, Dohrn.

History will show that the Obama administration had been exposed. Holder had to react to the SFPOA because of the forcefulness with which it made its case. Damage control was necessary. Otherwise, why would it have acted so quickly? That confidence on the part of the SFPOA was only made possible by the testimony of Grathwohl. In much the same way that Obama could not deny his relationship with Ayers – though not for a lack of trying – Holder's department couldn't deny why it was attempting to silence the SFPOA; the reason had to do with Grathwohl.

There is another aspect to what Grathwohl uncovered that is so critically important and it has to do with the intelligence value of what he discovered. In 1982, he provided a view behind the curtain of what the Weather Underground's intentions were. In 2008, that view took on added significance because of who was headed to the White House.

In the days and months before and after Obama's election, very powerful people would view those two minutes from 1982 and were provided with critical intelligence that the US government would have taken much more seriously in previous years.

The Weather Underground consisted of young leftist radicals who wanted to take down the government of the United States. By themselves, they were little more than a national nuisance. They were underestimated until Grathwohl revealed how they had planned to align with foreign enemies. The Weather Underground was aware of its limitations but Grathwohl revealed how it planned to compensate for them.

Ayers and company didn't plan to take down America by themselves, though they certainly didn't mind creating that illusion; it kept others deceived. It also afforded the Weathermen a heightened sense of importance.

The Weather Underground viewed themselves as part of an international movement that would work collectively to overthrow the US Government. That movement included the Cubans, the Russians, the Chinese, and North Vietnamese elements that were willing to work with the Weather Underground to further such an agenda. During the Obama administration, other foreign elements interested in the same goals would rise – illegal alien Mexican drug cartels and radical Islamists were among them. Disturbingly, the administration did more to hamstring efforts to confront such elements than it did to neutralize them.

Grathwohl's 1982 appearance in *No Place to Hide* served to provide intelligence about the belief system of people with very close associations to the 44th President of the United States. The United States government had access to that intelligence but it didn't prevent Barack Obama from a presidential run. In 2008, the American people gained access to that intelligence. When this reality made itself available on *YouTube*, some very powerful people took notice. Who could have imagined that the actions of a man in 1969 – 1970 would have such far-reaching implications so many years later?

In 2008, Grathwohl presented Americans with information collected during the Nixon administration, revealed during the Reagan administration, and mass distributed via the internet on the eve of the Obama administration.

It remains to be seen if this humble man from Cincinnati will live to see the fruits of his labor but one thing is for certain. He was always at his best while flying under the radar and he did so for years after infiltrating the Weather Underground.

As Grathwohl told me, "One day people will realize that there are people who hate us just because we're US."[61]

 **CHAPTER 5**

## DAVID CONN
### vs.
# JIM JONES

## ■ STEALTH HERO

If ever there existed a man who had a right to feel scorned by those he rightfully warned, it was David Conn. After doing so much to expose the evil that manifested itself in the cult known as the Peoples Temple – led by Jim Jones in Ukiah, CA – Conn was virtually ignored by those who should have heeded his words in the years prior to the massacre that took the lives of nearly one thousand people in Guyana, South America on November 18, 1978.

An extension of grace might have been warranted had those entities and individuals humbled themselves after the cultic holocaust. Instead, Conn was virtually cast aside. After all, he wasn't viewed as a real journalist; he was just a guy unafraid to do a journalist's job without pay or recognition while willing to face danger that real journalists would not – in a world without blogs. His work – coupled with the accuracy of his predictions – thoroughly embarrassed the liberal media establishment. Rather than acknowledge him, those media entities practically committed plagiarism by omitting his contributions.

As is so often the case, heroes were in abundance after the Jim Jones threat was gone. Once Goliath fell, those who wanted to re-write history far outnumbered those who were willing to pick up the slingshot and do battle before his death. Conn was also the watchman whose trumpet was ignored for years as Jones successfully intimidated political, religious, and media establishments. Had any one of those entities stood up, Jones would have been put down long before he joined his followers in mass suicide. Instead, the cult leader grew while a man not belonging to any of those societal pillars began chopping him down nine years before, in 1969.

Ironically, Conn is not bitter. On the contrary, he spends much of his time in critical self-reflection – even today – almost torturing himself over what he could have done differently; he never gloated. Paradoxically, while journalists should have humbled themselves after the Jonestown massacre, it was Conn who humbled himself and reached out to God, seeking forgiveness.

Most people envision their arch enemies as entities with a face, someone or something that can be the object of determined ire and planning. In the case of Jim Jones – a control freak – his arch enemy wasn't revealed to him until years after Conn had gotten a significant head start. When that arch enemy was finally revealed, Jones ran scared and would ultimately hit each member of his own flock between the eyes before proving himself more cowardly and self-destructive than Goliath.

## ■ MONKEY BUSINESS

Like serum and anti-serum, Conn and Jones shared something in common that would benefit the former more than the latter; both were members of one of the largest protestant denominations in 1965 – the Disciples of Christ. It was the same denomination to which former United States President Lyndon Baines Johnson belonged. Jones was an ordained minister back in Indianapolis and Conn was an elder at Barrett Avenue Christian Church (BACC) in Richmond, CA.[1]

In an interview I conducted with Conn, he explained that Jones was extremely cunning and strategic in finding a home with a church like Disciples of Christ because the denomination prided itself on minister autonomy.[2] Jones would exploit that at every turn and as a member, Conn's experience and connections were both assets; he understood the autonomous culture within the Disciples of Christ and was able to reach out to the denomination's leadership. Although he had virtually no luck prodding that leadership into action, the rejection only further validated his suspicions and emboldened his resolve, which ultimately led him to pursue other avenues.

At about the time Conn left his church, Jones would soon arrive in Northern California to reestablish the one he left behind in Indianapolis in 1965. Jones was able to use fear to get many of his followers to join him in his relocation westward by predicting that the world would suffer a holocaust in 1967 – presumably nuclear – and Northern California was one of the few safe places to be.[3]

When I asked Conn about what may have been the real impetus for Jones wanting to leave America's heartland for Ukiah, he pointed to the likelihood that Jones saw a better opportunity to exploit the religious, political, and media establishments in the extremely liberal bastion of northern California than he would have been able to do in a state like Indiana.[4] Jones was an opportunist so such a scenario made sense. Aside from that, he thoroughly exploited all three of those entities and leveraged each one to his advantage.

Jones didn't make it onto Conn's radar until 1969 and it happened as a direct result of the polarizing effect the preacher from the People's Temple had on people. Conn had two good friends – Elmer Mertle and Larry Tupper – who were dichotomous catalysts responsible for sounding Conn's alarm bells. All three knew each other from BACC. Mertle was a co-worker of Conn's at Standard Oil (Chevron) and sang the praises of Jones. It struck Conn as creepy but it wasn't until Tupper approached him and conveyed the sentiment that Jones was exactly the opposite of what Mertle described, that Conn's antennae went up for good.

The monkey business he witnessed at the People's Temple after driving three hours to catch a Jim Jones service in 1970 convinced him that Tupper was onto something. Conn spoke of how Jones singled him out at the very beginning of the service and asked Conn to stand up to answer questions before commencing. What Conn witnessed only further bolstered Tupper's claim. After an alleged tumor extraction took place in a restroom, the foreign body was paraded up and down the aisles during the service. Conn was not permitted to examine the tumor and immediately knew an extremely charismatic, fraudulent, and dangerous pastor was representing the denomination to which Conn once belonged.[5]

The nine year crusade Conn would subsequently find himself fighting was the result of journalists, politicians, and religious leaders who either failed to act or succumbed to the will of a madman.

As the saying 'monkey business' relates to Jim Jones, it wasn't just a figure of speech. At one time, Jones sold living monkeys to raise money for his early church. In hindsight, it was a sick foreshadowing relative to the allegorical meaning of the term.[6]

## ■ DISCIPLES OF CHRIST

Prior to 1969, Conn was an admitted liberal. That changed as he continued to witness the avowed Marxist, Jones. Until he left BACC in Richmond, CA – his local branch of the Disciples of Christ (DOC) in 1965 – Conn was an elder who knew how the denomination worked; he knew its structure; he knew its culture. It gave him what he thought would be an advantage after witnessing firsthand the fraud that was Jim Jones, upon visiting Peoples Temple in Ukiah in 1970. Surely, the seventh largest protestant denomination in the United States would want to act on information Conn could provide.

As is a common theme in this book, what Conn discovered was an aspect of human nature that prefers the path of least resistance and willful ignorance over righteous action in the face of evil, especially when the person housing that evil possesses the ability to make that path appear primrose. Jones was clever and he had charisma. It served him well – for a while.

Conn left BACC over the church's handling of issues involving race. Interestingly, both Mertle and Conn left for similar reasons.[7] Afterward, Mertle gravitated toward a Marxist preacher who knew how to exploit the worst of human nature and grew his flock by doing so. In fact, Jones's tactics mirrored those of Community Organizing founder Saul Alinsky, whose mantra consisted of the phrase, 'rub raw the sores of discontent.'[8]

Most of Jones's flock consisted of black members who would take their own lives one day. Conversely, Conn saw through the Marxist Messiah.[9] He saw a man who was willing to deceive and intimidate while fostering a culture of paranoia that encouraged its followers to blame unnamed and unidentified villains as the culprits which only warranted further paranoia. At one point, Jones even staged his own shooting with firecrackers and fake blood; it simply created another opportunity he exploited – a miraculous recovery from an injury that didn't exist.[10]

After witnessing the fraudulent Jones in action, Conn was able to leverage his experience with BACC to schedule a lunch with Elizabeth Kratz, the regional president of DOC responsible for Jones's region. During that lunch, Conn expressed very forthrightly his concerns about what Jones was doing. He pleaded with Kratz to investigate and explained to me her reaction:

> "I filled her in on what I could see was obvious, just a big charade put on by Jones but she just could not really believe, she had heard so much about his social work and his community organizing that even she was enthralled in spite of my warnings."[11]

A little bit later, Conn explained to me that Kratz ultimately did visit the Peoples Temple in Ukiah but that her visit was announced in advance and the very controlling Jones was able to prepare; Kratz was showered with a hospitality that only served to reinforce any inclination she may have already had toward willful ignorance. Conn continued:

> "She did decide to go up and see his church up north but when she got there, Jones was all prepared and he just had his people ready to praise her and treat her like a saint. And she came back just enthralled with him. It was amazing what he could pull off."[12]

Had DOC taken Conn's words seriously regarding Jones, the latter could have been neutralized. Instead, Peoples Temple metastasized. DOC leadership had been successfully manipulated to the point of acquiescence to insanity. Even Jones himself echoed the sentiment in what appeared to be an autobiographical recording of his voice acquired after his death.

"I decided, how can I demonstrate my Marxism? The thought was, infiltrate the church."[13]

Jones was not satisfied with using his charm to neuter the church he infiltrated; it was a conquest that only served to whet his appetite for more power. Despite Conn's connections, Jones was able to graft his agenda into the religious establishment with charm and deceit. This not only emboldened him to extend his Temple's reach south to San Francisco; it gave him the confidence to go after two other very important pillars – media and politics.

## ■ THE MEDIA

After reaching the conclusion that the DOC had no interest in pursuing what Conn knew to be true about Jones, the Chevron employee made several attempts to contact various reporters within the media establishment; the fish weren't biting and Conn was incredulous.

There was one major exception and his name was Lester Kinsolving. At the time, Kinsolving was a religious writer for the *San Francisco Examiner* and he was the only reporter who would pursue Conn's warnings; he decided to investigate the Peoples Temple in 1972.

Ukiah, which sits approximately 120 miles northwest of San Francisco, was nice but Jones began setting his sights on church expansion to the south. With the Disciples of Christ sufficiently neutered, Jones was already on the inside of one powerful entity. Another key establishment he needed on his side was the fourth estate. In San Francisco, it would be much more difficult to keep the lid on the full range of activities that took place inside the Peoples Temple so the Marxist Messiah got creative.

Jones did have a bit of an advantage in this regard. He was both charismatic and a creature of the left; the media in northern California was as liberal as there was and his aim was to control it as best he could. In early 1973, Peoples Temple attempted to buy some sympathetic press when it allocated $4400 to be spread out among various media entities including the *San Francisco Chronicle*, the *Los Angeles Times*, the *Oakland Tribune*, the *San Francisco Examiner*, the *Ukiah Daily Journal* and others. *KGO-TV*, San Francisco even benefited. Not surprisingly, the *Chronicle* and the *Times* received the largest amounts, ostensibly because they had the largest audience.[14]

The payments were billed as "commendation" awards and were issued to show support for freedom of the press. Not so coincidentally, the man responsible for distributing them had a very political agenda and wasn't interested in a free press at all but a very favorable one. He was so radical that there was no way for him to succeed without a compromised media. Jim Jones sought power and the money that Peoples Temple awarded to those entities was intended to help him get it, either through favorable coverage or via editors who would turn a blind eye to his activities after having their memories jogged about how gracious the Peoples Temple had been. Interestingly, the one entity that returned the money was the one where a reporter named Lester Kinsolving worked – *The San Francisco Examiner*.

A few short months prior to Jones's attempt to buy favorable press, Kinsolving had written a series of eight extremely damaging articles about the Peoples Temple with Conn providing the lion's share of insider information via sources who had confided in him. In addition to his own firsthand accounts, Conn put Kinsolving in touch with very key individuals inside the Temple. Each article was scheduled to run on a separate day. A key figure in the articles was a man by the name of Timothy Stoen. At the time, he was both a high-ranking member of Peoples Temple and an Assistant District Attorney for Mendocino County.

Stoen would later serve a key role in Jones's attempt to infiltrate the San Francisco political structure but first, a brief overview of Kinsolving's eight articles.

## PART 1: THE PROPHET WHO RAISES THE DEAD
Sunday, September 17, 1972

Though Jones wouldn't kick a portion of that $4400 to the Ukiah Daily Journal for several months, the Journal was already firmly in his camp. Kinsolving reported that when he reached out to the Daily Journal to learn more about Jones, the editor of the paper instead went to Stoen, ostensibly to warn him.[15]

This prompted Stoen to proactively approach the Examiner with a letter in which the Mendocino County Attorney personally testified that he had witnessed Jones raise people from the dead and claimed the number to be "more than 40."[16]

It was shocking. An Assistant District Attorney was so enamored with Jones that he was willing to go on the record as saying his own pastor had raised multiple people from the dead. Stoen was a tremendous asset to Jones and the latter knew it but the kind of exposure Kinsolving was giving the Peoples Temple was not the least bit glowing; it certainly didn't help the cause.

## PART 2: 'HEALING' PROPHET HAILED AS GOD AT S.F. REVIVAL

Monday, September 18, 1972

This installment gave the reader some insight into the possible tactics of Jones as Kinsolving described how the pastor raised people from catatonic states without naming or identifying the nurses who were allegedly part of it.

Kinsolving then provided another example of this failure on the part of Jones and his followers to identify people, whose accounts are necessarily required to substantiate such claims. He quoted Jones as having said something about another pastor who, according to Jones, "propositioned two of our young choirgirls!" when the Marxist Messiah attempted to partner with said pastor's denomination.[17]

This afforded Jones the opportunity to take the high road by being more protective of his flock while also appearing more righteous. The added benefit – and endgame – was that he would have reason to demand privacy.

## PART 3: D.A. AIDE OFFICIATES FOR MINOR BRIDE

Tuesday, September 19, 1972

The third installment from Kinsolving wasn't kind to Stoen at all. For all intents and purposes, the author caught the Assistant D.A. in the potential commission of a crime after reporting that Stoen had performed a marriage involving one of the Temple's former members. After Stoen assured Kinsolving that he met all of the requirements necessary to preside over such a union, he would find himself unable to cite the state code that allowed him to do so.[18]

Kinsolving also reported on some mop-up duty Stoen had to perform relative to a return trip Jones made to Indianapolis.

Clearly, Kinsolving's investigations were exposing one of Jim Jones's most trusted confidants in Stoen. After the third installment had been published, it was becoming clear that Tim Stoen was not being portrayed positively by a major news publication in San Francisco. Stoen was a man who held political office in Mendocino County and Jones had big plans for him. Thanks in large part to Conn – a man Jones didn't even know at the time – Kinsolving was disrupting those plans in a major way.

## PART 4: PROBE ASKED OF PEOPLE'S TEMPLE
Wednesday, September 20, 1972

Again, Timothy Stoen was a central figure in Kinsolving's next article. In fact, Stoen's boss, Mendocino County District Attorney Duncan James was also featured. Like Stoen's, his wasn't a flattering portrayal. James came across as someone unwilling to comment or follow up on some very serious charges levied by a Baptist pastor in Ukiah who had called for the State Attorney General to launch an investigation into Peoples Temple only after he had reached out to the County Sheriff to no avail.[19]

Another bit of insight was revealed in Kinsolving's article and it had to do with the claims of Peoples Temple attorney Eugene B. Chaikin, who was quoted as saying that local law enforcement advised his clients to carry firearms because of threats. Undersheriff Tim Shae flatly denied this claim.[20] In light of other unsubstantiated statements made by Jones it would seem that he would be more than willing to victimize his Temple in order to justify having armed members. As time went on, people would come to learn that these were simply Marxist tactics being executed by Jones.

## COMMUNITY ORGANIZING

On the morning of September 19th – the day Kinsolving's third install-ment was published – the writer noticed an extremely large picket line outside the Examiner on his way to work. During an interview I conducted with Kinsolving, he explained:

"When I got to the Examiner, the editor – Tom Eastham – said, 'why don't you go out and greet your flock?' I said, 'Greet my flock?' He said, 'Yes, why don't you go out?' So I borrowed a policeman's hat and tried to take a collection. I didn't get any money. I got a few smiles but an awful lot of glares."[21]

Though the Examiner ran Kinsolving's fourth installment the next day, none of the subsequent articles ran; installments five through eight were never published. The newspaper's leadership succumbed to intimidation, community organizing, and threats of lawsuits. When I asked Kinsolving about this, he was noticeably aggravated, even more than thirty years later:

"They (the *Examiner*) killed the rest of my series. They never ran it!"

Kinsolving had a right to be angry, especially in hindsight. After all, he had been right when virtually every other journalist refused to listen to his warnings, which were made all the more credible by what Conn knew firsthand. Said Kinsolving:

"I went to thirty different…daily newspaper religion editors that I knew and begged them, I begged them! 'Go out and look, look into it if you don't believe me, go out…' Not one single one did it! And as a result of this neglect, of this outrageous behavior of all those newspapers, 916 of our fellow Americans were poisoned or led into committing mass suicide."[22]

Later in the interview, Kinsolving talked about the reaction of the media to the Jonestown massacre. In a normal world, one would right-fully assume that Kinsolving's fellow journalists would have lined up to apologize for not listening to him. Unfortunately, according to the

former *Examiner* reporter, the exact opposite happened, with one exception – Brit Hume.

The conversation then turned to Tom Eastham:

"If he hadn't let those people cut me off in the *Examiner* halfway through my reporting, it might just possibly have been reported in its entirety and might have stopped Jones before he killed so many people and I lay that right at the feet of Eastham and the rest of that crew at the *San Francisco Examiner*."[23]

Kinsolving appeared to encapsulate his own sentiment best – moments later with even fewer words – when he described the dereliction within his profession and the consequences:

"(it was) The bloodiest horror caused by journalistic disdain."[24]

## THE ARTICLES THAT WEREN'T
In 2010, Kinsolving made a bold claim: if his remaining articles would have been allowed to run, maybe something could have been done about Jones. Upon further review, he may have been right. After all, Community Organizing tactics were used after only three of his eight articles had been published.

Jones was clearly afraid of the truth being revealed.

As was the case in prior Kinsolving articles, the leader of Peoples Temple would have had to deal with extremely damaging press about his most important human asset – Timothy Stoen. Mendocino County's Assistant District Attorney had been skewered with facts.

## PART 5: THE PEOPLE'S TEMPLE AND MAXINE HARPE
1972, Unpublished
Maxine Harpe's death was ruled a suicide by the Mendocino County Coroner's office; her family called for the State Attorney General's office to investigate. She had ties to the Peoples Temple and the Peoples Temple had a significant amount of her money.

Timothy Stoen was fingered by Harpe's family as having been someone whose advice the deceased woman had once sought.

Though Stoen denied ever having spoken with Harpe, Kinsolving caught the Assistant District Attorney in a lie while citing a statement Stoen made that was published in the *Ukiah Daily Journal*. In it, Stoen said the following:

> "I never said at any time that I saw 40 people raised from the dead."[25]

It was stunning. In part 1, Kinsolving had published the contents of a letter he received from Stoen in which the latter admitted to seeing Jones raise "more than 40" people from the dead. In an article that would have been published one week later, Stoen's own words denied the claim.

In addition to proving that Stoen had lied, Kinsolving was able to raise questions about the county Sheriff as well as Stoen's boss, Duncan James.

## PART 6: THE REINCARNATION OF JESUS CHRIST – IN UKIAH

1972, Unpublished

In addition to witness reports that Jones encouraged his followers to refer to him as the Son of God, this installment from Kinsolving highlighted the pervasiveness of the Peoples Temple in Ukiah. According to statistics cited by the *Examiner's* Religion writer, nearly one half of the city's population was made up of people who belonged to PT.[26]

Another aspect of PT that was revealed was the "Catharsis Sessions," which involved subjecting members to intense periods of intimidation in front of their peers. During those sessions, people were forced to confess their deepest sins in front of the congregation while being intensely derided, sometimes by their closest loved ones **[See Chapter 4, p. 111]**.

Perhaps the most important aspect of Kinsolving's sixth installment was the window he provided into Jones's strategy. The Marxist Messiah had co-opted at least one of Ukiah's two radio stations and the area's lone newspaper. Broadcast and print media in Mendocino County had become a powerful arm of Jim Jones.

Said Kinsolving:

"If the civil government is awed, the communications media have proven downright subservient."[27]

## PART 7: JIM JONES DEFAMES BLACK PASTOR
1972, Unpublished

Here, Kinsolving reported more details about the pastor that Jones accused of propositioning two young girls. This happened after Rev. George L Bedford, along with other representatives from his church, had welcomed members of the Peoples Temple into their homes. It was quintessential defamation. According to Bedford, Jones wasn't even present when any alleged propositioning would have taken place – in front of multiple witnesses.

The motives of Jones were like that of any Marxist – to smear for personal advantage. In this particular case, Jones was attempting to acquire new members for his own church by stealing them from others while using gutter tactics to do so.[28]

## PART 8: FINAL: SEX, SOCIALISM, AND CHILD TORTURE WITH REV. JIM JONES
1972, Unpublished

Believe it or not, Jim Jones taught night school classes in Ukiah's public school district. According to multiple witnesses, Jones would go into very graphic detail about particular sexual acts. He also talked about both syphilis and his own extrasensory perception while teaching a class that had nothing to do with either subject.

Additionally, witness reports showed that Jones expressed reverence for the Soviet Union, Mao, and Fidel Castro while being persistently critical of the United States [See Chapter 4, p. 92-93].

Unspeakable accounts surfaced in Kinsolving's article about how Jones either personally mistreated children or condoned their mistreatment at the hands of others.

In a very telling excerpt from the last installment that would not run, the subject of Jones's classroom antics was addressed by one of his former students, who responded to a question about why Jones was allowed to get away with such abhorrent behavior.

Said Betty Bailey about why school authorities ignored her complaints:

> "..so many board members are either members of the People's Temple or are afraid of it."[29]

## ANOTHER LOST OPPORTUNITY

Without question, a common thread was running through all of the entities that could have done something to stop Jones but didn't. In each case, whether it was the Disciples of Christ, the media in general, the *San Francisco Examiner* in particular, Ukiah officials, or the local school district – that common thread was fear.

There was another person Kinsolving relied heavily upon when doing his research on Jones. Her name was Carolyn Pickering and she was a writer for the *Indianapolis Star*. Her notes on Jones relative to his Indianapolis connections were of great benefit to Kinsolving's work.[30]

It is important to note that one of the primary figures in Kinsolving's articles was Timothy Stoen. Later, Stoen would leave the Peoples Temple and become number one on Jim Jones's hit list; he also became incredibly remorseful. In fact, in 2010, Kinsolving appeared more impressed with Stoen than with those who were his media colleagues at the time:

> "He (Stoen) sent me a wonderful letter of confession and apology."[31]

Kinsolving was referring to a heartfelt letter he received from Stoen in 2005 in which the latter bared his soul – far more than all but one of Kinsolving's colleagues had done.[32]

In 1973, Kinsolving quit the *Examiner* and moved to Washington, D.C. As damaging as the articles were, Jones was emboldened by the fact that his Community Organizing paid off. The one media outlet that challenged him most, blinked first.

Conn provided much of the punch that allowed Kinsolving to hit Jones hard, though the blow was softened by the cowardice of the Exam-

iner. Years later, with the help of different writers, Conn would hit Jones with a haymaker by getting the Marxist Messiah to do battle with his own paranoia.

Regrettably, the collateral damage would be monumental.

# ■ CALIFORNIA POLITICS

Jim Jones wasn't just trying to grow his Temple by targeting metropolitan areas; he was aggressively leveraging his growing flock in order to gain power within the political structure of California in general and San Francisco in particular. In the early to mid 1970s, Jones became extremely well-connected with liberal Democrat politicians. It was also during this time that he would realize his greatest political victory; he exploited his own flock in order to achieve it.

## JONES COURTS BLACK POLITICIANS

His charisma, coupled with the overwhelming majority of blacks belonging to his Temple, helped Jones gain the support of multiple black politicians. Among them were State Assemblyman Willie Brown, Lieutenant Governor Mervyn Dymally, and Los Angeles Mayor Tom Bradley, who once said from the pulpit of the Peoples Temple while referring to Jones:

> "I am really pleased and inspired by what I have seen. Here truly is a man – Pastor Jim Jones – who is touched by God."[33]

Despite this despicable stain on Bradley's judgment, he would be re-elected multiple times until finally leaving office in 1993, a full fifteen years after the massacre at Jonestown.

Jones also successfully used his flock to infiltrate the NAACP. In fact, so many of his members joined the civil rights group that they were able to get Jones elected to the board in 1976.[34]

On January 15, 1977, Jones received the Martin Luther King, Jr. Humanitarian Award from one church in San Francisco; the date was significant because it was the forty-eighth anniversary of King's birth. At another church on the same day – the Peoples Temple – the Governor of California, Jerry Brown spoke after being invited by Jones.[35]

In what would prove incredibly embarrassing to those who bestowed the MLK Humanitarian Award upon Jones were the words that came with it:

> "...in recognition of his outstanding efforts to further the ideals of civil rights and civil liberties championed by Dr. King."[36]

Despite the plethora of signs that Jones was evil in the flesh, hype and euphoria in response to his persona simply trumped the facts. Tragically ironic is that his followers – most of whom were black – would one day be forced to end their own lives, which is the exact opposite of civil liberty.

Marxism has proven over and over again that it represents the exact opposite of everything it claims to champion. The lies Jones told illustrated that reality perfectly.

## A MAJOR POLITICAL VICTORY

The San Francisco Mayoral election of 1975 pitted Republican and trusted conservative John Barbagelata against former state Senator and democrat George Moscone. Everyone accepted the fact that it was going to be a close race but Jones had great interest in a Moscone victory. He knew that if he could contribute to that victory, Moscone would be beholden to the Peoples Temple. That is exactly what Jones set out to do and he would use many of the Community Organizing tactics that would later be made even more infamous during the 2008 Barack Obama presidential campaign, to do it – after being asked by Moscone personally for help.[37]

Jones had members of Peoples Temple bused in from Los Angeles and Redwood Valley (Ukiah) to knock on doors and get people to vote for Moscone. People were simply used as a means to further Jones's agenda. This account is from Vicky Moore, a one-time member of Peoples Temple:

> "We got out [of the buses] and went door to door, passing out leaflets, telling people where to vote. I woke up when I started doing things like that, because I didn't know enough

about Moscone to tell you which side of the street he lived on. All I was doing was mimicking what Jim said about him. I did it because...Jones said Moscone represented the cause, whatever the cause was."[38]

Moscone won by a meager 4000 votes and was clearly indebted to Jones more than anyone else. Nonetheless, Barbagelata pushed for an investigation into voter fraud but hadn't suspected Peoples Temple as being complicit. The responsibility for appointing someone to oversee the investigation fell to newly elected District Attorney Joe Freitas, who appointed none other than Mendocino County Assistant District Attorney Timothy Stoen.[39]

Said Dave Conn in one of our interviews:

"Moscone admitted that he wouldn't have been elected mayor without Jones. That was when... Jones was able to get his own henchman – Timothy Stoen – installed in the District Attorney's office there in San Francisco. The best spot, of course, was the Assistant District Attorney in charge of voter fraud. So that's where Timothy Stoen made his deep connections for Jones.... So Jones had his own man in a very high position in the District Attorney's office."[40]

Moscone's victory didn't just mean that Jones's people would move up within the political structure; it meant that Jones himself would move up as well. In a clear act of political back scratching, Jones was appointed by Moscone to the San Francisco Housing Authority in 1976.[41] A few months later Moscone announced that Jones would be named chairman.[42]

Perhaps more amazing than Moscone's political payback to Jones in the form of a cushy job with the Housing Authority that oversaw $14 million of taxpayer money was the way in which the new mayor relied on State Assemblyman Willie Brown to help make it possible.

## WILLIE BROWN

After Moscone assumed office, he attempted to satiate Jones by offering him a seat on the human rights commission. Based on Jones's reaction, Moscone must have realized he insulted the man who got him elected.[43]

Jones desired something that wielded far more power than that – a seat on the San Francisco housing authority commission. Such a position would put Jones on a board responsible for overseeing $14 million. Moscone was put in the awkward position of having to promote Jones despite the objections of existing board members who would vehemently oppose such an appointment. In light of the publicity Jones had gotten in recent years, it didn't make sense.

Nonetheless, in October of 1976 Mayor Moscone submitted Jim Jones's name for approval despite the attempts by some board members – John Barbagelata among them – to require any new members to go through a background check.[44]

In essence, Moscone was put in check by board members who opposed the notion of Jones being one of their colleagues. What Moscone did in response was beyond shady; he enlisted the help of State Assemblyman Willie Brown, who sponsored legislation that would allow the Mayor to appoint all board members without the consent of existing board members **(Appendix A)**. That legislation passed and Moscone proceeded to appoint Jones without having to go through the messy process of his appointment being vetted.[45]

After a few short months of seeing the Jim Jones circus accompany its namesake to the meetings, the board stood by virtually helpless thanks to Willie Brown; Moscone appointed Jones chairman in early 1976 **(Appendix B)**. Though objections ensued, Moscone assured board members that Jones was the man for the job. Existent members fell in line. After all, legislation that de-fanged them had passed without their vigilance, knowledge, or perceived ability to stop it.[46]

In one of the later articles that helped to expose Jones for the man he was, Willie Brown all but admitted that Moscone was beholden to the pastor of Peoples Temple. Brown was quoted as saying the following:

> "In a tight race like the ones that George (Moscone) or Freitas or Hongisto had, forget it without Jones."[47]

The article went on to refer to Brown – based on the assemblyman's own words – as "an admirer of Jones."

Conn described what happened between Jones and Brown thusly:

"Jones was able to manipulate the Mayor of San Francisco to the extent that the Mayor sent a young assemblyman up to Sacramento to push through a very special bill that would allow the Mayor to bypass the board of supervisors and appoint Jones directly to this high position of chairman of the housing commission. That young assemblyman…was the primary instrument for that tremendous jump in power for Jim Jones."[48]

Decades later, Conn would confront Willie Brown directly at an event sponsored by the Sacramentans for Accountable Government. At that event, Brown was featured opposite pollster Frank Luntz in what was billed as a "no holds barred" debate.[49] Conn also attended and was able to ask Brown about that bill he passed in 1976.

According to Conn, Brown interrupted Luntz during the debate by affirming that his word is always trustworthy. Here is how Conn explained the interaction:

"…it was just after he (Brown) interrupted Dr. Frank Luntz to say, 'I'm always candid.'"

Conn then used that opportunity to speak up, reminding Luntz of Brown's words just moments earlier; he then proceeded to address Brown:

"You may recall the time when Reverend Jim Jones was appointed to Chair of the Housing Commission, and the Mayor needed to bypass the Board of Supervisors, and the only way he could do it was to get the state statutes changed (sic), allowing him to circumvent the Board. So he sent a young Assemblyman up to Sacramento to get a special Assembly Bill passed. You and I know who that Assemblyman was, don't we?"[50]

Brown reportedly feigned ignorance and then for good measure, threw in an accusation that Conn must have had a political agenda. At that point, there were two men in the room who knew beyond a shadow of a doubt that Brown was lying – Conn and Brown.

Conn wasn't done. He approached Brown after the debate, following him up the aisle, even telling the former Assemblyman that he had a copy of the Bill in his possession. Brown still denied having any knowledge of it according to Conn, saying:

"I have no idea what you are talking about."[51]

It was shocking. Conn realized that he was having a discussion with a man who not only knew the truth but knew Conn knew it as well. Yet, Brown had the ability to lie with a straight face. Said Conn:

"I'll say one thing: that man can lie more smoothly than anyone I've ever seen, even to the face of someone who he knows has the full documentation."[52]

By any honest account, Willie Brown has blood on his hands; he poured gasoline on the Jim Jones fire in 1976. Yet, just a few years later, he would become Speaker of the California State Assembly – after the massacre at Jonestown. Subsequent to that, he would be elected Mayor of San Francisco and wouldn't relinquish the position until 2004.[53]

Like Los Angeles Mayor Tom Bradley, Brown was able to repeatedly win reelection despite the indelible stain of having provided support to one of the most evil human beings on the face of the earth during the twentieth century.

Brown's denial of any culpability only bolstered the claims against him; that denial served to implicate him as both a liar and a willing accomplice to evil.

## RALPH NADER

In 1975, the man David Conn used to work with at Standard Oil left the Peoples Temple with his wife. The event that served as the last straw for Elmer and Deanna Mertle had taken place a year earlier, when their daughter was paddled violently nearly one hundred times in front of countless witnesses at a church meeting overseen by Jones. Their daughter's buttocks looked like "hamburger" after the abuse was completed according to witnesses.[54]

Upon leaving the Temple, the Mertles feared for their safety and even had their names legally changed to Al and Jeannie Mills. Elmer Mertle was full of remorse; he sought out Conn and bared his soul. He also wanted to expose Jones and hoped that Conn could help.[55]

Despite the name change, the Mertles were still being tracked by the Peoples Temple. They reached out to renowned consumer rights activist and politician Ralph Nader in late 1976 for help. If someone like Nader would have taken up their cause, Jones very likely could have been stopped.

It was not to be; confiding in Nader actually put Deanna and her husband in even greater danger. In a book published in 1979, Jeannie Mills (Deanna Mertle) explained her attempt to reach out to Nader:

"I wrote an extremely guarded letter to him, telling of the cruel and inhuman things that Jones was doing. I enclosed several of Lester Kinsolving's articles and some of the articles from an Indianapolis newspaper from several years before when Jones had been encouraged to leave the area. I ended my letter saying, 'I have always respected you, and I know that you cannot be bought off. I am telling you these things as my last resort. I live in daily fear for my life. In fact, I am so afraid that I do not dare tell you my name. If you believe this letter, and would be willing to hear more, please put a classified advertisement in the personal section of the *San Francisco Chronicle* to Angela, and I will get in contact with you. You are the last hope I have that justice will prevail.'"[56]

Had Nader done nothing, a later claim by him that he never received Mertle's package would have been somewhat supported by plausible deniability. That's not what happened. Note that Mills gave instructions to Nader on how to contact her if he was willing to help. He did not do that either.

Instead of following the Mertles' instructions, Nader chose another course. Due to the fact that Jones's demise ultimately involved the death of a United States Congressman, the 96th Congress released its findings in 1979 and named Ralph Nader specifically, relative to the attempt on the part of Al and Jeannie Mills to seek his help.

Nader sent the letter to the District Attorney's Office in San Francisco. By some means, the letter filtered back to People's Temple and the writer soon thereafter received a threatening phone call that said "We know all about your letter to Angelo (sic)."[57]

At that time, Joe Freitas was the District Attorney of San Francisco. Willie Brown had already been quoted as saying Jones helped get Freitas elected. Nader ran in the same political circles. It is beyond a stretch to believe he knew nothing of this connection. Nader's actions were egregiously irresponsible. It was a betrayal of trust reminiscent of that perpetrated by Judas Iscariot.

Fifteen months after the massacre at Jonestown in Guyana, Elmer and Deanna Mertle were murdered; Jones had left instructions to get those "traitors."[58] There had been multiple incidents which had served to fuel Jones's anger relative to the Mertles after they defected. The information given to Nader that made its way to Jones had been one of them.

If one makes the argument that Nader's actions were not responsible for the deaths of Al and Jeannie Mills, it's a case that can be made; they were outspoken about the Peoples Temple after they left and had already become targets. Even if one takes that argument a step further and asserts that Nader did the right thing by going to Freitas, how can Freitas's office be excused for feeding the information to Jones?

Nader's betrayal coupled with his inaction meant that he was likely an indirect accomplice to not only their deaths but the deaths of nearly 1000 people two years after he made that despicably wrong decision.

## JERRY BROWN

As Jim Jones was gaining his foothold in San Francisco, a politician by the name of Jerry Brown was elected Governor in 1974. By all accounts, Brown knew full well that Jones was a power player in San Francisco politics. The governor visited the Peoples Temple and understood what a positive relationship with Jones meant to his political career.

During my interview with Kinsolving, the former *San Francisco Examiner* reporter expounded on Jones's relationship with the Governor:

"(Jones) became very powerful in the City of San Francisco and all of those Democratic politicians – including a young Jerry Brown – just catered to him."[59]

When I asked Kinsolving about Brown's trips to the People's Temple, he became noticeably disgusted as he admitted that Brown did so, "to his everlasting disgrace!"[60]

Amazingly, Brown won reelection eleven days before the massacre at Jonestown in Guyana, South America despite overwhelming evidence that he had had a relationship with Jim Jones that extended beyond mere elbow-rubbing and handshakes. The Peoples Temple pastor had already fled the United States as a result of the increased exposure that revealed an evil man whose character Brown should have known – and undoubtedly did.

Jerry Brown's ties to Jim Jones prior to the massacre should have destroyed his political career but they did not; the Governor continued to trudge ahead years after choosing not to seek reelection for a third term as Governor; that would come later. He would mount his most significant presidential campaign in 1992. After his hiatus from holding political office, Brown would eventually be elected Mayor of Oakland in 1998 and then re-elected in 2006 – by wide margins both times.[61]

In a case of sick irony, Jerry Brown was elected Attorney General for the State of California in 2006. The man who befriended a mass murderer and looked the other way – when bold red flags were vigorously raised and waved – became the top law enforcement officer of his state less than thirty years later. It was as much an indictment of Brown as it was of the media establishment that gave Jim Jones a pass for all those years. The blind eye they turned then was being turned again.

The apologies Lester Kinsolving didn't receive from his colleagues made sense in one respect. The media establishment that consisted of countless people, who refused to offer one, had picked up right where it left off. The correlation was palpable, especially in light of that establishment's loss of the one person who did apologize – Brit Hume.

During the 2008 election cycle, the Association of Community Organizers for Reform Now (ACORN) was at the center of a nationwide scandal involving voter registration fraud. It was a scandal that lasted many months, culminating with undercover videos a year later that revealed a willingness on the part of the group to enable and encourage fraudulent and illegal behavior, including sex trafficking and the prostitution of under aged girls.[62]

Interestingly, the tactics used by ACORN in getting out the vote were very similar to those used by the Peoples Temple decades earlier when George Moscone was elected Mayor of San Francisco. Putting Moscone over the top in the Mayoral election by using those tactics is what got Jones his seat on the housing commission in the form of political payback [See Chapter 1, p. 12].

One of the ACORN offices exposed by the undercover videos was in San Diego, CA. In October of 2009, Breitbart's *Big Government* site published the work of private investigator Derrick Roach, who noticed that the office had dumped thousands of documents in the dumpster out back. He then retrieved them only to find very personal information about the people ACORN had allegedly been helping.[63]

Coincidentally or not, the dump occurred days before a scheduled visit by Attorney General Brown. More suspicious than that, however, was an audio tape that recorded portions of an ACORN meeting at a San Diego restaurant. During that meeting local spokesman David Lagstein made an alarming admission; his people had been in contact with the Attorney General's office and ACORN had assurances that fault would be found with the filmmakers and not with ACORN, once the investigation was finished.

Said Lagstein:

"The Attorney General is a political animal as well  but certainly every bit of communication we've had with (him) has suggested that the fault will be found with the people who did the videos, not with ACORN."[64]

It was shocking on one level but predictable on another. As a Democrat, Jerry Brown relied on the work of ACORN out of political necessity. Granted, the recording of Lagstein would be considered hearsay in a court of law but the subsequent words from Brown himself on a radio interview only served to validate the claims of those who maintained he was beholden to such groups and corrupted as a result.

Even if someone were compelled to believe that Jerry Brown learned from his mistakes relative to his relationship with Jim Jones and the forces behind the Marxist Messiah, not only would such an extension of grace be misplaced but it would be debunked, in large degree, by Brown himself.

While appearing on a *KABC* radio interview with Peter Tilden, Brown didn't just bolster the credibility of the audio recordings that captured Lagstein. His bias in favor of ACORN was on display for all to hear. Remember, as California's Attorney General, Brown's job was to uphold the rule of law and prosecute cases of injustice perpetrated against his state. When questioned by Tilden about what Roach discovered in the ACORN dumpster, Brown offered only obscure and tangential responses before saying the following:

"...there's a lot of people who, you know, are going after ACORN, assigning them a significant causation of certain major events in our country and I think just, on the face of it, there seems to be a bit of exaggeration, to say the least."[65]

Inexplicably, Jerry Brown came full circle when he was elected in 2010 to the position he held when Jim Jones committed mass murder – Governor of California.

To underscore the point about how connected Jones was to California politicians, here is what Conn had to say to those who would extend him grace based on the notion of plausible deniability:

"These political types in San Francisco still came out and defended Jones...when these political types here in California claimed that they had no idea of what was going on later and said, 'well we just didn't know.' That is an outright lie because anyone of them – including Jerry Brown by the way – could have gone to the *Examiner* and read all eight of those articles just to re-trace any of their suspicions. They chose not to do that..."[66]

The church, media, and political establishments had all failed the people of San Francisco and California generally. Though Conn would be proven right, it was he who would continue to live in relative obscurity as many of those politicians successfully deceived constituents with the help of the churches that would remain silent; media that would inject bias into its coverage; and a political culture that would protect its own.

## ◼ THE UNMASKING

In 1977, David Conn was still working at Standard Oil. One of his very best friends was a co-worker by the name of George Coker. Coker was an American Indian and Conn so valued their friendship that the latter had heartfelt concern about the reputation of the American Indian Movement (AIM).

This concern caused Conn to approach Coker about a photo he had seen of AIM leader Dennis Banks with Jim Jones. As a trusted co-worker, Coker had been kept abreast over the years by Conn about what Jones was doing. Conn wanted to find a way to reach Banks so that he could relay what he knew about Jones so Banks could protect himself and AIM from future embarrassment.

At the time, Banks was facing extradition to South Dakota for his role in a stand-off with Federal agents at Wounded Knee **[See Chapter 4, p. 108]** in which AIM seized control of the town and faced off with Federal agents for seventy-one days. A US Marshall and an FBI agent were seriously wounded during the stand-off and two American Indians were killed.[67]

As an interesting aside, Banks fled to California and was given sanctuary by Governor Jerry Brown, who refused to extradite him.[68]

Unbeknownst to both Conn and Coker, Banks was closer to Jones than either had thought or imagined. Coker had an acquaintance named Leighman Brightman, who was another leader within AIM. Brightman had connections to Banks. Conn wanted a meeting with Banks so he could warn the AIM leader about the dangers and future embarrassment of being associated with Jim Jones.

Thanks to Coker's ties to Brightman, that meeting was arranged.

Conn was contacted on very short notice and directed to meet Banks at Brightman's house after midnight on March 23, 1977. Both Conn and Coker went and for three hours, Conn revealed everything he knew about Jones for the sole purpose of convincing Banks that unless the AIM leader distanced himself from Jones, the American Indian Movement would suffer dire consequences.[69]

Everything Conn said made its way to Jim Jones shortly thereafter because Banks was beholden to the pastor of Peoples Temple. All of Conn's sources were in immediate danger and would be terrorized within hours of that meeting. Conn himself would spend eighteen months in hiding.

Amazingly, as a result of the meeting, Conn found himself deeper inside Jim Jones's head than he thought he could be; that meeting served as the flashpoint for Jones's unmasking.

As Conn poured his heart out to Banks in the early morning hours, he referred to two people without naming them; it was not calculated or premeditated. It just happened that way. Those inadvertent omissions would prove to be the spark that lit the paranoid fuse that was an integral part of the Jim Jones persona.

First, Conn confided in Banks that he was in touch with a Treasury agent. Once word of this had gotten back to Jones, the Marxist Messiah panicked and began believing the worst case scenario – the Treasury agent must have been with the IRS, which must have been building a case against him, based on his shady financial dealings. Jones was right to be concerned about such a scenario but the reality was that no such investigation was taking place. The man Conn referred to was Jim Hubert, a low level employee whom Conn had been put in touch with by the other person he did not name but who caused more panic within Jones's twisted mind.

Second, the other person Conn made reference to was a reporter he had been in contact with. In reality, that reporter was George Klineman, who wrote for a relatively small publication. However, Jones's mind played tricks on him. He knew that *San Francisco Chronicle* writer Marshall Kilduff was planning to write what he thought was an innocuous article about his Temple but if Kilduff was privy to the information Conn had, the Marxist Messiah was face to face with a disaster.

Jones's ego had gotten the better of him in another respect. Conn told me during a phone conversation that if Jones would have laid low after receiving those meeting minutes, he would have been able to take him out with minimal trouble or media curiosity.[70] Instead, that meeting instigated an all-out propaganda war on the part of Peoples Temple. Conn was to be demonized; local media took notice. This lowly citizen had been tracking Jim Jones for over seven years without the pastor's knowledge. Jones was able to control the church, the media, and the politicians! How could this powerless, meager citizen have done so much damage?!

Remember, Jones still held the position of chairman of the San Francisco housing authority. On March 24th, while chairing one of those meetings, Jones simply collapsed hours after Conn's meeting with Banks. He was subsequently taken away in an ambulance; it should have been a paddy wagon.

Conn had demonstrated the best way to defeat evil. He got it to unmask itself.

## JONES FLEES TO GUYANA, SOUTH AMERICA

Upon learning that Conn was in touch with a reporter, Jones's paranoia told him that the reporter had to have been the *Chronicle's* Marshall Kilduff, who was working on an article about the Peoples Temple that was to appear in *New West* magazine. Those suspicions became part of Jones's reality and *New West* began receiving phone calls, letters, and threats as a result. The truth was that Kilduff had none of the access to the inside information or sources to that which Conn had.

*New West* and Marshall Kilduff were living the terrorizing reality that was intended for George Klineman, a man whose name Jim Jones didn't know. At one point, California Lieutenant Governor Mervyn Dymally even contacted *New West* in an attempt to dissuade them from moving forward.[71]

As if that weren't enough, Jones's foot soldiers began to target the owner of *New West* magazine, Rupert Murdoch (yes, that Rupert Murdoch) and even went after advertisers.[72] It was a case of foreshadowing as decades later, *Fox News* – another Murdoch entity under his *Newscorp* umbrella – would be subjected to very similar treatment.

Kilduff had material for an article but it was based mostly on political intrigue. Thanks to Conn, Klineman had the inside stuff. As a result of the increased pressure put on *New West* by the Peoples Temple, Klineman reached out to Kilduff; the two ultimately met and collaborated on the *New West* article that appeared in the August 1, 1977 issue. Conn's sources are what made the article so incredibly damaging to Jones.

Ironically, while Conn was the catalyst for Jones igniting his own paranoia, it was Jones himself who was responsible for what would be the explosive pairing of Kilduff and Klineman. It was a story that presented firsthand accounts from multiple people who escaped Peoples Temple.[73] Had Jones not panicked, those accounts most assuredly would not have been part of the article that ultimately flushed his Temple out of San Francisco and into Guyana.

The article so exposed Jones that he fled to Guyana before it was published.[74]

In the days and weeks after the *New West* article, more reporters began to write about the Peoples Temple. Among them were Tim Reiterman and Nancy Dooley of the *San Francisco Examiner*, both of whom relied on Conn as a primary source for their articles.

## DEATH OF A US CONGRESSMAN

As more suspicions about Jones were raised and became more public, a US Congressman took notice. Rep. Leo Ryan (D-CA) assembled a team to assist him in visiting the new location of the Peoples Temple in

November of 1978. Among those who joined Ryan was *Examiner* reporter Tim Reiterman.

Conn was adamant that the visit not take place. He knew Jones and not only pleaded with as many people as he could in an effort to prevent the trip but he successfully predicted what would happen. When he heard of Ryan's plans to go to Guyana to find out if people were being involuntarily held there, Conn said:

"Ryan will never make it. If he goes to Jonestown, he will never leave alive."[75]

Conn contacted Dooley and pleaded with her to listen and to pass along the message to Reiterman so that Ryan could be persuaded to call off the trip.

"I said, 'Nancy, I studied this guy's mind for eight years. There is no way that he's going to allow this to come off. He has some kind of plan of action. I know it.' And she said, 'Well, our people are going to tell Ryan everything we have on him on the way down,' and I said, 'That's not going to do it. You've only been on it for three or four months. You can't possibly know what an evil guy this man is.' And so, I told her right then that Ryan is not going to come out of South America alive."[76]

As Ryan's party attempted to leave Jonestown after the visit, armed members of Jones's cult approached them before they could board the waiting plane. Eighteen people were shot, including Ryan and Reiterman. Ryan became the only Congressman in United States history to die in the line of duty. Reiterman survived.[77]

Sadly, the worst was yet to come; Conn predicted that too. Once receiving the news about Ryan's shooting, Conn insisted that mass suicide would be next. He phoned *Examiner* reporter Nancy Dooley to warn her that unless authorities chose the proper course of action, all of the inhabitants of Jonestown would become victims and suffer the consequences of their own allegiance to an evil man.[78]

Conn's last prediction about Jim Jones was correct too. In the name of his twisted, Marxist God, Jones poisoned a flavor-aid concoction and got his flock of nearly one thousand people to drink it before he shot himself in the head.

Unfortunately, Conn's vindication came at the expense of a macabre reality. For years, he had been ignored by the people who could have prevented that reality from coming to fruition. Instead, the culture of fear and corruption had steadily provided nourishment to the evil which continued to grow until it blossomed, revealing an essence none could deny. The culture that had birthed Jones' power had been violently rebuked by the fruit of its own weakness.

During one of my phone conversations with David Conn, he expressed sorrow for Nancy Dooley and wished for a way to contact her but never could. He was never able to shake the sense that she had been much too hard on herself after the massacre. One of his most frequent prayers asked for her to be comforted.

A lesser man would have gloated.

## ■ BATTLE ASSESSMENT

The demise of Jim Jones was not exclusively about a madman who killed hundreds of people; it was also about a Marxist who revered the socialist movement and aligned with the Communist Soviet Union at the height of the cold war between the United States and the United Soviet Socialist Republic (USSR). In addition to being a psychopath, Jones was also an agent of America's enemy during a time of undeclared war.

One month prior to the massacre at Jonestown, Jones welcomed a Soviet diplomat named Feodor Timofeyev to his Temple. As he introduced Timofeyev to his congregation, Jones said the following:

> "For many years, we have let our sympathies be quite publicly known, that the United States government was not our mother, (pause) but that the Soviet Union was our spiritual motherland.[79]

By the time this meeting had taken place, Jim Jones had been severely weakened, thanks mainly to a chain reaction set in motion by David Conn. The power Jones acquired in California was astounding in retrospect. Had Conn not thrown a monkey wrench into Jones's plans, that power could have extended even deeper into American politics. It's a statement of fact to say that Conn didn't just prevent a powerful madman from acquiring even more power; he also prevented a domestic enemy from doing so.

Jones continued his introduction of Timofeyev:

"...I'm glad after many hours of the kindest, uh, benevolence of our consular of the Soviet Embassy, Feodor Timofeyev, spending hours and hours fulfilling our highest ideals, and our noblest expectations. We were not mistaken in allying our purposes, our destiny, with the destiny of the Soviet Union."[80]

After introducing Timofeyev, the Soviet representative from his country's embassy in Guyana spoke to Jones's flock. Here is a portion of what he said:

"I am very happy that I saw here in Jonestown the full (pause) uh, harmony of theory which have been created by [German socialist Karl] Marx, [German socialist Friedrich] Engels, Lenin, and uh, the practical implementation of this— some fundamental features of this theory, under the leadership or together with you, by Comrade Jim Jones, and I'd like to thank him for that.[81]

As is the case with every chapter of this book, the figure representing the unsung David is also someone who fought a patriotic battle for his country. Prior to 1977, Jones was well on his way to cementing significant power in not only the city of San Francisco but in the state of California after moving to a small town in that state, less than fifteen years earlier. Had he continued on that course without the interference of an American citizen by the name of David Conn, the power he could have ultimately secured is frightening to consider; it would have almost necessarily involved a cozy Soviet partnership as well.

Let there be no doubt that Jones was not just a madman but an enemy of the United States. In a letter to Timofeyev dated November 18, 1978 Peoples Temple representative Annie McGowan willed all

assets to the Soviet Union **(Appendix C)**. In addition to listing accounts and their specific dollar amounts, the letter said the following:

> "...regarding all our assets which we want to leave to the Communist Party of the Union of Soviet Socialist Republics...I am doing so on behalf of Peoples Temple because we, as Communists, want our money to be of benefit for help of oppressed people all over the world, or in any way that your decision-making body sees fit."[82]

Consider that on the same day Jim Jones ordered the assassination of a United States Congressman, his Temple bequeathed all of its assets to the Soviet Union. Yet, the politicians who supported Jones for so many years are still revered; in some cases, they are still in office.

A relevant aside would be the fate of another member of the United States Congress – Gabrielle Giffords of Arizona. Giffords was shot in the head little more than thirty-two years later, on January 8, 2011 by a man named Jared Loughner as she was meeting with her constituents in a shopping center parking lot. Loughner's *YouTube* page listed the *Communist Manifesto* as one of his favorite books.[83] The recovery of Giffords was nothing short of miraculous. Her condition was so grave at one point that she had been declared dead. In both cases – Ryan and Giffords – those who would assassinate did so in the name of Marxism to varying degrees.

It wasn't just Jim Jones that David Conn saved his nation from; it was the furtherance of Marxism, an ideology which makes many of its gains through intimidation and bully tactics.

There will be those who argue that Conn's missteps with Dennis Banks on that fateful night in March, 1977 led to the deaths of many. Others may argue that the politicians in and around San Francisco enabled those deaths. Taken together, those arguments would place Conn and those politicians on the same plane.

The truth is there could not be a clearer line of distinction between Conn and those politicians. The former erred while trying to help others by warning them about Jones – at great risk to his own personal safety. Politicians like George Moscone, Willie Brown, Ralph Nader, and Jerry Brown erred by aiding Jones's harming of others in the interest of furthering their own careers [See Chapter 7, p. 201]. A starker difference between motives may not exist.

It is worth underscoring that an everyday citizen armed with nothing more than a sling shot took down a man who had neutered all of the big guns that were supposed to be in place to defend against attacks on him.

# CHAPTER 6

## WAYNE PERRYMAN
### vs.
# DEMOCRATIC PARTY

## ■ CHANGING SIDES

As a black American from Seattle, Reverend Wayne Perryman did what a great majority of other black Americans did; he supported and voted for Democrats. In 1996, he worked very hard to re-elect Bill Clinton as President of the United States. Soon thereafter, Perryman did what so few – regardless of race – ever do. Armed with intellectual honesty, he allowed historical facts and undeniable truths to shatter the paradigm he had long embraced. In what can only be described as one of God's many paradoxes, Perryman was made much stronger by allowing himself to be broken.

Shortly after Clinton won reelection, Perryman was challenged by some younger members of his church to explore the history of the relationship between the Democratic Party and blacks.[1] It was a moment of truth. Had Perryman cordially demurred, the battle he would soon be called on to fight may never have been waged. Blessed with an extremely unique ability to do research, Perryman would one day build a case against the Democratic Party that would shatter the paradigms of anyone willing to be intellectually honest as well.

On average, black voters pull the lever for Democrats about 90 percent of the time. This has been the case for decades. The Democratic Party relies on that percentage for its success. Without it, electoral defeat would be all but assured in every election cycle.[2] While the Democratic Party has for so long relied on the black vote, black voters have been giving the Democratic Party their allegiance in droves. Perryman's research was certain to reveal exactly what the Republicans had done to black Americans that would cause the latter to so roundly reject them.

The opposite happened.

In his book *Unfounded Loyalty*, which was a direct result of that challenge posed to him by those young church members, Perryman instead uncovered a history that revealed an inexplicable lack of rejection for an historically hateful and racist Democratic Party on the part of blacks. If ever there was an entity blacks had reason to be repulsed by, it was the Democratic Party, which treated them in ways grotesquely similar to how Nazis treated Jews.

After conducting research that was so intense he could hear the screams of his ancestors, Perryman would find the resolve to go to battle with the entire Democratic Party establishment.

That establishment would have a fight on its hands.

## ▓ PRELUDE TO BATTLE

In 1993 – years before he would throw down the gauntlet with the Democratic Party – Perryman conducted a mock trial that laid the foundation for extremely tangible and significant results. It involved an interpretation of Biblical Scripture that had become widely accepted within many mainstream institutions – Genesis 9:18-27. It is about Noah and his three sons – Shem, Ham, and Japheth. Ham is widely accepted to have been the ancestor of the black race today. This portion of Genesis discusses how Ham mocked his father's nakedness after the latter had become drunk. When Noah awoke, he cursed Ham's son, Canaan.

> [25]He (Noah) exclaimed, Cursed be Canaan! He shall be the [a] servant of servants to his brethren!
>
> [26]He also said, Blessed be the Lord, the God of Shem! And blessed by the Lord my God be Shem! And let Canaan be his servant.
>
> [27]May God enlarge Japheth; and let him dwell in the tents of Shem, and let Canaan be his servant.[3]

While that passage makes it clear that Noah cursed Canaan, not Ham, a narrative had been put forth for hundreds of years that said European Christians pointed to the alleged 'Curse of Ham' when rationalizing the enslavement of the black race. This grossly simplistic and erroneous interpretation of Scripture had many pitfalls; it cast the righteous descendants of Ham as being victims of that curse and it didn't square with historical fact.

According to Perryman, the curse upon Canaan and his descendants ended when the Jews conquered the Canaanites.[4]

The trial that took place in California in 1993 highlighted the fact that publishers and various Encyclopedias had accepted a certain narrative as a valid interpretation of fact; slavery was the result of Ham's behavior toward his father and the subsequent curse placed upon him and his descendants.[5]

After the trial, Perryman wrote to the *Encyclopedia Britannica*, *Thomas Nelson Publishers*, and *Zondervan Publishing House*, among others. All three responded that they would be correcting the record. The Editorial Division of *Encyclopedia Britannica* conceded Perryman's point and told him they could no longer continue supporting the argument on the part of some that the curse could have been responsible for the enslavement of people of African descent:

> It is our belief that neither the biblical text in question, nor its treatment in the *Encyclopedia Britannica*, could be logically used to support such a claim.[6]

In response to Perryman's list of books published under the *Zondervan Publishing House* name that contained the erroneous historical account, Vice President and Editor-in-Chief, Stanley N. Gundry wrote to Perryman that those books would be changed:

> ...I have taken steps to make the necessary corrections, removing the "Curse of Ham" interpretation from the titles that you mentioned, and revising the text to more faithfully reflect what the Genesis 9 passage actually says.[7]

*Thomas Nelson Publishers* also honored the ruling of the mock trial. In a response Perryman received from the publisher's Vice President, Philip P. Stoner, he was assured that *Nelson's Illustrated Bible Dictionary* would be changed:

> I hope it will please you to know that we are in the process of thoroughly revising NELSON'S ILLUSTRATED BIBLE DIC-TIONARY and are correcting errors in the specific entries you listed in your letter...The original NELSON'S ILLUSTRATED BIBLE DICTIONARY was edited by the late Dr. Herbert Lockyer, Sr., who was apparently unaware of the issues you have raised.[8]

It was a sweeping and significant victory. Perryman was able to cut through the façade of widely accepted beliefs and prove unequivocally that those beliefs were based on a false premise; that premise allowed generations to construct and live under a paradigm that justified the oppression and persecution of an entire race of people.

In just a few short years after that victory, Perryman would be hard at work deconstructing another narrative, one that said the Democratic Party looked after the interests of black Americans. It was a seemingly logical conclusion based on voter registration numbers; Democrats received 90 percent of the black vote. Couldn't the only explanation be that the Republican Party had a history of persecuting blacks? Was this reality or the consequence of one party's successful use of dema-goguery and deception across generations?

After completing his research, it would be shown that like those who embraced the 'Curse of Ham' theory, the Democratic Party – more than any other establishment in American history – viewed black Americans as an inferior race to be demeaned, terrorized, abused, tortured, murdered, intimidated, and exploited.

## ▪ COMMON THREADS

Taken separately, the glaring incidents of racism and persecution toward blacks during the 1800s on the part of the Democratic Party might be successfully explained away by those with a vested interest in doing so. Perryman's ability to put historical events into a much broader context can only be met with silence by the fiercest defenders of the Democratic Party. In fact, many of the behaviors exhibited by Democrats during that time are not all that dissimilar from the behaviors of Democrats today [See Chapter 5, p. 133-134].

Prior to 1854, the Republican Party did not exist but slavery in the United States did. In 1844, the Democratic Party ran on a platform that defended slavery.[9] Those who wanted to end slavery – the abolitionists – were specifically targeted in this platform as people who should, in essence, mind their own business. This entrenched belief on the part of Democrats, that slavery was indeed a right, led to the birth of the Republican Party, which was formed primarily to put an end to slavery.[10]

Perryman highlights two very significant events that paint the Democrats of the 1800s as ideological ancestors of present day Democrats. The first involved the Kansas-Nebraska Act of 1854. This law – passed narrowly – allowed each state to determine for itself if slavery would be permitted. Perhaps just as relevant is the way this Bill was passed; Democrats successfully sent hundreds of people to Kansas and fixed the elections to guarantee a slavery-friendly legislature.[11]

A disturbing similarity between the Democratic Party of 1854 and the one of the late 20th and early 21st Centuries involves the Association of Community Organizations for Reform Now (ACORN), a group whose primary goal was to elect Democrats [See Chapter 1, p.12]. ACORN was charged with voter registration fraud in several states in the wake of the 2008 election.[12] A significant difference was that the Democratic Party relied heavily upon ACORN to secure black votes.

In 1854, Democrats hadn't yet acquired and didn't need the ability to delegate such a task; blacks didn't secure the right to vote until Republicans gave it to them when they sponsored – and then ratified – the 15th Amendment in 1870. Democrats would subsequently threaten, intimidate, and torture blacks to either vote Democrat or not vote at all.[13]

Also in 2008, before the election that saw Barack Obama become President, an ACORN official with the group's Project Vote affiliate – Anita Moncrief – revealed to a *New York Times* reporter – Stephanie Strom – that her group was given the lists of donors to various Democratic campaigns who had already contributed the maximum legal amount to their candidates. This list was to be used to solicit those donors to contribute to Project Vote, which overwhelmingly supported the Democratic Party in general and Barack Obama in particular. The brass at the *New York Times* angrily shut Strom down and the story was never fully told. Moncrief – a black American – subsequently soured on the Democratic Party and became a strong and outspoken opponent of the Democrats.[14]

Two modern day examples demonstrate one trait of the Democratic Party – voter fraud – seemed to be passed down from generation to generation. First, in 2004, Democratic candidate for Governor of Washington State – Christine Gregoire – was declared the winner in an extremely narrow election after multiple recounts put her ahead. This, despite evidence that there were more votes certified in King County than there were ballots cast. There was also controversy over missing military absentee ballots; military personnel historically vote Republican by a significant margin.[15]

In another example, Al Franken – a Democrat – seemed to be granted recount after recount in his race with incumbent Republican Senator of Minnesota, Norm Coleman in 2008. Once the recounts showed Franken had enough votes, he was declared the winner. By 2010, it was widely accepted by many objective observers that Franken won as a result of voter fraud.[16]

The Barack Obama administration showed great allegiance to public sector unions in the form of the Service Employees International Union (SEIU) and the American Federation of Labor – Congress of Industrial Organizations (AFL-CIO). This manifested itself in many ways but one involved a collective bargaining law in the state of Wisconsin. As the state legislature was on the cusp of passing a Bill that would restrict the ability of public sector unions to collectively bargain, the SEIU and a group known as Organizing for America (OFA) – the Community Organizing arm of the Obama administration – descended upon the State Capitol in Madison, WI from all over the country to aggressively protest the Bill.[17] Again, it was the Democratic Party that attempted to bully a state legislature to further an agenda, in much the same way it did in 1854.

Perryman points to a second incident that shows the Democratic Party for what it truly was. It involved the near murder of a Republican Senator from Massachusetts named Charles Sumner. In 1856 – in response to the Kansas-Nebraska Act – Sumner took to the Senate floor to argue vehemently against slavery. After his speech, he was physically attacked when a Democratic Congressman from South Carolina – Preston Brooks – beat him unconscious with a cane.[18]

While Brooks resigned due to pressure from the Republicans, he was soon thereafter re-elected despite committing the act of attempted murder in full view of his colleagues.[19] Ironically, Brooks returned to Congress well before Sumner, who took three years to recover and then returned to the Senate.[20] This pass granted to Brooks on the part of the Democratic Party in 1856 made the Party's support of Bill Clinton in 1999 look mild by comparison in degree only, not in principle.

Though Clinton – a Democrat – was impeached on two counts by a Republican-controlled House – perjury and obstruction of justice – not one Democrat voted in favor of that impeachment. Nor did a single Democratic Senator vote to convict Clinton, who went on to finish his term.[21] The Democratic Party closed ranks and smeared those who would hold Clinton to account by impugning their motives instead of enforcing the law.

As Perryman points out, in 1868 Democrats called Republicans "Ni**er Lovers" while boasting that America was a "white man's country." After the 15th Amendment was ratified, Republicans actually had to pass the Enforcement Act of 1870 and then the Force Act of 1871 to guarantee the rights of black voters would be protected under the 15th Amendment.[22]

Smears, fraud, and a disregard for the law are things the Democratic Party of old seems to share with its ideological descendants.

# ■ LINCOLN REACHES ACROSS THE AISLE

It may be the quintessential example of why reaching across the aisle – a practice championed by modern day Democrats when their Party is *not* in power and moderate Republicans when their Party *is* in power

– is a bad strategy. Abraham Lincoln selected a Democrat as his vice presidential running mate for his second term. Hannibal Hamlin, a radical Republican who vehemently opposed slavery, was the Vice President during Lincoln's first term. In a political move, Lincoln and his Party thought it best to appeal to a broader contingency of voters by putting Andrew Johnson on the ticket.[23]

A few short months later, Lincoln was assassinated by a Democrat named John Wilkes Booth, who sympathized with the Confederacy. This put a pro-slavery Democrat in the White House. Though history shows that Booth didn't kill Lincoln to put Johnson in power, the consequences of that assassination virtually mirrored those of an act perpetrated by someone with such a plan.

Just prior to Lincoln's assassination, Special Field Order #15 was issued by the president's Union General, William Sherman. That order called for each black family to receive forty acres and a mule as a form of reparation for slavery. The Republican Party made formal efforts to support that order.

Approximately one year later, Sherman's Bill was introduced and passed by a Republican Congress. It was not to become law because President Johnson vetoed it. As a result, every black family that had been issued those 40 Acres and a mule had to return them.[24]

At the 2004 Democratic National Convention in Boston, black Democrat Al Sharpton invoked this history but he got it very wrong while scoring political points:

> "It is true that Mr. Lincoln signed the Emancipation Proclamation, after which there was a commitment to give 40 acres and a mule. That's where the argument, to this day, of reparations starts. We never got the 40 acres. We went all the way to Herbert Hoover, and we never got the 40 acres. We didn't get the mule. So we decided we'd ride this donkey as far as it would take us."[25]

Take note of Sharpton's reference to Herbert Hoover. The implication was that blacks switched to the Democratic Party after Hoover, who was succeeded by Democrat Franklin Delano Roosevelt.

Continue reading to find out how racist the 32nd President of the United States was.

Sharpton is a political opportunist who has no concern for actual history. The fact remains; the Party that took away those 40 acres is the same one Sharpton hitched his wagon to. The Party that fought *for* those reparations is the same one Sharpton treats with contempt. He is rewarded by a Democratic establishment that continues to fail blacks in America. Al Sharpton is proof positive that at some point, the Democratic Party found a way around terrorizing and intimidating blacks in order to further its agenda. It found a way to use a select few of them to do the dirty work of smearing the opposition. In so doing, it has made painting the Republican Party as racist a primary goal.

Like Bill Clinton, Johnson was impeached but not removed from office.[26]

## ■ KU KLUX KLAN (KKK)

In 1865, the 13th Amendment was ratified; it abolished slavery. In 1868, the 14th Amendment was ratified; it granted citizenship to former slaves and their offspring born in the United States. Since amendments to the Constitution don't require the approval of the President, the Republican controlled Congress was able to ratify them without the consent of Johnson. In between the ratification of those two amendments was the formation of a hateful and racist group known as the KKK in 1866. It was a group formed by Democrats who felt threatened by the freedoms blacks were realizing as a direct result of Republican efforts.

The 15th Amendment, which gave blacks the right to vote, was introduced in 1869 and overwhelmingly supported by a Republican controlled Congress while being almost universally opposed by the Democrats in both houses. Not one Democrat in the House voted in favor of the Amendment, which was ratified in 1870.[27]

In conducting his research for *Unfounded Loyalty*, Perryman found a plethora of books penned by various historical experts who explained how the Democratic Party was the "Daddy" of the KKK, its armed wing. One of them was Professor Allen W. Trelease, who explained how the KKK reacted to passage of the 15th Amendment:

"Klansmen in disguise rode through Negro neighborhoods at night warning Negroes either to cast Democratic ballots or stay away from the poll...Klan activities created a reign of terror in many localities and sometimes had the desired effect of demoralizing Negroes and Republicans...Republicans of both races were threatened, beaten, shot, and murdered with impunity. In some areas Negroes stopped voting or voted the Democrat ticket as the Klan demanded."[28]

Perhaps this quote from Trelease – cited by Perryman – explains even more:

"Democrats by a kind of tortured reasoning, sometimes accused Negroes and Republicans of attacking and even killing each other so that the crimes would be blamed on the Democrats; investigations usually revealed that the Democrats had committed the acts themselves."[29]

Those inclined to insist that the Democratic mindset of the 1800s was more closely aligned with the Republicans of the 21st Century encounter a problem at this point, especially when factoring in the rise of the Tea Party in April of 2009. As constitutionally-minded conservatives rose up in protest against the big government policies being implemented at the time by a Democrat-controlled Congress and White House, Democrats used similar tactics, though not as violent.

On the one year anniversary of the Tax Day Tea Party, a man named Jason Levin founded a group called 'Crash the Tea Party.' The objective of the group was to infiltrate the Tea Parties in order to portray them as racist, hateful, and uneducated.[30]

In August of 2009, the office of Democratic Party headquarters in Denver was vandalized; windows were smashed. The Party chair Pat Waak immediately blamed the Tea Party but one of the assailants had been apprehended. Maurice Joseph Schwenkler was actually tied to a Democratic group and ultimately pleaded guilty.[31]

In perhaps one of the most surreal examples, a black man named Dyron Hart created a fake name on Facebook and used the photo of a white supremacist to identify himself. He threatened to kill blacks because Barack Obama had been elected President. Hart threatened three black students and ultimately pleaded guilty to threatening one of them.[32]

The examples of such behavior are too numerous to chronicle here but virtually all of them involve Democratic attempts to smear their opponents with staged events, contrived scenarios, and outright falsehoods. Disturbingly, elected officials were willing participants far too often, if not actively, then certainly in their silence.

In multiple instances, Democratic operatives in the 21st Century behaved very similarly to their counterparts of the 19th Century. The degree to which those tactics were implemented can be debated but the tactics themselves are identical. This ends-justifies-the-means mentality is espoused by the Democratic Party establishment to this day.

The ideological hero of the 44th President of the United States, Democratic President Barack Obama, was Saul Alinsky, who once wrote that "the end justifies almost any means..."[33] Hillary Clinton, Obama's Secretary of State, was also a student of Alinsky **[See Chapter 1, p. 4]**.

There were some minor differences between the Democratic Party tactics of the 1800s and those employed in the 1960s when it came to securing the black vote after ratification of the 15th Amendment. The Democrats used terror and intimidation to get what they wanted and then switched to manipulation and empty promises.

Perryman writes:

> From 1870 to 1930, the party used fraud, whippings, lynching, murder, intimidation, and mutilation to get their vote. In the 1930s and 1960s they switched from violence and intimidation to manipulation and voter's registration.[34]

In talking about the overriding agenda of the Democratic Party, Perryman says that it has been...

> ...to either destroy the African American or make him his perpetual servant for profit.[35]

That is an either/or proposition but the founders of the KKK and Jim Crow laws would be proud of the Democratic Party today when it comes to abortions. Groups like Planned Parenthood have been destroying black American families while simultaneously profiting from that destruction for years. *LifeNews* reported that while blacks only make up 13 percent of the US population, 36 percent of all abortions are performed on black babies.[36] Planned Parenthood receives taxpayer dollars along with the overwhelming majority of its support from the Democratic Party.

That same article focused on a controversial billboard that went up in New York City in 2011. It said, 'The Most Dangerous Place for an African American is in the Womb.' The billboard – put up during Black History Month – caused a great deal of controversy and ultimately came down due to political pressure. None other than Al Sharpton was one of the more prominent voices who objected to it. He said:

> "The billboard was offensive, especially during Black History Month, and I had intended to hold a press conference… in front of the billboard to protest the message of racial profiling and against a woman's right to choose."[37]

The tragic irony is that in defending the right of black women to kill their babies, Sharpton unwittingly aligned himself with the KKK's ideals out of loyalty to none other than the Democratic Party. It is the Republican Party platform – if not all party members themselves – that rejects abortion. Again, anyone who claims that the Democrats of old seized the righteous mantle while the Republican Party of old descended into a pit of racism needs to look at these facts.

The Democratic Party seemingly pulled off a major coup. While perpetuating a culture of death, it was somehow able to convince blood relatives of those it killed, to willingly endorse the murder of their own family members.

In 2003, black comedian Dave Chappelle performed a very controversial skit for his short-lived television show in which he played the role of a "black white supremacist" named Clayton Bigsby. The plot was made possible because Chappelle's character was blind and able to rise through the ranks of the Ku Klux Klan, having the ability to effectively communicate the message of the racist group while wearing a hood.[38] It's an allegory that relates directly to many of the black leaders within the Democratic Party who are blind to history. As a consequence, they help convince 90 percent of the black electorate to vote Democrat.

Chappelle, who converted to Islam years before his television show, serves as an interesting case study in this regard.[39] The Islamic world has a history of enslaving black Africans across several centuries. By some accounts, the figure is estimated to be approximately 14 million people between the seventh and twentieth centuries.[40]

An added twist of irony involved the reaction of the KKK to a Florida pastor in the summer of 2010. Terry Jones planned to burn several Qur'ans on the ninth anniversary of the September 11th attacks. Though the burnings never took place, the KKK took notice prior to the scheduled event.

The KKK website decried the plans of Jones and referred to the act of burning the Qur'ans as "completely UNACCEPTABLE... despicable, and un-American."[41] Lost on the racist group was its own history of burning crosses. The disturbing reality is that in this one case, the KKK, the Muslim world, and a black American comedian were all on the same page.

Was the lion lying down with the lamb or was the wolf lying down with sheep?

Perryman pointed out that in 1871, Democrats attempted to stop blacks from voting in the wake of the 15th Amendment's ratification. He cites the testimony of a black man named John Childers of Alabama in front of a Joint Select Committee. Childers explained that he voted Democrat out of fear and that he was intimidated at the polling place. Here is an excerpt of his testimony:

> "At the last election... there was a man standing here in the court-house door; when I started to the ballot-box he told me he had a coffin already made for me, because he thought I was going to vote the radical [meaning Republican] ticket."[42]

On Election Day in 2008 – the same election that saw Barack Obama become President – two members of the New Black Panther Party, dressed in military garb, were standing in front of a Philadelphia polling station. One of the men – King Samir Shabazz – was brandishing a nightstick. The other man – Jerry Jackson – was an official Democratic Party poll watcher.[43] A firsthand account from that day quoted Shabazz as saying, "You're about to be ruled by the black man, cracker."[44]

A lawsuit was filed against the two men as well as against the New Black Panther Party by the US Justice Department under the outgoing George W. Bush administration. The defendants failed to respond and the government won a default judgment. The Justice Department under the incoming Democratic Obama administration dropped all charges against the defendants.

A career attorney within the Voting Rights section of the Justice Department – Christopher Coates – later gave sworn testimony to the US Commission on Civil Rights in which he said he was instructed by superiors at the Department of Justice not to bring voting rights cases against minority defendants.[45]

The color of the individuals at the polling station that day notwithstanding, the behavior exhibited by both men is more historically consistent with the Democratic Party than it is with the Republican Party; it was racist in nature.

Moreover, in a *National Geographic* video documentary about the New Black Panther Party in 2009, King Samir – armed with a bullhorn – instructed people on a crowded street what they needed to do in order to secure their freedom:

> "You want freedom? You're gonna have to kill some crackers (white people)! You're gonna have to kill some of their babies!"[46]

As it was in the 1800s, this type of hatred was directed toward Republicans and blacks who sided with them. Differences between then and now are again, matters of degree, not of spirit.

Consider the Ku Klux Klan Act of 1871, which was introduced by Republicans. It was intended to prevent the KKK from terrorizing blacks and white Republicans. In one of his many examples of stellar research, Perryman found the words of a Republican Senator from Michigan at the time – William Stoughton – who shared the contents of an interview the Senate Investigation Committee held with a Klan member named James E. Boyd. Boyd said he was:

"...initiated into the Ku Klux Klan as an auxiliary of the Democratic Party."[47]

Stoughton then shared his views with the Senate and warned that the Democrat-controlled south was descending "into a state of blood-shed and anarchy."

Two people who had a significant influence on Barack Obama revered anarchy beginning in the 1960s. One was Frances Fox Piven who, along with her husband, devised a strategy to hasten the fall of capitalism by overloading the government bureaucracy with entitle-ment demands that eventually could not be met. The subsequent collapse would lead to anarchy.[48] The out-of-control spending policies of the Obama administration led many to believe that the President endorsed the strategy.

The other person with close ties to Obama who espoused anarchy was Bill Ayers, founder of the Weather Underground [See Chapter 4]. In 2002, Ayers said the following in a radio interview:

"I considered myself partly an anarchist then and I consider myself partly an anarchist now. I mean, I'm as much an anarchist as I am a Marxist which is to say I find a lot of the ideas in anarchism appealing."[49] [See Chapter 5, p. 124]

The warnings from a Republican Senator about a Democratic Party with a desire for anarchy in 1871 seemed to ring true with some of its more prominent faces in the 21st Century as well.

Stoughton's 1871 speech struck a nerve with a Republican Congressman from Mississippi named George McKee. Stoughton brought up the fact that Klansmen from Alabama had recently descended upon Meridian, Mississippi at the behest of the Klansmen from his state; several people were killed, both black and white. McKee spoke about what became known as the Meridian massacre:

"...amongst all this red list of slaughter you do not find the name of a single Democrat. The dead and wounded, the maimed and the scourged, are all, all Republicans."[50]

Perryman chronicles countless cases of the downright despicable and inhumane cruelty to blacks at the hands of the KKK and the Democratic Party but two of those cases seem to illustrate the barbarism best; it was akin to how Islamic terrorists treat their victims.

First, in 1899, a black man named Sam Hose was stripped and chained to a tree surrounded by logs soaked with kerosene. Perryman writes what transpired:

"...they cut off his ears, fingers, and genitals, and skinned his face. While some in the crowd plunged knives into the victim's flesh, others watched...the contortions of Sam Hose's body as flames rose, distorting his features, causing his eyes to bulge out of their sockets and rupturing his veins. The only sounds that came from the victim's lips, even as his blood sizzled in the fire were, "Oh my God! Oh, Jesus!"[51]

What happened next was not the least bit dissimilar from what happened to the two Israeli soldiers in Ramallah detailed in another chapter of this book [See Chapter 2, p. 46-47].

The second example occurred in 1918 after a black woman named Mary Turner pledged to have the men who lynched her husband, prosecuted. At the time, Turner was nine months pregnant. A mob dragged her from her home and hanged her from a tree. Perryman writes of the despicable, inhumane acts that then took place:

While she was hanging from the rope, they cut open her womb, the child spilled out, and when the baby cried, they crushed the baby's skull with the heels of their boots.[52]

It was as if the murder of Turner's baby laid the foundation for the culture of abortion the Democratic Party endorses today. The two aforementioned cases are endemic to how blacks in the American south were treated at that time. The treatment of human beings under Jim Crow laws, the KKK, and the larger umbrella of those groups – the Democratic Party – served as a precursor to what would happen across the Atlantic Ocean just a few decades later.

Shortly after his book *Unveiling the Whole Truth* was released, Perryman appeared on my radio show and explained this very thing:

> "The Democratic Party is responsible for approximately the death of over 30 million black people; it's called the black holocaust that no one ever talks about because the Democratic Party was not only responsible for slavery; they were also responsible for Jim Crow and the Ku Klux Klan and every racist institution in America."[53]

When people hear the word 'holocaust' it immediately conjures up images of Nazi Germany and Hitler's barbaric persecution of the Jews. This charge by Perryman would put the Democratic Party on par with the Nazi Party.

He convincingly did just that.

## ■ NAZIS AND DEMOCRATS

The English translation of the word, 'Nazi' is National Socialist Party. That was Hitler's Party. In the early 21st Century, Democrats in the United States insisted that there was a very clear line of distinction between that type of socialism and the type they thirsted for.

Shortly after Barack Obama's inauguration in January of 2009, *Newsweek Magazine* had a cover story entitled, "We Are All Socialists Now." The case made by *Newsweek* was that America was indeed headed towards being a European style, socialist nation.[54] Getting significant credit for this fact in the article was the prior administration, which was Republican and led by George W. Bush, who never seemed interested in using the veto pen, especially when it came to spending bills.

In fairness to *Newsweek*, the Republican administration that preceded the Democratic one did steer the United States toward economic socialism but Obama's administration took the wheel and shifted into overdrive.

An historical example provided by Perryman perhaps explains why a Republican administration would so willingly do the Democrats' bidding; it had to do with the path of least resistance. In 1877, the Republicans made a deal with the Democrats; they "reached across the aisle" in the interest of compromise and it proved disastrous – as it almost always does.

Ironically, what became known as the Compromise of 1877 was the result of an extremely close election – the closest until the 2000 election between Republican George W. Bush and Democrat Al Gore. In 2000, Gore won the popular vote but lost the electoral vote, which was mired in controversy over what happened in Florida. In the election of 1876, circumstances were amazingly similar. Republican Rutherford B. Hayes was pitted against Democrat Samuel J. Tilden. The results were so close that an election commission was created to help determine a winner.

Ultimately, the election went to Hayes in return for his Party agreeing to the removal of federal troops from the south.[55] These troops had gone a long way in preventing blacks from being terrorized by members of the Democratic Party and its KKK arm. The compromise only served to open the floodgates of terror against blacks at the hands of the Democratic Party. Both Sam Hose and Mary Turner – whose gruesome deaths were described earlier in this chapter – quite possibly, suffered their horrendous fates as a result of this compromise.

Amazingly, there are people who vote Democrat today – many of them black – and are taught that the Compromise of 1877 is reason to demonize the Republican Party; many refer to that Compromise as 'The Great Betrayal.'[56] The argument from those on the left is that the Republican Party, which was responsible for the 13th, 14th, and 15th Amendments turned their backs on the black Americans they were instrumental in liberating.

Nation of Islam leader Louis Farrakhan spoke to a crowd about the Compromise of 1877 and said the following:

"There was a great compromise of 1877. It's called 'The Great Betrayal of the Negro.' In 1865, the 13th amendment legally abolished slavery but just 12 years later, in 1877, a decision was taken by the leaders of America that would have profound consequences for the Black man and woman long, long into the future. The Compromise of 1877 is arguably the most devastating single event in the history of Blacks in America..."[57]

Ironically, it is the "radical" Republicans or Tea Party of the 21st Century whom the Democratic left paint as racist that would agree with such an assertion. The Republican Party of 1877 gave in to an evil Democratic Party, in part, to avoid a second civil war. Democrats of the 21st Century who indignantly assign blame to the Republican Party for having done so don't identify the Party that actually ruled like the Nazis after that compromise; it is the Democratic Party that *should* be the real object of derision for people like Farrakhan.

Giving in to the compromise was wrong. Many of the arguments against it are akin to the conservative arguments of the early 21st Century; Republicans should not compromise with Democrats when the outcome is the result of a compromise of principle. Two prominent examples of Republican Senators who have historically done this are John McCain of Arizona and Lindsey Graham of South Carolina, both of whom have a disturbing history of compromising the principles of the Party they represent; it is reflected in their votes.

In the liberal mind, the Democratic Party can transform its ancestors into unidentified bogeymen if it means creating a straw man out of the Republican Party. Blaming others for what you are indeed guilty of is the worst form of denial; it prevents reconciliation with both the past and with those wronged.

In *Unfounded Loyalty*, Perryman drew very distinct parallels between what happened to blacks under Democratic rule and what happened to Jews under Nazi rule. In the aggregate, the sheer number of similarities between the treatment of both as conveyed by Perryman should cause every registered Democrat to re-examine the Party to which he or she belongs, especially in light of what Perryman would later discover about how the Party would react to his request for an apology; there will be more on that later in this chapter.

As for the historical similarities the Democrats share with the Nazis, the list is extensive.[58] Here are some of the examples:

- Jews and blacks were both denied rights as citizens through legislation
- Jews and blacks were not allowed to attend school with Germans and whites
- Jews and blacks were both forced to work in hard labor camps without compensation
- Jews and blacks had their citizenship taken away by Nazis and Democrats
- Jews and blacks were prohibited from marrying Germans and whites
- Jews and blacks had businesses and property confiscated by Nazis and Democrats
- Jews and blacks had their houses of worship destroyed by Nazis and Democrats
- Jews and blacks were forced to live in ghettos by Nazis and Democrats
- Jews and blacks were terrorized, tortured, and murdered at random by the SS and KKK
- Jews and blacks were prohibited from running for public office by Nazis and Democrats

Perryman rhetorically asks why any black American would join the Democratic Party when a Jew would never join the Nazi Party. He also noticed something that would be at the crux of his biggest battle; Germany apologized for the holocaust it was responsible for while the Democratic Party had not apologized for the holocaust *it* was responsible for. To even further underscore the point, it is today a crime in Germany to deny that the holocaust took place.[59] Additional irony is

provided by the fact that the Ku Klux Klan is a group that has historically denied the holocaust as well.[60] Yet, the Democratic Party consistently receives 90 percent of the black vote while distancing itself from the KKK, a group it formed to do its bidding.

Something is very wrong.

## KRISTALLNACHT AND THE EARLY 1900S

With what is known about how blacks were treated in the United States by the Democratic Party and its armed wing – the KKK – perhaps there is even more that can be gleaned from the origins of Nazi history. The tactics of Hitler's henchmen had so much in common with those employed by the Democratic Party in the United States against blacks – for decades prior to Hitler's rise to power – one is right to suspect the Nazi leader studied those tactics before employing them himself.

Translated into English, the term 'Kristallnacht' means *The Night of Broken Glass*. It was used to describe the actions of Nazi youths who went into Jewish towns in Germany on the nights of November 9th and 10th, 1938 and rioted; countless windows were shattered. It was sheer lawlessness on the part of the Nazis. They torched synagogues and destroyed businesses. Thousands of Jews were arrested and put into concentration camps **[See Chapter 4, p. 92-93]**. Hitler's men allowed the anti-Jewish riots to take place and labeled such acts as nothing more than random violence.[61]

Leading up to these nights of terror, the Nazis had been incrementally placing increased amounts of pressure on the Jewish community; Jewish shops were ordered to be boycotted; Jewish children were restricted in public schools; Jews were denied German citizenship and prohibited from participating in elections; economic opportunities were denied.[62] It all sounds so reminiscent of what the blacks went through in the United States. The Nazis, while applying that increased pressure, were just waiting for an opportunity to exploit for their advantage.

That opportunity came when a very bad decision was made by a relative of one of the families that was forced to move to Poland. That decision involved assassinating a German official at the German embassy in Paris. The Nazis allowed Kristallnacht to take place while blaming the Jews for a conspiracy that killed a German official. It gave them the excuse they needed to crack down even harder.

Approximately 20 years earlier – in Houston, Texas – a group of black soldiers had reached their breaking point with the Houston police after one of those soldiers had been arrested and beaten for no reason. There were deaths that resulted after fellow black soldiers heard the news and went into town looking to fight back in a way not all that dissimilar from how the family member of a victim of Kristallnacht reacted.

Courts-martial followed and nineteen black soldiers were sentenced to death. Sitting Democratic President Woodrow Wilson did not prevent those executions. The soldiers disobeyed orders not to go into Houston, clearly an ill-advised choice but in much the same way that continued oppression of Jews in Germany would cause one person to lash out, black soldiers in Houston had been pushed to a breaking point as well.[63]

Speaking of Woodrow Wilson, about thirty years before the 28th President of the United States took office, he became close friends with a man named Thomas Dixon at Johns Hopkins University.[64] Dixon was a staunch Democrat who authored a novel entitled *The Clansman*, which also became a stage play and later a movie that stoked hatred for and violence toward blacks.

## POWER OF PROPAGANDA

Thomas Dixon's stage play – *The Clansman* – opened in Atlanta, GA in 1904. The play glorified the KKK and portrayed blacks as savage animals who were always lying in wait to attack and rape white women. Perryman writes that after an Atlanta newspaper reported that white women had been raped, it was the blacks who were savagely beaten – by whites. In cases where blacks fought back, many were killed. Perhaps most egregiously, the newspaper's report was false.[65]

Ten years later, Dixon's novel was made into a movie entitled *The Birth of a Nation*. Like the stage play before it, the film helped to stoke hatred toward an entire race of people. Membership in the KKK grew as a result and whites who attended the movie openly attacked blacks after watching it.[66] The film was also the first to be shown inside the White House, which was occupied at the time by none other than Dixon's friend, Woodrow Wilson.[67]

After writing twenty-two novels, Dixon was rewarded in 1938 – by Democratic President Franklin D. Roosevelt (FDR), who appointed him clerk of the United States Court, Eastern District of North Carolina[68] in 1938 – the same year the Nazis blamed the Jews for what led to Kristallnacht.

It's also interesting to note that FDR, the 32nd President of the United States rewarded someone else who was a member of the KKK to a position of far greater power, in 1937. Hugo Black was appointed to the Supreme Court of the United States by FDR despite the former being a card-carrying member of the KKK. Prior to his nomination, Black was a trial attorney in Alabama and was backed by the Klan in a case involving the murder of a Catholic priest by a Methodist preacher named E.R. Stephenson, who was also a member of the Klan and a Democrat.

When Father James Coyle married the daughter of Stephenson and a Catholic Puerto Rican man, the elder Stephenson became enraged and shot Coyle dead.[69] The future Supreme Court Justice was also anti-Catholic – in addition to being a member of the KKK – and defended Coyle's murderer. Stephenson was ultimately acquitted on the grounds of self-defense and Black later lied about his own ties to the Klan in order to be confirmed as Supreme Court Justice.[70]

In much the same way that *The Clansman* wrongly appealed to some twisted form of honor by getting Democrats to believe they were actually protecting women by terrorizing blacks, Adolf Hitler appealed to a sense of patriotism in Germans who believed they were defending their country.

Almost one year after Kristallnacht, Hitler and his henchmen devised a scheme to draw Poland into war. That scheme involved extremely deceptive tactics and three SS units that donned Polish uniforms; each unit was to attack three separate targets, including a radio station, on the German side of its border with Poland. Former Hitler youth Hilmar Von Campe explained what happened in his book *Defeating the Totalitarian Lie*:

> ...a number of political inmates held in the nearby concentration camp Sachsenhausen were murdered and outfitted in Polish uniforms then distributed around the three targets as fallen enemy combatants. One German civilian, Franz Honiok, who had done nothing wrong, but lived in the area, spoke Polish and was known to be friendly with the Poles, was arrested by the Gestapo, killed and left lying at the doorsteps of the radio station. His death was carried out to make people believe that he was the person who had given a victory speech over the radio. The bodies of these murdered people disappeared once the press had registered, and reported on them.[71]

Von Campe then explained how Hitler was able to get German citizens to believe him:

> Hitler lied, murdered, and started a war. I was 14 years old at that time. We only heard the official story, the party line, since the only media outlets, newspapers, and radio were controlled entirely by the Nazis.[72]

Remember, Professor Trelease wrote that after ratification of the 15th Amendment, Democrats actually accused blacks and Republicans of killing each other so the Democrats could kill without blame. The facts were that it was the Democratic Party – with the help of its KKK arm – that was guilty of such acts. These tactics were no different than the ones Hitler himself used to start war.

## DEMOCRATS, GERMANY, AND TURKEY

After World War II, Germany apologized for what it had done as a nation to the Jews. There was a concerted effort on the part of that nation to reconcile with its very ugly past. As mentioned previously, it eventually became a crime to deny the holocaust in Germany.

There was also a holocaust that took place in what is today Turkey. The perpetrators were the Ottoman Turks and the victims included over 1 million Armenian Christians during World War I. Like Germany, the Ottoman Empire was defeated. Unlike Germany, Turkey did *not* apologize for *its* genocide. In fact, today, it is a crime in Turkey to describe the slaughter of so many Armenians *as* genocide; Turkey is in holocaust denial.[73]

A modern day example is that of Orhan Pamuk, an extremely well known novelist in Turkey. After writing about the Turkish holocaust, the backlash was reminiscent of what happened to blacks in America who dared to vote against Democrats. When he called attention to his country's past, Pamuk's books were burned, his photo was shredded, there were threats against his life, and he was forced to leave the country. He was even charged with insulting the Turkish state in the process.[74]

Like blacks in America for so many years, Armenians in Turkey lived as second class citizens (sound familiar?); they were not afforded the same rights as the Muslim Turks (sound familiar?); neither property nor life was protected by law (sound familiar?); they were denied participation in government (sound familiar?).[75]

When challenged about their genocidal history, Turks who refuse to admit the truth claim that the Armenians who died in WWI died at the hands of inter-ethnic strife.[76] This would have meant that the Armenians killed themselves; such a claim is eerily reminiscent of what Trelease said about the KKK blaming those it murdered – both blacks and Republicans – for killing each other.

Even in the decades after passage of civil rights legislation that many Democrats – including Al Gore, Sr. – voted against, Republicans are demonized as the racist descendants of those who tortured, terrorized, and lynched blacks. The Democratic Party has been hugely successful at getting blacks to believe that the Republican Party magically changed its core beliefs from protecting and defending blacks to persecuting them after it had shed so much blood *for* them. Equally amazing is the Democratic Party's ability to win the support of those it persecuted without ever having apologized *for* that persecution.

Once Civil Rights legislation became a reality the Democrats could not fight, they changed tactics by projecting what they were guilty of onto their opponents. Prominent racist Democrats from the 1960s included Alabama Governor George Wallace (D), Arkansas Governor Orville Faubus (D), and Alabama Public Safety Commissioner Bull Connor (D). Yet, despite all of this rich history of Democratic racism, 90 percent of blacks in America vote for the Party that perpetuates that racism while blaming its opponents; it's proof positive that projection – accusing your opponent of what you are guilty of – works, until the truth comes out.

Before WWII, the Democratic Party more closely aligned with the Nazi Party. After the war, Germany's attempts at reconciliation were substantial and the Democratic Party found itself more aligned with the Ottoman Turks in its denial of the truth.

## ■ MLK, LBJ, AND ROBERT BYRD

The path to what the Democratic Party perceived as political victory changed drastically once it became apparent that blacks in America had been granted civil rights. Prior to passage of civil rights legislation, Democrats found it much easier to overtly intimidate and terrorize blacks with the use of its militant arm – the KKK – to get the black vote. Such tactics would no longer work after the Civil Rights Act of 1964; it passed in the House with far more support from Republicans than Democrats.

In the Senate, Minority Leader Everett Dirksen (R-IL) decried the seemingly endless Democratic filibuster to prevent the Bill's passage and diligently re-worked the language. Two very prominent Democrats participated in that filibuster. One was Al Gore, Sr. (D-TN) whose son would go on to become Vice President under Democrat Bill Clinton and later the poster child for the extremely fraudulent Cap and Trade legislation based on man-made global warming propaganda; the legislation was designed to re-distribute the world's wealth under the guise of protecting the environment. The other was Robert Byrd (D-WV), who filibustered for 14 hours and would later be known – until his death in 2010 – as the "conscience of the Senate" by his Democratic colleagues.[77]

Byrd was an interesting study in that he was a microcosm of the shift within the Democratic Party from a Party of intimidation to one of exploitation. He was once not just a member of the KKK but the leader of his local chapter.[78] At Byrd's funeral, Bill Clinton eulogized the deceased Senator and excused his past affiliation with the KKK as "fleeting" and necessary to get elected so he could make up for it by helping people as a legislator.[79] It was a lie intended to excuse the evil past of a Democrat and by extension, the much broader evil that was the Democratic Party's past.

Bill Clinton's words carried the echo of holocaust denial. Yet, the Democratic Party continued to receive overwhelming support from black Americans.

On March 28, 1968 Martin Luther King, Jr. was leading a march on City Hall in Memphis, TN to show support for city sanitation workers. When the protest turned violent, many pointed to King as having been responsible.[80]

One of King's most ardent detractors was Senator Robert Byrd, who threw down the gauntlet one day later, on the Senate floor. In a fiery speech, Byrd's words were directed squarely and forcefully at Democrat President Lyndon Baines Johnson. In it, Byrd warned Johnson that MLK's planned marches on the US Capitol had to be stopped.

> "Yesterday, Mr. President, the Nation was given a preview of what may be in store for this city by the outrageous and despicable riot that Martin Luther King helped to bring about in Memphis, Tenn.
>
> If this self-seeking rabble-rouser is allowed to go through with his plans here, Washington may well be treated to the same kind of violence, destruction, looting, and bloodshed."

In making reference to the Memphis riot, Byrd said of King publicly to Johnson:

"Ostensibly, Martin Luther King went to Memphis to do the same sort of thing he has promised to do here – to 'help poor people.' He has billed his Washington march as a 'poor people's crusade.' In Memphis he went to lead striking garbage workers in a march to 'help' them, but today, in the aftermath of Thursday's stupid and tragic occurrence, the Negroes he purportedly wanted to help are far worse off than they would have been if he had never gone there, for many are in jail and many are injured – and most certainly race relations have been dealt a severe setback across the Nation, as they have been in Memphis."

Byrd finished his speech thusly:

"Apparently the hoodlums in Memphis yesterday followed King's advice to break laws with which they did not agree. This has been a cardinal principle of his philosophy – a philosophy that leads naturally to the escalation of nonviolence into civil disobedience – which is only a euphemism for lawbreaking and criminality and which escalates next into civil unrest, civil disorder, and insurrection."[81]

Senator Robert Byrd was warning President Johnson – in no uncertain terms – to stop Martin Luther King, Jr. from marching on Washington, D.C.

Two days later, Johnson – who had referred to King as "that ni**er preacher"[82] – would make his now famous speech to Americans in which he declared he would not "seek" nor "accept" another term as President.[83]

Four days later, King was assassinated.

Again, when Democratic Congresswoman from Arizona, Gabrielle Giffords was shot in the head at a town hall event on January 8, 2011 Democratic operatives did all they could to pin her shooting on the "rhetoric" from the right. As more information came out about the shooter [See Chapter 5, p. 151], that despicable strategy became less and less tenable.

In reality, when such a standard is applied to Robert Byrd in 1968, six days prior to the assassination of Martin Luther King, Jr., the Democratic Senator from West Virginia had the blood of a civil rights icon on his hands. The man convicted of King's murder was also a Democrat.[84]

Yet, only a few short months prior to the Giffords shooting, a former Democratic President praised Byrd and dismissed his association with the KKK; Clinton then used very twisted logic to argue that Byrd only joined the Klan to get elected. If Byrd did pledge allegiance to a violently racist group just so he could get elected, what would explain his incendiary speech – as an elected Senator – to Lyndon Johnson that called on the President to stop the "rabble-rouser" King?

In short, Clinton's eulogy of Robert Byrd epitomized a significant problem within the Democratic Party – revisionist history and holocaust denial.

## ■ PERRYMAN DOES BATTLE WITH DEMOCRATIC PARTY

Upon completing his book *Unfounded Loyalty*, Perryman decided to take action. After all, his research unearthed multiple skeletons that were previously buried in the Democratic Party's past. On November 7, 2004 he sent a letter to Democratic National Committee Chairman, Terry McAuliffe. The purpose of the letter was to seek an apology from the Democratic Party for its racist history.

Perryman included the graphic depictions of the deaths of Sam Hose and Mary Turner, described earlier in this chapter. After chronicling several historical instances in which the Democratic Party was responsible for the persecution of blacks, Perryman included the following in his letter to McAuliffe:

> Despite these factual truths, the Democratic Party has never issued or offered an apology to African Americans in its 212-year history.[85]

Members of the Republican Party who opposed slavery before it was abolished and adamantly supported its extinction after the 13th Amendment was ratified, were referred to by Democrats as "Radical

Republicans." Perryman highlighted this historical fact while making a larger, unassailable point:

> From 1792 to 1960, the "radicals" in the Democratic Party weren't spokespersons for African Americans (sic); they were the assassins that brought terror and death to African Americans.[86]

Perryman closed his letter to McAuliffe by pointing to the willingness of Christian publishers to set the record straight with respect to *The Curse of Ham*, discussed earlier in this chapter. It was a battle Perryman fought more than a decade earlier – and won. In that case, the apology he sought was granted.

Would Terry McAuliffe and the Democratic Party mirror those Christian publishers as well as the Germans after World War II, who repented of the holocaust their nation was responsible for? Would he issue an apology on behalf of his party or would he behave like the Turks when pressed to admit the truth about the Armenian genocide **[See Chapter 10, p. 336]**?

Choosing the first path would lead to healing and reconciliation. Choosing the second path would lead to further holocaust denial and potentially, more wickedness.

## THE RESPONSE

Terry McAuliffe became the outgoing DNC Chairman shortly after Perryman's letter. He was replaced by radical liberal Democrat Howard Dean; the baton had been passed. Either Dean would apologize for his party's past or he would choose another course.

Whether the decision not to respond to Perryman's letter was made by McAuliffe, Dean, political consultants, or was simply a consequence of the transition from one chairman to the other, made little difference. When Perryman filed suit in response to the non-response he received, the actions of the Democratic Party spoke volumes.

Led by Dean – for all intents and purposes at the time of Perryman's extensive brief – The Democratic Party responded to that brief, which was filed with the United States District Court in the Western District of Seattle, by hiring one of the most powerful law

firms in the country – Perkins Coie. Coie's flagship office was in Seattle and had an office in Washington, D.C.[87]

This response was significant because it showed that Dean and the Democrats were willing to go to extreme lengths in order to avoid meeting the very fair demands in the *Prayer for Injunctive Relief* requested in Perryman's brief; there were four requests:

- Defendants issue a formal apology
- Defendants fund educational projects correcting the record
- Defendants pay Plaintiff's legal expenses
- Defendants pay anything further deemed by the court[88]

In essence, any defense mounted by the Democratic Party involved refusing to issue an apology for its evil past; a refusal to endorse education that revealed that evil past; and a refusal to compensate those (Perryman) who had the gall to demand such things. Denial, the perpetuation of lies, and unaccountability continued to define the Democratic Party.

Attorney for Perkins Coie – David Burman – filed a *Motion to Dismiss* Perryman's case on the grounds that the plaintiff did not have standing. Perhaps most telling was Burman's willingness to concede – if only in a backhanded way – Perryman's premise when making his argument. Hidden in Burman's motion was a veiled denial:

Conceding the horrors of slavery and racism, and even accepting for the purpose of this motion that the Democratic Party in the past supported or acquiesced in those horrors, nowhere does the complaint make the required showing of any "concrete and personalized injury" necessary to confer standing...[89]

Notice that in his motion, Burman conceded to something Perryman did not assert. The Perkins Coie attorney inferred that part of the plaintiff's argument was that the Democratic Party either supported or submitted to entities not affiliated with it who then committed evil against blacks. Perryman's complaint was not that the Democratic Party stood idly by during a holocaust. On the contrary, the claimant asserted that the Democratic Party was the driving force in that holocaust.

Inherent in the *Motion to Dismiss* was a form of holocaust denial. The District Court ruled in favor of the Democratic National Committee and granted the motion, which cited the Supreme Court case *Lujan v Defenders of Wildlife*. In his appeal to the Ninth Circuit, Perryman would rip the comparisons between his case and *Lujan* to shreds.

## APPEAL TO THE NINTH CIRCUIT

To understand the differences between *Lujan* – which was defeated at the Supreme Court – and *Perryman* it's important to distinguish between the awards sought by each. In the case of Lujan, the plaintiff sought *monetary* damages based on speculation that injuries could theoretically result if an endangered species was made extinct. In Perryman's case, he argued for a mere *apology* based on actual injuries suffered.

Writing for the majority in *Lujan*, Supreme Court Justice Antonin Scalia even stipulated that in order for a party to have standing, it must establish that an injury has actually been suffered. In *Perryman*, the DNC conceded that the plaintiff had indeed suffered actual harm, saying that injuries were:

"...inflicted on all African Americans over two hundred years and affect the entire African American community."[90]

Perryman also argued that, unlike the plaintiff in another case cited by the DNC, he was not seeking monetary damages.

In making the distinction between his case and *Lujan* with respect to injuries incurred vs. injuries of a hypothetical nature, Perryman argued in his appeal:

In the *Lujan* case, there were no particularized, concrete, or injuries in fact, because there were no injuries. The entire case was based solely on the possibility that injuries may occur as a result of damage to endangered species. In *Lujan*, the court was simply saying plaintiffs cannot bring a matter to court on the possibility of an injury sometime in the future.[91]

The Democratic Party had to walk a very thin line. Perhaps that is why it hired such a powerful law firm. If it denied that Perryman had been injured, it risked being perceived as dismissive of an individual who represented a voting bloc it so desperately needed. If it accepted Perryman's premise, it had to accept responsibility for having terrorized the ancestors of that voting bloc.

The case cited by the defendant was highly suspect because the issue at the heart of *Lujan* (future injury) did not apply in *Perryman* (past injury).

As part of Perryman's Reply Brief, he suggested that the Nazi Party in Germany was likely inspired by the Democratic Party for the two hundred years prior to the rise of Hitler to prominence. The brief then chronicled the similarities between the two parties outlined earlier in this chapter.

Perryman was asking for little more than an apology similar to that issued willingly by Germany after World War II. Yet, his appeal was dismissed. The Ninth Circuit seemed more than willing to protect the Democratic Party from having to apologize for atrocities it was responsible for; the Defendant was willing to spare no expense to avoid having to issue that apology.

Said Perryman in the conclusion of his appellant brief:

> The Defendants have argued that the Appellant's injuries are the same as the injuries inflicted on African Americans over a two-hundred-year period. But what they failed to report is that they were the ones who inflicted these injuries.[92]

The degree to which the Democratic Party fought Perryman spoke volumes and is very telling with respect to its stance. Had it voluntarily apologized before being sued, it could have pointed to an actual point in time when it reconciled with its ugly past. Instead, it refused while fighting tooth and nail to deny its involvement *in* that past.

Perryman's appeal was unfortunately – and unsurprisingly – denied by the very liberal (Democrat) Ninth Circuit.

Paradoxically, the more the Democratic Party dug in its heels to defend itself, the more it implicated itself in holocaust denial – with the help of the American Judicial system.

## APPEAL TO THE UNITED STATES SUPREME COURT

The odds of the Supreme Court taking Perryman's case were indeed long but that didn't stop him from submitting a thirty-two page *Petition for a Writ of Certiorari*.

Perhaps it was those long odds that helped inspire Perryman to throw, what in football is called a 'Hail Mary' pass by identifying the Supreme Court itself as having been complicit in the persecution of blacks.

The plaintiff stated in his introduction:

> It was the United States Supreme Court's decisions in key civil rights cases that gave the Respondent (the Democratic Party) the legal authority to inflict the alleged injuries on those whom the District Court referred to as the "entire African American community."[93]

During the period in question, the Supreme Court had consistently ruled in favor of the racist policies and laws implemented by the Democratic Party. The court's rulings reinforced Jim Crow laws and in *Scott v Sanford* (the Dred Scott decision), the Supreme Court ruled that blacks were to be regarded as property, not people. Five of the nine Justices who decided Dred Scott were from families that owned slaves and seven of the Justices had been appointed by pro-slavery presidents (Democrats).[94] Less than one hundred years later, Democrat President Franklin D. Roosevelt appointed KKK member and Democrat Hugo Black to the Supreme Court.

The decision by Perryman to single out the Supreme Court's complicity in an ugly past was intended to put the current Justices face to face with a hard reality that involved the body each represented. In naming the Court specifically, Perryman put its Justices on the spot. If they rejected his plea for relief, they would be put in the same box as the Defendant – the Democratic Party – which was unwilling to admit

to its own despicable history. If the court ruled in favor of Perryman, it too could come clean with its past.

Said Perryman in his supplemental brief to the Supreme Court:

Two hundred years ago the Respondents found ways to use this very court and the law to enslave us, beat us, terrorize us, and murder us, and now they are using this same court and the law to keep from apologizing to us.[95]

John Childers – a black man – was interviewed by the Senate Select Committee in 1871 about being intimidated by Democrats. One answer given by Childers perfectly illustrates how the Democratic Party of intimidation and threats morphed into the Party of welfare entitlements.

Coincidentally, Perryman included that answer in his *Writ of Certiorari*:

"I have had threats that if we all would vote the Democratic ticket we would be well thought of, and the white men of the county – the old citizens of the county – would protect us; and every struggle or trouble we got into we could apply to them for protection, and they would assist us."[96]

The Democratic Party used to secure the black vote with negative reinforcement – by withholding punishment. It does the same today with *positive* reinforcement – through welfare programs and empty promises. Blacks who voted Republican then, were killed; today, blacks who vote Republican are smeared as "Uncle Toms" and "sell-outs" who long for the days of slavery. In both cases, the "Party of White Supremacy" (Democratic Party) was and is more concerned with the black vote than it is – ironically – with the *welfare* of blacks *who* vote. In a kind of *soft* slavery, many black Americans who vote Democrat don't even know they're being exploited in such a way.

In his supplemental brief, Perryman argued that because the Supreme Court denied blacks their Constitutional rights in the past while pointing to the rule of law as justification, it should overturn the lower courts' rulings, which used the rule of law as justification to avoid reconciliation.[97]

The Supreme Court declined to hear Perryman's case and, in so doing, unwittingly implicated itself in the perpetuation of holocaust denial. While the argument can be made that the Supreme Court has to sift through a much greater volume of cases than do the lower courts, it is nonetheless on record as having chosen to sweep not only the Democratic Party's ugly history under the rug, but its own as well.

## PERRYMAN CONFRONTS SUPREME COURT

Truth is a mighty sword and to the unbeknownst chagrin of every Justice who denied or dismissed *Perryman*, he or she is now on record as having stood by while the history of the country's most racist political party was given a pass. There is little to no difference between these judges and the ones who presided over the Nuremburg trials when it comes to the charges each had the opportunity to deliberate over. There *is* a dramatic difference between the two groups of judges when it comes to the decisions rendered. Make no mistake; the decision not to hear a case is a decision rendered.

After the Supreme Court decided not to hear *Perryman*, the plaintiff wrote a letter to Chief Justice John Roberts, who presided over a very balanced court at the time, with Justice Anthony Kennedy often providing the swing vote.

The purpose of Perryman's letter was to garner an apology from the Supreme Court relative to its very racist decisions in the past. In the letter, Perryman assured Roberts that all he wanted was the court to acknowledge that it has rendered decisions it is not proud of.

Perryman argued that past racist decisions rendered by the Supreme Court were not based on right or wrong but on the personal prejudices and party affiliations of the Supreme Court's justices.[98]

When Perryman did not receive a response from Roberts, he sent a letter to each member of the Supreme Court. In it, he said:

> Is there any compassion on the bench? Or has the court become like many of those whom they have convicted – cold individuals that offer no remorse for the harm that they caused others.?[99]

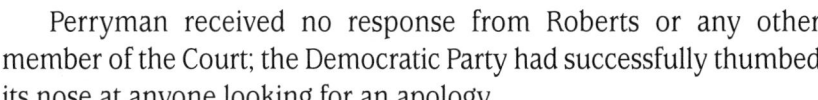 

Perryman received no response from Roberts or any other member of the Court; the Democratic Party had successfully thumbed its nose at anyone looking for an apology.

## ■ BATTLE ASSESSMENT

At first blush, it may appear that Wayne Perryman fought valiantly in defeat. If viewed in the context of not getting the apology he sought, such an argument is conceded. When the apology he didn't receive is viewed in a much broader context, one that includes history not yet written, it's certain to be a far different story.

Perryman's efforts did not lead to an explosive public revelation but his work is so bitingly relevant that it is almost certain to become a time bomb for future researchers. Such people will one day find much less resistance from future descendants of the Democratic Party. When they do, those researchers – and future plaintiffs – will be armed with not only Perryman's massive compilation of evidence that now includes shameful court decisions, but with the names of Democratic Party officials (Terry McAuliffe and Howard Dean) as well as District, Appellate, and Supreme Court Justices who participated – to varying degrees – in holocaust denial.

In much the same way that Perryman was able to unearth that which the Democratic Party attempted to keep buried, the truth will come out one day; it will show that instead of coming clean and confessing past sins, the Democratic Party hadn't confessed because it wasn't contrite.

In the United States, there is a disturbing dynamic at work. Justice is repeatedly denied to defendants and plaintiffs when the opposing side belongs to an elite political class or federal entity with the power to influence the outcome, even while holding the 'smoking gun.' Perryman's story illustrates this dynamic perfectly; so does the story of Peter Paul, J.D. Cash, and Lt. Col. Anthony Shaffer **[See Chapters 1, 8, and 9]**.

The Democratic Party is one such entity. It is one of the two political pillars in a two-party system. The power it has amassed over the years is beyond formidable. It's a living, breathing organic beast and it will defend itself at all costs. Perryman was a threat to it and was in many ways destined to be defeated in the short run. In the long run, he's destined to be victorious. His short term victory detailed earlier in this chapter serves as no better example of foreshadowing.

When Perryman was able to get publications to rescind what they had put forth as a legitimate interpretation of Scripture relative to the 'Curse of Ham' he did so after a false narrative had been pushed as fact for hundreds of years. Research helped him to determine the origins of such falsehoods. Enough time had passed that those responsible for pushing such a narrative were not so emotionally or ideologically tied to it that they would martyr themselves to prevent a correction of the record. In fact, the opposite happened.

The truth came out along with the racist past of those who viewed the plight of blacks as being Biblically justified. There were two groups of people: those who believed that such an interpretation was correct or warranted and those who passionately rejected its premise. The same applies to the plight of blacks under the Democratic Party: those who ignore and excuse its past and those who think it should come clean.

Practically every account of the Democratic Party chronicled by Perryman involved people who are no longer living; each contributed to his case. His work may likely one day do the same and all who ignored, dismissed, or marginalized him are now on record in much the same way that racist Democrats of the 18th, 19th, and 20th centuries are. Ditto for those who defended the 'Curse of Ham' that Perryman officially debunked.

In setting the record straight with the 'Curse of Ham,' Perryman was the last man to chop at the very old tree that fell very hard. That doesn't mean he chopped it all himself. When it comes to the future of the Democratic Party, the inverse may very well be true. He will not have delivered the final blow but he will have given it the hardest whacks.

As the saying goes, "The bigger they are, the harder they fall." That saying applies to the growing legacy of the racist Democratic Party, which is being chopped down as it tries to grow to the sky. Make no mistake; Perryman will have been one of the many who swung the axe that chopped at the Democratic Party until it was felled.

# CHAPTER 7

## O'NEAL DOZIER
### vs.
# REPUBLICAN PARTY

### ■ THE CONNECTED PASTOR

As I walked into the office of Rev. O'Neal Dozier more than one hour before his Sunday service at the Worldwide Christian Center was about to start, I took notice of the number of 8 x 12 photos that adorned his walls. Each frame held a picture of Dozier standing next to a very prominent and powerful person in American politics: President George W. Bush, Florida Governor Jeb Bush, Florida Governor Charlie Crist, Secretary of State Condoleezza Rice, Supreme Court Justice Clarence Thomas, Oklahoma Congressman J.C. Watts, and many others.

I had come to know Dozier several years earlier but had never met him in person. Through coincidence and timing, I had the opportunity to do so. Another person profiled in this book, Walid Shoebat, was scheduled to speak at Dozier's church that day [See Chapter 10, p. 339].

Just prior to entering Dozier's office, my father – who accompanied me as a curious observer – and I were standing outside when we noticed the words on the marquee in front of the church. Never one to back down from the politically incorrect or socially inflammatory, Dozier's very public announcement did not disappoint. In capital letters, his signage boldly stated:

SPEC GUEST SPKR EX-MUSLIM EX-PLO MEMBER
WALID SHOEBAT SUN MAR 13TH AT 11AM & 5PM[1]

Shortly after we noticed the marquee, a police cruiser from the Broward County Sheriff's Office pulled up next to us as we stood waiting in the parking lot. After lowering my head into the passenger side window, the female officer said she was assigned to this location and was looking for a place to park. She then expressed concern over the marquee while seeming both familiar *with* and confused *by* Dozier's willingness to be such a lightning rod for controversy. She even rhetorically asked why the letters on the marquee couldn't have been smaller.

Sometime after the officer parked across the street, Shoebat arrived and as the three of us stood outside waiting to be let in, a very nice Jewish man approached us and introduced himself. He had come specifically to see Shoebat speak and expressed great appreciation for what the former terrorist was doing for Israel.

We were soon ushered into Dozier's office; the pastor arrived shortly thereafter.

Shoebat, who is very used to having to ask pastors what rhetorical territory is off-limits before speaking from the pulpit, was pleasantly surprised when told by Dozier to say "whatever the Holy Spirit moves you to say."[2]

Just prior to Dozier's introduction of Shoebat, it was brought to the former's attention that a leader with the Council on American Islamic Relations (CAIR) was in attendance. Dozier could have asked Nezar Hamze – the Executive Director of CAIR's South Florida chapter at the time – to leave based on views the pastor had expressed years earlier about Islam but he was noticeably more concerned with leading his congregation. Hamze's presence, coupled with Shoebat's message, was ostensibly the kind of mixture that precipitated a police presence in the first place. Instead, Dozier welcomed the CAIR leader with the hopes – no matter how faint – that a conversion might take place.

In the 1800s, Republicans who wanted to abolish slavery were known as 'radical' Republicans. **[See Chapter 6, p. 171]** Today, Dozier is considered by the Democratic left as being radical because he opposes abortion and homosexual marriage; he supports the second amendment as well as capital punishment; he is against affirmative action and advocates for prayer in schools; he is against illegal immigration and rejects political correctness in virtually every circumstance but especially when talking about the dangers posed to western civilization by Islamic fundamentalism.

He's also a black American.

Dozier was born in South Carolina in 1948, the son of sharecroppers; he attended high school during the racially tumultuous 1960s; he served two years in the Army and is a Vietnam veteran; after graduating from Bethune Cookman, Dozier had short stints in the NFL with the Chicago Bears and New York Jets; he then went on to get his law degree from John Marshall Law School in Atlanta, GA. He later founded the Worldwide Christian Center just a short drive north of Fort Lauderdale, FL – in Pompano Beach – in 1985.

As a Pastor whose message very much resonated with the religious right, it made good political sense for Republican Party candidates to align themselves with Dozier. After all, here was a black conservative whose help moderate Republicans could use to ingratiate themselves with social conservatives as well as with blacks. An alliance with Dozier would also help blunt charges of racism. Politically, aligning with Dozier was a no-brainer. It was good for business – and votes.

Dozier was also a minority within a minority. While 90 percent of the black community traditionally voted Democrat, in him the Republican Party had a charismatic pastor who publicly and unapologetically championed practically every plank in the Republican Party platform. Just outside the liberal bastion of Fort Lauderdale lived a social, fiscal, and Christian conservative who also happened to be black.

## ■ APPOINTED BY GOVERNOR JEB BUSH

In 2001, Dozier was appointed to the 17th Judicial Circuit, Judicial Nominating Commission in Broward County, Florida by Republican Governor Jeb Bush. Though Dozier never practiced law, his degree gave him the credentials necessary to sit on the Commission. He would interview and screen judicial nominees, an opportunity he termed a "blessing." His church website explains how Dozier viewed the appointment:

"...an opportunity to honor God and to promote right-eousness and godliness through the selection of 'God-fearing candidates' and 'good judges regardless of color.'"[3]

Far too often, well-intentioned men sacrifice their principles at the altar of political cowardice (some call it political correctness) once they are appointed or elected. Dozier spoke boldly before he was appointed to this political position. It remained to be seen whether he would maintain his forthrightness and honesty or rationalize any reticence to display it in the name of some abstract, nebulous greater good.

Dozier's initial term was only for two years. Upon completion of that term, he was re-appointed to an additional four-year term in 2003 by Governor Bush.[4] It didn't take long for the Florida pastor to find himself at the center of controversy.

The *Daily Business Review* reported on some interview questions posed to nominees by Dozier and another member of the committee. Dozier admitted to asking candidates if they were "God-fearing."[5] This line of questioning raised objections from a Fort Lauderdale lawyer. Bush was under pressure from anti-religious groups to remove Dozier from the committee. Dozier eventually agreed to refrain from that line of questioning but not before making his sentiment known:

"Why is everyone so against God? Are people who oppose the question saying people should have no respect for God?"[6]

Attorneys who objected to Dozier's comments pointed to Article VI of the United States Constitution, which states in part:

"...no religious test shall ever be required as a qualification to any office or public trust under the United States."[7]

The founding fathers of the United States fled religious persecution as well as a government that mandated a state-run, protestant religion. Dozier was being an advocate for neither persecution nor a state-run religion with his question. In fact, one could argue that he was simply trying to get nominees to outwardly agree with the verbiage already emblazoned on American currency: "In God we Trust." The mandate of King George III, that every subject be a member of the Protestant denomination is far different from asking a man if he is "God-fearing."

The acquiescence borne of fear that is inherent in political correctness – which is nothing more than a politically correct way of saying 'cowardice' – is also a religion, one not of God but of His adversary. It is a religion that portrays itself as a defender of religious freedom while exploiting the worst in human nature. All the while, it champions its own righteousness, which is the epitome of a very prideful and dangerous religion – one that is, ironically, devoid of reverence for God.

Dozier didn't stop there. During the interview in which he explained his line of questioning, he was asked about his public denunciations of homosexual behavior. He said in response:

> "If someone has a problem with calling it nasty and disgusting, they don't have a problem with me, it's with God. Those are His words."[8]

To underscore his point, Dozier cites a very short verse in the Christian Bible. Leviticus 18:22, which states:

> You shall not lie with a male as with a woman. It is an abomination.[9]

The Florida pastor defended his line of questioning by saying he wanted to be sure that any nominee with a bias in favor of homosexuality would not allow such a bias to "push the homosexual agenda."[10]

The returns were coming in. By all accounts, Dozier was incorruptible. His principles were taking precedent over any desire for political influence. It was refreshing and though Jeb Bush did not give in to the demands that Dozier be relieved at that time, the Governor's office did consult with the pastor over his comments.[11]

## ■ CHARLIE CRIST CAMPAIGN

Florida Attorney General Charlie Crist, a Republican, launched his gubernatorial campaign in 2006; Jeb Bush was ineligible for a third term. Initially, the Attorney General welcomed the support of Dozier as both a member of the campaign and its advisory council. At a breakfast in May of that year, in response to a revelation that the Florida pastor told Crist two years earlier he'd had a dream that Crist would be the next governor, Crist said the following:

> "...the reverend has a very strong faith in his heart and he's a good man. I'm very grateful for his help and his support and his belief."[12]

Governor Bush's comments were sought and though he didn't respond directly, he said the following about Dozier:

> "Far be it from me to judge about people's faiths and what occurs because of it. He is very sincere. Rev. Dozier's a good man."[13]

It is worth noting that in addition to Dozier being right about Crist's gubernatorial victory, both Bush and Crist were willing to accept Dozier's claim of divination as long as it was either advantageous or harmless, politically. If such a claim had been perceived as ridiculous on its face, would either man have so ingratiatingly accepted the endorsement?

## ■ DOZIER BECOMES A REPUBLICAN PARTY PARIAH

Rev. Dozier fell out of favor with the Republican Party as a direct result of comments he made about Islam on the *Steve Kane* radio show in July of 2006.[14] The reason for Dozier's appearance on the show was to talk about the attempts of the Islamic Center of South Florida (ICOSF) to build a mosque near his church. As recently as 2009, ICOSF was listed as being owned by the North American Islamic Trust (NAIT), which was identified in a 1991 Muslim Brotherhood document as being a member group.[15] Screenshots posted on the *Americans Against Hate* website proved that NAIT owned the ICOSF, which validated Dozier's concerns **(Appendix A)**.[16] NAIT, along with CAIR and ISNA, was named as an unindicted co-conspirator in the Holy Land Foundation trial, the largest terrorism financing trial in American history.[17]

When discussing his views about Islam on the air, Dozier waded into politically hot water, calling it a "dangerous" and "evil cult."[18]

During the interview, a left wing reporter from the *Broward New Times* named Bob Norman had the opportunity to ask Dozier a few questions as well. Norman reported shortly afterward that he asked Dozier if the Bush brothers – President George and Governor Jeb – supported his stance on Islam. In response, Dozier said, "I haven't talked with them about this, so I don't know."[19]

According to Dozier, Norman then pledged to find out how George and Jeb felt about the views expressed during that radio interview. This was a polite way for Norman to say he was going to make life difficult for Dozier, who very soon thereafter received a phone call from Governor Bush's office.

Said Dozier:

> "It was his (Jeb Bush's) senior adviser on the phone. She asked me if I said that on the air and I said, 'Yes, I did.' She said, 'Well now that you have said that, you can no longer be on the Judicial Nominating Commission.' She said, 'Jeb Bush wants you off of the Judicial Nominating Commission right now.'"[20]

Initially, Dozier rejected the adviser's insistence on his resignation but ultimately relented under consistent pressure from the Governor's office.

The Governor wasn't the only Bush to suddenly reject Dozier. Jeb's older brother occupied the White House at the time. Dozier explains how his access to George W. Bush was cut off as a result of his comments:

> "I continued to be invited to the White House, but my level of closeness to President George Bush suffered. I once sat in rooms of twelve to fifteen people, engaged in intimate conversations with the President. After my stand against the building of the mosque I found myself in far more formal gatherings of a hundred or more."[21]

In July of 2006 – when Dozier made his politically incorrect comments – it must have made politically correct sense for both George and Jeb to ostracize him. Crist, on the other hand, had a conservative base to woo. A significant contingent of that base liked Dozier. Crist, who didn't secure the Republican nomination[22] until September 5th, officially jettisoned Dozier just a couple of weeks later.

On September 23rd, Crist's campaign released a statement explaining why Dozier was removed from its advisory panel:

"Charlie Crist believes that we must not confuse those who practice any religion with a prayer toward peace with extremists who pervert religion to further a radical cause."[23]

Contributing to the Crist campaign's uneasiness was Dozier's distribution of cartoon pamphlets in the area, which denounced Islam. Lost on Crist was the fact that the reason he had to deal with the politics of a black pastor in South Florida had everything to do with the chord that pastor was striking with the voters whose support Crist very much wanted.

At the time of his dismissal from the Crist campaign, Dozier said:

"I am really hurt about it. There's no place for those who want to do the work of God in politics. Politicians want you to support them, but they are not going to support you."[24]

In a very short time, Dozier lost his access to President George W. Bush, was forced to resign by Governor Jeb Bush, and was cast aside by then future Governor, Charlie Crist, once he was no longer useful. The political risk of being perceived as an ally to Dozier was apparently too great for two Republican administrations and one Republican gubernatorial campaign.

Conversely, Dozier's decision to align with the Republican Party in the first place was not risk-free. In so doing, he faced the very real prospect of fewer congregants and a bad public image among the vast majority of black Floridians who despised the Republican Party. Dozier took significant political risk with the Republican Party. When faced with the opportunity to reciprocate, Republican leaders turned their backs on him.

## FIGHTING THE MOSQUE

The impetus for Dozier's much publicized comments about Islam and the subsequent political fallout was a proposed mosque that was to be built near his church. The mosque was to be a gargantuan 29,000 square ft in size; it would significantly dwarf Dozier's church, which was slightly more than 10,000 square ft. One of Dozier's concerns was what he saw as an attempt by Islamic leaders to recruit vulnerable minorities. He made it a personal mission to prevent construction of the mosque as early as 2006.

During an interview with Shalom TV, Dozier explained why he was so adamantly opposed to the mosque's construction:

"This neighborhood is a predominantly black neighborhood. There aren't any Muslims living in this neighborhood. Now the only reason they want to build a mosque here, of that size, is to recruit young blacks, young Hispanics, who are vulnerable to the Islamic cult, into their mosque."[25]

Ironically, Dozier also argued that he was a victim of Affirmative Action relative to the proposed mosque. According to him, the City of Pompano Beach had previously issued a mandate that said no more houses of worship would be built in the community. The property in question was to be developed by a local contractor, who had agreed to build affordable housing after entering into an agreement with the city. That deal fell through and the contractor returned the land to the city. According to Dozier, the ICOSF applied for and received a special exception to build the mosque on property that was not available for religious houses of worship.[26]

Perhaps even more important than religious discrimination relative to Pompano Beach's zoning inconsistencies were the ties ICOSF had to terrorist groups. This was an objection Dozier had raised repeatedly but was smeared as a bigoted pastor. Instead of coming to his side, Republican leaders saw him as radioactive. Conversely, all three Republican leaders mentioned previously, exhibited coziness with groups that have proven connections with Islamic terrorists.

Shortly after Dozier found himself at the center of controversy over Islam and the proposed mosque, an article at *Front Page Magazine* revealed some very telling and indisputable facts about the ICOSF Imam, Hassan Sabri, whose website once linked to one of the unindicted co-conspirators in the HLF trial – the Islamic Society of North America (ISNA). Remember, earlier in this chapter, it was revealed that ICOSF was owned by another co-conspirator – NAIT.

In 2002, Sabri participated in an event that featured multiple Islamic extremists, including Sami Al-Arian, who was convicted of financing terrorist activities in his role as leader of the Palestinian Islamic Jihad (PIJ). Also present at the event was Ahmed Bedier, who would later become a spokesman for the Council on American Islamic Relations (CAIR), still another co-conspirator in the HLF trial. The Florida Executive Director of CAIR at the time – Altaf Ali – was also in attendance with Sabri.[27]

Again, it cannot be overstated that CAIR and fellow unindicted co-conspirators in the HLF trial like ISNA, all have connections to the Muslim Brotherhood, as does the Islamic group al-Qaeda, which attacked America on September 11, 2001.[28] Any attempts to dismiss Dozier's assertions as paranoia would prove grossly unfounded.

In short, Dozier's concerns then have been validated with each passing day until now and beyond. In fact, events since 2006 indicate that one of the following two scenarios must be true. Either Dozier knew more than the Republican leaders who were responsible for knowing more than he did or he was more politically courageous than they were.

The assumption that Dozier had less to lose than George W. Bush, Jeb Bush, or Crist by taking the stance he did is offset by those Republican leaders having more to gain – the defense of America as an example – by taking the same stance. Additionally, an argument could be made that the nation itself had more to lose in the long run than Dozier did in the short run, if those leaders didn't side with him.

## BUSH BROTHERS AND CRIST CHOOSE SIDES

Dozier became radioactive to the Republican Party in 2006 – if the reactions of some of its prominent members are any indication – for his comments about Islam. The forces behind the proposed construction of a mosque in his church's neighborhood should have garnered critical attention from President George W. Bush and Governor Jeb Bush. Instead, Dozier was ostracized as a bigoted villain while the forces behind the mosque not only escaped political fallout but continued to enjoy a righteous portrayal courtesy of Republican leaders who facilitated the demonization of a Christian pastor.

In the days after the September 11th attacks, President George W. Bush appeared at a Washington, D.C. mosque with the Executive Director of CAIR – Nihad Awad – at his side **[See Chapter 10, p. 302]**. Seven years prior to that, Awad said he was a supporter of the "Hamas movement."[29]

Still, President Bush said the following less than one week after 9/11 from inside the mosque:

"...let me quote from the Qur'an itself: 'In the long run, evil in the extreme will be the end of those who do evil, for that they rejected the signs of Allah and held them up to ridicule.'

"The face of terror is not the true faith of Islam. That's not what Islam is all about. Islam is peace. These terrorists don't represent peace, they represent evil and war."[30]

Bush spoke those words while standing shoulder to shoulder with a man – Awad – who openly supported the aspirations of a group that shared one of Hitler's primary objectives – extermination of the Jews. Less than five years later, O'Neal Dozier would call Islam a "dangerous and evil cult" while pointing to a group that wanted to build a mosque near his church. That group, whose mosque was owned by NAIT, had very close ties to CAIR, which portrays itself as the best Islam has to offer while having extensive ties to both the Muslim Brotherhood and Hamas – the group Awad expressed support for in 1994. Why were Awad's words and views not enough to make *him* a pariah?

In August of 2006, about a month after Dozier made the comments that forced him out of the Judicial Nominating Commission, it was learned that British intelligence agents prevented an Islamic terrorist attack involving airlines that traversed the Atlantic. In response, President Bush said that in this instance, America was not in a "war with terrorism," but that it was "at war with Islamic fascists."[31]

CAIR responded almost immediately to what it perceived as incendiary rhetoric from the President. Dozier points out in his book that CAIR took such umbrage at Bush's words that the group sent the President a letter that said, in part:

> "Unfortunately, your statement this morning that America is at war with 'Islamic fascists' contributes to a rising level of hostility to Islam and the American-Muslim community."[32]

Never again did George W. Bush utter such words in public. Unlike Dozier, political intimidation trumped courageous honesty. Yes, it's true that the stakes of being president are much higher than those that come with being on the Judicial Nominating Commission in Broward County but as Scripture says in Luke 12:48:

> For everyone to whom much is given, from him much will be required; and to whom much has been committed, of him they will ask the more.[33]

When Dozier stood by his own words, he traded away political influence for honesty. When George W. Bush refused to stand behind *his* own words, the President ceded a degree of political influence by not being honest.

The fact remains that George W. Bush chose CAIR over a Christian pastor who rightfully chose – at significant political expense – to warn America about the group. The President of the United States himself also turned his back on Dozier and kowtowed to a group with known ties to terrorist organizations.

Accepting a premise that Bush was unaware of CAIR's background requires an assumption that a South Florida pastor knew more about the group than did the President of the United States. It is simply not believable. Dozier was thrown to the wolves, CAIR remained in good standing while donning sheep's clothing, and the shepherd looked the other way.

In 2005, Governor Jeb Bush had some peculiarly kind words for CAIR in the form of a letter that was sent to the group just prior to its annual banquet in Orlando. At the fundraiser, attendees were reportedly encouraged to contribute to the creation of a CAIR office in Orlando. Though Governor Bush did not attend, his letter to the group said in part:

> "It is a great pleasure to extend greetings and best wishes to all attending the Florida Chapter of the Council on American-Islamic Relations (CAIR-FL) annual banquet...I commend your contributions to the protection of civil rights and freedom of religion...Once again, congratulations on your accomplishments and my warmest greetings and best wishes on your continuing success."[34]

In addition to the letter from Governor Bush, CAIR also received letters from other prominent politicians. One of them was none other than Florida Attorney General at the time, Charlie Crist, whose letter expressed similar sentiment. After politely declining the invitation due to "previous commitments," Crist extended his "best wishes for a wonderful event."[35]

As early as 2004, more than a year prior to this banquet, Islamic expert Daniel Pipes said the following about CAIR:

> "...despite its terrorist associations and legal tribulations, the Council on American Islamic Relations (CAIR) is gaining acceptance among the gullible, the ignorant, or the foolish as a legitimate 'civil liberties group.'"[36]

Perhaps no one demonstrated this phenomenon more than Governor Charlie Crist himself. A simple contrast between how he treated Dozier on one hand and the treatment he gave to a man named Muhammad Musri on the other, illustrates the larger problem perfectly. Crist's campaign jettisoned Dozier before the election in 2006 but Crist embraced Musri all the way to the end of his own administration in 2010.

As the Imam of an Islamic group known as the Islamic Society of Central Florida (ISOCF), Musri headed a group with connections to CAIR; both groups belonged to the Fiqh Council of North America. Some of the groups listed as members of Fiqh in 2005 were entities that later became unindicted co-conspirators in the Holy Land Foundation trial. Listed as member organizations were the Islamic Society of North America (ISNA), the Muslim Students Association (MSA), the Muslim Public Affairs Council (MPAC), and the Muslim American Society (MAS).[37]

As for Musri, he held significant positions with the Crist administration while Dozier remained radioactive.

In an article by Patrick Poole that appeared on the *Big Peace* website in 2010, it was revealed that Musri served on Crist's Faith-Based and Community Advisory Council; Musri was also appointed by Crist to the governor's 2010 Sunshine Census Committee. That's not the worst part. Thanks to an undercover video posted by Poole, it was revealed that Musri held a fundraiser for Hamas inside his mosque in 2009. Individuals who spoke at that fundraiser included British Parliamentarian and terrorist sympathizer, George Galloway, who is on record as being an admirer of Fidel Castro, Saddam Hussein, Hugo Chavez, Mao Zedong, and Joseph Stalin.[38] Mahdi Bray of the Muslim American Society (MAS) also spoke and helped raise funds for Hamas.[39]

Conspicuously absent in the wake of this revelation was the very public declaration from Crist that he would no longer support Musri. Again, the contrast between how Crist reacted to news he appointed an anti-Semitic individual to positions of influence in his administration compared with how he treated a man who attempted to warn the public about such people years earlier, was very stark. The denunciation and silence displayed by the governor in both instances respectively, was grossly misplaced.

This bizarre contradiction was perhaps best explained by Dozier himself during an interview with *Shalom TV*; the Florida pastor said the following in 2011:

"The agenda is to advance itself (Islam) throughout the world – and the rest of the world, they simply back up because they want to be politically correct. That is their greatest weapon against us. As long as we remain politically correct and refuse to call Islam what it is, Islam will continue to grow in this country and throughout the world. What's going to stop its growth is for people like my good friend George W. Bush, Dick Cheney, and the rest of them – Barack Obama – and all of them were to stop getting on television and telling people what a beautiful religion Islam is...Everyone wants to belong to a good, beautiful, peaceful religion. It (Islam) is not that. They're saying these things for political reasons...Our politicians are selling out our country and selling out Israel simply because they want to win in office."[40]

What is political correctness? Everyone knows it when they see it but what is at its essence? Is it something that has been renamed because the truth about what it really is strikes at the core of how all men fear being viewed? Is political correctness a term that is synonymous with cowardice or the path of least resistance?

In a short *YouTube* video by Bill Whittle where America is identified as a 'Turncoat Nation,' he explains how the term 'turncoat' came to be. Soldiers would turn their coats inside out in order to avoid being identified by what they perceived to be a superior enemy. Such men were not necessarily ideologically opposed to the side whose uniform they wore. Instead, they decided that their best chance of survival involved switching sides in a very literal sense.[41]

In the 1992 film *Scent of a Woman*, Al Pacino played the role of a retired Marine who had been blinded in combat. He was a jaded, embittered man who had made a lot of mistakes in his life. During the climactic scene in the film, Pacino's character decided to put his selfish nature aside and defend a young college student he had grown to admire because he saw in that student a person he failed to become himself. Instead of resenting the young man named Charlie, Pacino stood up for him in front of a school board and a student body that thirsted for a fall guy.

Before finally driving home his point and ultimately defending Charlie successfully, Pacino loudly proclaimed the following:

"I always knew what the right path was. Without exception, I knew. But I never took it. You know why? It was too damn hard!"[42]

Whenever a man fails to do what's right, the reason can almost always be narrowed down to one of three possibilities: laziness, cowardice or wickedness.

At the very essence of this book is a story about how one man, who wielded an incalculable amount of earthly power, was defeated by a boy who was the conduit for infinitely righteous spiritual power. The boy chose righteousness over fear while everyone around him chose the inverse, even those who had more earthly power than he did.

Not so coincidentally, the boy who slew the giant was able to do so with a faith that could not co-exist with any of the things that cause a man to fail to do what is right.

## A TERRORIZING GIANT IN THE LAND

Dozier's trials with members of the Republican Party – including the Broward County Executive Committee – in the wake of his comments about Islam, partly served as the inspiration for one of his most powerful sermons, which he delivered to his church in the weeks after being alienated by the Party's most powerful state and national leaders. Dozier informed me that *CNN* was in town that weekend to produce a news segment about him and filmed the entire sermon from the church's balcony. He again did not mince words.

As he directed the congregation to turn to 1 Samuel and the story of David and Goliath, Dozier asked the question, "Did you know that America, like Israel, is being terrorized by a giant in the land?"

In Biblical Scripture, Goliath is described as the giant the Israelites refused to confront; it didn't end there. They allowed the giant to disgrace them, to humiliate them, and to defame their God without consequence from them. In Dozier's sermon, Goliath was portrayed as one of Islam's forefathers and America as Israel's Judeo-Christian ally who is dealing with a similarly intimidating enemy in much the same way:

> "There is a giant in the land today and this giant is doing the same thing Goliath did. He is disgracing America! He is making shame America! He is defaming America! He is putting America down! Who could this man be? This man, who has everyone running, this man, who has the greatest of the greatest men of the earth running for cover, duckin' and dodgin', who could this man be who has brought terror in America?"[43]

In light of the political battle Dozier was engaged in, the metaphor was palpable. He was calling out those politicians who rejected him, politicians who were charged with defending the homeland and who had exponentially more power at their disposal to do so. The implication was clear. Dozier was comparing the likes of George W. Bush, Jeb Bush, Charlie Crist, and any other politician who deferred to political correctness – to the Israelites who cowered in the face of Goliath and the Philistines. If they were the Christians they claimed to be, the faith of these politicians demanded much more than what they were giving.

Inherently, Dozier was comparing Crist and the Bushes to the disciple Peter and his denial – three times – of being associated with the Truth in the flesh. Dozier wasn't done:

> "In like manner today, the men of the nation of America are afraid of the giant and they are fleeing from this giant. Yes, men of great stature like political leaders and men of God. Even pastors are afraid to antagonize this giant...They are afraid to oppose and to counteract this giant. They are afraid to make an enemy of this giant so therefore we say all of the politically correct things in order not to antagonize this giant."[44]

Goliath terrorized the Israelites. Their fear fed Goliath's confidence that he would certainly rule over them. He was so convinced because of his great size coupled with the fear instilled in his opponents *by* that size. In one of Dozier's most ingenious allegories, he compared the *size* of Goliath in the Old Testament with the size of the Islamist *movement* today:

"Is the enemy who has come to terrorize us (America), is he of great size? Yes, he is of great size. He is of great numbers, great numbers."[45]

After comparing the decision of the Israelites not to confront Goliath with the decision of western leaders not to confront very real Islamic threats, Dozier continued:

"...and the politicians considered not. They said in their hearts, 'no, we will not take on this giant because there are so many of them and it may hinder my election.' Oh, my friends, we're in for a fix!"[46]

As Dozier subsequently and rightly pointed out, one of the human reactions to fear is to deny what causes it. Israelites who denied Goliath's existence were compensating for their own fear, which is a strongly undesirable human emotion; people who are afflicted with it will deny it exists within them. Internally, it's extremely uncomfortable. Externally – when people perceive you as cowardly – it's extremely dishonorable.

The result is often a vigorous defense of those emotions through rationalization and arguments that, on their face, might seem cogent. In reality, they are no more than fronts that hide a cowardly core. The symbolism of Dozier's message was too rich to dismiss as abstract. He was accusing America's political leaders – Republican leaders specifically – of being cowards who wanted to portray themselves as righteous while denying the true threats. Such behavior had become expected from the Democratic Party. The degree to which these politicians treated Dozier so disrespectfully spoke volumes and Dozier's sermon only drew more attention to their behavior.

To illustrate this point, just a couple of years later, in 2008, more than 75 percent of Jewish voters pulled the lever for Barack Hussein Obama as President of the United States. They did so despite overwhelming and irrefutable evidence that Obama would not be kind to the state of Israel. Obama had a racist, anti-Semitic pastor named Jeremiah Wright for twenty years. Wright published the terrorist manifesto of Hamas – written by Hamas leader Mousa Abu Marzook – in his church's newsletter in 2007.[47] This reality was widely revealed more than six months prior to the election but Obama still secured nearly 80 percent of the Jewish vote, despite his pastor's affinity for the words of a man who led a group that has the destruction of Israel in its charter.[48]

This is to say nothing of the support Obama received from avowed anti-Semite Louis Farrakhan, who referred to him as "the Messiah." How about former PLO operative Rashid Khalidi, who was a staunch friend of Obama in Chicago? On the eve of the 2008 election, the *Los Angeles Times* refused to release video of Obama and Weather Underground founder Bill Ayers [See Chapter 4], at Khalidi's farewell dinner, ostensibly because doing so would have been incredibly damaging to the future president.[49]

On May 31, 2010 a flotilla with origins in Turkey attempted to break an Israeli blockade of Gaza. Fortunately, Israeli cameras recorded the subsequent confrontation, which showed armed, militant Palestinians who had portrayed themselves as peace activists. Israelis killed nine flotilla members in self-defense.[50] Obama's friend, Bill Ayers, was part of the *Free Gaza Movement*, which sponsored the flotilla [See Chapter 4]."[51]

In May of 2011, Barack Obama gave a speech while at the US State Department, during which he called for Israel to return to its 1967 borders. Making the speech more incendiary was the fact that one day later Obama would publicly meet with Israeli Prime Minister Benjamin Netanyahu in the Oval Office of the White House.

At the very public press conference afterward, Netanyahu schooled Obama inside the President's own office, in full view of cameras. The Israeli Prime Minister rebuked Obama by publicly rejecting the President's words from one day earlier.

Despite all the evidence to the contrary, Jews voted overwhelmingly for Obama in 2008. In light of the dynamic that existed just prior to David's slaying of Goliath, perhaps we are provided a window into why Obama garnered so much of the Jewish vote – fear.

Sure, liberal Jews will deny this but they do so at their own peril, especially when it comes to the Barack Obama administration.

Dozier tapped into this reality two years prior to Obama's election:

"Have you seen this man who is increasing in numbers in your country, in the very midst of your eyes? Have you seen this terrorizing man who is coming up, increasing in numbers, who is now, perhaps 2 percent of the population? What's going to happen as this man rises up to 4 percent, 5 percent, 8 percent, 10 percent, 15 percent, 20 percent of the population? What's going to happen with this man? Do you believe...this man would become more brave, would become more intolerant toward the American view? Could it be the strategy of this man to increase in numbers so that he could take over?"[52]

The *CNN* cameras rolled as Dozier expounded on the words he expressed a few short months earlier in a south Florida radio studio. Backing down did not appear to be part of his makeup. Without mentioning names, Dozier explained to his congregation – and to *CNN* – why the likes of George, Jeb, and Charlie chose to defer to nefarious entities instead of confronting them:

"Why are men running? Some are running because they fear for their lives. Others are running from the giant because they reverence man and the things of this world more than they do God...Things like power! Things like political offices! Things like political appointments! Things like worldly prestige! Things like money!"[53]

Political leaders were being accused of cowardice and wickedness from the pulpit. It was something the vast majority of pastors would not do, at least not from a right-wing perspective and especially not with *CNN*'s cameras rolling. The likes of Jeremiah Wright would call for the destruction of America while giving at least one Hamas leader a platform to do so as well. Yet, somehow, the mainstream media found Dozier's pro-America, pro-Israel message far more controversial while right wing pastors in general hadn't the courage to preach such a message, let alone with similar conviction.

Barack Obama distanced himself from Wright only after it became politically necessary, not because it was the right thing to do. Republican leaders distanced themselves from Dozier because of a perception that it was politically necessary, despite it being the wrong thing to do.

As Dozier wrapped up his sermon, he outwardly imagined what he thought God might be saying about the cowardice that exists within the leadership of America:

"God says, 'My Church, of all people should stand! My Church, I have not given you the spirit of fear but of power... Why are you running?' Sooner or later, someone has to challenge this giant...Someone has to challenge this giant before this giant gets into the heart of our government and begins to twist and turn our governmental system towards his way of thinking. Someone has to challenge this giant."[54]

Fortunately or unfortunately, public figures are judged by their words and actions. As the years pass, legacies can age like a fine wine or like one that turns to vinegar. Dozier's words in 2006, though uncomfortable for many at the time, have rung true for an increasingly large number of people since.

Conversely, the legacies of George W. Bush, Jeb Bush, and Charlie Crist continue to sour, at least in this one regard. George has earned a reputation as the President who spent recklessly and cleared the way for Obama by abandoning conservative principles in his second term. He also failed to identify the true Islamic threat to America; Jeb continued to fight a 'moderate' label as well as continued opposition to the Bush name, thanks to his older brother; Charlie embarrassed himself when he refused to drop out of the Florida Senate race in 2010 after being defeated by Republican Marco Rubio in the primary. The Governor then revealed his insatiable hunger for power when he disgraced himself further by running as an Independent in the General election; Rubio still won.

In 2011 – five years after Dozier made his controversial comments – an organization named *The United West* posted a video of an interview with a Lebanese Christian in Dearborn, MI – one of the most heavily populated Muslim cities in America. In the interview, the Christian man explained how the Muslim community discriminates against him for his religion. At one point, he explained the resistance he received when attempting to ring his Christian church bells:

> **Christian Male:** At Sunday masses, why can't I ring the bell? I used to enjoy it back in Lebanon. I used to ring my bell. Here, if you go to Hamtramck, you hear the mosque...they're praying out loud on a speaker in front of the mosque at 5 o'clock in the morning. Why can't we ring our bell if they can do that?
>
> **Interviewer:** Who's stopping you from ringing the bell?
>
> **Christian Male:** The City
>
> **Interviewer:** Yet, the City allows the loud speaker for the call to prayer?
>
> **Christian Male:** I don't even know if the City knows about Hamtramck because they're all Muslims.
>
> **Interviewer:** Wow. So this is a closed city. This is the Middle East here in America?
>
> **Christian Male:** Sort of. I was shocked. There is more people here with scarves more than there is back in my country. I came here thinking I'm going to see America but I'm just basically in Libya.[55]

Remember, Dozier warned his congregation as well as *CNN* news cameras of this very thing five years earlier when he said, "Someone has to challenge this giant before this giant gets into the heart of our government and begins to twist and turn our governmental system towards his way of thinking."

Who *will* challenge the giant Dozier rightly identified publicly in 2006? It has clearly grown in power and prominence since then.

## ■ LAWSUIT

As Dozier was left abandoned by the Republican Party, he still had a battle to fight. A citizen named Rodney Wright was the plaintiff in a lawsuit against CAIR, CAIR Florida, and the Islamic Center of South Florida but Dozier was an integral part to its litigation.

While the defendants attempted to have the case dismissed, Dozier wanted to obtain access to CAIR's financial records. Said Dozier in 2007:

> "What we're trying to do right now, is we need to come up with the funds to do an adequate discovery. We need to do a very good one, depose all of the various persons on the other side, get all of the pertinent information, get their financial affidavits. We want to get copies of their books. We want to be able to get into their bank accounts."[56]

Imagine if Dozier had had the backing of the Republican Party's leadership. By threatening to drag CAIR's records into discovery, Dozier had the Islamic organization on the ropes save for two things – money and influence. Instead of prominent Republicans distancing themselves from Dozier, perhaps the Republican-led Justice Department could have taken a look at the pastor's claims. If he was right, it was an issue of national security. Perhaps CAIR could have been designated as a terrorist organization. Instead, a Florida pastor was left to fend for himself after being ostracized by a government whose primary responsibility is protecting its citizens.

The strategy of using discovery to get CAIR to back down was not unprecedented. A man named Andrew Whitehead was sued by CAIR over the information he had posted to his website, which chronicled the intentions of the group. CAIR objected to Whitehead's accusations and sued him. Whitehead, who had no money, was left virtually defenseless until attorney Reed Rubenstein of Greenberg Traurig provided him with pro-bono counsel. Ultimately, Whitehead won a huge victory against CAIR, which suffered a humiliating defeat. Though the details of the settlement weren't revealed, it was reported that CAIR withdrew its complaint as it became apparent that the group would have to reveal documents that would be quite damaging.[57] Ultimately, CAIR backed down.

Again, if a private attorney was able to get CAIR to withdraw its lawsuit against a citizen who posted factual items about the group on his website, just imagine how quickly Dozier could have succeeded with a US Justice Department on his side against such groups. Instead, he was on his own.

In an interview I conducted with Dozier in 2008, the pastor discussed the controversy that was dominating the news at the time. It had to do with a media double standard that existed when it came to Barack Obama's pastor, Jeremiah Wright, who had been exposed as a racist; it was the closest Barack Obama would come to having his campaign derailed:

"I had Governor Jeb Bush, Governor Charlie Crist, President George W. Bush, all of them stepping away from me because of my comment against Islam… I believe that according to the teachings of the Qur'an and the Hadith that Islam is a very dangerous and evil cult. Now, if I'm thrown under the bus for that, because my friends George W. Bush, Governor Bush, Charlie Crist believed that I hurt them in their association with me, what does that tell us about Obama?…I would have been thrown under the bus for nothing if Obama is going to get a pass on something this ugly… which I believe was much greater…this man (Wright) damned his own country and he talked against white people and Jews…If Obama searches to become the frontrunner for the Democratic Party in spite of what this man said, I should be vindicated."[58]

It's a point that cannot be honestly argued. The left circled its wagons when it came to Jeremiah Wright and Obama; the right had retreated when it came to being associated with Dozier. While the Florida pastor embraced Jews and Christians, Wright damned America as he embraced a Hamas leader – and Obama still got elected. Ironically, that Hamas leader – Marzook – helped found the group with strong connections to CAIR.[59]

Interestingly, Dozier points to the attorneys in the lawsuit against the ICOSF as the ones who were reticent about going to the mat with CAIR.[60] In a conversation with this author, Dozier said that two separate attorneys had decided to take the case; both failed to aggressively pursue victory and ultimately backed out.

"The first attorney wanted to use the case to fundraise for himself," Dozier said. "The second attorney backed down out of fear that his firm would suffer sanctions proposed by the defendant." The result was a withdrawal, though without prejudice; this allowed for the possibility of a future lawsuit on the same grounds. Dozier does not dismiss the possibility that such a lawsuit may still be filed one day. "It is most certainly on the table," Dozier said.[61]

One of Dozier's arguments all along had been that the intention of the mosque's backers was to recruit "angry black people."[62] When I had the opportunity to ask him about this assertion, he said the following:

"Islam – the Qur'an – is a very dangerous instrument. It preaches hate; it preaches killing; it preaches against the American way of life. We don't need our young blacks, who are already turning against America, who already believe that they have been set aside, they have been neglected by America. We don't need a group coming in here, telling them that they have been or a group coming in, putting down the American way of life...They say that their plight is similar to ours, as African Americans, and I totally disagree with that."[63]

At the time of the lawsuit, CAIR's Florida Director was Altaf Ali. In an interview, Ali explained why ICOSF was so interested in building a Mosque at the selected location:

"They picked that spot because they were sympathetic to the black struggle and believed the feelings were mutual, especially since the persecution after 9/11."[64]

What more could have possibly validated Dozier's charge? The spokesman for the opposition conceded the argument. Yet, Dozier was viewed as a bigot for accurately enunciating the sentiment of his opponent.

About a week after resigning from the JNC, Dozier said the following about Jeb Bush and the latter's unwillingness to defend him; he also made a harrowing prediction:

"I see this as my job for the sake of soul-winning, that we call a spade a spade and an ace an ace...Governor Bush, I believe one day, if he doesn't understand that Islam is a cult, that Islam is very, very dangerous and evil; it is evil and dangerous because of what the Qur'an teaches and I believe one day that his eyes will be opened to this fact."[65]

Something happened soon thereafter which convinced Dozier that George W. Bush actually agreed with him.

Although the invites to the White House slowed down significantly, there was one in particular that had been scheduled after Dozier's comments and subsequent ouster from the JNC. At that White House visit – Dozier would tell me during the writing of this book – President Bush shook his hand and referred to him as the "right reverend." The pastor said the two men locked eyes for a brief moment and Dozier said he knew right then that Bush knew the pastor had spoken the truth. Dozier said it was as if the President wanted to express support for his position but either couldn't or wouldn't give it publicly.

Some weeks after that incident, in talking about the refusal of our leaders to deal with the threat facing our nation, Dozier said:

"If I see it and you see it and the American citizens see it, I know our heads see it. They must see it. They have more information than we have. So yes, they understand it but it is not politically correct to say it. We are in this political correct thing...it is killing America. It is killing us gradually."[66]

Dozier was ready to fight for his flock but the lawyers retained to defend it did what the highest ranking state and national political leaders chose to do; they took a pass.

## ■ VINDICATED IN NEW YORK

In the summer of 2010 – exactly four years after Dozier was demonized as an Islamophobic bigot for protestations against a mosque being built in his neighborhood – New York City was becoming embroiled in an eerily similar controversy over the Ground Zero mosque, which was a project that was to be built two blocks away from the site once home to the World Trade Center towers that were destroyed in the September 11th attacks [See Chapter 10, p. 319].

One of the biggest defenders of the mosque was New York's once Republican mayor, Michael Bloomberg. In a teary-eyed speech, Bloomberg compared any resistance to construction of the mosque to the persecution of religious groups in early American history. He invoked the First Amendment of the Constitution as a defense; he did not want anyone to prevent construction of the mosque based on these grounds:

"The government has no right whatsoever to deny that right – and if it were tried, the courts would almost certainly strike it down as a violation of the US Constitution..."[67]

Less than one year earlier, Bloomberg's office welcomed an unindicted co-conspirator in the 1993 World Trade Center bombing to City Hall for a roundtable discussion in the wake of the Fort Hood shooting that killed 14 people [See Chapter 9, p. 287, Chapter 10, p. 333]. Siraj Wahhaj met with Bloomberg and the city's Police Commissioner. In the wake of a public relations disaster, the mayor's office pleaded that it was unaware of Wahhaj's background.[68]

That statement was either a lie or something that conveyed a level of such gross incompetence that someone should have been fired.

The parallels were blatantly obvious. Bloomberg was behaving like the political leaders Dozier had been dealing with. By welcoming the enemy, Bloomberg emboldened the efforts *of* that enemy to defeat those who the mayor was charged with protecting. The word used to describe that behavior is so obvious; it need not be stated here.

Publicly, Bloomberg would find significant resistance to his position. In essence, the polls mirrored the position of Dozier, who resided more than 1,000 miles to the south. Constitutionally, Bloomberg was on even shakier ground. By invoking the First Amendment, he negated the fact that Islam is a political system – in addition to being a religion.

In countries like Saudi Arabia and Iran, Sharia law *is* the supreme law of the land.[69] In such countries, a Constitution like the one we have in the United States simply cannot co-exist. It is an either-or proposition. If Islam were just a religion, the First Amendment would apply:

> *Congress shall make no law respecting an **establishment of
> religion**, or prohibiting the free exercise thereof*;[70]

However, Islam is not just a religion; it is also a political system
that consistently seeks to creep into other systems until it becomes
the supreme law of whatever land it establishes a foothold in. Therein
lies the rub. As the Center for Security Policy's Team B II report points
out, Article VI of the US Constitution is what should preclude anyone
from accepting the First Amendment argument espoused by Islamists:

> *This Constitution, and the laws of the United States which
> shall be made in pursuance thereof; and all treaties made, or
> which shall be made, under the authority of the United States,
> **shall be the supreme law of the land***;[71]

As a Christian and a Vietnam veteran, Dozier understands this as
well as anyone. He was ahead of the curve when it came to the
Ground Zero mosque but there were still some who insisted that his
warning bells were nothing more than the sounds of religious bigotry.

In an article that appeared in the *Miami Herald*, the controversy
surrounding the Ground Zero mosque was used as an opportunity to
resurrect Dozier's opposition to the mosque in *his* neighborhood as
"bigoted" while arguing that such "bigoted" behavior had magically
gone mainstream and Dozier was somehow the precursor.[72] It was an
attempt to bait that fell flat. It collapsed under the weight of people
who were actually trying to prevent the bigoted foundation of religious
intolerance from being built just a stone's throw from where America
was attacked.

The proof of this is further explored in another chapter but the
words that Ground Zero mosque Imam Feisal Abdul Rauf spoke in
English did not square with what he said to Arabic audiences **[See
Chapter 10, p. 320]**. Those who bought the lie that the Ground Zero
mosque was about "interfaith dialogue," "tolerance," and "First Amendment" freedoms were deceived; many continue to be.

Dozier's concerns were not only validated in Pompano Beach, FL.
They were adopted and acted on in New York City four years after he
raised those concerns.

Further proof of this – as well as an actual comparison – is demonstrated in the words of the Imam leading the Mosque Dozier is fighting – Imam Hassan Sabri.

When asked if his agenda was as nefarious as Dozier believed, Sabri said, "No, just the opposite. It's actually the promoting and understanding of Islam."[73] There is that narrative of Feisal Abdul Rauf again; Islam is about peace, tolerance, and understanding. In 2004, in the wake of the Madrid bombings, Rauf suggested that the West needed to "understand" the point of view of the terrorists.[74]

He went further, even taking the side of America's enemies in WWII:

> "The Islamic method of waging war is not to kill innocent civilians. But it was Christians in World War II who bombed civilians in Dresden and Hiroshima, neither of which were military targets."[75]

Lost on Rauf was the fact that such decisions were made to prevent future loss of life while Islamic terrorists seek to end the lives of innocent people who disagree with them.

As was the case in Pompano Beach, the protesters of the Ground Zero mosque had an effect on construction. Despite getting all necessary municipal approvals and political support, the construction of the mosque was indeed hampered by the size and intensity of the protests.

The forces behind the mosque in Dozier's neighborhood had been dealing with a similar situation in the form of resistance led by the pastor. As of this writing, the mosque in Dozier's neighborhood is still not built.

## ■ TEA PARTY VINDICATION

The George W. Bush administration's lurch toward the left in its second term opened the door for the Barack Obama administration. Republican voters were disenfranchised. They resented their politicians, primarily because the Party forgot its principles; Congress spent like Democrats and Bush avoided the veto pen like the plague. The ongoing wars in Iraq and Afghanistan didn't help either. Dozier enunciated perfectly the frustration of conservatives when it came to our war efforts:

> "We constantly hear that we're fighting the war on terror but we don't hear who it is we are fighting. We're fighting Islamic fascism...You must identify the enemy if you're going to win the war."[76]

This was another reason the Republican Party lost support from conservative voters. Wars were not supposed to become politically correct experiments with our military servicemen. They were supposed to be fought against an identifiable enemy with all the force we could muster to defeat that enemy as quickly as possible; that didn't happen.

Barack Obama was billed as the alternative to Bush. Unfortunately, though many saw Obama for who he was, many were deceived. The good news was that while Obama doubled down on Bush's spending policies, a consequence of his recklessness was the awakening of a contingent of people who got in touch with the spirit of America's founding fathers. The Tea Party was born early in Obama's administration and showed up in droves all across the country on April 15, 2009 – tax day.

Dozier became part of this movement and actively participated. He supported practically everything it stood for and viewed it as something God would support. His defense of the Tea Party was consistent. As a black conservative, he knew that he had to stand up for the group that was being demonized in the media as racist and unwilling to 'spread the wealth.' In a short *YouTube* video shot on a street corner in Fort Lauderdale, Dozier echoed the sentiment:

> "The Tea Party is not racist and the people here are Godly people. They're standing for God. They believe in God...God would never ordain a government to take from the rich and give to the poor...God is not a socialist. God is not a Robin Hood."[77]

The Republican Party was no longer getting a free pass from its voters and the situation in Dozier's district was no different from what was going on in the rest of the country.

There was one exception. Dozier had been considered radioactive by the Republican Party establishment. Would Tea Party candidate and military veteran Lt. Col. Allen West be different? Like Dozier, West was outspoken against the radical Islamic threat to America. He also had a very tough uphill battle to unseat the Democrat incumbent but ended up winning in a route.[78] Unlike Dozier's experience with other Republican politicians, West did not reject him. In fact, shortly after getting elected, West spoke at Dozier's church as Congressman-elect. The church was celebrating both its 25-year anniversary as well as the end of a mortgage that had recently just been paid off.

After walking up to the pulpit with his Bible in hand, West talked about the power to influence:

"Your mission is how (you) are to influence a nation... Influence is a power to affect others; the power to produce an effect because of wealth, position, or ability.[79]

West then read from the Bible:

If My people who are called by My name will humble themselves, and pray and seek My face, and turn from their wicked ways, then I will hear from heaven, and will forgive their sin and heal their land. – 2 Chronicles 7:14

The very fact that West was speaking from the pulpit of Dozier's church as a Republican – elected to Congress after the pastor had been rejected by the Party West represented – was not only a testament to Dozier's ability to influence but to do so despite the Party's attempt to take his ability to influence, away.

Unlike those who rejected him, he did all of this without compromise.

## ■ BATTLE ASSESSMENT

In 1985 – the same year Dozier's church opened – the film *Rambo: First Blood Part II* was released. It starred Sylvester Stallone as a Vietnam veteran who was called upon to covertly return to Vietnam years later to rescue surviving POW's that were said to still be alive. He was told by the bureaucrat in charge that he was *not* to engage the enemy and *not* to rescue any POW's he finds; he was to do nothing more than take their pictures.

After completing the mission, Rambo was to rendezvous with a helicopter and be lifted out of hostile territory. At the moment of truth, Rambo ignored an unlawful and immoral order. Instead of leaving the POWs behind after taking pictures, he took what POWs he could with him to where the helicopter was to pick him up alone. When the bureaucrat was told over the radio that Rambo had POWs with him, he ordered the mission aborted; all were left behind. Rambo would later confront that bureaucrat in a climactic final scene. The bureaucrat's excuse was that he was just following orders.[80]

O'Neal Dozier made a decision some time ago to do battle on the front lines in a fight that his conscience – through prayer – told him was one that needed to be fought. In uttering those fateful words on the radio in 2006, he did not ask Republican leaders to engage in the fight with him. He merely asked that they not abandon him. That request was ignored. It was not enough that he stressed he was speaking for himself only and not for others. It was not all that dissimilar from a platoon leader and a General leaving an infantryman stranded during a fire fight. Those inclined to dismiss such a comparison don't see the fight as Dozier does. He saw war up close in Vietnam and he sees it rapidly approaching today.

In the film, the reason Rambo was not allowed to bring those POWs home was a political one. It would have had consequences that the leaders and bureaucrats did not want to have to deal with. If they were rescued, politicians would feel the heat of a public relations disaster; there could have been increased tensions with other nations. The same can be said about why Dozier and those who supported him were abandoned. If political leaders admitted he was right, perhaps they would have increased problems in the Middle East; maybe OPEC would cut back on oil production. Groups like CAIR are very wealthy and have powerful lobbying arms; it's possible the administration didn't want to upset those relationships.

At some point, the right thing must be done regardless of consequences. In Dozier's mind, that's what he did. While he paid a price, the Republican Party establishment paid one as well. What establishment leaders did to Dozier was not an isolated case. It was a microcosm of how it conducted business generally. The Tea Party recognized this in great numbers. The line of distinction that once clearly separated the Republican and Democratic Parties had blurred at best and shifted to separate the people from their government at worst.

Though not an actual party, there was an inverse relationship between the rise of the Tea Party and the decline of the Republican Party establishment. Dozier was embraced by the party on the rise. Everywhere he went, people were telling him how much they supported him for standing up to what those they elected would not. Sure, the left wing smear merchants stepped up their attacks but it wasn't because they resented Dozier any more than they had previously; it was because he had become a greater threat. Republican establishment politicians, who are afraid of such attacks, do what they have to in order to avoid them. Often, that involves doing exactly what both Bushes and Charlie Crist did; ditch your friends so your enemies – both political and real – leave you alone, which they never do anyway.

In this sense, Dozier has been victorious against a political establishment by challenging it years before it was more roundly exposed. In speaking the truth when it was politically incorrect to do so, he is today on the right side of history while those who cast him aside are on the wrong side.

There is still another battle Dozier is fighting. In some respects it is symbolic and in other respects, it is very real. The forces behind the mosque that is to be built in his church's neighborhood are paying very close attention to Dozier. CAIR's South Florida Director, Nezar Hamze makes regular visits to Dozier's church.

As a member of CAIR, Hamze is well aware that the lawsuit Dozier was intricately involved in named the former's organization as defendants. Dozier is already on record as saying when the conditions are right, that lawsuit could very well be resurrected and re-filed. In the meantime, CAIR obviously wants to know what Dozier is up to.

Sometimes the best way to fight attempts at intimidation is to refuse to be intimidated. I witnessed Dozier's refusal firsthand. On the morning former Muslim terrorist, PLO member, and Muslim Brotherhood activist Walid Shoebat was scheduled to speak at Dozier's church, Hamze was in attendance. Shoebat spent more than an hour laying out the case that Islam is the religion of the anti-Christ [**See Chapter 10, p. 339**]. Before entering the church, Hamze must have seen the marquee in front; it was the same marquee that a Broward County Sheriff's deputy wished hadn't been there.

There is a reason Dozier is on CAIR's radar. If he were to win any lawsuit against them over the mosque, it would represent a tremendous victory. CAIR also doesn't want extensive discovery; the Whitehead case proved that.

A conservative black pastor exhibited more courage than – among others – the President of the United States, two Florida Governors, the Broward County Republican Party, the City of Pompano Beach, two attorneys who wouldn't litigate the case, and his local police officer.

That's why he's in this book.

# CHAPTER 8

## J. D. Cash
## vs.
# DEPARTMENT OF JUSTICE

### ■ THE GROUND SHIFTED

Imagine an event so significant and so earth-shaking that it compelled you to completely change your career choice at the age of 43. Then imagine taking an entry level job in your new field only to embarrass the alleged best in your new profession. Throw in a touch of historic national importance and you have the profile of someone who garners references to blue moons when efforts are made to describe the frequency with which such people come along.

Such is the profile of a man named J.D. Cash. After the Oklahoma City bombing on April 19, 1995 that caused the deaths of 168 people, he became a journalist for an incredibly small newspaper in south-eastern Oklahoma. He was so good at digging that Cash arguably altered the course of national events at multiple points along the way. His style was disarming and he gained trust almost effortlessly. He was friendly and gained friends. He was easy to talk to and heard much. He had a dogged determination to get to the truth despite smear merchants who dogged him once they realized that ignoring him wouldn't work.

Cash was a man authorities and mainstream media outlets tried to marginalize and dismiss. After all, he was a middle-aged novice work - ing in a market that media establishment types didn't even view as being worthy of their scorn, let alone their attention.

When Cash approached the *McCurtain Daily Gazette*, he had hoped to do enough research to leave an historical account of what happened at Oklahoma City. He did not expect – after more than ten years – to become so thoroughly disgusted with his own government. He granted the FBI and Department of Justice what he believed to be a healthy deference until his discoveries revealed a systemically corrupt and bureaucratic illness. Unlike so many others, Cash refused to look away and insisted on looking deep while keeping his head down without losing focus.

J.D. Cash made his government very, very uncomfortable when it was more than warranted and that is largely what makes him a patriot.

## ■ A CAVEAT

The conspiracy theories relative to the Oklahoma City bombing are dwarfed only by those that swirl around the attacks of September 11, 2001 which were perpetrated by Islamic Jihadists. Those who subscribe to the notion that they were perpetrated by the US government give those Jihadists a pass while asking Americans to accept an absurd premise in defiance of their own eyes.

Much of the conspiratorial sentiment surrounding 9/11 was fueled by how the Oklahoma City bombing was investigated. As the weeks, months, and years went by, the very legitimate questions about how the bombing was handled by the Department of Justice caused Americans to be suspicious of their own government. The grandiose conspiracy theories and manufactured questions that surrounded 9/11 can, in part, be attributed to the unanswered questions about Oklahoma City [See Chapter 9, p. 257].

J.D. Cash became a journalist after the Oklahoma City bombing. His work has percolated with an enduring credibility, poised to one day boil with vindication. Though he did garner the interest of the 9/11 conspiracy theorists based on his findings that implicated the US government, Cash managed to keep a safe, factual distance from them as well; he resisted the temptation to connect dots that were too far apart.

Though he disagreed vehemently with her, Cash's work should in no way diminish that of former Oklahoma City television reporter Jayna Davis, who authored an extremely powerful book about John Doe #2 being a member of Saddam Hussein's Republican National Guard. In her book, *The Third Terrorist*, her accounts are solid, credible, backed up by multiple witnesses, and thoroughly researched.[1]

However, while the reporting of J.D. Cash draws many conclusions that differ significantly from those of Davis, there is a common thread that ran through the work of each investigator – the US government had questions to answer and it refused to do so. Cash's investigations led him down a path that exposed government lies, corruption, and coverups. So did the investigations of Davis. The difference was that Davis's findings pointed to an Islamic connection in general and an Iraqi connection in particular. Cash's did not; his work honed in on the Feds and Neo Nazi groups from Elohim City in Oklahoma. In light of what's been learned about the historical alliance between Nazis and Arab Muslims in World War II, perhaps Davis and Cash were both right.[2]

In addition to his thoroughly researched work, what makes Cash's story relevant to the theme of this book – in large part – is where and when his journalism career began.

## ■ JOURNALIST AT AGE 43

Prior to becoming an investigative journalist, J.D. Cash was a mortgage banker with a law degree from Tulsa University.[3] After the Oklahoma City bombing, Cash's life would change dramatically. As a lifetime Oklahoman, the bombing hit home and he was compelled to do something that could make a difference. He was also motivated by the fact that a friend of his who worked for Housing and Urban Development (HUD) was killed in the explosion.

In the days after the bombing, Cash showed up at the office of the *McCurtain Daily Gazette*, located in Oklahoma's McCurtain County. He was eager to contribute in some way and wanted to try his hand at investigative reporting so he asked *Gazette* publisher Bruce Willingham if they'd take a look at his work.

"I told him we'd take a look at it but that there was no guarantee we'd run any of it," Willingham told me in a phone call during the writing of this book. To Willingham's surprise, Cash's work included quotes from a witness who had previously been unwilling to speak with anyone before.

"One of the things that amazed us was J.D.'s ability to get people to talk to him," said Willingham. "There was one witness in particular who wouldn't talk to anybody – but he talked to Cash."[4] Willingham went on to explain that Cash was extremely personable and developed strong rapport with many of the witnesses he interviewed and fought for. They trusted him at a time when truth was in short supply.

Willingham was almost as equally impressed with Cash's fact checking. "Early on, I did my due diligence on all of his work to make sure he wasn't loose with the facts and that everything was sourced properly. It eventually got to the point where I didn't even need to check it."[5]

Amazingly, Cash's very first article won him an award for investigative reporting from the Society of Professional Journalists. It was unheard of; a loosely deputized, 43 year-old male with no journalism experience or degree won a journalism award for his first article in a paper with a circulation of 6,500. He had done an investigation into the possibility that C-4 was being stored in the Murrah building at the time of the explosion. His source included a fire marshal that Cash quoted as saying he witnessed the Feds hauling C-4 out of the building.[6]

Cash, by all professional standards a journalistic novice, would uncover things that should have left every member of the national media thoroughly embarrassed for not having uncovered themselves [See Chapter 5, p. 147-149], let alone journalists writing for newspapers in cities home to more people than resided in all of McCurtain County times ten.

McCurtain County is in the far southeastern corner of Oklahoma; it shares a border with Arkansas to the east and Texas to the south. It would be a literal corner piece of any Oklahoma jigsaw puzzle partitioned by county. The population of the entire county has consistently hovered around 35,000 for years.[7] To say the audience Cash was attempting to reach was small would be an understatement. What made his reports so powerful – in addition to his ability to get so many sources to talk – would eventually be their staying power, despite the reach of the paper that published them.

Cash overturned rock after rock, exposing levels of corruption that thoroughly embarrassed the Department of Justice – and its various agencies – on multiple occasions. Key to this was an uncanny perception on the part of multiple witnesses and government employees who knew things, to confide in Cash. Willingham admitted to me that word got back to the *Gazette* – courtesy of local government officials – that the Feds were paying attention to Cash's work and attempted to discredit it.[8]

Cash trudged ahead, writing prolifically for the *Gazette*, while ignoring its low circulation numbers; they didn't matter. He was on fire for the truth and the *Gazette* was his medium. Though initially minimal, the readership of Cash's articles continued to grow – thanks to the internet – long after the print editions had been recycled or discarded.

In an interview Cash granted to a radio program called, The Intel Report on July 22, 2005 he revealed that as the years passed after the Oklahoma City bombing, members of various law enforcement agencies provided him with information in the form of memos and other documents. The information started coming in from local law enforcement contacts, then county, state, and federal agency officials. Cash further stated that as each FBI agent confided in him, that agent was subsequently relieved and dismissed. Cash said the following during that interview: "As about as fast as they'd tell me something, they'd lose their job."[9]

He went on to say that those sources dried up for some time but that eventually other sources approached him, insisting they be identified only as "Department of Justice officials." Many of those officials worked at the highest levels.[10]

In the days and weeks after the bombing, a family who had lost children in the explosion began to raise seriously legitimate questions about the behavior and statements from officials at the Alcohol Tobacco and Firearms (ATF) division of the DOJ. The mother of two children who died in the explosion – Edye Smith – was demanding answers to questions about why no ATF officials were killed in the blast when they had offices on the 9th floor of the Murrah building.

According to Ambrose Evans-Pritchard, author of *The Secret Life of Bill Clinton*, Smith pressed the ATF about their agents' collective ability to escape injury and received a variety of inconsistent answers.[11]

According to Evans-Pritchard, the ATF appeared to double down in response to media inquiries about Smith's claims when Lester D. Martz, field office special agent in the Dallas office made a specific claim about one of his colleagues – Alex McCauley – that was subsequently disproven; Martz claimed that the Oklahoma resident agent in charge survived a five story fall while in an elevator shaft during the explosion.[12]

Smith and her father Glenn Wilburn smelled a coverup and actually worked closely with Cash to expose the lies they believed were being told by ATF leadership. Cash aided Smith and her father in contacting the elevator company. The ensuing statements from Midwestern Elevator Company, as well as measurable facts, would cause the ATF to change its official story.[13]

Later, in a phone interview with Cash, Martz revised his story, saying that McCauley's fall must have created the *sensation* of falling five stories; McCauley must have "imagined" such a fall.[14]

This would not be the last time the Feds were caught in contradictory statements.

Another testament to the trust that Cash had garnered with the families of bombing victims was the invitation he accepted from Wilburn. As Wilburn was growing increasingly angry with what he viewed as blatant lies from his government, he embraced Cash by insisting that he stay with him and his daughter. Cash would essentially commute back and forth from Oklahoma City to his home in Isabel, four hours away.[15]

It wasn't just victims' families that Cash was able to develop symbiotic relationships with. In fact, he even became friends with the court-appointed investigator for Timothy McVeigh. Amazingly, the new journalist was able to leverage his skillful ability to befriend would-be sources in order to develop a relationship with someone who was defending the man accused of murdering the children and grandchildren of the people who had welcomed Cash into their home.[16]

While Cash had no journalism experience, that didn't mean he couldn't call on what professional experience he did have for his investigations. Evans-Pritchard relayed a story from Cash in which the IRS had planned to lease one of his buildings years earlier, when Cash was a mortgage banker. The deal never went through because the Criminal Investigations Division of the IRS wanted to store C-4 in the building. This experience raised Cash's antennae after the Oklahoma City bombing. After all, if the IRS stored explosives in its buildings, why wouldn't the ATF – which had offices in the Murrah building? It was his reporting on this subject that won him the award from the Oklahoma Society of Professional Journalists mentioned earlier.[17]

## ■ CASH AND JOHN DOE #2

The now infamous sketch of John Doe #2 is the sketch of a man never apprehended nor officially presented in human form to the American public. John Doe #1 was McVeigh. The other man convicted of the Oklahoma City bombing was Terry Nichols, who, based on his features, was clearly not John Doe #2. So who was the man in the sketch? Multiple witnesses, who insisted McVeigh was in the company of multiple persons in the days before the bombing, were disgusted with the FBI's apparent insistence that their memories were lacking. Sentiment was widespread throughout Oklahoma – to the tune of 70 percent according to one poll – that the FBI had no real interest in pursuing the answer to that question.[18]

As witnesses in Oklahoma City were becoming frustrated with what they perceived to be deaf ears belonging to FBI agents, Cash and Willingham were providing information to an FBI agent whose superiors likely weren't expecting to have to deal with.

In 1997, Cash and Willingham presented information to FBI Special Agent Ricardo J.W. Ojeda that showed a connection between Timothy McVeigh and the Aryan Republican Army, which had a base in Elohim City, located in northeastern Oklahoma. Although Ojeda was fired by the FBI after a national television appearance on *CBS* in which he was critical of his employer, it was not known if what he learned from Cash and Willingham had anything to do with his willingness to be so publicly critical of the agency for which he worked.[19]

In light of the evidence presented to Ojeda by Cash and Willingham, it wouldn't be that much of a leap to consider the possibility that Ojeda's boldness was bolstered by what he saw from the *McCurtain Daily Gazette*.

Cash's ability to get people to talk to him may or may not have had something to do with his coming into possession of a surveillance tape from a strip club named "Lady Godiva's" in Tulsa. Nonetheless, the owner of the club presented a videotape to the *Gazette* that was recorded on April 8, 1995 – eleven days before the bombing. On that tape, a female employee can be heard making a shocking claim to other employees.

In 2001, Cash spoke about what was on the tape presented to both he and Willingham by the club owner: "She is heard in the tape telling other women in the room that one of her customers told her she would never forget him 'come April 19.'"[20]

Additionally, Cash spoke about his interview with the woman whose voice is heard on the videotape. After showing her pictures of various people, the woman identified McVeigh as well as men named Michael Brescia and Andreas Strassmeir. Cash further relayed that the woman said Brescia was the one paying for drinks.[21]

Cash continued to exhibit relentlessness when it came to pursuing his leads; he even upped the ante. A man named Dennis Mahon, who allegedly had strong connections to Elohim City, was interviewed by Cash, who determined that Mahon was a high ranking member of the Ku Klux Klan **[See Chapter 6, p. 161]** and the #2 man in the White Aryan Resistance (W.A.R.).[22]

In an interview, *McCurtain Daily Gazette* publisher Willingham said the following about FBI agent Ojeda:

"Ojeda probably does have some bad feelings (because of his firing). But the other side of that is that at the time the [night club surveillance] tape was revealed to him...he said he was surprised that [the FBI] wasn't taking more interest in it."[23]

An indisputable reality is that in Ojeda, the FBI had an agent who was inspired to pursue an investigation based on the evidence presented to him by Cash and Willingham. Again, Cash's due diligence in pursuit of that evidence should not be given short shrift. Based on how the pleas from Ojeda to his superiors were rebuked, the FBI was faced with another embarrassing revelation. In that sense, it was a small victory for Cash.

Moreover, members of the ARA were indicted on January 30, 1997 for bank robbery. Among them were Michael Brescia, Mark W. Thomas, Peter K. Langan, Scott A. Stedeford, Kevin W. McCarthy and Richard Guthrie. At least two of those individuals – who Cash learned from his interviews with Mahon – had connections to Elohim City.[24]

In 2004, the *Associated Press* reported that the FBI had suspected McVeigh was working with bank robbers – before the bombing – who belonged to the Aryan Republican Army. Keep in mind that this was well over seven years after Cash was conducting interviews with Mahon and getting this information firsthand. A wet-behind-the-ears reporter for an extremely small newspaper had scooped the *Associated Press* by just under a decade.

Government documents never before released only served to bolster Cash's claims that the bombing had a significant Aryan Republican Army component with multiple players. One of the ARA members who provided additional information to the *AP* was Langan, who implicated three of his colleagues.[25]

Could one of the ARA members from Elohim City have been the infamous John Doe #2? In a radio interview Cash gave to Scott Horton on the *Weekend Interview* Show[26] in Austin, TX on November 26,

2005 he asserted with the utmost confidence who he believed John Doe #2 was:

**Horton:** "Any idea who John Doe #2 in the sketch is?"
**Cash:** "That's Mike Brescia. There's no question who that is. I was told who he was from day one."

Later in that interview, the prospect of an Islamic connection to the Oklahoma City bombing was brought up. Cash scoffed, calling the utter notion "crap" and insisted that Terry Nichols never went to the Philippines; there was no connection between Nichols and Ramzi Yousef. At one point, in an effort to demonstrate the absurdity of the idea, Cash said that if Nichols ever went to the Philippines to learn how to make bombs, the locals would have eaten him. He even said that anyone who wrote stories or books about an Islamic connection to Oklahoma City were frauds.[27]

Although he didn't name Jayna Davis specifically, it wasn't much of a leap to envision her as the target of such a charge. After all, at the time of the interview with Horton, Davis was riding the wave of an extremely successful book tour and got multiple national media interviews.[28] Cash rejected, out of hand, any Islamic involvement whatsoever in the Oklahoma City bombing; he told Horton that Arab Muslims and neo-Nazi groups hated each other, dismissing the groups' common hatred for the Jews as any type of incentive for them to work together.

If a mutual hatred existed, it didn't square with recent ancestral history. The Muslim Brotherhood aligned with Hitler in WWII and the Grand Mufti of Jerusalem was put in charge of Nazi Muslim troops [See **Chapter 10, p. 296**].[29]

Conversely, his research and investigative work is unmatched. Cash may have been right about Brescia being John Doe #2; he made a great case for it. By Cash's own admission, he didn't have all the answers and didn't pretend to. With how layered and complex the case had become, dismissing an Islamic connection seemed premature as long as those layers hadn't been fully peeled back.

To illustrate the point, Mark Hamm – an author whose work Cash respected – identified McVeigh and his colleagues as having used tactics that Americans would become all too familiar with after 9/11 because al-Qaeda operated in similar fashion. Hamm referred to McVeigh and other members of the ARA as having relied on "leaderless resistance," whereby "one cell did not know about other cells," and "of those cell members who were known, perhaps they were only known by their first name or code names."[30]

If this was indeed the case, Cash could have had so much investigating to do relative to the neo-Nazi connection that a larger plot involving an Islamic connection may have gotten short shrift; his plate was certainly full with what information he did have. Perhaps he was at least mildly predisposed to pursue a neo-Nazi angle exclusively. Evans-Pritchard wrote that Cash was in the middle of writing a novel on Nazi gold when dramatic real life events in Oklahoma City served as the catalyst for his writing intense non-fiction for the *McCurtain Daily Gazette*.[31]

Nonetheless, neo-Nazis as well as the Department of Justice certainly would have preferred that Cash had been focused on that novel instead of on them; he would expose both in a big way.

## ■ INFORMANT(S)

In a phone interview with *KTOK 1000* News Director Jerry Bohnen in Oklahoma City, I asked about the most powerful news stories written by Cash. Without hesitation, he pointed to Cash's work relative to ATF informant Carol Howe, who had infiltrated Elohim City in the months before the Oklahoma City bombing.

Bohnen, a seasoned news professional in Oklahoma City who had developed a solid relationship with the *McCurtain Gazette* reporter was, like Willingham, amazed at Cash's ability to get people to talk to him. Howe was no exception. As national media outlets sought her out, Howe seemed willing to talk only with Cash.

In a 1997 article written by Cash that featured excerpts from an interview he secured with Howe, he reported she revealed to him that in her communications with her handler – a woman who would later be identified as Angela Finley – more than 70 reports were filed by

Howe before the bombing, about the intentions of the residents at Elohim City. Those intentions involved specific interest in federal buildings in Oklahoma.[32]

In light of all the information Howe had provided to her handler – very specific information – it's not surprising that the level of embarrassment on the part of the Feds would have caused them to be concerned about Howe talking to the media. The *McCurtain Daily Gazette* got virtually exclusive access to Howe. No doubt, this was attributable – at least in part – to Cash's personable nature; he had that uncanny knack.

A consequence of Howe confiding in Cash would be realized years later when the judge who presided over the trials of both McVeigh and Nichols made a startling admission in closed chambers. The transcript of that private meeting somehow ended up in the hands of Cash and the *McCurtain Gazette.*

In a shocking revelation, the transcript revealed that judge Richard P. Matsch acknowledged he had received Howe's informant file several months previously but had not read it.[33] What more important document could there have been in these cases? It made no sense that an informant for the ATF inside Elohim City, whose submitted reports totaled more than 70, would be brushed aside. Why would Matsch ignore such a crucial compilation of evidence?

In an article written by Jon Dougherty, it was reported that the details of the closed door meeting between Matsch and Nichols' attorneys pointed to an extremely fortuitous bounce for the Feds and an anti-climactic event for those wanting to hear Howe testify as a government informant. Matsch's ruling allowed Howe to be painted as a white supremacist instead of as someone who signed a contract with the ATF, passed multiple lie detector tests, and provided actionable intelligence to the federal agency – intelligence that embarrassed the ATF because they didn't act on it [See Chapter 1, p.17].[34]

In the November 26, 2005 interview Cash gave to Scott Horton, the former shed some light on why Howe was used as an informant. Policies implemented at the highest levels served to hamstring lower levels.

"At the time that this bombing occurs, Janet Reno had issued a set of parameters to the FBI as to what they could and could not do about infiltrating private organizations and churches, and so forth. Elohim City was off-limits at that time and...apparently what has happened is the ATF, the FBI, and everybody was trying to figure out a way of getting around those directives and so they were using all sorts of little tricks. For instance, the ATF used Carol Howe who ostensibly was to investigate a Klan leader by the name of Dennis Mahon with Flight Aryan Resistance. They sent her out to his favorite place, Elohim City, and used her to gather information."[35]

Another alleged informant for the Feds was a man named Andreas Strassmeir, a German military officer. According to Cash's claims in the interview, Howe was directed to gather intelligence on Dennis Mahon only but the complexity of what Mahon was involved in led her to report on what was going on inside Elohim City in general and another individual in particular – Strassmeir.

In the interview with Horton, Cash was adamant that Strassmeir and Howe were both informants for the Feds, though not working together. Another group with an informant inside was the leftwing group, Southern Poverty Law Center (SPLC), led by Morris Dees – more on that later.

In an article written by Cash and his trusted co-author, Charles Rogers, information about a man named David Hollaway was introduced courtesy of an FBI form known as a 302, which had been fed to Cash by one of his many trusted sources. That document revealed that Hollaway admitted to having had discussions with McVeigh two days before the bombing.

Conversely, Hollaway's lawyer insisted his client never even met McVeigh, despite the official FBI document that said otherwise – in Hollaway's own words.[36]

Another indication of Cash's effectiveness was a story he broke that tied Strassmeir to McVeigh in 1996. Strassmeir fled the United States, at least in part, as a result of that connection being revealed.

The *Gazette* reported at the time that it was Hollaway who helped Strassmeir escape from the US via Mexico, to Berlin.[37]

Sometime after arriving back in Berlin, Strassmeir agreed to an interview with Ambrose Evans-Pritchard for the latter's book, *The Secret Life of Bill Clinton*. Many believed the Oklahoma City bombing was a sting gone wrong. In his responses to Evans-Pritchard's questions, Strassmeir seemed to implicate himself as an accomplice to murder:

> **Evans-Pritchard:** "There comes a time in every botched operation when the informant has to speak out to save his own skin, and that's now, Andreas."
>
> **Strassmeir:** "How can he? What happens if it was a sting operation from the very beginning? What happens if it comes out that the plant was a provocateur?"
>
> **Evans-Pritchard:** "A provocateur?"
>
> **Strassmeir:** "What if he talked and manipulated the others into it...The relatives of the victims are going to go crazy. He's going to be held responsible for the murder of 168 people...Of course the informant can't come forward. He's scared...right now."[38]

If Strassmeir was a provocateur at Elohim City, it would mean that he was largely responsible for the destruction at Oklahoma City. That outcome resulted in the deaths of 168 people. His reticence to talk, coupled with his eagerness to flee the US after the *McCurtain Daily Gazette* tied him to Timothy McVeigh meant he felt the burden of that responsibility in a very real and heightened sense.

Moreover, the notion that Strassmeir was scared for this reason was backed up by the claims made by Carol Howe. She reportedly told her superiors that Strassmeir wanted to bomb federal buildings.[39]

Once again, indications were that the *McCurtain Daily Gazette* – with a circulation of 6,500 – managed to have an impact on international events; Cash's reporting was a direct contributor to an alleged FBI informant's panicked decision to flee the country [**See Chapter 5, p. 146**].

In the official Timothy McVeigh biography by Lou Michel and Dan Herbeck, McVeigh admitted calling Elohim City on April 5, 1995 in an attempt to reach Strassmeir to discuss availability of the compound as a hideout after the bombing. McVeigh also told the authors that he'd had political discussions with Strassmeir on occasion. Proof of the phone call is a matter of public record.[40]

A teletype from FBI Director Louis Freeh on January 4, 1996 wound up in the possession of Cash and the *Gazette*. It corroborated what the authors of McVeigh's biography had reported. A man named Andreas Strassmeir was indeed a person at Elohim City McVeigh had tried to contact on April 5th.

The memo said: "Prior OKBOMB investigation determined that (name redacted) had placed a telephone call to (name redacted) on 4/5/95 a day that he was believed to have been attempting to recruit a second conspirator to assist in the OKBOMB attack."[41]

Obviously, the redacted names referred to McVeigh and Strassmeir. Cash continued to put pieces together.

## ■ SOUTHERN POVERTY LAW CENTER

Perhaps one of Cash's most alarmingly bizarre and ironic finds involved the far left organization known as the Southern Poverty Law Center (SPLC) – co-founded by Morris Dees – and FBI documents from an FOIA request **(Appendix A)**. In light of Cash's claim that he was in possession of a 1996 teletype that revealed communications from FBI Director Louis Freeh about the agency's relationship with SPLC, the following statement about Dees, which is still on the SPLC website as of this writing, is curious at best:

> Known for his innovative lawsuits that crippled some of America's most notorious white supremacist hate groups, he has received more than 20 honorary degrees and numerous awards.[42]

In the November 26, 2005 interview with Horton, the subject of the SPLC came up. Cash sufficiently highlighted the gross hypocrisy between SPLC's charter and the alleged mess they were involved in at Elohim City. Cash said the following in that interview:

"I couldn't understand why I was getting singled out when I started after these Nazis. I thought the Southern Poverty Law Center was about getting rid of the Klan...When I started in on this Strassmeir, making these connections to Elohim City and all the Nazis over there, they started in on me! And this was right after the bombing and now I know why – because they were sitting right in the middle of a sting operation."

A short time later, Cash explained why he thought his claims were indisputable.

"What else do you need but a memoranda from Louis Freeh, a series of teletypes talking about the FBI's relationship with the Southern Poverty Law Center and the fact that the SPLC is sitting at Elohim City with informants when Tim McVeigh is putting together the very last minutes of his plan?"[43]

Cash's claim was that because the FBI had been handcuffed as a result of the rules set forth by Attorney General Janet Reno with regard to what entities they could investigate, the SPLC was used to infiltrate these agencies. Once sufficient information had been gathered to meet Reno's criteria, federal agencies could then be engaged. The 1996 teletype from FBI Director Louis Freeh was critical to the corroboration of this charge. Cash went on to allege that after the FBI had taken control of certain operations from SPLC, some SPLC informants would stay on.[44]

According to a story in *World Net Daily* on January 6, 2004 Morris Dees even conceded that his group had someone working at Elohim City but would not elaborate on why. He even attempted to use some of his civil rights capital by intoning that his organization had successfully sued many a white hate group.

"A lot of hate groups don't like me," Dees said. "I'll tell you...when you put them out of business and take their double-wides (mobile homes), they don't like it. We've sued a lot of these vicious hate groups over the years."[45]

The racial implication that hate groups live exclusively in trailers notwithstanding, there is a significant difference between suing hate groups and having representatives acting as informants inside a compound that was home to several alleged conspirators in the Oklahoma City bombing. The burden of proof should have been shared by SPLC.

In the same January 4, 1996 FBI memo that linked McVeigh and Strassmeir, the SPLC was identified as having had an informant at the compound. The relevant portion said: "(redacted) telephone call from Timothy McVeigh on or about 4/17/95, two days prior to the OKBOMB attack, when (name redacted), per a source of the SPLC, was in the white supremacist compound at (redacted), Oklahoma, notes the director."[46]

These revelations were clearly embarrassing to the Feds and Dees but Cash would soon exhibit a level of investigative fortitude that no other journalist seemed interested in matching.

In the July 22, 2005 interview Cash gave to the *Intel Report*, he said that shortly after the 1996 teletypes came into his possession in 2003, his editor – Willingham – informed him that Morris Dees was scheduled to appear at Southeastern State University, which was 50 miles away from the *Gazette*.

Cash relayed that both he and Willingham were in attendance at the Morris Dees press conference. After letting other reporters – who Cash said acted like Dees was "the second coming" – finish their innocuous questions, Cash and Willingham approached Dees to ask him about the January 4, 1996 FBI memo. What ensued was a testament to on-the-ground reporting. Cash explained Dees' reaction to his question about the memo:

> "He's just about to die. He said, 'do you have it with you?' I said, 'no, obviously I don't because I don't want to share it with you. Not at this time. I just want to ask you some questions.' He goes, 'how did you get it?' I just looked at him and he said, 'you got it from a FOIA.' And he's sitting there thinking, 'how can they be so stupid?' And I said, 'Let's just talk about it.' I said,

'number one, why were you there?' He said, 'we were there but if I had to tell you, I'd kill you first before I would tell you.'"

After several minutes, Dees was walking away when Cash confronted him about something no other reporter would dare to:

"I walked up to him and I said, 'well now that you've had years to think about this, what do you think about Andy Strassmeir now?' He gave me the coldest go-to-hell look that I've had in a long time and he said, 'I am not going to talk about that man. I will never talk about him.'"

Cash went on to say that he believed David Hollaway was the SPLC informant at Elohim City and that he was using Strassmeir to get information. Hollaway and Strassmeir had been roommates before and after the bombing.[47]

Once again, the objective observer should be struck by the fact that a reporter for the *McCurtain Daily Gazette* was confronting a very powerful person with facts obtained by sources within government agencies – sources that trusted him – in order to hold that individual accountable. In this case, armed with documents received via FOIA requests, Cash did just that while much larger media outlets seemed unwilling to even barely scratch the surface.

In an article on the *CBS News* website dated January 21, 2005 it was reported that the FBI had been fighting a FOIA lawsuit. Among the documents requested in that lawsuit was an un-redacted copy of the January 1996 teletype. The FBI claimed that they had no documents matching that request **(Appendix A)**.[48]

A small problem with that claim was that Cash had a copy of the redacted teletype in question and willingly gave it to the attorney who filed the lawsuit. Once again, the FBI found itself in an extremely embarrassing position – thanks to Cash – when the attorney provided the redacted teletype to them, essentially saying 'here's the document, now look again.'

According to the *CBS* article, the FBI's response was that the search they had already conducted was reasonable and that they shouldn't be required to produce the documents.

Later that year, thanks to Cash's investigations, the FBI would find itself in yet another untenable position. In an October 21, 2005 article, Cash reported that the federal judge in the FOIA case ordered the FBI to release the documents in question. The DOJ attorneys argued that the names in the memos should not be made known. Here is part of their argument as to why:

> "Names and identifying information of third parties who were (and, possibly, still are) of investigative interest to the FBI have been redacted and withheld from release...Being a suspect or person of interest in an FBI investigation – in particular, the FBI investigation of the bombing of the Murrah Federal Building – carries obvious negative connotations and stigmas...Accordingly these third parties have a significant privacy interest in the nondisclosure of their names and other information that would lead to their identification."[49]

Cash closed the article by pointing out that the federal attorneys who prosecuted McVeigh and Nichols claimed to have exhausted all investigative leads with regard to Elohim City being a place that housed co-conspirators and found nothing. If true, the argument given to keep names redacted was fallacious. It was logical to conclude that the SPLC was being protected by the Justice Department under George W. Bush, which seemed to go out of its way to protect the Clinton administration on multiple occasions [See Chapters 1, p.16, Chapter 9, p. 261].

The name of the attorney who filed the FOIA lawsuit was Jesse Trentadue. By all accounts, he had no interest in getting to the bottom of any coverup of the Oklahoma City bombing; that was not his motivation. He wanted nothing more than to get to the bottom of a case involving his brother Kenneth, who died in an Oklahoma federal prison center under extremely suspicious circumstances on August 21, 1995 – four months after the bombing. Unfortunately, Jesse would be stonewalled in ways not all that dissimilar from what the families of bombing victims experienced when they demanded answers.

In 2003, Cash would begin investigating the Trentadue case and his reporting implicated people at the highest levels in the Department of

Justice – including a man who would eventually become Deputy Attorney General at the time Jesse began getting close to the truth in 1997.

## ■ THE TRENTADUE CASE

To understand why Kenneth Michael Trentadue was picked up near San Diego in the summer of 1995 and then transported to the Federal Transport Center (FTC) in Oklahoma City in a Department of Justice jet, it's important to remember that a grand jury in the bombing case referred to "others unknown" when handing out indictments for McVeigh and Nichols.

McVeigh was known to have consorted with bank robbers – the 'Midwest bank robbers' to be exact. *Fox News* reported in 2005 that one of the gang's members – Peter Langan – told *Fox* that members of his group participated in the Oklahoma City bombing.[50]

On January 30, 1997 six men were indicted in Pennsylvania for robbing banks. All were members of the Aryan Republican Army (ARA). One of them – Michael Brescia – was identified by Cash as John Doe #2. Langan was one of the others indicted.[51] If Brescia was John Doe #2 and hadn't been arrested until early 1997, that obviously meant that such a suspect was still at large at the time of Kenneth Trentadue's arrest in the summer of 1995.

Kenneth was no saint. He had indeed robbed banks at one time. He had a tattoo on his left arm that resembled the tattoo on the left arm of the alleged John Doe #2. He even drove a pickup truck that matched a similar description of the one at Oklahoma City a few short months earlier. These factors taken together led to his ending up at the FTC at DOJ / taxpayer expense.[52]

Cash's reporting seemed to afford him the frequent ability to begin paragraphs in his articles with, "Documents obtained by the *McCurtain Daily Gazette* show…" In the case of Cash's first installment of the Trentadue case, that statement was applied to the fact that the officer who arrested Trentadue noted the would-be detainee's former alias – Vance Paul Brockway.[53] It was the Brockway name being tied to bank robberies that may have been the final straw for the Feds sending Trentadue to the FTC. It was Cash's ability to tie all of these things together eight years later that made him such a nemesis for the Feds.

The facts surrounding Trentadue's past, coupled with the seemingly logical conclusions that could be drawn about his ties to the Oklahoma City bombing – the tattoo, the truck, the history of bank robberies, etc. – could have given the Feds added confidence that they were on solid assumptive ground relative to this detainee being someone they could press hard with minimal consequence.

If so, they were wrong.

Kenneth had an older brother. His name was Jesse and he became an extremely successful attorney with a practice in Salt Lake City, UT. In typical J.D. Cash fashion, the *McCurtain* journalist befriended Jesse and would make his brother's case the subject of a five part series in his reporting. Cash revered Jesse's skills as an attorney and took up his cause, seeing an opportunity to expose the despicable way the Feds handled the case of Kenneth Michael Trentadue, who wound up dead on August 21, 1995 in a prison that was supposedly suicide proof; that prison was the FTC.

In a way similar to how Cash ingratiated himself with Edyie Smith and her father Glenn Wilburn in the days and weeks after the bombing, there seemed to be a connection taking place between Cash and the Trentadue family. When one reads Cash's articles about what happened, professionalism and journalistic integrity is quickly discernable but so is a high level of personal investment; he virtually adopted the familial cause while giving it voice.

The first sign that the Feds were in trouble came on the morning of Kenneth's death, when the FTC warden contacted the mother of both Kenneth and Jesse to inform her that one of her sons – Kenneth – had committed suicide. Earlier, while being booked, Kenneth did not tell the authorities about his wife and young child – only about his parents; that may have been his biggest mistake. Perhaps it sent the signal that he was a bit of a lone wolf with a family that didn't care much about him; if that was the message received by the FTC, they would soon regret it.

As Cash reported in part one of his five part series on the death of Kenneth Trentadue, the warden was not expecting the answer she got from Kenneth's mother after telling her that her son had committed suicide and that the FTC would like to cremate the body.

After the warden seemed to be caught off-guard by the prospect that Kenneth had a wife – Cash reported that Kenneth only gave the FTC his parents' contact information – the boom was lowered against the Feds.

Stunned but suspicious, the mother of the deceased told the prison official, "Yes, he's married and he also has a 2-month-old child and his brother is a lawyer. We'll get back to you!"[54]

Some time after that call, the Oklahoma Medical Examiner's investigator and her associate arrived at the FTC to pick up the body and investigate the cell where Trentadue was found dead. While the two were allowed to take the body, their attempts to access the cell were repeatedly denied by the Feds, who said they were handling the investigation – despite such an assertion being contrary to state law.

In a clear example of how Cash was able to take away any vestige of plausible deniability from the Feds relative to that claim, he accessed records that showed both the M.E. and her assistant were only at the FTC for a total of twenty minutes.[55]

Clearly, if those two officials had been allowed to investigate the scene, a visit longer than twenty minutes would have been recorded. The Feds had an extremely worthy opponent who found evidence over and over again that backed up his reporting. It bolstered his credibility throughout the state. Perhaps his ability to help his sources back up their claims also contributed greatly to his ability to garner even more sources.

The Medical Examiner's lead investigator at the time was Kevin Rowland. After viewing the body and determining suicide was not the cause of death, Rowland contacted an FBI agent to report his findings. Cash even managed to get his hands on a memo from that agent to his superiors subsequent to that discussion. In it, recipients were notified that the Medical Examiner's office was likely going to rule Trentadue's death a homicide. It also said that FTC employees were being steered in the direction of avoiding polygraph tests.[56] **[See Chapter 1, p. 20]** On one hand, FBI officials seemed to have their work cut out for them. On the other hand, they had to have been flummoxed by this obscure reporter's findings – it was like he had several people on the inside working for him. They had to have been wondering how a 'nobody' reporter always seemed to be onto them. Yet, news entities with a much broader reach and far more resources continued to focus on much lighter fare.

As is the case with any puzzle, each piece is critical. In 1999, the Office of the Inspector General for the US Department of Justice released a report about Trentadue's death. In it, the OIG found that Trentadue's cell was cleaned prior to Bureau of Prisons investigators arriving on the scene.[57] This was a stunning admission on the part of the OIG but it was made even more so after factoring in the behavior of the FTC when the Oklahoma Medical Examiner's investigator was denied access to the cell before it was cleaned. If the OIG report hinted at a coverup, the behavior of the FTC prior to the arrival of Bureau of Prisons (BOP) investigators pointed to one when coupled with what the OIG did concede. It was Cash who featured these two realities prominently in one article, not to mention the FBI memo mentioned earlier.

Regardless of how embarrassing the OIG report would be to the Feds, the most important thing to the latter was the report's conclusion. Was the death a suicide or was it a homicide? The key to that determination was the chief medical examiner; his name was Dr. Fred Jordan and for three years, it was clear that he thought Kenneth Trentadue was murdered.

In early 1997, Jordan granted a rare television interview to the Oklahoma's *Fox* television affiliate *KOKH* to talk about the case. During that interview, Jordan was adamant in his insistence that the government was either incompetent or worse. Said Jordan during that interview:

> "I think it's very likely he (Trentadue) was murdered. I'm not able to prove it. I have temporarily classified the death as undetermined. You see a body covered with blood, removed

from the room, as Mr. Trentadue was, soaked in blood, covered with bruises, and you try to gain access to the scene and the government of the United States says, 'no, you can't.' They continue to prohibit us from having access to the scene of his death, which is unheard of in 1997...There are questions about the death of Kenneth Trentadue that will never be answered because of the actions of the United States government...It was botched or worse – it was planned."[58]

As part of Cash's research in 2003, he got a quote from Jesse Trentadue regarding Jordan. Once again, the *McCurtain* reporter landed something extremely telling and it had to do with Jordan's state of mind at the time:

"Jordan repeatedly told us this was a murder, but because the crime scene had been destroyed, he had to list the manner of death as unknown. He also looked at my mother, Carmen and sister in the eye and told them he would never go back on them."[59]

The vehemence with which Jordan conveyed his level of emotional investment cannot be understated because something would change his mind before the OIG report was released in 1999.

As the chief medical examiner in the state of Oklahoma, the sole responsibility for determining the cause of Kenneth's death rested with Jordan. The Feds even released reports saying that suicide was the cause but for three years, Jordan would not budge.

Signs that Jesse Trentadue was getting too close for DOJ comfort would soon appear in Cash's five part series of articles on the story. If not for the *McCurtain Gazette*, which had already developed a significant following by the time Cash began investigating the story in 2003, some incredibly disturbing facts about the US government may not have been published by any publication of consequence; being a publication of consequence on these stories was something the *McCurtain Gazette* was able to claim, thanks to Cash.

Jesse told the *Gazette* that he had gone all the way to Janet Reno's office for answers in the weeks and months after his brother's death.

Eric Holder had assumed the role of Deputy Attorney General in June of 1997, the year when Jesse learned that the FBI had not done any significant investigation of Kenneth's death, despite receiving a medical examiner's report that said the death should be investigated as a homicide.[60]

The FBI agent assigned to the case seemed to be more interested in informing his agency about the whereabouts, movements, and statements of Jordan than in getting to the truth about Trentadue's death.

Cash and the *Gazette* actually obtained a memo written by Jordan in December of 1995 in which the latter phoned the office of Eric Holder (at the time, Holder was not yet the Deputy Attorney General but he was a high ranking member within the DOJ). That memo shows that Jordan's call to Holder was an attempt to urge the FBI to conduct a full investigation into Trentadue's death. Jordan never did reach Holder.[61]

It would seem more than reasonable for someone like Holder to accept or return the call of the Oklahoma state medical examiner who wanted an investigation into the death of a man who died while in federal custody. Add to that a potential link to the Oklahoma City bombing and it should have been a top priority for Holder. It apparently wasn't, at least not in terms of getting to the truth – more on that later. Holder would later become the US Attorney General under Barack Obama in 2009. While there, his Department developed quite the reputation for stonewalling and obfuscation.

Jordan seemed resolute. He assured the Trentadues that he would not buckle under federal pressure to change his ruling relative to cause of death. He was the biggest obstacle for the Feds. If he ruled the death a suicide, the Feds could breathe easy. It would mean no federal grand jury or indictments. All roads to a successful coverup went through Medical Examiner Fred Jordan. For Jordan, it was a double-edged sword. Yes, he had the power to make life difficult for some very powerful people but he would also be subjected to intense intimidation as a result.[62]

Ironically, as Cash reported, Jordan would not budge as long as the FBI and the Bureau of Prisons (BOP) attempted to pressure him. That all changed after the Oklahoma County District Attorney Bob Macy inter-vened. Shortly after Macy took over, Jordan ruled the death a suicide.[63]

According to the *Gazette*, Macy hired a man named Tom Bevel to investigate the case. Bevel had also been hired to assist in writing the OIG report that would ultimately be released in 1999.[64] Once again, Cash was connecting dots that should have been connected by major media outlets and shouted from the rooftops. If he had gotten even a little support from one major news outlet, this case could have exploded onto the national scene, exposing corruption at the highest levels of government. Perhaps Jordan wouldn't have been successfully strong-armed either. Posterity is a funny thing, however. Cash added a number of significant facts to the historical record through his reporting that simply could not be easily dismissed.

Cash reported that before Bevel went to work for the DOJ and OIG, the Trentadues trusted him as a member of Macy's team, charged with investigating the death. After all, the state was essentially an alleged ally of the Trentadues against the Feds – or so it was thought.

Ironically, Bevel helped to point out a series of absurdities – in what is known as the "Wintory Report" – one would have to believe in order to accept the notion that Kenneth committed suicide. The report was done before Bevel switched sides and began working for the Feds. Had he been an agent of the DOJ at time the "Wintory Report" was drafted, one would have been right to question his credibility.

Nonetheless, after working for the Feds, Bevel would use that report as the basis for his suicidal conclusion, according to Cash. In part five of Cash's series on Trentadue's death, he included the relevant portion of the report:

> The Government claim that after the guards last saw Trentadue alive and in bed at 2:38 a.m., Trentadue used a pencil to write a suicide note on the wall of his cell, but did not sign that note with his own name. Next, he patiently tore a sheet into dozens of strips. He then constructed a ligature from those strips of bed sheet. Once that ligature was manu-factured, Trentadue re-made his bed, climbed the wall of his

cell and wove the bed sheet rope into a metal vent above his sink. Trentadue then tried to hang himself and was momentarily successful, but the bed sheet rope broke. Trentadue fell, hitting his buttocks on the edge of the sink but doing no injury to his buttocks. The impact of his body on the sink caused Trentadue to ricochet across the cell headfirst into the corner of a metal desk at the end of his bunk, producing a major wound on his forehead.

The Government claim that the force of that impact caused Trentadue to rotate 180 degrees and careen across his cell to smash his head, leaving blood and hair on the wall of his cell and tearing extensive areas of skin off of his back. Despite striking the desk with such force, the impact does not disturb a cup of coffee or any of the papers on the desk.

The Government claims that while unconscious from his two head wounds, Trentadue rolled over on his stomach and bled profusely, depositing large pools of blood on the floor of his cell. When Trentadue regained consciousness, he attempted to get up but struck the back of his head on the metal stool attached to the desk, causing a third major wound on the back of his head. This third blow to his head further dazed Trentadue, who then crawled on all fours, with his clothing smearing the blood on the floor.

The Government claim that Trentadue finally got to his feet and staggered around, leaving blood deposits on the walls and floor of his cell. He then stumbled to his bed and lay down to regain his senses.

After a while, Trentadue used two plastic toothpaste tubes or a plastic knife to cut his throat, leaving blood on his pillowcase, sheet and blanket. When that second suicide attempt failed, Trentadue reconstructed the bed sheet and successfully hanged himself.[65]

The report's depiction of events was ludicrous. Perhaps it was the best the Feds could do in light of the investigative journalism that was taking place in southeastern Oklahoma. Cash was not done, however. He would not disappoint those looking for a crescendo in his five part series. In part five, he implicated a man that would one day become the Attorney General of the United States as being personally involved in the coverup of Kenneth Michael Trentadue's death.

## "THE TRENTADUE MISSION"

In part five, Cash reported some very serious charges levied by Jesse Trentadue against the Department of Justice. Jesse's claim was that while he confided in certain federal officials he thought were in search of the truth, they were actually using the information against the Trentadue family to aid in the coverup.

According to Cash, the Medical Examiner (Jordan) did not declare Kenneth's death a suicide until July of 1998 while Jesse maintained that a federal grand jury returned a "no bill of indictment" nearly one year earlier. How is that possible if the medical examiner hadn't ruled on the cause of death yet? Based on the fact that Kenneth was in solitary confinement at the time, a homicide ruling would have necessarily implicated federal officials. Jesse is quoted in Cash's article as having claimed that the Grand Jury's ruling was kept quiet so that the Justice Department could work on the coverup.[66]

Cash then reported Jesse's very serious charge: the meetings amongst DOJ leaders were all part of what was called "The Trentadue Mission" and that none other than Deputy Attorney General Eric Holder chaired many of those meetings.[67] A serious charge indeed but Cash obviously felt comfortable reporting it because of what his contacts were able to provide him. In this case, it was an email dated October 1, 1997 by Juliette Kayyem who worked for the DOJ at the time. The subject line of the email said, "The Trentadue Mission" **(Appendix B)**. Here is the text of that email as published by the *McCurtain Gazette*:

"This is like coordinating the invasion of Normandy. We are on for Monday; the declination memo is done. Is this OK with Eric's schedule (I can call whoever does that.) I talked to Faith and she is going to think about the best way to approach

Hatch and possibly Dorgan, and I will get back to you. Also, we will be contacting the FBI and Jesse Trentadue at the same time (about 2 hours before the press release.)"[68]

The press release referred to in that email was ultimately released on October 9, 1997. In it, the DOJ announced it had found no wrongdoing on the part of the FBI or the BOP relative to Kenneth Trentadue's death. Obviously, the public stance on the part of the Feds, that suicide was the cause of death would only serve as a high stakes incentive to apply more pressure to Jordan, who would eventually buckle nearly one year later.

## SENATE JUDICIARY COMMITTEE

At the time of the DOJ press release on October 9th, Senator Orrin Hatch (R-UT) was the chairman of the Senate Judiciary Committee. His committee was looking into a possible investigation of the Department of Justice's findings. On October 10, 1997 Hatch answered questions after his meeting with Deputy Attorney General Eric Holder the night before.[69] The purpose of that meeting was ostensibly to prevent that congressional investigation.

Hatch appeared convinced that Trentadue's death was not the result of a suicide and that indications of a coverup were very strong. Hatch was asked about that:

> **Hatch:** "I was disappointed in these findings. There are just too many unexplained facts, too much brutality apparently done and frankly, no answers. I can't understand that.
> **Reporter:** Does it have the aroma of coverup?
> **Hatch:** Yep, it has the aroma of coverup.

The relevant portion of Hatch's exchange with the press went on for nearly eight minutes. Throughout, Hatch didn't mince words about his certainty that the Trentadue case needed to be investigated and that the DOJ's report was not sufficient.

Here are some additional quotes from Hatch during that Q&A:

"They (DOJ) have not found any criminal liability here. On the other hand, they can't explain the tremendous inconsistencies of what happened in this particular instance."

"There's a lot wrong with this case and I hope somebody will get to the bottom of it but apparently the Federal government hasn't been able to do so."

"Somebody other than Trentadue beat…beat Trentadue up. The injuries that he suffered on his body do not appear to have been self-inflicted, neither does the actuality of his death."

"Somebody has not told the truth here and somebody in my opinion is covering up."

"It just appears to be a tremendous injustice as we sit here right now."

The degree to which Cash's work played a role in Hatch's public display of opposition to the handling of the Trentadue case may be up for debate but it *did* play a role.

The admission by the chairman of the Senate Judiciary Committee that a coverup took place in a case with such strong connections to the Oklahoma City bombing should dramatically shift the burden of proof to the federal government, not only in the Trentadue case but in the much larger investigation of the Oklahoma City bombing.

J.D. Cash's work is backed up by witnesses, documents, and unmatched investigative reporting. If Senator Hatch believed there was a coverup with respect to Trentadue's death – which would almost necessarily align him with the conclusions of Cash's five part series – shouldn't the multiple other stories penned by Cash warrant increased credibility as well?

The admission by Hatch went a long way in doing just that. If members of the federal government were indeed involved in a coverup relative to a death suspected of having ties to the Oklahoma City bombing, why should a coverup of the bombing itself not be suspected?

Cash had already made that case.

Even after Hatch expressed these concerns following that private meeting with Eric Holder on October 9, 1997 the former Senate Judiciary chairman inexplicably and egregiously cast a "Yea" vote to confirm Eric Holder as Barack Obama's Attorney General on February 2, 2009.[70] The video interview with Hatch clearly proved he knew the details surrounding the case of Kenneth Michael Trentadue. His vote for Holder in 2009 was unprincipled and unconscionable.

## ■ BATTLE ASSESSMENT

In terms of the David vs. Goliath metaphor as it relates to J.D. Cash, the stone he slung – in the form of countless articles – is still flying through the air. The trajectory could have it one day landing between the eyes of the United States Department of Justice, an entity that has come under increased public scrutiny over its handling of other matters since.

Historians will one day look back at the bombing of the Murrah Federal Building on April 19, 1995 with greater intellectual curiosity than exists today. If they are honest in their desire for *the truth*, they will inevitably have to include the work of J.D. Cash before arriving at a conclusion. In fact, the exposing of the DOJ may just be a fait accompli – in large part – because of his work.

Unfortunately, when that day comes – and if you believe the truth always wins out, it will – Cash will not see it. He died on May 6, 2007 of liver disease combined with pneumonia.[71] A man who began his journalism career in 1995 would, in the twelve years that followed, do what the vast majority of supposed seasoned journalists were averse to doing after being in the profession for decades – investigative reporting. He did so because he was driven by a sincere desire for the truth while others may have placed a higher priority on rising through the ranks, impressing their peers, or simply choosing the path of least resistance.

Cash chose instead to fight for those who cried out for justice with loud hearts but muted voices. His sources trusted him – some outright loved him. In order to fight successfully as the little guy with a purpose, one must almost necessarily fight unabashedly for the *cause* of the little guy. This was perhaps Cash's biggest strength. In the world of journalism, he was the little guy who left a mark that is bound to have staying power long after the big guys are forgotten.

People often feel powerless in the fight to make a difference at the highest levels of American government, relegating themselves to obscurity if they view any attempt to engage in the fight as an exercise in futility. More analytical minds might apply the law of diminishing returns to attempts at affecting change on such a large scale – time could better be spent elsewhere, the thinking goes. Cash proved all such paradigms are incredibly flawed. Though he has closed his eyes for the last time, his work helped to set the alarm clock that should wake us all up.

The stone he slung before his death is still flying through the air and it's still on course.

# CHAPTER 9

## LT. COL. ANTHONY SHAFFER
## vs.
# DIA BRASS

### ■ HANDLING OF OKLAHOMA CITY AND 9/11

The Federal Government's handling of the Oklahoma City bombing rightfully fueled increased suspicion about a coverup [See Chapter 8]. Unfortunately, that healthy skepticism helped give birth to outlandish conspiracy theories in the wake of the September 11th attacks. Many people believed that the United States government actively participated in the attacks and that the buildings fell not because Arab Muslim men flew jetliners into them but because the World Trade Center towers were the target of a controlled and covert demolition on the part of the Bush administration.

The theories are so absurd that they shouldn't be mentioned here save for one reason; they arose in part due to a lack of transparency on the part of the US government and became accepted as fact by people who became known as "Truthers." Though the theories are without merit, the reasons *for* them warrant at least a modicum of pity for those who subscribe to such beliefs. The United States government is not guilty of a sin of *commission* when it comes to September 11th but evidence supports the notion that it committed a grave sin of *omission*. In other words, the "Truthers" may be right about one thing: blood is on the hands of those who are not Muslim.

Specifically, a data mining operation known as Able Danger was designed to identify and track individuals and relationships within al-Qaeda terror networks. At first, it relied upon unclassified, open source information that connected members of the group, creating maps and link charts of known and suspected terrorists. General Peter Schoomaker, who headed up the Special Operations Command (SOCOM) at the time, helped develop the program, which had been requested by the Chairman of the Joint Chiefs of Staff, General Hugh Shelton. One year before September 11th, when Gen. Schoomaker retired, the program was scrapped by his replacement, General Holland after the Defense Intelligence Agency (DIA) withdrew its support as well. After 9/11, the government not only engaged in behavior that was eerily reminiscent of how it behaved in the wake of the Oklahoma City bombing but there is strong evidence that suggests the 9/11 attacks could have been prevented had the Able Danger program been allowed to continue. Evidence explored in the previous chapter pointed to a botched sting operation at Oklahoma City that involved the ATF and a coverup to prevent accountability. There is also strong evidence of a coverup with respect to Able Danger, for similar reasons.

Lt. Col. Anthony Shaffer was an integral part of Able Danger; he later revealed what he knew about the program to members of the 9/11 Commission while he was assigned to Army Intelligence in Afghanistan, two years after the worst attack on American soil. Unbeknownst to him, his next tour of duty would be against his own government when he returned home. After his tour of duty in Afghanistan, for which he received a Bronze Star, Shaffer reported back to DIA headquarters in Clarendon, VA and was greeted by a security officer who escorted him to see a senior officer in HUMINT operations at DIA. Instead of returning his DIA security badge, they informed Shaffer that his security clearance had been suspended and he would be reassigned to Fort McNair pending disciplinary action for "three serious items" the DIA IG had found him guilty of committing: accepting an undue award for work on Able Danger before 9/11, $67 in excess call forwarding fees, and an invalid $180 travel voucher (so much for a hero's welcome).

## ■ HUMINT ABSORBED BY DIA

Though Shaffer concedes that bureaucracies consist of good people who do what they can to overcome the pitfalls inherent in such systems, he has an inherent aversion to bureaucratic machinations.

Shaffer explained in his book that he was subsequently approached by Navy Capt. Scott Phillpott and given a thick briefing book shortly after the General told him he'd been re-assigned:

> I remember opening the briefing book, starting to read, and then stopping. *Oh my God. This is the A ticket.* The ultimate mission. We were taking the gloves off and going after al-Qaeda.[3]

Shortly after joining the team, Shaffer recommended it enlist the help of the Army's Land Information Warfare Center (LIWA) to help provide much more data than what Able Danger had been able to acquire on its own. Shaffer had previous experience with LIWA and described their platform as "Google on steroids."[4]

In his written testimony to the House Armed Services Committee on February 15 2006, Shaffer adamantly asserted that his team had identified Mohamed Atta – ringleader of the 9/11 attacks – as early as January of 2000, nearly two years before the attacks.[5] In his book, Shaffer recalls the details of that discovery; he wrote that both he and Captain Phillpott stared at Atta's face on one of the Able Danger charts Shaffer had taken with him to SOCOM to use in briefing Schoomaker.[6]

However, it wasn't just Atta who had been identified; he was only one of multiple members of the "Brooklyn Cell" that the Able Danger team had discovered. The discovery also identified three of the other 9/11 hijackers (the first four to enter the US).[7] This cell to which Atta belonged included associates of Omar Abdul Rahman, the "blind Sheik" behind the 1993 World Trade Center bombing.[8]

In the weeks after Shaffer had taken his charts to SOCOM, things began to change. SOCOM lawyers took significant interest in LIWA's handling of the Able Danger project and began to put up obstacles to furtherance of the research. The articulated concerns were that the program was uncovering data on US persons, violating Army Regulation 380-10.

Interestingly, the same technology had been used, quite successfully, months before it was decided to use it aggressively against al-Qaeda.

In early 1999, after the development of technology that would birth Able Danger, an experiment was run at LIWA that included the mining of data relative to the transfer of sensitive military technology to China. According to former senior analyst Michael Maloof, who worked on the project, the Office of the Defense Secretary's Legal Counsel ordered the entire study be destroyed.

A request from Rep. Curt Weldon (R-PA) – who served on a US National Security Select Committee – to FBI Director Louis Freeh for an espionage investigation fell on deaf ears and the program was subsequently shut down. According to Maloof, the legal counsel in the Office of the Joint Chiefs of Staff ironically pointed to the potential for spying as the reason for shutting down the operation at LIWA.[9] The data mining process cast such a wide net that eventually, the future National Security Advisor and Secretary of State Condoleezza Rice's name appeared on a list of people tied to business transactions with Chinese military officials.[10]

In addition to Rice, Defense Secretary William Cohen allegedly appeared on the list as well. Both were previously linked to a suspected Chinese spy and missile scientist named Hua Di by their interactions with him at Stanford University.[11] A former senior Defense official at the Information Dominance Center (IDC) within the Army's LIWA operation at Fort Belvoir, Virginia – where Able Danger would operate from – even told Shane Harris, author of *The Watchers* and a reporter for the *National Journal*, that Hillary Clinton's name showed up in their search, and after that, the program was not continued.[12] He also reported that top brass at the Department of Defense (DoD) was alarmed enough to notify the House Intelligence Committee that the first lady's name had shown up during the China data harvest.[13]

In the spring of 2000, all of the data mined relative to al-Qaeda was destroyed along with the data mined about transactions with China. The conservative blogger "AJ Strata" rightfully speculated that everything might have been destroyed in a "moment of political panic."[14]

In May of 2000, the man largely responsible for having compiled the enormous cache of data relative to al-Qaeda was ordered to delete everything. Army Major Erik Kleinsmith later testified that he complied with that order.[15] Such an order had to have come from, at minimum, the highest levels of DoD and possibly the Clinton White House.[16]

Shaffer would later testify that the reasons given for the data purge at LIWA were absurd and that the DoD lawyer who used that argument was being "deceptive." The argument that the program couldn't continue because of its infringement on the rights of US persons didn't pass Shaffer's smell test. He cited two exceptions to the US persons rule which existed within the regulation itself. It specifically allowed analysts to collect and retain the following information:

**2.** Publicly available information. Information may be collected about a United States person if it is publicly available.

**3(c).** Persons or organizations reasonably believed to be engaged or about to engage, in international terrorist or international narcotics activites.[17]

As mentioned previously, the data collected during Able Danger at that point was already publicly available. In targeting al-Qaeda, the program was going after individuals believed to be active terrorists.

Prior to being hassled by Army lawyers, the Able Danger team had been growing impatient with all the resistance it was getting from DIA, which didn't want to share the data with SOCOM. The hands of the Able Danger team had become increasingly tied at LIWA. Ultimately, this fact and the deletion of their data led to the decision by Gen. Schoomaker to move the operation to a Raytheon facility in Garland, TX.

Before the move, SOCOM came into the possession of a hard drive full of the data from DIA that the Able Danger team had requested. Though the act of getting the hard drive was difficult enough, when Shaffer's team received it, the data on the hard drive was scrambled, creating more work for those who were actually fighting to protect the United States.[18] This hard drive, which Shaffer pushed for and received – with the help of his deputy – proved invaluable because it included some classified information his team was able to incorporate with the

unclassified, open source data it would acquire at Garland, using the same techniques it employed at LIWA.

By July of 2000, Able Danger was being put back online at Garland. In October of that year, Able Danger identified a very real threat in the country of Yemen just days before the bombing of the USS Cole on October 12th.

At the House Armed Services Committee Hearing that would take place years later, the Congressman most knowledgeable about Able Danger – Rep. Curt Weldon – grilled fellow Republican Stephen Cambone, Defense Undersecretary for Intelligence, on many fronts. One of them included what Able Danger had uncovered about Yemen before the lives of 17 sailors were needlessly ended after their ship had docked for re-fueling:

> "...that naval officer... had three options on that day. He could have refueled the ship at sea. He had two other harbors. If he would have had any indication that there was a problem with Aden in Yemen, he would not have gone there. He was never given that information.
>
> We're playing with a man's career, and we're playing with the loss of 17 sailors' lives. Some of those families are out in the audience today."[19]

At the 2006 hearing, Cambone and several other officers admitted Able Danger had identified a problem in Aden but claimed it was not "actionable intelligence." The intelligence about Yemen prior to the Cole bombing was given to Central Command (CENTCOM) at the request of Gen. Schoomaker but was never given to Lt. Commander Kirk Lippold of the USS Cole. Was there a desire to cover this reality up and, if so, did that desire contribute to the demise of Able Danger? Why else would a program be ended as soon as there was proof it worked?

At about the time of the Cole attack, Gen. Schoomaker was in the process of retiring. His successor – Gen. Charles Holland – showed little, if any, interest in Able Danger according to Shaffer; the program was in the process of dying a slow death. Another superior officer Shaffer had to contend with was DIA Maj. Gen. Rod Isler. Shaffer writes that Isler ordered him to "cease all support" to Able Danger and that it wasn't his job to "chase terrorists."[20] Here is a relevant excerpt from Shaffer's written testimony:

Scott Phillpott calls me in desperation in the May 2001 timeframe on my mobile phone. He asked if he can bring "the ABLE DANGER options" that ABLE DANGER had come up with to DC and to use one of my STRATUS IVY facilities to do the work. I tell him with all candor that I would love nothing better than to loan him my facility and work the options with him (to exploit them for both Intel potential and for actual offensive operations) but tell him that my DIA chain of command has directed me to stop all support to him and the project.

In good faith, I ask my boss, COL Mary Moffitt if I can help Scott and exploit the options – and that there would be a DIA quid pro quo of obtaining new "lead" information from the project. She takes offense at me even mentioning ABLE DANGER in this conversation, tells me that I am being insubordinate, and begins the process of removing me from my position as chief of STRATUS IVY. As a direct result of this conversation, she directs that I be "moved" to a desk officer position to oversee Defense HUMINT operations in Latin America.[21]

Less than four months later, America was hit by Islamic terrorists whose ringleader had been identified and tracked by Shaffer's group. This public claim – that Atta had been identified – would become a significant bone of contention between DIA Brass and Shaffer. The showdown between one man and a powerful bureaucracy would eventually reveal that the DIA would be much less willing to assert its insistence that Atta was *never* discovered before 9/11 than Shaffer would be willing to insist he *had* been; it was a claim the Lt. Col. would not deviate from in the face of extreme intimidation.

Though he would eventually become the most outspoken, Shaffer wasn't the only member of his team who made the claim. Even the New York Times acknowledged that at least five people who worked on Able Danger insisted they had uncovered Atta before 9/11.[22] In both his testimony and in his book, Shaffer recounted how one of his Able Danger colleagues at LIWA – Dr. Eileen Preisser – showed him a chart after 9/11 that proved again, Atta had been discovered beforehand. The realization hit Shaffer that the chart he took to SOCOM in January of 2000 had contained a gun that the world saw smoking on 9/11 – but it had been destroyed before it could be analyzed.[23]

Signs of a coverup, in quite the literal sense, reared their heads before 9/11, while Able Danger was still being operated out of LIWA. As the SOCOM lawyers were wringing their hands over the issue regarding targets being US persons, Shaffer's team was told they could no longer process data on such individuals. The lawyers even extended this courtesy to non-US citizens who were legally inside the country on visas. In other words, the best way to escape detection was to literally walk right through the front door and apply for a visa at an American embassy overseas. On his next trip to SOCOM, Shaffer noticed that many of the people on the eye-popping chart he had taken with him to SOCOM before, suddenly had Post-it notes covering their faces; this included most of the photos of the Brooklyn cell. The lawyers were, in effect, protecting the 9/11 attackers from the Able Danger dragnet.[24]

Frustrated, Shaffer decided to approach the FBI. If his team was unable to track individuals he knew were connected to, or members of, al-Qaeda – simply because those individuals were in the country legally – perhaps the FBI could pick up where Able Danger left off. It's worth noting that Shaffer was willing to do what so many bureaucrats would not – share information. Unfortunately, he couldn't do it alone.

In his written testimony, Shaffer described three separate meetings he arranged between SOCOM and the FBI at which the information put together by his team, including what they had on Atta and three of the other hijackers, was to be communicated. All three of the meetings were cancelled by SOCOM lawyers who didn't want to get too close to something they viewed as having the potential of becoming politically radioactive. The FBI never gained access to the very actionable intelligence that Able Danger was no longer allowed to develop.[25] An appropriate allegory might be a relay race at the Olympics in which an American fan runs onto the track and intentionally disrupts the baton hand-off between two runners on his own country's team. Like Peter the disciple, SOCOM leaders denied the truth three times.

In 2009, an undercover FBI operative named Elie Assaad came forward and told *ABC News* that he met Mohamed Atta at a radical mosque in Florida in early 2001. Unfortunately, despite his suspicions about Atta, Assaad's superiors had told him to focus on other radicals instead, who they saw as easier targets. Imagine what could have happened if that undercover agent had the Able Danger intelligence at his disposal. Unfortunately, he did not, so we will never know.[26]

Perhaps most emblematic of the 'see no evil' mentality that can exist within a bureaucracy is what happened when Col. Shaffer attempted to brief the deputy chief of human intelligence at DIA about Able Danger in the context of another project known as DORHAWK GALLEY. The meeting took place after the Garland, TX data had been transferred to SOCOM in the fall of 2000.

During the Armed Services Committee hearing, Shaffer explained that when he began speaking to the Deputy Chief of HUMINT at DIA about issues related to the US person debate the SOCOM lawyers were intricately involved with, that Deputy Chief walked out of his own office while saying, "Oh, my God, I can't see this." Shortly after relaying that testimony in open session to the Committee, Shaffer admitted that he initially thought the man was joking.[27]

If not directly, that deputy's behavior was rewarded indirectly in the form of a promotion, while the entity responsible for promoting him attempted to simultaneously destroy Shaffer's career. The man who abruptly walked out of his own office – when he couldn't bear to listen to the truth that may have prevented 9/11 – was subsequently promoted to a new office, one that had 'Deputy Director of Defense Intelligence Agency' stenciled on the door; he was promoted to the *number two* position at DIA.

In the years subsequent to Able Danger, Shaffer would find himself fighting a domestic enemy he later identified in his written testimony as "the bureaucracy." It would be his second battle over Able Danger. Ironically, the opening salvo was fired in a briefing room at Bagram Airbase in 2003.

Unbeknownst to him, Shaffer had picked a fight simply by doing what he thought was right and his country would punish him for defending it.

## ■ COVERUP AND REPRISALS

9/11 Commission investigators, led by Executive Director Philip Zelikow, visited Bagram Airbase in October of 2003 and made themselves available to anyone with information that might help contribute to the final report. Shaffer got permission from his superior officer in Afghanistan to meet with Zelikow about Able Danger.

Zelikow, a Republican, was astonished by the information Shaffer provided to him and even gave Shaffer one of his business cards. As he handed it to him, Zelikow told Shaffer, "What you said today is very important," and he asked Shaffer to contact him upon returning to the United States.[28] Ostensibly, this meant that Zelikow wanted to include the details about Able Danger in the final 9/11 Commission report. For some reason, Zelikow's astonishment inexplicably gave way to disinterest soon thereafter.

As a friend and adviser to Condoleezza Rice of the National Security Council during the Presidential transition process in 2000 and 2001, Zelikow may have been directly involved in the decision not to prioritize terrorism or the al-Qaeda threat above other issues when the data mining program was shut down.[29] In fact, he claimed to have recused himself from parts of the 9/11 Commission investigation that dealt with the time he served on the Bush transition team.[30]

However, when he learned about Able Danger, which took place, in part, during that time frame, Zelikow asked Shaffer to contact him directly. The meeting in Bagram played a key role in exposing perhaps one of the biggest coverups in American history and Shaffer's ability to later produce that business card substantially bolstered his credibility; it would torpedo Zelikow's.

Something definitely happened between the time Shaffer was handed that card and when he attempted to contact the 9/11 Commission's lead guy. Upon doing the latter in early January of 2004, Shaffer was told by Zelikow's office that the Executive Director didn't need any more information about Able Danger.

This newfound indifference on the part of the Commission seemed to coincide with treatment of Shaffer that was completely unwarranted. In his written testimony, Shaffer explained how he was treated shortly after his attempts to contact Zelikow's office:

> Immediately after I notified the chain of command on my contact with the 9/11 commission, my life became strange. I was scrutinized and harassed on virtually every issue I had to deal with...I was threatened with disciplinary action if I did not show up every day in military uniform. In other words I was treated like a brand new recruit rather than a seasoned two decade professional who was preparing a team and himself for a deployment into a combat zone.[31]

Here was a man who had just returned home from a string of harrowing experiences in Afghanistan being punished for attempting to give a Commission – the sole purpose of which was to investigate what went wrong before 9/11 and how to prevent future breakdowns – information that should have been an integral part of its research. Shaffer had provided the Commission with a golden opportunity to meet and even exceed its stated goals. As the Executive Director, Zelikow punted and blamed Shaffer for the long snap.

In a case of shockingly palpable irony, the DIA bureaucracy attempted to strip Shaffer of one of his most prized medals, the Defense Meritorious Service Medal (DMSM); it had been awarded to him, in part, for his work on Stratus Ivy, which included his work on Able Danger.[32] Shaffer was also awarded the Bronze Star for his valor in Afghanistan in 2003 as an intelligence officer and since speaking with Zelikow at Bagram, the military had consistently questioned whether he deserved it.[33]

In 2005, when Rep. Curt Weldon told the American people the story of Able Danger for the first time, the 9/11 Commission responded that Able Danger wasn't "historically significant."[34] A powerful indictment of that assertion came courtesy of former FBI Director Louis Freeh, who wrote an editorial that appeared in the *Wall Street Journal* as the details of the Able Danger coverup were beginning to surface later in 2005. Freeh did not mince words when it came to his disdain for the 9/11 Commission's decision to exclude an investigation of Able Danger in the final report:

> The Able Danger intelligence, if confirmed, is undoubtedly the most relevant fact of the entire post-9/11 inquiry. Even the most junior investigator would immediately know that the name and photo ID of Atta in 2000 is precisely the kind of tactical intelligence the FBI has many times employed to prevent attacks and arrest terrorists. Yet the 9/11 Commission inexplicably concluded that it "was not historically significant." This astounding conclusion – in combination with the failure to investigate Able Danger and incorporate it into its findings – raises serious challenges to the Commission's credibility and, if the facts prove out, might just render the Commission historically insignificant itself.[35]

Freeh also referenced Navy Captain Scott Phillpott who, like Shaffer, was one of the people who worked on Able Danger and was adamant the team had identified Atta both by name and by photograph. The former FBI Director was familiar with the fact that Phillpott had briefed one of the 9/11 Commission's staffers before the final report was released.

A short time before his editorial appeared in the *Wall Street Journal*, Freeh appeared on *Meet The Press* with Tim Russert and informed viewers that if the FBI had been given access to Able Danger's findings, the 9/11 attacks may have been prevented.[36]

At this point, it's important to introduce Jamie Gorelick, Eliot Spitzer, and Dietrich Snell.

Shockingly, Gorelick was named as one of the 9/11 Commission members despite her very questionable handling of the Oklahoma City bombing investigation as Deputy Attorney General under president Bill Clinton [See Chapter 8]. Her name was also synonymous with the creation of the infamous wall of separation that prevented intelligence from being shared between the CIA and FBI.[37] If ever there existed a profile of someone whose actions contributed to the difficulties encountered by Shaffer when it came to setting up meetings between SOCOM and the FBI, Gorelick seemed to fit the bill, based on her implementation of policies that encouraged such behavior.[38] Choose any fox and henhouse metaphor you'd like – chances are none will come close to accurately describing how ill-advised the decision was to appoint Gorelick to the Commission. Then again, her presence may have been more symptomatic than causal when it came to the Commission's agenda and conclusions.

Before serving as the Governor of New York who would later resign in disgrace for his role in a prostitution ring, Democrat Eliot Spitzer was that state's Attorney General. He was serving in that capacity both before and after the 9/11 Commission report was released. One of the US Attorneys for New York who worked for Spitzer at the time was Dietrich Snell, who also served as a staffer for Gorelick in her capacity as a 9/11 Commission member.

Though Shaffer was the first member of Able Danger to approach the 9/11 Commission before its report had been released, he wasn't the only one. The other person to do so was Scott Phillpott, who went to Dietrich Snell in the latter's capacity as a staffer for Jamie Gorelick.[39] Rep. Weldon relayed what Phillpott testified to about that meeting with Snell:

> "In July of '04, a Navy Officer, Annapolis Grad (Phillpott), voluntarily goes in to de-brief the 9/11 Commission staff and he mentions that he will swear on his entire life career, that he identified Mohamed Atta in January of 2000 and that his team had a chart with Mohamed Atta's name on it and face on it but also that he saw that chart over and over again; it wasn't a 'one time' glance. And he also told Dietrich Snell that they tried to transfer that information to the FBI. This was Dietrich Snell's response: **'What do you want us to do with this information? We go to print in ten days.'**"[40]

During the House Armed Services Committee hearing, Weldon spoke of the Committee's efforts to get Dietrich Snell to testify about his meeting with Phillpott but New York Attorney General Eliot Spitzer prevented it.[41]

In Shaffer's testimony, he described an experience he had that was not all that dissimilar from the one Phillpott had with Snell. It occurred during his first meeting with Weldon, after the final 9/11 Commission Report had been released. Shaffer gave Weldon the same presentation he gave Zelikow at Bagram in 2003. Weldon then instructed his Chief of Staff, Russ Caso, to contact the Commission to find out why Able Danger was not mentioned at all in the final report. After speaking with Chris Kojm, the Deputy Executive Director under Zelikow, Caso came back and told both Weldon and Shaffer why there was no mention of Able Danger in the report. According to Kojm, "it did not fit with the story we wanted to tell."[42]

It was this response from Kojm that solidified Weldon's desire for an investigation into why Able Danger was ignored by the 9/11 Commission.

## ■ HERO INVESTIGATED

Shortly after returning home from Afghanistan in late 2003, Shaffer learned that the Inspector General's office of the DIA (DIA IG) was investigating him. The findings against him would ultimately be so petty that it was beyond obvious he had become the victim of a witch hunt. Shaffer was even told by a superior officer that the DIA was trying to find a way to rescind his Bronze Star.[43] All of this was taking place before Shaffer had even taken Zelikow up on the latter's request to be contacted upon Shaffer's return to the US. Shaffer was being punished simply for talking to Zelikow in the first place.

After finally being allowed to return to Afghanistan, Shaffer was contacted by a superior, albeit sympathetic officer who instructed him that some powerful, unnamed forces were going after Shaffer hard. When Shaffer objected to an alleged complaint that he'd been running "unsafe convoys," that superior officer confided in him that those forces were looking for anything they could to use against him.[44]

Once the DIA IG's findings were completed, arrangements were made to have Shaffer return from Afghanistan as quickly as possible. He was informed by a DIA Colonel that "three serious items" had been found. They were:

1. Undue award of the Defense Meritorious Service Medal
2. Misuse of a government phone totaling $67
3. Filing a false voucher in the amount of $180

Ultimately, Shaffer's Defense Meritorious Service Medal was not withdrawn. Ironically, he had earned it in the first place, for his work on Able Danger. Keeping the medal was a victory in itself because it implicitly meant the DIA conceded that Able Danger was an actual operation and that Shaffer had done an exceptional job in his capacity there.

As for the misuse of a government phone, it occurred over a period of 18 months, when Shaffer was the commanding officer of a DIA operating base. During that time, he occasionally had calls forwarded to his personal phone at a charge of $.25 each.

Lastly, the false voucher involved a required trip Shaffer took to an Army base for training he needed to complete in order to receive a promotion. He expensed the cost of the trip and the DIA argued he was not authorized to do so, despite the fact that they had approved his request for reimbursement at the time. To illustrate the absurdity of this charge, even if Shaffer hadn't expensed the trip, he would have been fully within his right to deduct it from his taxes.[45]

Before being dismissed, Shaffer was informed that his security clearance had been suspended; it would ultimately be permanently removed when he was fired by the DIA.

In a speech on the House floor, Rep. Weldon put this reality in perspective when he compared the treatment received by Shaffer with that of former National Security Adviser under President Bill Clinton, Sandy Berger.[46] Just prior to testifying before the 9/11 Commission, while reviewing records from the Clinton administration at the National Archives, Berger took classified documents, hiding some in his pants and socks; he successfully destroyed some of those documents.[47] Though Berger was guilty of felonious behavior, the punishment didn't fit the crime. In fact, his security clearance was merely suspended for three years.[48]

Conversely, the DIA went as far back into Shaffer's past as it could in order to justify permanently revoking his security clearance. To illustrate how clean Shaffer was and the lengths the DIA was willing to go to smear him, consider that they dredged up an admission made by Shaffer himself in 1987 as part of the process to get his clearance in the first place, which he ultimately received. Shaffer admitted that when he was fourteen years old, he took government pens from an American Embassy and shared them with his friends.[49] By pointing to this incident, the DIA was actually implicating itself for having issued the security clearance despite having this information when it did so. The DIA even went so far as to smear Shaffer for amassing $2000 in personal debt.[50]

Along those lines, after the DIA had suspended Shaffer's security clearance, the agency committed two laughably egregious acts relative to both that suspension and the charges the agency decided to levy against him. After suspending Shaffer's security clearance for offenses totaling approximately $300, the DIA sent Shaffer's attorney seven boxes. Ostensibly, they consisted of his personal items. According to a speech given by Weldon on the House floor, those boxes contained classified information as well as government property, to include a "multi-hundred dollar GPS system" and 25 government pens.[51]

Sandy Berger confessed to stealing and destroying classified documents from the National Archives prior to testifying in front of the 9/11 Commission and received a ridiculously light punishment. A man guilty of felonious behavior was given a virtual pass while a hero's career was given the death penalty for defending his nation.

It was reported in 2007 that the Vice Chairman of the 9/11 Commission, Democrat Lee Hamilton, accepted a position on the board of a company named Stonebridge International. This matters because Stonebridge was founded by none other than Sandy Berger, who was the company's chairman at the time of Hamilton's arrival.[52]

## DOD IG INVESTIGATION

In 2005, Congressman Weldon worked with fellow members of Congress to hold hearings on Able Danger. When Shaffer was called as a witness in February of 2006, the DIA tried to prevent him or any other witnesses from testifying. While most witnesses agreed not to, Shaffer refused to be silenced.

In his written testimony, Shaffer named names; he called out those individuals whom he viewed as being complicit when it came to either shutting down Able Danger or participating in its coverup. Shaffer identified such people as being more concerned about their careers than with defending their country. At the top of that list was the man who walked out of his own office when Shaffer attempted to brief him. That man's name was William Huntington and Shaffer alleged that Huntington directed two officers who were former members of HUMINT, to lie to Congress.[53]

This was huge. A Lt. Colonel, who was in the process of being railroaded, didn't back down in the face of a very powerful DIA machine, which had enough teeth to be used as the attack dog for both DoD and the White House. In essence, Shaffer formally accused the Deputy Director of Defense Intelligence Agency of being corrupt, more interested in career advancement and self-preservation than in truth and justice for his fellow countrymen. Rarely had this type of gauntlet been thrown down at this level, in the face of such a bureaucratic behemoth, on such a public stage.

Nearly two years before submitting this written testimony, Shaffer's security clearance had been suspended. Curiously, that suspension occurred shortly after he informed superiors within his chain of command that he'd had contact with the 9/11 Commission about Able Danger. That chain of command included Huntington.[54]

Bureaucracies are historically known for having powerful, nameless members. After Shaffer's testimony, the DIA's list of nameless members became noticeably shorter.

Within days of giving his testimony, DIA began the process of permanently revoking Shaffer's security clearance and firing him from the DIA. Incredibly, they claimed the timing of all this was just a coincidence and that it was not in retaliation for his Congressional testimony.

In Rep. Weldon's speech on the House floor in October of 2005, the Congressman announced that he had called for an independent investigation into the treatment of Lt. Col. Anthony Shaffer at the hands of DIA.[55] That investigation would be conducted by the IG at the DoD. Unfortunately, to say it was short on justice would be an understatement.

Typically, OIG investigators are careful to *portray* objectivity with varying degrees of nuance. As much as Inspectors General attempt to remain neutral, there is inherent pressure from the leadership of the offices within which IG's operate. This is one of the reasons that Inspectors General are to be protected by Congress from Executive Branch political interference. Consider the example of IG of the Corporation for National and Community Service, Gerald Walpin. When he went against the grain of the Obama administration in 2009 by insisting that abuses had taken place involving Obama ally and Sacramento Mayor, Kevin Johnson, he was fired.[56]

The DoD IG investigation into the reprisals of Lt. Col. Shaffer was emblematic of this tendency. The final report was long on denials and short on factual substance. The first sign of trouble was on the first page, with the introductory letter to Stephen Cambone, the Under-Secretary of Defense for Intelligence. The DoD IG reported directly to the same DoD official who Weldon had accused of a coverup, and the IG report was addressed to him (Cambone).[57]

Much of what readers were expected to believe was presented as conclusions to be taken on faith and without substantiation. The premise that readers were expected to accept was that the DoD IG was impartial. Once such a premise is rejected – or at least not accepted blindly – the report is rightfully questioned. The conclusions appear very biased, which is exactly why readers should not *assume* IG's are impartial; they work within very powerful agencies and *can* be compromised, Shaffer's treatment at the hands of the DIA notwithstanding.

For example, very early in the final report, four witnesses who were said to have identified Mohamed Atta prior to 9/11 were referenced and subsequently dismissed as having recollections that were "not accurate."[58] Attempts to bolster these claims consisted of vague generalities that did not serve to assuage IG skeptics in the least.

That leads to Major General (MG) Geoffrey C. Lambert. The OIG report identified him as someone who reported directly to Gen. Schoomaker "on issues related to Able Danger."[59] This admission immediately placed someone between the Able Danger team and the head of SOCOM. That may seem rather innocuous in the context of the OIG report but a book entitled *Horse Soldiers* identified Lambert as someone who confirmed Atta had been identified before 9/11:

"It had taken him (Lambert) about ten seconds to figure out who had masterminded the attacks, and who had carried them out. For the past several years, he had observed a top-secret intelligence program called data mining that had identified one man, an Egyptian by the name of Mohamed Atta, as a serious terrorist with links to a Saudi named bin Laden, who was a financier of terrorist training camps for men like the Egyptian. Months earlier, the people involved in the program had tried telling the FBI what they had discovered, but Army lawyers had discouraged the disclosure, even though the project had identified the hijackers. Lambert figured they knew everything there was to know about Osama bin Laden and his military training camps in Afghanistan, but none of the legal minds could decide if the surveillance was lawful. Now Lambert felt sick that more effort had not been made to warn someone. (Lambert, extremely upset, later agreed with lawyers that the information not be shared with the FBI.)"[60]

Lambert invoked comparisons to the prodigal son by admitting he was wrong; here's the irony. Those involved in either shutting down Able Danger or covering it up would have been welcomed as prodigal sons themselves, by those who knew of their guilt. Instead, the guilty doubled down on their own complicity by taking the painful truth out on the innocent. In many ways, it's the worst part of human nature – bearing false witness out of pride.

The IG report seemed to draw a line of demarcation between Able Danger team members who claimed they had seen Atta, and the superiors of those individuals. However, the report also painted Lambert as being in the camp of opposition to the claims of Shaffer, Phillpott, and Preisser; that fact makes the admission by Lambert very powerful indeed.

The IG report also misrepresented the recollections of the Chairman of the Joint Chiefs of Staff credited with directing SOCOM General Schoomaker to commence with the Able Danger program. The IG seized upon Gen. Hugh Shelton's inability to recall the name "Able Danger" while ignoring his admission – nearly a year before the report was released – that he authorized a data mining program to target al-Qaeda.[61] The *McClatchy News Service* posted an article detailing the results of its interview with Shelton in which the General made that clear:

> ...under his direction, Shelton said, Gen. Peter Schoomaker, now Army chief of staff, set up a team of five to seven intelligence officers after Shelton was promoted to chairman of the Joint Chiefs of Staff in 1997 and Schoomaker succeeded him as Special Operations commander.
>
> The program began at Special Operations headquarters at MacDill Air Force Base in Florida, Shelton said, but it was expanded later and moved to Fort Belvoir, VA, outside Washington. Schoomaker briefed Shelton on the program's progress in late 1997 when Shelton made a return visit to his old command post in Florida.[62]

Of course, Able Danger was indeed moved to Fort Belvoir; that is where LIWA was located. So why did the IG act like Shelton was not familiar with the program? Did they bother to ask him any detailed questions? This was an egregious omission by the IG and it demonstrates beyond a reasonable doubt that the IG was either complicit in or compromised by a coverup.

The IG report seemingly had a case against one of the charges made by Shaffer regarding the boxes DIA had sent back to him.

Shaffer opened the boxes in the presence of his attorneys and claimed that an expensive GPS system was among the items returned to him. This was relayed by Rep. Weldon during the speech in which he called for the investigation.[63]

The IG made the claim that the GPS system in question was issued to Shaffer while he was in Afghanistan and that it had never been returned to DIA, which meant they could not possibly have included it in one of the seven boxes of personal belongings they sent to Shaffer's attorney. In other words, their paperwork must be right and Shaffer must be lying as a result. Curt, at *Flopping Aces*, had this to say about the IG's claim:

> "While reading the report you cannot help but notice how much credibility they put on commanding officers while reducing the credibility of lower level officers. They basically call Shaffer a liar and cast his whole testimony in a bad light by suggesting he stole a GPS unit. They spend quite a bit of time on this incident, one in which it could easily have been a mix-up, either Shaffer forgot it was in his deployment bag (this one has happened to me personally while I was in the Marines) or some other kind of mix-up. But the time they spend on this incident smells to me. They cast all his testimony and memories away because of it."[64]

It's worth noting that the DoD IG did concede that a box which contained the GPS system was sent to Shaffer along with his "personal" belongings. It also conceded that the box did contain accessories and software for the GPS system in question. It is therefore easy to see how Shaffer may have assumed that the entire GPS system had been shipped to him, after emptying all of the boxes.[65] Since the DIA was interested in splitting hairs, it should be noted that the box itself, as well as the GPS accessories and software, was government property as well; the government parted with those items unjustifiably. Someone should be held accountable, using DIA standards, of course.

To underscore the point that too much attention was focused on attempting to discredit Shaffer, the IG report referred to the date of

October 12, 2000 as the date when the decision was made to announce the Able Danger program would be winding down, to dissolve completely two months later. Something else happened on that day – the bombing of the USS Cole. At best, the IG glossed over the fact that the plug on Able Danger was pulled at such a coincidental time. At worst, it was pulled so abruptly because of the warnings that preceded the bombing. The report did not rightfully acknowledge the warnings about Yemen, which originated with Able Danger and were passed up the chain but never given to the USS Cole commander, even when discussing the key issue of whether or not the Able Danger program had been shut down prematurely.[66]

Although the IG report made a mildly convincing case in some of the narrow issues it focused on, one of its pillars was torpedoed with a business card.

In the report, 9/11 Commission Executive Director Phillip Zelikow corroborated Shaffer's account in that the two met at Bagram but denied that Shaffer mentioned anything about having identified Mohamed Atta. In fact, Zelikow recollected that there was no way Shaffer could have identified Atta because nothing else would have "drowned it out."[67]

This account runs completely counter to Shaffer's claim that Zelikow handed him his business card after the presentation and instructed Shaffer to contact him upon Shaffer's return to the states. The reason given by Zelikow, according to Shaffer, was that the information he presented was too "important."[68]

Interestingly, further testimony cited by the IG involved the allegation that there was no way Shaffer could have mentioned Atta during the meeting with Zelikow at Bagram. The reason was that it would be too explosive and memorable. This brings us full circle if the premise that the DoD wanted to coverup Shaffer's claims carries weight. If Shaffer did mention Atta and the 9/11 Commission wanted to ignore it, wouldn't this be exactly how they would do so if Shaffer pressed the issue?

Is it too far-fetched to believe that the 9/11 Commission representatives would close ranks around Zelikow to defend their report's credibility? After all, he was having difficulty explaining why one of his business cards was in Tony Shaffer's possession.

Administrator of the Able Danger Blog, Mike Kasper, made an extremely salient observation regarding another gross discrepancy in the report. First, consider this from page 87 of the IG's report about an evaluation given to Shaffer by his boss, Captain Andersen:

> We considered CAPT Andersen's testimony that one factor in his overall assessment of LTC Shaffer was that he had exhibited poor judgment by failing to inform his superiors before he met with the 9/11 Commission staff (October 2003).[69]

Note the implication. By not informing his superior officers back at DIA of his intention to meet with the 9/11 Commission, Shaffer received a lower evaluation score. Despite overwhelming evidence that Shaffer did in fact notify his superior officers at Bagram, the IG report published this blatant contradiction to Andersen, just three pages later:

> DIA officials did not issue LTC Shaffer an unfavorable OER (Officer Evaluation Report) for his protected communications to the 9/11 Commission. The OER would have been issued absent those protected communications.[70]

Did you catch that? According to his boss, Shaffer exhibited "poor judgment" in approaching the 9/11 Commission but the DIA didn't issue an unfavorable review based on poor performance. If Andersen was right, the DIA was derelict. If the DIA was right, Andersen was out of line and should have been reprimanded.

Neither faced consequences. So much for Shaffer's "protected communications."

For the record, one thing the IG report conceded was that Shaffer did receive government pens in the boxes that were supposed to contain personal property only. This served as vindication for DIA's attempt to smear him over his confession years earlier that he had taken government pens as an adolescent.[71] Someone placed those pens in one of those boxes but no one lost their security clearance over it.

In short, the IG report was extremely biased and portrayed the image of a bureaucracy that was willing to go to extreme lengths to smear persons who threatened that bureaucracy. Those lengths included labeling patriotic Americans as liars. Conclusions of the report included a determination that Shaffer, Phillpott, Preisser, and others were all liars because neither Mohamed Atta, nor "any of the other 9/11 terrorists" had been identified by any of them prior to 9/11.[72]

Congressman Weldon requested the IG investigation in order to find out how we failed to prevent the greatest attack on American soil since Pearl Harbor. The IG's conclusion consisted of one, solitary sentence:

> "We recommend that the Director, DIA, review procedures concerning disposition of personal belongings when abandoned by DIA employees and procedures for rendering military performance reports to ensure that Service requirements are met."[73]

Those pens must have really gotten under DIA's skin.

## OIG REBUTTALS

Rep. Curt Weldon's staff adviser on national security issues was Peter Pry, who also happened to be a former CIA military analyst.[74] Two questions Pry raised after the release of the report had to do with both timing and methodology. The IG's report was released just a few weeks prior to the 2006 elections and was in the hands of the press before any member of Congress had the opportunity to review it. Pry rightfully underscored the fact that the subject matter of the report was "highly sensitive" and should have been presented to Congress first.[75]

With respect to the methodology used in the investigation, Pry puts the inherent conflict of interest best:

> After all, the DoD Office of the Inspector General is part of the Department of Defense and the careers of its personnel depend upon the Department. Common sense suggests that in some cases DoD may not be trustworthy to investigate itself.[76]

Pry then chronicles multiple examples in which the DoD IG compromised its investigations in order to appease its master. A discrepancy in the IG report highlighted by Pry involves the assertion that the IG could not find any evidence that Atta had been identified by Able Danger prior to 9/11. The report then concedes that any such evidence, had it existed, was destroyed on orders by the DoD.[77] If the evidence was gone, how could the IG draw a conclusion based on evidence it knew was missing? One way was to imply that anyone who claimed to have seen it was a liar, regardless of their credentials.

One of the would-be 9/11 hijackers was apprehended approximately one month before the attacks. Pry made the case that if Able Danger had been allowed to continue, many more dots could have been connected:

> Since the purpose of Able Danger was to discover al-Qaeda terrorists, the detection of Mohamed Atta and other 9/11 terrorists by Able Danger would, contrary to the Inspector General, have constituted the establishment of a possible link with al-Qaeda. The 9/11 Commission concluded that the discovery by the FBI of the least important of the 9/11 terrorists, Zacarias Moussaoui, about one month before 9/11, constituted the best opportunity to stop the airliner hijackings and attacks on New York and Washington of September 11, 2001. Surely, the discovery by Able Danger of the 9/11 ringleader, Mohamed Atta, about one year before 9/11, would have been an even better opportunity to prevent the September 11 catastrophe.[78]

In much the same way that the IG focused on Shaffer's GPS system, it also focused disproportionately on charts instead of on actionable intelligence. In its efforts to discredit Shaffer and others by constructing a narrative that painted the picture consisting of charts that didn't exist, the IG overlooked something more important – the data.

The IG report was so biased that while it attempted to discredit Shaffer, Phillpott, and Preisser, it completely ignored the backgrounds of each. Shaffer still possesses that Bronze Star; Phillpott was promoted after Able Danger to the level of a Destroyer commander, and Preisser is a double Ph.D.

One of the things the IG hung its hat on was the situation with the GPS unit. The report strongly asserted that the unit was not among the personal items it sent to Shaffer. Pry, on the other hand, reports that two attorneys were present when Shaffer opened the box that contained the GPS unit. The testimony of those two attorneys was not included in the final IG report.[79]

In essence, the IG report smeared good people; it clearly portrayed Shaffer, Phillpott, Preisser and others as liars. According to Pry, it was obvious that the witnesses were cross-examined by a prosecutor more than they were questioned by an investigator.

Rep. Weldon also released a statement on the IG report, saying:

> "Acting in a sickening bureaucratic manner, the DOD IG cherry-picked testimony from witnesses in an effort to mini-mize the historical importance of the Able Danger effort. The IG narrowly focused their investigation on the witnesses recol-lections of the 9/11 hijackers and a chart. The report trashes the reputations of military officers who had the courage to step forward and put their necks on the line to describe impor-tant work they were doing to track al-Qaeda prior to 9/11."[80]

Perhaps Weldon best illustrated the disparity between the amount of time the IG spent with Shaffer, Phillpott, Preisser, and others compared with how much time it spent with individuals on the other side. For example, Weldon stated:

> "The FBI agent that was tasked with setting up meetings between Able Danger and FBI officials – meetings that were block(ed) by DoD lawyers – was not interviewed in this report, yet it concluded that 'Able Danger members were not prohib-ited from sharing intelligence information with law enforce-ment authorities.'"[81]

While Able Danger whistleblowers like Shaffer, Phillpott, and Preisser were busy getting called in until the IG could make their minds right, an FBI agent who could have corroborated one of Shaffer's most disturbing claims, was avoided entirely.

The fact remains, if the IG report was correct, subordinates put their careers on suicide missions over a lie. It doesn't make sense. If those subordinates were being honest, the IG went to the mat in order to *protect* a lie that, if revealed, would destroy the careers of those who covered it up as well as those who defended it. *That* makes all the sense in the world.

After firing off his stinging rejection of the OIG report, Weldon would soon find himself in dire electoral straits just a few short weeks later; he was in the middle of a hotly contested reelection campaign when the FBI raided his daughter's home. No charges were filed and all of Karen Weldon's property was returned. Weldon lost that reelection bid to Democrat Joe Sestak, who would be at the center of controversy himself, just a few short years later when he confessed that the Obama administration offered him a job to drop out of his Senatorial primary race with Arlen Specter.[82]

If not for the efforts of Rep. Curt Weldon, Shaffer may have been completely destroyed. Weldon stood tall *for* him and stood toe to toe *with* the power structure in Washington. Weldon's vociferous appetite for the truth angered the establishment and eventually led to a raid on his daughter's home two weeks prior to Election Day in 2006. That raid was enough to create the *perception* that Weldon had done something wrong. It was the perfect "October surprise" for his political opponent. In reality, no one in authority ever spoke to Weldon's daughter and all of her belongings were returned to her. News cameras covered the raid but not the return of what was taken.

Weldon lost reelection – he insists – because of that raid.[83] In a phone conversation with the former Congressman, he explained to me that there was a vested interest in his defeat as the political power structure did not want to see him with subpoena power.[84] Weldon was one of the few Congressmen who put his country first in this case. Shaffer benefited greatly from his patriotism and readily admits as much. He still lost his top level security clearance and career at DIA.

However, he kept his position in the Army reserve, in part, thanks to Congressman Chris Shays (R-CT), who also lost reelection after helping Shaffer regain his basic security clearance and keep his post in the Army, where he had never had clearance issues.[85]

A few short years earlier, there was a raid that *didn't* happen in Pakistan, despite Shaffer's insistence that it should.

## ■ THE EXPENSE OF VINDICATION

In hindsight, much of what Lt. Co. Anthony Shaffer dealt with in Afghanistan was a foreshadowing of the battle he would have with DIA at home. While at Bagram Airbase in 2003, it didn't take Shaffer long to understand that no matter what US forces did in Afghanistan, al-Qaeda had an unfair advantage because Pakistan was off-limits to American troops. As long as the American dog was on a leash, the al-Qaeda cat could taunt it; Shaffer knew this and grew increasingly frustrated with that reality. The passage of time would prove the Bronze Star winner right in a big way.

At one point, he was briefed on what became known as the "al-Qaeda Hotel." It was a base in Wana, Pakistan that served as a command post for the enemy. Shaffer's challenge was to figure out a way to identify and go after High Value Targets (HVT); he would have to overcome the American bureaucracy and its lifeblood of insanity.[86]

Shaffer wanted to go on offense by going into Pakistan.

After drafting a plan and presenting it to the Commander of the US and coalition forces in Afghanistan, Lt. Gen. John Vines, Shaffer was ecstatic upon hearing Vines' reaction; it was one of approval. In fact, Vines stated that one of the reasons he was so pleased with Shaffer's plan relative to the al-Qaeda Hotel was the extent of its integration – a refreshing change.[87]

It was a change that didn't last.

Gen. Vines was relieved of his duty after an unexpected medical condition. He was replaced by General David Barno. Shaffer explained that the reaction he got from Barno was exactly opposite from that of Vines. Barno didn't want to go into Pakistan at all. His inexplicable intransigence baffled Shaffer, who attempted to explain to Barno that Pakistan's intelligence was actually supporting al-Qaeda.[88]

According to Shaffer's firsthand account, Barno's reaction consisted of the words, "I don't care," but that wasn't all. The General's directive to Shaffer was to "give the Pakistanis the intelligence."[89]

Shaffer explained his demoralized state thusly:

> "In some ways, I felt like I did after the September 11 attacks. Through Able Danger, my team and I had done everything in our power to prevent a disaster, but others had made bad decisions that resulted in our failure to help prevent those attacks."[90]

It was like good cop vs. bad cop, Jekyl and Hyde, or the two faces of Zelikow. There was the Zelikow with a sense of urgency, who handed Shaffer his business card, and there was the one who refused to meet with Shaffer afterward. The same phenomenon almost seemed to manifest itself in the form of Vines and Barno respectively.

Despite being told by Barno to pass on his intelligence information about Wana and the "al-Qaeda Hotel" to Pakistan, Shaffer didn't do it. He speculated that this also contributed to the increased pressure that was applied to him by the DIA and suspected that either Barno or his staff had something to do with giving that information to Pakistani Intelligence.[91]

## BIN LADEN KILLED

On May 1, 2011 the world received news that al-Qaeda's leader, Osama bin Laden had been killed by Navy SEALS who covertly raided bin Laden's compound without the knowledge of the Pakistani government. As details emerged, it became known that bin Laden's compound, where the al-Qaeda leader had been living for years, was a very short distance from the Kakul Military Academy, where Pakistani army officers were trained.[92]

The circumstances of bin Laden's assassination vindicated Shaffer in two respects. First, Shaffer had insisted, for years, that the best way to target al-Qaeda leaders was to cross into Pakistan; this is ultimately how bin Laden was killed. Second, the proximity of bin Laden's compound to an official Pakistani military academy carried with it nearly unimpeachable evidence that the Pakistani government was supporting al-Qaeda leadership at worst, and allowing it to operate under its nose, at best.

Given those facts, the claims of Shaffer in an article that appeared in *Playboy* after the release of his book in 2010 certainly carry added weight. For example, Shaffer strongly suggested that had Gen. Barno given him the green light to carry through with Operation Dark Heart, al-Qaeda's number two, Ayman al-Zawahiri could have been a casualty long before bin Laden was and that the operation could have "broken the back of al-Qaeda." Shaffer had reported that Pakistani Intelligence was working with al-Qaeda, which is why he was so shocked that Barno had, for all intents and purposes, instructed him to pass his intelligence on to the enemy. The author of the *Playboy* article, Peter Lance, attempted to get a comment from Barno but the General never responded.[93]

Did the killing of Osama bin Laden shine the light on a microcosm of a much larger problem? If Barno was too ashamed to be interviewed, is it too much of a leap to consider that the DIA would have been too ashamed to admit that the 9/11 terror attacks could have been prevented?

Perhaps the only path to victory for America will be revealed when its own bureaucratic leaders and establishments come clean. Otherwise, those entities will continue to fight, tooth and nail, men like Shaffer, instead of the enemies they swore an oath to protect their country from.

Those enemies are only made stronger by our own corruption.

## ANWAR AL-AWLAKI

While many will argue that Able Danger could have prevented the 9/11 attacks, few will believe that an al-Qaeda leader was invited to dine at the Department of Defense *after* those attacks took place. Allow that to sink in. American patriot, Lt. Col. Anthony Shaffer had his security clearance taken away because he embarrassed DIA Brass while defending his nation. Yet, Anwar al-Awlaki was invited to a DoD luncheon to speak *after* September 11, 2001.

In the days after the September 11th attacks, al-Awlaki was interviewed by the FBI at least four times because of his relationship with three of the 9/11 hijackers – Nawaf al-Hazmi, Khalid al-Mihdhar, and Hani Hanjour. Yet, just a few short months later, al-Awlaki was invited to attend a DoD luncheon because the secretary of the Army "was eager to have a presentation from a moderate Muslim."[94] At the time of this luncheon, the Secretary of the Army was George W. Bush appointee, Thomas E. White, Jr.[95]

After Jihadist Nidal Malik Hasan murdered 14 people and injured 32 at the Fort Hood, TX Army post on November 5, 2009, al-Awlaki soon found himself at the top of the CIA's kill or capture list because of his correspondence with Hasan as well as his connections to the Christmas Day bomber Umar Farouk Abdulmutallab and the would-be Times Square bomber Faisal Shahzad.[96]

Despite this very predictable future reality, the arrogant culture of denial at the Pentagon that led to Awlaki's lunch date was off the charts. According to a former high-ranking FBI agent, the DoD bristled at any attempt to vet people who were invited for political reasons that were not to be questioned.[97]

Anwar al-Awlaki was born in New Mexico, an American citizen. In 2002, an arrest warrant was issued for him on charges related to passport fraud, according to the *Denver Post*. After being detained briefly at JFK airport, al-Awlaki was released when it was learned that the warrant had been withdrawn. In a case of tragic irony, al-Awlaki eventually returned to the place he called home – Yemen. It was the same place where the USS Cole had been attacked.[98]

As the Fort Hood shooter's case dragged on, Hasan's attorney John Galligan grew increasingly frustrated with the lack of evidence provided in discovery. In particular, there were allegedly at least 18 e-mails between Hasan and al-Awlaki before the shooting. Well more than one year after the shooting, the DoD had not provided Galligan with more than 9 of them. In addition to the absence of these emails, there was also a White House intelligence report on the shootings that had been withheld from Galligan. Army lawyers refused to allow Galligan to see the documents.[99]

Two days after it was reported that Galligan still had not received proper security clearances for the case after more than 20 months, he was no longer Hasan's attorney. Though no official reason was given for Galligan's departure, it was no secret that he was very frustrated with DoD's intransigence when it came to releasing information.[100]

Shortly after Osama bin Laden's killing, *Fox News* released newly discovered details about the luncheon al-Awlaki attended at the DoD. National correspondent Catherine Herridge reported that courtesy of a Freedom of Information Act (FOIA) request, *Fox* came into possession of an email that originated with the Defense Department's Office of General Counsel (DoD OGC).[101]

That e-mail was essentially an announcement of al-Awlaki's scheduled appearance as well as an invitation to more than 70 people who were copied. Most, if not all of those copied, were members of the DoD OGC. The vast majority of the names were redacted, including that of the woman from whom the e-mail originated (**Appendix A**).

In addition to boasting about how Council on American Islamic Relations (CAIR) president Nihad Awad had expressed interest in showing up at the luncheon, the author was more than willing to sing al-Awlaki's praises a mere two months after 9/11, in the e-mail that was essentially broadcast throughout the DoD OGC. Here is an excerpt:

> "I had the privilege of hearing one of Mr. Awlaki's presen-
> tations in November and was impressed both by the extent of
> his knowledge and by how he communicated that informa-
> tion and handled a hostile element in the audience. I particu-
> larly liked how he addressed how the average Middle Eastern
> person perceives the United States and his views on the inter-
> national media."[102]

In hindsight, the "hostile element" in the audience, demonized by the woman who penned the e-mail, deserves an apology from her. In many ways, this too is a microcosm of a much larger problem. Shaffer was demonized by forces within the DoD who seemed more interested in running interference for either those who would do us harm or powerful individuals who could not afford the exposure.

The author of the e-mail also referred to al-Awlaki as the Imam at the Dar Al-Hijrah "Church" (mosque) while touting his credentials. This is significant because that mosque was operating as a front for Hamas operatives, according to the Investigative Project on Terrorism (IPT).[103]

In this case, the DoD was caught red-handed. As al-Awlaki's reputation grew more and more notorious after the Fort Hood shootings, he caused the DoD more and more embarrassment. This embarrassment had a cascading effect as well. It wasn't just the DoD that had been willfully duped.

Less than two years after Hasan's jihadist attack on Fort Hood, Pfc. Nasser Abdo plotted a follow-up attack there. If not for the vigilance of a local gun store owner in Killeen, TX, Abdo may have been successful in detonating a bomb at a restaurant before shooting patrons as they fled; that was his plan.[104]

In 2010, Abdo had filed for conscientious objector (CO) status because, as a Muslim, he said he could not fight fellow Muslims in good faith. Two anti-war groups – Courage to Resist and Iraq Veterans Against the War (IVAW) – supported Abdo in this regard. Prior to his arrest, Abdo had gone AWOL from Fort Campbell, KY after being charged with possession of child pornography.[105]

Obviously embarrassed, Courage to Resist scrubbed the page on Abdo's conscientious objector fight from its website. In many ways, Courage to Resist and IVAW shared something in common with DoD OGC; the desire to wish one reality into existence was snuffed out by the reality that *did* exist.

These entities shared something else in common – Anwar al-Awlaki. *ABC News* reported that Abdo mentioned him upon his arrest and then shouted Nidal Malik Hasan's name as he was being led out of the courtroom after being charged.[106]

Al-Awlaki duped the DoD and less than ten years later, he had managed to get his protégés to dupe others.

If al-Awlaki was able to do all of this, what kind of embarrassment would the disregard of Mohamed Atta, the ring leader of the 9/11 attacks, which killed 3,000 and took down the World Trade Center, have caused?

The extent to which the DoD was willing to go in order to destroy Lt. Col. Anthony Shaffer more than answers that question. In 2011, al-Awlaki was killed in Yemen when his convoy was hit with Hellfire missiles launched from two Predator drones in a CIA-led operation.

During a radio interview in the spring of 2012, Shaffer made a bold claim about why al-Awlaki was killed:

> "Anwar al-Awlaki had a documented relationship with the US Government and the Federal Bureau of Investigation...before 9/11...they were covering their tracks."[107]

A few days later, *Fox News'* Catherine Herridge wrote that FBI Director Robert Mueller was having to answer questions from Congress about why the FBI allowed al-Awlaki to be set free in 2002 upon re-entering the US. At the end of her report, Herridge cited former FBI agents who asserted there were only two reasons why FBI agents would do this. One of those reasons involved al-Awlaki working with the FBI as an informant or "friendly contact."[108]

## ◼ DIA CENSORSHIP

In 2010, as the first printed copies of Shaffer's book were being prepared for shipment, the DIA – along with the Department of Defense – ordered that the shipments be halted; it wanted significant portions of the book redacted. Despite a security review of Shaffer's book by the Department of the Army, which approved the completed version, some very powerful people saw things differently. Shaffer maintains that DIA was following directives from the White House. If true, this meant that the Obama administration was behind the attempt to censor Operation Dark Heart.

The DIA expressed a concern for national security if Shaffer's book was released but some of what the agency wanted removed sounded like a case of 'thou doth protest too much.' DIA did not want Operation Dark Heart to include details of Shaffer's meeting with Zelikow at Bagram, nor the assertion that Able Danger had identified Mohamed Atta long before 9/11 but how could it be classified, if their claim was that it wasn't true? There was no record of Able Danger included in the final 9/11 Commission Report and DIA didn't want Shaffer's account about presenting it to the Commission's Executive Director appearing in his book.[109]

Not only did Shaffer's published version eventually include both of these things but he came out swinging on page 2 against the forces responsible for all the book's redacted pages:

> ...the United States squandered the momentum it had after defeating the Taliban in Afghanistan after the September 11 attacks. Official timidity, bureaucratic foot-dragging, over-analysis – I saw it leading up to the September 11 attacks, I saw it in Afghanistan while I served there, and I still see it today.[110]

The collision course Shaffer was on with DIA brass had been set in motion years before his work on Able Danger, when HUMINT was absorbed by the bureaucracy. The collision itself took place years after his work on Able Danger. Neither DIA brass nor Shaffer knew what the other was in for.

Though the words "able" and "danger" would appear multiple times in the 585-page 9/11 Commission report, not once would they appear consecutively, as the name of a program that could have prevented the Act of War perpetrated against the United States on September 11, 2001.[111]

## ◼ BATTLE ASSESSMENT

Perhaps the greatest vindication for Lt. Col. Anthony Shaffer regarding his insistence that the US needed to target terrorists in Pakistan came just a few short months after the killing of Osama bin Laden. While speaking in front of the Senate Armed Services Committee, chairman of the Joint Chiefs of Staff Admiral Michael Mullen expressed exactly what Shaffer attempted to convince Gen. Barno of nearly a decade earlier; Pakistani Intelligence (ISI) was collaborating with terrorist networks. In particular, Mullen singled out the Haqqani network, a terrorist group that had been implicated in attacks on Americans in the region:

"The Haqqani network...acts as a veritable arm of Pakistan's Inter-Services Intelligence Agency."[112]

In essence, the highest ranking military officer in the United States Armed Forces told the world that the view held by Shaffer eight years earlier was correct. It was most certainly a powerful and welcome acknowledgment.

Those who serve in the US Military are prepared to make the ultimate sacrifice for their nation. Shaffer demonstrated countless times that he was willing to go to those lengths. He put himself in increased danger constantly and willingly, not because he had to but because he wanted to show that he wasn't one of those aloof DIA guys who looked down on combat soldiers. His love of country included a desire to find a way to break down the walls that separated him from others who felt the same way.

It paid off because it was *that* mentality that played a key role in Shaffer being awarded the Bronze Star. In many ways, that award would eventually be a source of strength for him; it served as a shield against the evil bureaucracy he would ultimately face; it was a shield that bureaucracy attempted to usurp. The attempt was made for a reason; the Bronze Star carried weight and power. In an unforeseen way, Shaffer was given that power because he decided to humble himself in order to serve alongside those who assumed he wouldn't do so.

Though Shaffer demonstrated that he was willing to make the ultimate sacrifice, history has proven that he was willing to do the next most selfless thing as well; he was willing to sacrifice his entire career in defense of his nation.

Most everyone knows what the right path is but few ever take it, not because they don't want to but because pressure forces them to abandon it. Lt. Col. Anthony Shaffer didn't have that problem. He sacrificed his career for his country. He went down swinging and stands tall when telling his story, while bureaucrats hide behind redactions that reveal their cowardice.

There is no telling how far up the ladder Shaffer could have climbed professionally. He possessed a Bronze Star and the Defense

Meritorious Service Medal, both of which are highly prestigious awards and the DIA attempted to rescind them both. Had he made the decision not to talk to Zelikow and play the game, Shaffer could conceivably hold a much higher rank today but he would have been compromised goods; he would have achieved such a position by staying quiet when circumstances demanded shouting. That reality doesn't bode well for the current crop. For insisting that the truth be told, Shaffer was punished by those who wanted it silenced.

What was their motivation for doing so? Was it because Shaffer was blowing the cover on further covert activity? If so, why wasn't he brought into the loop and given the facts? Was it because the notion of self-preservation he eschewed was given more value by those who smeared him? If so, why weren't there systems in place to promote Shaffer above such people?

Shaffer has the right to sleep well at night and should do so. Conversely, those complicit in the campaign to smear him channeled the spirit of Judas Iscariot and Benedict Arnold. The former betrayed the truth and the latter betrayed his nation.

Like others in this book, Shaffer may not have delivered the fatal blow to Goliath but he landed a significant blow nonetheless. It is so much more than so many others can claim. Shaffer willingly put his career on the firing line; he watched its execution from a front row seat. There are people whose careers were dealt mighty blows, not because their superiors held them accountable but because a politically wounded man named Lt. Col. Anthony Shaffer did so by telling the world their names as his career took its final breaths.

The ultimate sacrifice Shaffer was *willing* to make physically *was* made politically but at great expense to those who pulled the trigger.

# CHAPTER 10

## WALID SHOEBAT
### vs.
# ISLAMIC FUNDAMENTALISM

### ■ FEMALE CATALYSTS

Prior to 1993, Walid Shoebat was an enemy of the United States. After that, he became one of her patriots. Though he was the son of an American mother who was a devout Christian, his father was an anti-Semitic Arab Muslim. When one examines his family history, the odds of such a pairing are made even longer by the affiliations of his ancestors, who had personal relationships with Adolf Hitler's favorite Arab and Sir Winston Churchill respectively.

His is a story not only of love conquering hate but of the catalytic nature women possess when it comes to the success of the men in their lives. Walid's mother sowed the seeds of his conversion from Islam to Christianity, despite being held captive in a Bethlehem village against her will by her Muslim husband, Walid's father. She prayed secretly and sought opportunities to subtly introduce her son to Christianity at great risk to her physical well being. She would unwittingly be the catalyst for the amount of openness he would have to his wife's spiritual influence years later.

Not only did Shoebat's wife Maria play the critical role in his conversion but she too was a catalyst. After unwittingly taking the baton from her mother-in-law, she sowed the seeds of her husband's drive to convert as many people as he could to Christianity. Ironically, the attempt by Walid's father to use a Christian woman to give him Muslim sons would backfire in a major way.

One of those sons was born with the ability to debate ever so sharply his points; he could speak Arabic as well as English and would become an uncompromising Christian who would one day open eyes and change hearts on a massive scale.

## ■ DICHOTOMOUS HERITAGE

Shoebat's fraternal grandfather was the chieftain of the family's village, Beit Sahour-Bethlehem. As such, during World War II, Daud Shoebat welcomed a man named Haj Amin al-Husseini to his village on occasion. The relevance of al-Husseini cannot be understated; as the Grand Mufti of Jerusalem, he was allied with the Nazi leader. In fact, on November 28, 1941 a meeting took place between Hitler and the Grand Mufti. The minutes clearly demonstrate that al-Husseini was eager to formally and publicly align with Nazi Germany. While Hitler welcomed the invitation, he wanted to wait until Germany conquered Russia before making the alliance official and public.[1]

The history books have been written. Germany did not conquer Russia and the foundation for clear lines of distinction being drawn between Muslims and Nazis had been laid. The truth is that the old saying about the 'enemy of my enemy is my friend' could not have been better exemplified than it was between the Arab Muslims and the German Nazis in World War II. Both viewed the Jews as their common enemy **[See Chapter 8, p. 233]**.

The face of the Nazi/Islamic enemy in World War II belonged to Sir Winston Churchill. Amazingly, Walid Shoebat had a familial connection to him as well. There is documented evidence of a friendship between Churchill and Shoebat's maternal Great Grandfather, F.W. Georgeson. Once the mayor of Eureka, California in Humboldt County, Georgeson welcomed many famous personalities to his city. In 1929 Georgeson was the editor of *The Humboldt Standard* newspaper, which reported on September 9th of that year that Churchill was welcomed to the Eureka Inn by Georgeson himself.[2] Years later, the *Humboldt Times-Standard* reported that Churchill included Eureka on his family trip specifically so he could meet with his "old friend, Frederick Georgeson."[3] **(Appendix A)**

While Shoebat's heritage is certainly dichotomous, so too was the life he would lead. After being indoctrinated into a Muslim culture which consisted of passionate Jew hatred, he would become a terrorist in the 1970s. He was recruited by a man named Mahmoud Al-Mughrabi, who was a bomb maker in Yasser Arafat's Fatah. Shoebat was to take a bomb hidden in a loaf of bread and detonate it in front of Bethlehem's Bank Leumi in 1976. He has consistently maintained that he threw the bomb on the roof at the last minute after fearing for the safety of some Palestinian children he saw nearby.[4]

On another occasion – before departing for the United States in 1978 – Shoebat tells of an attempt to lynch a Jewish soldier in which the IDF member had been isolated by a mob of angry Palestinians – that included Shoebat – on what is known as 'Land Day,' which would have been in March. The soldier, according to Shoebat, attempted to apprehend a Palestinian who had hit him with a stone. Instead, the group captured the soldier and nearly bludgeoned him to death before he escaped. Shoebat openly admits to participating in that beating.[5]

After already having served some time in a Russian Moscovite prison in Jerusalem for civil unrest, Shoebat was eager to leave and moved to the United States in the summer of 1978. After living in California, he moved to Chicago. It was during his time there that he hit his lowest point. In a figurative sense it involved a stint with an Imam named Jamal Said. In a literal sense, it involved the basement where he resided on the south side of Chicago; the rats were huge. He would serve as a recruiter for the PLO and Muslim Brotherhood, assuming a role similar to that of terrorist Mahmoud Al-Mughrabi, who recruited him to commit the Bank Leumi bombing. During his time in Chicago, Shoebat sought to recruit volunteers to fight in Lebanon.[6]

There was a great uncle on his mother's side who perhaps foreshadowed a completely different life that was about to open up for him. His name was Pete and he convinced Walid to move out of that basement and stay with him. Despite the Christian home he was now living in, Shoebat was still a committed Muslim.

That would change when he moved back to California, where he would meet his future wife Maria, a Catholic. The two were married in 1991 much to the chagrin of Maria's family; to say they had reservations about their daughter marrying a Muslim would be an understatement. Unbeknownst to them, Walid's transformation may have already been taking place.

In 2010, Shoebat spoke at Six Flags in New Jersey; he told the audience about when he discovered critical thinking. Though he had conveyed the story countless times before, he seemed to steal the show on this occasion. He relayed a story of his trip to Israel in 1991:

My uncle took me all over the streets. All over the walls, graffiti. What did the graffiti say? The most common graffiti on the walls…"We knock on the gates of heaven with skulls of Jews." That's Nazism!

I said, "What is this?" He said, "You're asking too many questions."

I said there has to be a different way to go to heaven besides knocking on the gates with skulls of Jews…I got criticized by my own family for asking too many questions. They asked me, 'Why are you asking too many questions?' I said 'I have over ten years in America and America has something you don't have – Critical thinking!

Critical thinking!'[7]

In 1993, after two years of marriage, Shoebat rejected his life of terror upon reading the Bible; it was a challenge his wife Maria put to him. No doubt, his discovery of critical thinking opened the door relative to his willingness to take her bet. He did just that and they both won. Maria had saved her husband and her husband would soon minister to a multitude of souls with a brand of speaking that would leave his audiences wanting more, regardless of duration. When it came to energizing a crowd, Walid Shoebat would soon become the equivalent of Bruce Springsteen, with one exception – Shoebat wasn't a liberal. Speaking of liberals, Shoebat would soon learn that in addition to fighting Islamic fundamentalism, he would also have to overcome a powerful western media sympathetic to the Islamic cause.

One of the first things he would do after realizing he had been brainwashed was to save his mother, who was still living in Beit Sahour-Bethlehem. Shoebat's mother, a Christian, married his Muslim father in 1960 after meeting him in Humboldt, California. Shortly thereafter, she was taken on a trip to the Middle East for what she thought would be a short visit to her husband's homeland. At the time of Shoebat's conversion to Christianity in 1993, she was still there, held against her will.

After his conversion, Shoebat was compelled to save his mother from slavery. The weight of what he had done to her coupled with what, in hindsight, he realized she had done *for* him by planting Biblical seeds whenever she had the rare opportunity to do so, *drove* him. His efforts paid off when his mother landed in San Francisco in 1994.

Shoebat had tapped into the Churchillian side of his family and would not look back except to warn others.

## ■ THE CONTROVERSIAL TRUTH

Speaking of Churchill, an extremely salient quote is attributed to him that seems almost tailor-made for Shoebat's story; *"A lie gets halfway around the world before the truth has a chance to get its pants on."*[8] The latter would discover soon enough that truer words had never been spoken.

It would be more than ten years after his conversion to Christianity that Shoebat would start reaching vast numbers of people with his message via cable and broadcast air waves as well as through speaking engagements.

In the summer of 2003, Shoebat did a radio interview on the *Tovia Singer* show after appearing on the *Michael Savage* show as a caller who was afforded more time than most receive. The Singer interview was heard by the man who would one day manage Shoebat's publicity – Keith Davies. Upon hearing that interview, Davies was compelled to reach out to Walid. From that point forward, the former Muslim terrorist would begin reaching much larger audiences.

Davies, an Irish Jew whose great-grandparents immigrated to Ireland from Russia in order to escape persecution, moved to the United States in the early 1990s. As an interesting aside, Davies claims to have a familial connection to the man who slew Goliath with God's help, by tracing his roots back to the founder of Hasidic Judaism, Baal Shem Tov whose ancestry, Davies says, has been traced back to the Biblical King David.

Almost immediately after getting in touch with Shoebat, Davies began doing whatever he could to get him heard. The next big radio interview took place on the *Janet Parshall* show. The inertia was no longer at rest. Shoebat's first book – *Why I Left Jihad* – was in the works and would later be released in 2005.

Shoebat's strength is that he possesses a unique ability to use very few words when cutting through lies and hypocrisy. In *Why I Left Jihad* he makes the point that when he was a terrorist who sought the eradication of the Jews, he was identified as a "freedom fighter." It wasn't until he began loving the Jews that he was labeled a "racist" by many of the same people.[9]

At the essence of why his message is so controversial is how it is delivered. Sporting an uncanny knack for communicating with allegories and humor, he entraps his adversaries with arguments that are irrefutable.

For example, in his speeches, Shoebat often relays a trip he made to Great Britain in 2005 for an interview with the *BBC*. He tells the story thusly:

> "They had these three 'so-called' scholars who wanted to rebut what I was talking about... Typical of the liberal media, the first interviewer says, 'Mr. Shoebat, it always takes two to tango.' I said, 'no sir, that's another myth. It does not take two to tango. There's usually a rapist and there's a rape victim. What did the victim do to tango? If it takes always two to tango, tell me, what did the Jews do to tango in Nazi Germany, sir?' So the second person said, 'They must have done something.' I said, 'Tell the English people what did the Jews do to

tango in Nazi Germany." He realized he just shoved his own shoe in his mouth."[10]

Shoebat's ability to expose lies and cowardice – which serve as the foundation for political correctness – is controversial but his insistence that the similarities between Nazism and Islam are beyond coincidental, most assuredly provide additional fuel for the fire.

## OBSESSION

In 2006, a controversial documentary film about Islam was released entitled, *Obsession: Radical Islam's War Against the West*. There were stark comparisons drawn between Nazi Germany and the rise of militant Islam. Shoebat was one of the featured speakers in the film and in many ways, spoke with the most authority because, after all, it was his grandfather who was friends with Hitler's favorite Arab, Haj Amin al-Husseini.

At a point in the film when the meaning of 'Jihad' is discussed, Shoebat said the following:

"Yes, Jihad does mean 'self-struggle,' 'struggle within' but so does 'Mein Kampf.' Mein Kampf means 'my struggle' but what struggle? Nazism had a struggle with what?"

As the rhetorical question hangs in the air, Shoebat delivers another blow to those he claims refuse to admit the truth.

"I watched anti-semitism since I was a young kid and now the world is reaping, these eggs are hatching and what's coming out is literally something that comes out of Nazi Germany."[11]

One of the perks of being a radio talk show host is having the ability to interview people like Shoebat. I first did so in 2007.

He had just released his second book, *Why We Want to Kill You: The Jihadist Mindset and How to Defeat it*. It is a roadmap for those who want to know how America's enemies think. Yet, major media appearances seemed to be drying up for him. There was a sense that people wanted to hear his personal testimony but not the sound of the alarm bell he was ringing.

The debate about Islam then was somewhat different than it is today. People were more careful about how things were phrased when it came to Islam. There was more concern then that alienating 'moderate' Muslims would be counter-productive in the 'War on Terror.' I asked Shoebat about this concern and this is how he responded:

"If you look at Nazism when it began to rise, there was a few Oscar Schindlers and some righteous Germans. I guess this argument would say, 'the way to defeat Hitler and Nazism is to kind of bank on the Oscar Schindlers of the world.' The Oscar Schindlers of the world will do righteous things like save a few Jews during Nazism but by far, you are not going to liberate Germany from Nazism by supporting the Oscar Schindlers because they will be killed. So it is a minuscule investment. It's too late because the movement began in the 70s and is growing all over...By far, Islamic fundamentalism has won in the arena of the Middle East and it is too late for us to try to bank on the Oscar Schindlers at this moment."[12]

The premise was simple, straightforward, and easy to understand. Yet, the disease known as political correctness had infected the highest levels of government within the United States. The strategy of not alienating 'peaceful' Muslims was set in motion in the days after September 11th. Then President George W. Bush spoke at the Islamic Center of Washington, D.C. on September 17th and said, "Islam is peace." Present at that media event was none other than the Executive Director for the Council on American Islamic Relations (CAIR), Nihad Awad.[13] **[See Chapter 7, p. 201]**

CAIR would later be identified as an unindicted co-conspirator in the Holy Land Foundation trial, the largest terrorism financing trial to date.[14]

Only a few short months after his meeting with Awad in the days after 9/11, President Bush's Justice Department would shut down the Holy Land Foundation for funding Hamas. CAIR immediately chastised Bush, calling the action "unjust" and "disturbing."[15] CAIR now had something invaluable it could use to bolster its credibility – a photo of its Executive Director standing next to the President of the United States less than a week after the September 11th attacks.

Shoebat's claims are bolstered by that reality upon further analysis. When he was in Chicago in the early 1990s, he had a mentor named Jamal Said, a man he identified as being a member of the Muslim Brotherhood – a group Shoebat spent time with as an activist while in Chicago. One would think the President would want to stand with someone like Shoebat in the days after 9/11 instead of with a group having strong ties to the same Muslim Brotherhood.[16]

Remember, Shoebat's grandfather, as chieftain of his village, was a close personal friend of the Grand Mufti of Jerusalem, al-Husseini, who was a close friend of Hitler.

Inexplicably, while Hitler was rightfully demonized by the victors of World War II, his Arab ally al-Husseini not only escaped virtually unscathed but was named leader of the Muslim Brotherhood in 1946 – after his alignment with Hitler during the war.[17] This is the same Muslim Brotherhood that spawned Hamas and CAIR. Awad, the man who Bush stood with six days after September 11, 2001 was the leader of a group residing under the Muslim Brotherhood umbrella; it was the same umbrella under which al-Qaeda resided.[18]

Enter the name Abdullah Azzam, who was a close personal friend of the man responsible for the September 11th attacks, Osama bin Laden.[19] Azzam was killed in 1989 and credited with the formation of the group known as al-Qaeda; he was also a founding member of Hamas. Bin Laden once referred to him as, "the main pillar of the Jihad movement in the modern times."[20]

Shoebat had the following to say about Azzam and Said during that 2007 interview, in which he discussed a ribbon cutting ceremony one month earlier:

> "Abdullah Azzam was the colleague of my mentor, Jamal Said…They had a ribbon cutting celebration in Chicago in which the mayor of Chicago (Richard M. Daly) was present. The Muslim Society there – Jamal Said – was donating a park for the community and there was the mayor like nothing was happening."[21]

In order to come full circle, perhaps we could look at an interview that took place between the *Fox News* Channel's Bill O'Reilly and Ahmed Rehab, the Executive Director of CAIR in Chicago[22] on August 6, 2008. The subject was the resignation of the national coordinator for Muslim American Affairs of the Obama campaign, Mazen Asbahi. Rehab vouched for Jamal Said, claiming to know him personally and referred to him as a "great American faith leader."[23] Attempts were made to get Shoebat on O'Reilly's show based on Rehab's comments and Shoebat's association with Said but they were unsuccessful.

Shoebat may have illustrated this point more than a year earlier when he spoke about the western media's response to Islamic fundamentalism:

> "The media that you have is not building the American confidence. The media that you have is building the enemy's confidence. The confidence level by far for the Islamists has increased as a result of the American or western response to radical Islam."[24]

Why would America's top rated cable news show – *The O'Reilly Factor* – have a representative from CAIR on the program with no opposing guest? The adversarial role fell to O'Reilly by default but he was either unaware of CAIR's ties to terrorism or unwilling to broach the subject. Given that O'Reilly and his producers are in the news business, it is a stretch to accept the premise that CAIR's associations were unknown to them.

Again, Shoebat seemed to provide the best explanation over a year earlier:

> "It seems that we have a war on terrorism yet terrorism is working. Terrorism is fear. That's the definition of terrorism in one word. It's fear and the only way westerners can fight fear is fearlessness. You can't fight fear with fear."[25]

As mentioned earlier, Ahmed Rehab's superior – Nihad Awad – stood with George W. Bush six days after 9/11; Awad is on record as supporting Hamas;[26] Hamas is a group belonging to the Muslim Broth-

erhood; the founder of Hamas, Abdullah Azzam was a close friend of Osama bin Laden; Jamal Said was a colleague of Azzam; and Ahmed Rehab vouched for Said. Jamal Said was the mentor of Shoebat who fit perfectly the profile of a human intelligence jackpot, right? When dealing with the theoretical, yes!

In reality, Shoebat had been virtually shunned by those who actually set and implemented policy. The importance of George W. Bush's public stance with Awad and other Islamist leaders in the days after September 11th needs to be underscored. So soon after it was attacked, the United States not only refused to identify the enemy that attacked it but stood with those who had ties to that enemy. This concerted attempt to prevent the alienation of the 'moderate' Muslims would prove to be a major miscalculation.

Shoebat possessed all the characteristics of someone the United States should have treated as a primary human asset; he was a human intelligence *goldmine*. He knew the language, he knew the history, he knew the enemy, and more important, he was invested in the defeat of that enemy while being passionate about victory for America. Yet, he was not listened to by the policy makers and decided to speak to those who *would* listen – talk radio audiences as well as churches and universities.

## STUCK MOJO CONNECTION

On Christmas Eve, 2006 I had the opportunity to interview a man named Rich Ward, lead guitarist of a rock band from Atlanta named Stuck Mojo. At the time, Ward's band had found itself in the middle of some controversy over a song it had recorded called *Open Season*. The video for the song went viral on the internet; it had a heavy metal sound with politically incorrect and edgy lyrics to match, directed at the radical elements within the Islamic world. It was something that hadn't been done before.

The song was from an album the band had recently released called *Southern Born Killers*. One of those songs was titled, *For the Cause of Allah* and featured excerpts of Shoebat's various media interviews as a central component. When I asked Ward about the inspiration for the song, he revealed a strong respect for Shoebat's work and talked about how he wanted to incorporate violins to convey tension and marching drums to symbolize war; it was a war the west still hadn't identified but one a heavy metal band from Atlanta understood.

The band, which featured a black lead singer, leaned conservative politically and found itself the target of leftwing attacks over their new song. In fact, during the interview, Ward conveyed what it was like to be in a band made up of black and white musicians that was also identified as being 'racist.'[27]

I spoke with Shoebat less than four months later and I was eager to learn what he thought of the song – surely, he had already heard it. I thought I would end the interview with it.

To my surprise, after asking him what it felt like to be a rock star, he didn't know what I was talking about. "Rock star? I am not a rock star." When I explained to him that a rock band named 'Stuck Mojo' had produced a "Walid Shoebat song," he said, "Can you sing it for me?" Obviously, that wasn't possible so he had to settle for me playing part of it going into the next commercial break.

## ENCOUNTER AT UNIVERSITY OF WISCONSIN-MILWAUKEE

Being a public figure whose views are the source of so much controversy is a bit easier to manage when you're doing phone interviews or traveling a short distance by car to the nearest television studio.

However, Shoebat has also taken his testimony to the road; he travels nearly every weekend to a church or a university in an attempt to convey what he knows to be the truth. His regimen often consists of constant radio interviews during the week – even long after another author's book tour would have been a distant memory – and weekend travel to one of the rare churches that is willing to stand up to the potential consequences of providing a forum for the controversial truth.

He told his story and made his case to an audience of nearly 1000 people at the University of Wisconsin-Milwaukee (UWM) on December 4, 2007. The Conservative Union at UWM sponsored the event. Security was high as the Muslim Students Association (MSA) had scheduled

a panel after Shoebat's speech to defend Islam. Interestingly enough, the same man who would later be on the O'Reilly Factor to defend Jamal Said unopposed – Ahmed Rehab, Executive Director of CAIR Chicago – was part of that panel. It is also worth noting that Shoebat was one man while the panel that was put together to rebut him consisted of six people representing the Muslim perspective.[28]

After his speech was over, the floor was opened up to questions. Members of the CAIR event that was about to take place, had made their way into the room where Shoebat was speaking. One of the Muslim questioners took issue with his use of the term "croaked" to describe Yasser Arafat's death – a word Shoebat used earlier in his speech. That same person had a problem with Shoebat using the term "hijacked" to describe what they were doing to his event. Rather than attack the claims Shoebat had made, the questioner just got increasingly angry. Even Rehab, who was standing nearby made a small effort to calm him down.

A portion of the exchange went like this:

> **Audience member:** Ours is more of a religion [inaudible] you're making us look bad because you don't know what you're talking about.
>
> **Shoebat:** Yeah? Do you feel like coming up to the stage and beating me up?
>
> **Audience member:** [Shouts inaudibly]
>
> **Shoebat:** I am so glad you're here. Do you know why I'm glad you're here?
>
> **Audience member:** Because you're [inaudible]
>
> **Shoebat:** No, because it shows your true colors.[29]

At that point, the audience member was escorted away as the crowd cheered. None of the issues Shoebat had presented were confronted. Instead, the Muslim students attempted to intimidate – quite unsuccessfully – and attack his character. The *UWM Post* also reported that the MSA itself questioned Shoebat's credibility, calling him a "phony purveyor of hate, fear and violence."[30]

If the premise is accepted that when one side is losing a debate, the next course of action is ridicule and personal attacks, Shoebat's opponents have been losing big for quite some time. The charges levied by the MSA were no different. In one instance, the MSA attempted to discredit Shoebat's account of his time in Chicago by misspelling Jamal Said's name so that when people did an internet search for him, there was no way to validate any connection. Shoebat conveyed this during his December 4th speech at UWM:

"I began to realize that in my culture, you can't change your mind. I changed my mind and I want to speak at a university and the Muslim Students Association was up in arms. Why? In Michigan, the MSA issued edicts, leaflets outside how I'm such a false guy, how I'm made up, how I'm a Zionist conspirator, I'm a lying fabricating liar. In fact, they said even the mentor of Walid Shoebat, Jamal Said…they said there is no Jamal Said. He doesn't exist. I said, 'if you get your spelling correct…you would google the name and find out for yourselves.' They haven't even issued an apology for their mistakes (Shoebat said the name was spelled 'Sayed' by his critics)."[31]

**Note:** As of this writing, when entering the name 'Jamal Sayed' into the Google search engine, the user is not made aware of any potential misspelling.

The attacks from the MSA – along with other Muslim individuals and groups – would soon come from liberal media sources that attempted to paint Shoebat as a fraud.

Eventually, the former terrorist would find himself spending precious time defending his own honor, character, and reputation against those he was trying to warn of a very serious threat. In fact, he would be forced to spend far more time clearing his name than two writers in particular – Jorg Luyken at the *Jerusalem Post* and Christopher Hedges, formerly of the *New York Times* – spent attempting to smear him. There will be more on this later.

I interviewed Shoebat after his appearance at UWM. His comments about the MSA's tactics relative to their appearance at his event shed additional light on the group:

"Every University we go to is the Muslim Students Association. We have MSA at 150 campuses across this country and rarely ever anybody goes to respond to them. It's only me and David Horowitz so we need to focus on the students."[32]

It's important to understand the purpose of the MSA. It is a group that was established by members of the Muslim Brotherhood itself and actually serves to achieve multiple objectives. It encourages its members to rise through the political ranks of their respective university's student union. Ultimately, this teaches the Muslim students how to navigate through a political system, albeit a collegiate political system; it nonetheless provides training for those Muslim students on how to navigate upward through larger political systems. It also teaches them how to acquire power. Once they are successful, they can then use what they've learned to do the same thing in the US political system.[33]

Yet, as Shoebat mentions, interest on the part of American students to counter these efforts has been spotty at best. Conversely, the Muslim student groups are very organized. Instead of arriving at planned events coordinated by energized conservative student groups, Shoebat often has to do the energizing himself while having to deal with hostile opposition.

## UNWELCOME HOMECOMING

In October of 2008, Shoebat would speak at the University of Nevada at Reno (UNR). He was invited to speak there – along with Kamal Saleem – at the request of a student named Zakaryia Ezzat, who had recently converted from Islam to Christianity.

Like Shoebat, Ezzat was the son of a Muslim father and a Christian mother. His father was Egyptian and his mother was a Scottish-American protestant. Until he invited Shoebat to speak, he had kept his newly chosen religion secret for various reasons. After his friends saw that he had invited two former Muslims to speak at the university, it didn't take long for Ezzat's Christianity to become known by the Muslim community. Once that realization happened, he was branded as "ignorant of Islam, racist, and islamophobic."[34]

The event was a relative success with approximately 750 people in attendance. A few short months later Ezzat would coordinate another event, this time in a town where Shoebat's parents met – Humboldt, CA. Years later, Shoebat would meet his future wife not far from there, in Walnut Creek.

While attending the Young American Foundation conference in Santa Barbara weeks earlier, Ezzat met the president of the Humboldt State University (HSU) conservatives and began the process of coordinating the event.

On February 18, 2009 Shoebat spoke at HSU in Arcata, CA but not without incident. Unfortunately, there was no security detail and the local police only had two female police officers on the scene. Ezzat became even more concerned when he received word before the event that there was a planned protest. "Ten minutes into the event, I looked to my right and saw a person in a ninja-type mask crouched low to the ground," he said. "There were about 50 people nearby holding pro-Palestinian signs who were yelling and pushing their way toward the stage."

Ezzat had ridden to the event with Shoebat and both were somewhat concerned about the potential for violence beforehand; each knew that security would not be at a level Shoebat was used to. As they were talking about what to do, Ezzat said Shoebat told him, "If anything happens, I don't want you to get in the middle of it." That garnered Ezzat's respect and when something *did* happen, he *did* get in the middle of it. "We had announced beforehand that signs would not be permitted so when this group was charging the stage with signs, I was jumping on and off the stage in order to confiscate them," Ezzat said.

Nonetheless, according to Ezzat, the event was not cut short and continued despite the fracas. "At one point," Ezzat says, "Walid looks at me during one of my multiple trips on stage while he's speaking and says, 'I can take these guys.'"

As one can imagine, the perspective held by those opposed to the controversial speaker was that the students who charged the stage were simply fighting anti-Muslim bigotry and Islamophobia.

On the day after the event, a leftwing student who was in attendance wrote an account called, "Walib(sp) Shoebat vs. Humboldt State University." His take on things was fairly different:

> Walib proceeded to recite his prepared notes, not without taking time to share nasty responses with the people in the crowd who were speaking out against him. As time progressed, his fairly romantic presentation about Islamic ideals and terrorism in the Middle East became bitter and hateful as his increasingly grotesque point of view was met by an increasingly disgusted and vocal audience.[35]

Notwithstanding the notion that "nasty responses" to disruptive rabble-rousers are possible, if you're giving a speech and are consistently interrupted by catcalls, hecklers, and people rushing the stage, are you going to be polite in your response? Should you be? Apparently lost on this individual – aside from the misspelling of Shoebat's first name – was the fact that a speaker who was authorized to speak should be afforded the opportunity to do so. In typical leftwing fashion, the implication was made clear; if they don't like your speech, it should be shut down.

Shoebat said the following in an interview after the event at Humboldt State University:

> "Here I'm trying to witness to these people, very gently. First half hour, the jeering and the screaming and the foul language and the attacks and everything else. They attacked my family, they attacked my American side of the family...My great-grandfather was the mayor of Eureka, California (where Humboldt is). Here, the first day of my life I went there to speak at the university, I was attacked and they said my grandfather was a slave owner and I said, 'you don't even know my grandfather's name.' So much bad language, so much attacks, physical to the

podium…Finally, I called somebody a name, I got upset because they were so aggressive. All that I got was an email from somebody who was a Christian who said that because I yelled back at these people that I have not been a good Christian…They don't want to fight the real fight."[36]

Shoebat often sees himself as a man on an island. To the Muslims, he's an apostate who at a minimum should be completely discredited and at maximum, killed for leaving the faith. To the American left, he's a fraud and purveyor of hate who needs to be marginalized; and on the Christian right, he's viewed as either too extreme or someone whose views are correct but so controversial that most cower at the thought of publicly standing with him.

It is the latter group that most disappoints Shoebat. In his mind, these are people who are charged with revealing the truth, no matter the consequences. Yet, so many refuse to do so even when they know what the truth is:

> "I get churches who cancel on me because they say we're afraid of repercussions but we will pray for you…I had my own pastor…I brought Bus 19 (for the 19 hijackers on 9/11) so we can expose terrorism, radical Islam to the American people and he wanted to put the bus in the back of the church because he was afraid of repercussion. It's the same situation as when David dealt with Goliath. You had all the brothers afraid and yet young David wanted to fight Goliath and they're all afraid."

In keeping with that theme, perhaps one of Shoebat's most stinging rebukes of those who are charged with leading Christians with the truth but choose not to preach it, has to do with a very familiar passage in Scripture, namely from Matthew 10:16. Always thought-provoking, Shoebat makes a point that is very hard for any Christian to argue:

> "Jesus said, 'I send you as a sheep amongst wolves.' He didn't send us to have a conference on how we can have

church growth and bring in more tears and more fluff. I'm not against church growth but that's not the focus...There is persecution and perseverance in this war because wolves kill sheep and if we have no wolves in our life, we better start questioning whether we're really sheep. You have to really name your wolves."[37]

Shoebat's message is controversial, yes; so is the truth. In fact, the most controversial things in this world are rooted in truth. The truth hurts; it hurts when people are brutally honest. People don't want to hear it because it's often very uncomfortable. Some even lie to themselves to avoid facing it. In the film, *A Few Good Men*, Jack Nicholson's character famously barked, "You can't handle the truth."

Shoebat's argument, especially for Christians, is that faith should always trump fear. It's not an easy commission but that shouldn't make it any less spiritually mandatory.

## ■ FIGHTING 'FRAUD' ALLEGATIONS

In early 2008 – when liberal writers levied accusations that Shoebat was a fraud – the latter would be embroiled in yet a new fight.

Two articles in particular served as figurative bombs set right next to Shoebat's character. One was from Christopher Hedges, a writer with a resume that included many years with the *New York Times*. The other article was penned by a virtual unknown whose hit piece was inexplicably published in the *Jerusalem Post* just a few weeks later.

In both cases, neither man spent the time necessary to gather enough facts about an individual before issuing such sweeping character assassinations. Both articles would have made Saul Alinsky proud as ridicule, insults, and innuendo were all packaged as journalism. The contempt each man held for Shoebat was obvious and in both cases the clout of the author and publication respectively, was used as a weapon against their target.

Hedges' article focused on Shoebat and two other former terrorists – Kamal Saleem and Zachariah Anani. Hedges referred to the men as "the three stooges," saying that:

"These men are frauds, but this is not the point. They are part of a dark and frightening war by the Christian right against tolerance that, in the moment of another catastrophic terrorist attack on American soil, would make it acceptable to target and persecute all Muslims, including the some 6 million Muslims who live in the United States."[38]

That narrative seems to play right into Shoebat's claim that when he was a terrorist who hated the Jews, he was a "freedom fighter" but once he became a Christian who loved everyone – including Muslims – he became a fraud who declared war on tolerance. Just over a year after Hedges' article, Shoebat put it another way saying, "During my terror days when I lied to westerners, they believed me. Now that I'm telling the truth, I am called a liar."[39]

When a journalist – especially one with a history like Hedges – decides to levy accusations against an individual, the burden of proof should fall exclusively on that journalist to make the case. That burden should necessarily be made heavier in direct proportion to how much reach, respectability, and credibility that writer has accumulated. In the case of Hedges, it should have been a heavy burden. Instead, he accused another human being of lying without doing the necessary due diligence to back up the charge:

"Shoebat claims he first came to the United States as part of an extremist 'sleeper cell.'"[40]

Note the implication. Instead of doing the research required to either prove or disprove Shoebat's claims, Hedges intentionally leads the reader to believe Shoebat is lying because only a few paragraphs earlier, he called the former terrorist a "fraud." By putting the words "sleeper cell" in quotes, he performed the equivalent of sarcastically underscoring his premise before gathering the facts. It was journalistic malpractice.

The burden that should have belonged solely to Hedges was, by default, placed squarely on the shoulders of the man whose character he attempted to assassinate.

The other writer who would attempt to discredit Shoebat as a fraud was Jorg Luyken, whose article appeared in the *Jerusalem Post*.[41] Part of Shoebat's testimony involves a man named Mahmoud al-Mughrabi, who he says recruited him while the two were in a Moscovite prison in Jerusalem. Shoebat says it was al-Mughrabi who directed him to bomb Bank Leumi in Bethlehem in the late 1970s. Luyken began his column by alluding to that claim but did not make any further reference to it. It's understandable why, when one does the work on al-Mughrabi that Luyken should have done.

Upon doing the research Luyken didn't do, it's learned that al-Mughrabi was not only a real person but a very bad one. In fact, he was one of those killed by Israeli war planes in the fall of 1985 in what was termed Operation Wooden Leg.[42] The strike was carried out in response to the murder of three civilians by the armed wing of the PLO, Force 17 – on an Israeli yacht docked in Cyprus days earlier. According to intelligence sources, PLO leader Yasser Arafat was staying at PLO headquarters in Tunisia. As it turned out, he was not there but al-Mughrabi was; he would also be among the dead. Video footage of the aftermath was captured by *Al-Jazeera*.[43]

On a side note, when one contrasts the difference between the Islamic terrorists – who days earlier had murdered three Israeli citizens – with the care exercised by the Israeli Air Force in response, that contrast couldn't be more stark. The IAF took great pains, through precision strikes, not to have any collateral damage. In fact, they even went so far as to attack during the middle of the week, at a time when minimal tourists were present.[44] That al-Mughrabi was among the dead should not only bolster Shoebat's claims but should – in light of the IAF's precision – serve as strong testimony that al-Mughrabi was indeed a terrorist. After all, he was killed at Arafat's PLO headquarters in Tunisia.

Now that it's been established that a man named Mahmoud al-Mughrabi was a bad guy who Shoebat claims mentored him, is there any evidence that al-Mughrabi was housed in that Moscovite prison Shoebat talks about? The answer is, yes.

In fact, al-Mughrabi had a communist sympathizing lawyer who helped him perpetuate the notion that he was being mistreated in prison. Shoebat claims the conditions inside would actually cause people below the poverty line to commit crimes in order to get in so they could live better. During the writing of this book, he spoke about what it was like inside the prison:

> "If American prisoners tried Israeli prisons, they would all apply for a transfer to Israel. Palestinian prisoners are masters of exaggeration. Each inmate at the Moscovie (aka Meskubieh) had his own bed and we were provided an in-the-cell shower. We ate three full meals a day which included a choice of tea or sweet punch."

According to Shoebat, this did not stop al-Mughrabi from using his lawyer to help further his claims of abuse. Remember, it was in this prison at which Shoebat claims he met and was mentored by al-Mughrabi, to bomb Bank Leumi in Bethlehem.

So, what about proof al-Mughrabi was there? A consequence of al-Mughrabi using a leftist lawyer to further his fallacious claims was that there would be a record of his whereabouts when he did so. In a United Nations report on alleged Israeli abuses of Palestinian prisoners, 44 prisoners were interviewed, with more than 20 agreeing to be named; al-Mughrabi was one of those who agreed to reveal his identity.[45] The time of that report – the summer of 1977 – is around the same time Shoebat claims to have met al-Mughrabi.

Another source who corroborated the story of Shoebat relative to al-Mughrabi's death was none other than Edward Said, the Columbia professor and PLO apologist under whom Barack Obama studied in the early 1980s. In his book, *Blaming the Victims*, Said describes the events surrounding the death of al-Mughrabi.[46] Between *Al-Jazeera* and Said, that makes two Arab sources – not western – whose accounts add credence to Shoebat's story.

In September of 2010, Shoebat recounted to me his first encounter with al-Mughrabi that perhaps served as an ice breaker when the two would later meet in prison:

"I first spotted Mahmoud al-Mughrabi during a demonstration on the Temple Mount in Jerusalem. He was firing what seemed a low-caliber pistol when an Israeli post guard fired back and hit Mahmoud Al-Jneidi instead. I was right behind Jnedi who took the bullet. Jneidi was killed. Later on I was imprisoned with Mahmoud Al-Mughrabi at the Moscovite Prison, Jerusalem Central Prison... I recognized him from that event on the Temple Mount when Jnedi was killed. We became friends and I was recruited into the P.L.O. to do a bombing operation after I came out of prison. He gave me his address: Judo Star Martial Arts Institute on Bab Al-Wad Old city Jerusalem. We met several times planning an operation; we concluded that I could use my US Passport to hijack an airliner and to start off we could blow up Bank Leumi in Bethlehem. Al-Mughrabi assembled a bomb which I planted on the roof of Bank Leumi Israel in Bethlehem."[47]

Luyken did not address any of this – ostensibly because it didn't fit his premise or agenda. He then proceeded to address Shoebat's claims that he delivered a bomb to the office of Bank Leumi in Bethlehem. The way Luyken dealt with Walid's claim that the bomb he was carrying exploded on the roof of Bank Leumi was laughable in what it lacked – research and sources. Writes Luyken:

Shoebat's claim to have bombed Bank Leumi in Bethlehem is rejected by members of his family who still live in the area, and Bank Leumi says it has no record of such an attack ever taking place.[48]

Luyken wrote a news story that would have the effect of identifying a man as a fraud without doing the required research to back up his claim. Absent from the article is who he contacted at the bank.

Moreover, when a writer's work deals with the potential of destroying another human being's reputation – as was the case here – shouldn't other sources have been checked? How about newspaper archives? How about police reports? If those things were checked, Luyken seemed content not to mention them while merely saying that an unnamed person at the Bank told him there was no bombing. These sources are conspicuous in their absence. Besides, the bank in question had been closed down years earlier.

Serving as an example is a *New York Times* article referenced by Luyken. He cites the claims by "Academic professors" that the accounts of Shoebat and others about committing terrorist acts in the 1970s were unlikely because "violent religious ideology" didn't become prevalent until the "late 1980s."[49]

Once again, had Luyken done his research, he could have disproven the premise provided to him by the *New York Times*. If "violent religious ideology" didn't become prevalent until the "late 1980s" how does Jorg Luyken explain a rash of terrorist acts – including multiple bombings – in Israel between September of 1977 and October of 1978 that were documented by the United Nations General Assembly? The total count during that timeframe was well over one hundred fifty incidents. In fact, a bombing in Bethlehem is recorded in December of 1977 outside a courthouse. Coincidentally, there was a courthouse adjacent to Bank Leumi in Bethlehem.[50] Though Shoebat believes his bomb exploded in late 1976, this evidence disproves the assertion that "violent religious ideology" didn't start until years later.

What about the members of Shoebat's family, who Luyken said rejected Walid's claim that his bomb went off on the roof of Bank Leumi? While Luyken did report the reason given by Shoebat for their denial – to protect his cousin who was with him at the time of the bombing – he did not report any witness accounts who remember the bombing.

For example, James Yateem – a Palestinian Christian who now lives in the United States – claims to have been a childhood friend of Shoebat. In a phone interview I conducted with Yateem, he stated that he remembered the bombing. While Yateem confessed that he couldn't remember if he heard the explosion or saw it in the news, he said that the village was so small that news traveled fast and everyone knew. He also remembered Shoebat claiming responsibility for the bombing shortly afterward. Details about the bombing were fuzzy for Yateem but he was adamant that it had occurred.

Moreover, Shoebat has been in contact with a former IDF officer who was stationed near his village in the late 1970s and can corroborate significant aspects in his story. Luyken did not pursue this essential lead either.

## ■ THE GROUND ZERO MOSQUE

In the summer of 2010, a controversy of national significance resulted from the proposed construction of a mosque two blocks away from what is known as 'Ground Zero' – the site where the twin towers of the New York Trade Center once stood. The mosque was facing growing public opposition. "Cordoba," the name given to the Mosque, also raised the eyebrows of the educated – it's the name of a city in Spain that was once conquered by the Muslim Moors; a Christian church was transformed into a Mosque. Even the most liberal of sources could not deny this happened.[51] In the internet age, it didn't take long for American citizens to figure out the significance of the name. In fact, the Cordoba Initiative would eventually rename the Mosque Park 51 because of the burgeoning controversy.[52]

Ironically, elected caretakers of both the city and state of New York respectively – Mayor Michael Bloomberg and Attorney General Andrew Cuomo – stood with the Cordoba Initiative and defended construction of the mosque while Shoebat worked tirelessly to expose the man behind its construction as someone with a hidden agenda and nefarious intentions. Despite overwhelming public opposition to the mosque, Cuomo would win the gubernatorial race later that year in a landslide.

Ever the critic of any Islamic leader, Shoebat went to work on researching the background of the Imam leading the initiative, Feisal Abdul Rauf. As a former Muslim terrorist who speaks both Arabic and

English, he saw an opportunity to show that Rauf's words to one audience did not mirror his words to another.

He went to work, researching Arabic websites – and struck gold; Shoebat unearthed a quote from Rauf in an article the latter had written entitled, *Sharing The Essence of our Beliefs*. Shoebat translated the article into English, which revealed a disturbing reality:

"If someone in the Middle East cries out, 'where is the law', he knows that the law exists. THE ONLY LAW THAT THE MUSLIM NEEDS EXISTS ALREADY IN THE KORAN AND THE HADITH. People asked me RIGHT AFTER THE 9/11 ATTACK as to why do movements with political agendas carry [Islamic] religious names? Why call it 'Muslim Brotherhood' or 'Hezbollah (Party of ALLAH)' or 'Hamas' or 'ISLAMIC Resistance Movement'? I answer them this – that THE TREND TOWARDS ISLAMIC LAW AND JUSTICE BEGINS IN RELIGIOUS MOVEMENTS, because SECULARISM HAD FAILED TO DELIVER WHAT THE MUSLIM WANTS, which is life, liberty and the pursuit of happiness.[53]

This revelation vindicated those who suspected such things of the multiple Islamic groups that portrayed themselves as peaceful. Here was an Arabic-speaking man who was translating the words of America's adversaries into English and he was – in large measure, ignored. In one paragraph, Rauf proved skeptics of the moderate Islamic movement correct. The only interpretation that can reasonably be made with respect to this translation is that the intent of Islamic front groups is to deceive others. The irony of the aforementioned excerpt is that secularism failed according to Rauf's words while his biggest advocates in the west other than Islamists – the left – advocate secularism.

Just a few days later, Shoebat would come across an even larger discovery – Rauf, while being interviewed on Egyptian radio had made some shocking claims months earlier. Among them was that words from his book were incorporated into President Barack Obama's Cairo speech in June of 2009. Here is an excerpt from Rauf's interview, dated February 5, 2010:

> "We have to look at it [as] how to engineer solutions. At the Cordova Initiative we think of ourselves as an engineering shop. Yes. We have an analytical approach. Our work has been that. IN THE BOOK CHAPTER 6, I WROTE ABOUT THIS BLUE PRINT as to WHAT HAS TO BE DONE BY THE US GOVERN-MENT, what has to be done by the Jewish community, what has to be done by the Christian community, what has to be done by the Muslim community, what has to be done by educators, what has to be done by the media. For example, IN MY BOOK IN THE ARABIC VERSION page 293, what did I write? WHAT ARE THE THINGS THAT THE UNITED STATES NEEDS TO DO. IF YOU EXAMINE THIS CHAPTER YOU WILL FIND THAT THE (OBAMA) SPEECH IN CAIRO WAS ALL TAKEN FROM THIS SECTION *[Section 6]*.[54]

Shoebat's discovery was so significant that he began garnering interest, once again, from large radio shows and even the *Fox News Channel*. At one point, while I was discussing his interview schedule with him on the phone, he seemed to be surprisingly less than excited at the prospect of doing an interview the next morning on the *Bill Bennett* show before catching a flight. I was somewhat perplexed by his reticence to appear on one of the most listened to radio shows in America and asked him why he wasn't eager to do the interview.

In a distinct Arabic accent, he responded, "Mr. Barrack, (pause) do you have any idea what it is like for an Arab to do a radio interview about terrorism on a cell phone while in an airport?" I had to concede the point because it never crossed my mind; I also couldn't help but laugh for having missed what – to Shoebat – was quite obvious.

During an appearance on a segment of *Fox & Friends*, hosted by Brian Kilmeade and former White House Press Secretary Dana Perrino, Walid expounded on his translation of Rauf's words, which he was holding in his hands:

**Shoebat:** When he decries terrorism, what he means, he does not agree with the methodology of the terrorists but he agrees with the same goals and this is why he agrees with Hamas in the Arabic language and the goal is to establish…an American-style Islam in the US…

**Kilmeade:**…What are you reading from?

**Shoebat:** I am translating the Arabic because I don't listen to what this guy says in English. There's plenty of information about what Feisal Abdul Rauf stated in the Arabic language.

A short time later, Shoebat explained what Rauf meant when he spoke of using *peaceful* means to achieve his objectives.

**Shoebat:** He's saying we need to have Muslims in America basically advance the cause through peaceful means. This is what he means by 'peace.' 'To advise the governors and the government institutions. We also suggest that the governors and political institutions to consult Muslim religious institutions and Muslim personalities.' …In fact, he was talking on Egyptian radio, telling them how to lure Americans, saying the way you reason with westerners is the way you deal with a girl you want to date. You must cover yourself as a typical Muslim and appear as a westerner, and then you can engage. That was his exact words.[55]

Shoebat was opening the enemy's playbook and showing America what was inside. He demonstrated through translation that Rauf wasn't interested in peace as an end in itself but as a means to another end – Sharia law. He also provided viewers a window into the way Islamists think – that westerners should be manipulated into believing they are revered by the likes of Rauf when, in fact, they are being exploited like adolescent girls by an older man.

A few days later, Shoebat appeared on the *The O'Reilly Factor* which featured Laura Ingraham as the guest host. Opposite the former terrorist was Rev. Barry Lynn, executive director of Americans United for Separation of Church and State.[55] As a liberal, Lynn took the position of defending Rauf and siding with the New York City mayor while Shoebat reiterated many of the same points he put forth days earlier. What placed the exchange even more squarely in Shoebat's favor was the fact that Lynn attempted to defend a position on a subject Shoebat was far more qualified to discuss – the alleged peaceful intentions of Rauf.

While Shoebat cited the sources he researched to find Rauf's Arabic writings and comments, he also explained Rauf's deceptive use of innocuous words and phrases. He recited Rauf's words about why there are so many Islamic groups with different names (quote above). This was not only part of a segment on a news show but in a sane world, it would be considered intelligence gathering. The point was entirely missed – or avoided – by Lynn, who decided to seize on another part of the translation – namely Rauf's use of words like "peace" when communicating his agenda.

Lost on Lynn was the fact that he himself was playing right into the hands of Islamic leaders like Feisal Abdul Rauf by accepting what the Imam said at face value without truly understanding the meaning behind the words, despite having them translated for him by an Arab-speaking Christian. Lynn was either being played, too prideful to defer to an expert, or part of the game and on the side of the Islamists.

He said in response to Shoebat's claims:

> "I think it would help a great deal if people like our other guest here would also acknowledge that in the very thing he claims to have translated, he (Rauf) talks about the peaceful progress of Sharia. Well, good grief, are we supposed to be terrified now because a religious group that constitutes one percent of the people in America and, by the way one percent of the Muslims in America, most of them don't even want Sharia law…"[56]

Lynn did not address Rauf's response to the question about why it is necessary to have so many different Muslim groups. The translation – according to Shoebat – was that Rauf expressed "Islamic law begins in religious movements." This should have been an explosive claim that Lynn would have wanted to defuse if it was unfounded. Instead, he decided to focus on another portion of the words Shoebat translated. He decided to focus on Rauf's "peaceful" intentions:

"He (Rauf) says it's peaceful. If we cannot deal, sir, with (Rauf) here, if we cannot deal with him here, then what in the world do you want us to do in dealing with so-called moderate Islamic factions in Afghanistan and Iraq? If this gentleman is not moderate enough for you then we better pull out of the middle east right now."

It smacked of denial. Lynn actually seemed to be admitting that a reality Shoebat expressed was simply too scary to face. The mere prospect that Rauf may be a radical was a possibility that Lynn was either unwilling or unable to entertain. While such a view may be somewhat understandable, Shoebat's argument was that it was an extremely dangerous position to hold.

After September 11, 2001 Walid was incredibly frustrated by the thinking in the United States. Never before had Americans been so ignorant about the motivations of their enemy. At some point, he was compelled to find a way to educate people. In the days after 9/11, prevailing sentiment was that Islam was a religion of peace, as mentioned earlier in this chapter; even the president of the United States – George W. Bush – went out of his way to make the distinction.

The tone had been set. When it came to Islam, political correctness was alive and well. Shoebat had his work cut out for him. In his line of work, victories are small and don't come all that often but when the Ground Zero mosque controversy reached a fever pitch in the summer of 2010, he had some time to reflect and despite there being so much work left to be done, he took some solace in how far Americans had come. Public sentiment in opposition to the mosque had reached as high as seventy percent; it was a number that was unfathomable just nine years earlier. Shoebat had his head down, working to educate Americans for nine years; he encouraged many to educate themselves and each other.

Less than a decade earlier the views held by him were considered "Islamophobic" and "extreme." In August of 2010, a *CBS News* poll found that seventy-one percent of Americans agreed with him by opposing the mosque. It was a small but significant victory. All of a sudden, the former Muslim terrorist had found himself in the majority when it came to opposing the furtherance of an Islamic agenda under the guise of Constitutional protections. Perhaps progress was being made after all.

However, while Shoebat found himself part of a significant majority, it did not include *CBS News*, whose analysis of the poll results included questions about what could have caused so many Americans to become Islamophobic.[57]

## RAUF OUT AS GROUND ZERO IMAM

In January of 2011, the *New York Times* reported that tensions between Rauf and his partner, Sharif el-Gamal are what led to Rauf stepping down as the public face of the Imam leading the project. If one accepts that public statements about reasons behind such departures don't tell the entire story, there was more to Rauf's stepping aside.

The *Times* article even hinted at what such a reason may have been:

> "By most accounts, both Mr. Abdul Rauf and Mr. Gamal were surprised over the summer when their project drew such emotionally charged opposition, despite receiving the approval of Community Board 1 and the Landmarks Preservation Committee."[58]

It is logical to conclude the surprise felt by both men helped to fuel any tension that grew between them. Though he was certainly not the only one, there is no question that Shoebat had a significant role in exposing who Rauf really was. Others included *Jihad Watch's* Robert Spencer and Pamela Geller of the *Atlas Shrugs* website; both were extremely active in garnering opposition to the project.

The vacancy left by Rauf was filled by a man named Abdallah Adhami and research on him began soon after he was named Imam of the Ground Zero mosque. Aaron Klein of *World Net Daily* uncovered audio of Adhami from just a few months earlier saying that Islamic apostates – people who leave the faith – have the right to do so but that they do not have the right to spread their new faith:

> "The Qur'an distinguishes between public and private apostasy…In Islam, in the Qur'an, theoretically, if you look over the Qur'an from cover to cover, you literally have the right to the choice to reject God's message. The only thing you do not have the right to do is to spread this conviction, lest you, quote unquote, pollute others."[59]

This was an interesting discovery in that Adhami spoke these words a few short months after Shoebat's translations helped to expose Rauf's true intentions and just two months prior to his being named head of the Ground Zero mosque. In the abstract, Adhami seemed to be speaking directly to Shoebat, himself an Islamic apostate who proselytizes in support of Christianity and against Islam.

## ■ TRANSLATING 'SON OF HAMAS'

In 2010, a book entitled *Son of Hamas* was released. It was written by a man named Mosab Hassan Yousef, the son of a founding member of Hamas. Mosab garnered several high profile media interviews, including Sean Hannity's television show on the *Fox News Channel*. His story captured the attention of many; he had converted to Christianity from Islam and helped Israel by spying on Hamas.

Less than a year after the book was released, Shoebat had again made a huge discovery, in a way similar to how he unearthed Feisal Abdul Rauf's intentions – he listened to what Yousef said in Arabic.

After studying Yousef's interviews on Arabic media outlets, Shoebat uncovered someone who wasn't what he claimed to be. Here are portions of what Shoebat was able to glean from an interview given by Yousef to Al-Arabiya in which Mosab explained he is still fighting alongside the Palestinians to defeat Israel (translated from Arabic into English):

> "During my tours in universities and even churches, [I found] the real support for Israel stems from the church in the West...We need to understand the difference between "revenge" and "resistance" and once the Palestinians do, we will have our victory against Israel."[60]

The implication of these words was more than just somewhat clear. Shoebat charged that Yousef was planning to infiltrate the American churches based on the premise that he had turned from his ways. Mosab's Arabic indicated he hadn't changed from his ways at all.

Mosab went on to say that "Israel is the problem and occupation must end."[61]

There was more. Shoebat also uncovered an interview Mosab gave to an Arabic-language show entitled *Daring Question*. During this interview, according to Shoebat's translation, Yousef referred to Hamas leaders as being "heroes and glorious defenders" and said he thought they needed to use smarter tactics – like the ones he was employing.

A caller to the show was asked by the host about a hypothetical situation in which school children (presumably Israeli) were about to be killed and whether the caller believed such a situation should be reported. Yousef interjected when the caller did not respond with an answer:

> "If I was in your shoes, you should not report it to Israel. I do not encourage anyone to give information to Israel or collaborate with Israel. If anyone hears me right now and they are in relation

to Israeli security I advise them to work for the interest of their own people – number one – and do not work with the [Israeli] enemy against the interest of our people. They should collaborate with the Palestinian Authority only (Shoebat translation)."[62]

Shoebat's translations of Mosab left him to conclude that Mosab disagrees only with the means of Hamas, not with the ends of the group. This is not dissimilar from Feisal Abdul Rauf, whom Shoebat uncovered as having used peaceful means to push an agenda that matches that of suicide bombers – an agenda that involved Sharia law.

The difference between Rauf and Mosab is one of nuance only. In the case of the Ground Zero mosque, Rauf wanted to further Islam through deceptively peaceful means. According to Shoebat's translations of Yousef's Arabic, the latter wants to destroy Israel by deceptively portraying himself as a Christian and influencing the church. Both men were exposed by a former Muslim terrorist who is passionately attempting to warn Americans about that deception.

## ■ A CONGRESSMAN'S WIFE

As the sexual twitter scandal involving Rep. Anthony Weiner (D-NY) was unfolding in the summer of 2011, his wife, Huma Abedin, was brought into the unwelcome spotlight. In addition to being the spouse of Weiner, Abedin was also the Deputy Chief of Staff for Secretary of State Hillary Clinton.

Abedin had first started working for Clinton in 1996 and ultimately became one of Hillary's closest and most trusted aides. Though it had been reported during Hillary's 2008 presidential campaign that Huma was a practicing Muslim, there was little interest, reason, or ability to explore Abedin's background at great length.[63]

The scandal involving Weiner prompted Shoebat to conduct a cursory search of Abedin's background. What he discovered was far more than he had expected to find.

As he searched Arabic sites on the internet, Shoebat inadvertently stumbled across a blog that had acquired and published a list of 63 very dangerous leaders of a Muslim Brotherhood entity. One of the members on that list was Huma Abedin's mother, Saleha. This list consisted of the leaders of an extremely secret group known as the Muslim Sisterhood. It is a group that shares the goals of the Brotherhood and works actively to further them.[64]

In addition to Huma's mother belonging to a group that seeks the destruction of the United States, Shoebat also discovered that Huma's sibling, Hassan Abedin, did as well. Hassan, Huma's brother, is listed as a fellow at the Oxford Centre for Islamic Studies (OCIS). This is significant because the OCIS was founded by Islamists and several of Hassan's colleagues are members of the Muslim Brotherhood.[65]

Huma Abedin's father, Syed Z. Abedin, died when she was 17 but prior to his death, he founded the Institute for Muslim Minority Affairs (IMMA) with Saleha. There is overwhelming evidence that al-Qaeda godfather Abdullah Omar Naseef worked very closely with both of Huma Abedin's parents.[66] This puts nearly every member of Huma Abedin's immediate family under the suspicion of working with al-Qaeda. Such a discovery would be alarming enough on its own but when viewed in the context of Huma's role as Secretary of State Hillary Clinton's close advisor, alarm bells don't just ring; they scream.

Still, do the associations of Huma Abedin's mother, father, and brother implicate her? Is such an inference no more than guilt by association? The FBI technique intended to screen Character, Associations, Reputation, and Loyalty to the United States (CARL)[67] notwithstanding, giving Huma Abedin the benefit of the doubt is made more difficult by what has been scrubbed from the IMMA website.

Upon visiting the IMMA website in 2011, Saleha S. Mahmood (Abedin) is listed as the Editor and Hassan Abedin is listed as an Associate Editor.[68] Huma's name does not appear. However, as recently as 2008, it once did. Courtesy of a screenshot captured by the *Anti-Mullah* blog, Huma Abedin once served as an Assistant Editor with IMMA **(Appendix C)**.

Shortly after two articles were published by Shoebat and this author about the Abedin family connection to the Muslim Brotherhood, the *New York Post* reported that Huma was taking time off from her job as Hillary Clinton's Deputy Chief of Staff and had moved to an "undisclosed location."[69]

About one month later, the *Post* reported that friends of former Rep. Anthony Weiner said that the former Congressman admitted to having to convince three women – Huma, Hillary, and Saleha – that he had been cured of his sex addiction. Weiner's sexual appetite is not why such news is important. The lines of communication that continued to exist between him and those three women is.[70]

Once again, Shoebat's translations caused quite the stir. Still, the DHS expressed no interest in supporting him or following his lead.

## ■ CNN SMEAR

A few weeks before Shoebat exposed Huma Abedin's familial connections to the Muslim Brotherhood, he spoke at a DHS Conference in Rapid City, South Dakota. It was a small venue, not uncommon to the stops along Shoebat's speaking circuit. What was uncommon was the appearance of *CNN* reporter Drew Griffin. A national correspondent from a cable news network showing up at such a conference was indeed curious.

The stated position of Griffin – and his producer Kathleen Johnston – for appearing at the event was to interview several of the multiple speakers and report on the event but according to Shoebat and Davies, the *CNN* reporters seemed to have interest in them exclusively. In particular, Griffin allegedly appeared more interested in discrediting Shoebat than in discussing the substance of his presentation.

It soon became apparent to both Shoebat and Davies that *CNN* was pursuing the same angle reporters Luyken and Hedges had before. At the core of Griffin's narrative was a premise that said Shoebat was a fraud.

Ultimately, Griffin's report appeared in two parts on *Anderson Cooper 360*, about two months after the DHS event.[71] It was exactly the 'hit piece' Shoebat suspected it would be. In an extensive rebuttal, Shoebat's foundation claimed to have "unimpeachable sources" that CAIR colluded with *CNN* to carry out "this political assassination."

That rebuttal referred to assertions made by Griffin in Rapid City that didn't make the final report; the claims Shoebat made only seemed to bolster the charge of *CNN*'s collusion with CAIR. In raw footage, according to Shoebat, Griffin made the claim that Shoebat had charged $13,000 for speaking that day. Shoebat's rebuttal included the following:

"Griffin simply was repeating an article written by CAIR, which falsely claimed that he (Shoebat) was paid $13,000. Anderson Cooper should review the entire interview, which is damaging to *CNN*. What Griffin did was simply rely on an article written by CAIR (Council of American Islamic Relations) based on an old article in which 3 x-terrorists were paid $13,000 in an event at the Air Force Academy in Colorado Springs. Griffin then changed his story to include the correct amount."[72]

In one of the most egregious omissions in Griffin's final report, the *CNN* reporter attempted to debunk Shoebat's claim that the latter served time in the Israeli prison with Mahmoud al-Mughrabi, mentioned earlier in this chapter. Griffin reported that his team checked with that prison to see if the name "Shoebat" showed up in its records. Though Griffin reported he was told there was no record, he omitted a very crucial fact.

Shoebat's website explained further in its rebuttal:

"When Mr. Shoebat was arrested he turned in his U.S. passport and not his birth certificate or I.D. card. His U.S. passport had a different last name. Mr. Shoebat was born in Bethlehem and since his mother was a U.S. citizen he was under her passport as a child. When he matured he held his own passport, which used his mother's information, which is not under the name 'Shoebat.' We offered to clarify all this to *CNN*...on the condition to keep the documents private. *CNN* refused to offer privacy."[73]

Additionally, in a letter to *CNN* Executive Director Tim Lister before the final report aired, Davies informed Lister that Griffin had informed

Shoebat in Rapid City that he had contacted Bank Leumi in Bethlehem to verify Shoebat's story that the latter's bomb exploded on the roof of the bank. This was not possible because the Bank Leumi branch in question was closed in 1996. Though Griffin's final report did not include this claim, both Davies and Shoebat insist it was made in Rapid City, on camera.

A few days prior to the DHS Conference event, CAIR national spokesman Ibrahim Hooper called on the South Dakota Department of Public Safety (DPS) to drop its endorsement of Shoebat specifically.[74] Aside from CAIR, there was no real entity that so publicly called attention to this event. In addition to Shoebat claiming to have unimpeachable sources that prove CAIR colluded with *CNN*, Hooper's active involvement in leading a campaign to prevent Shoebat from speaking in Rapid City, seems to lend credence to the charge.

Moreover, if anyone's credibility should have been questioned, Griffin was a prime candidate based on an interview he conducted with then Vice Presidential candidate, Sarah Palin prior to the 2008 election.[75]

While citing an article written by conservative Byron York that appeared in *National Review*, Griffin took a quote from York completely out of context while furthering the narrative that even conservatives doubted Palin's bona fides. Here is the York quote Griffin presented to Palin as being from a conservative:

> "I can't tell if Sarah Palin is incompetent, stupid, unqual - ified, corrupt or all of the above."

Curiously, Griffin couldn't name the author of the quote when Palin asked him for it but a quick check showed that York's quote was meant to indict people like Griffin, not Palin.

Here is York's quote in full:

> "Watching the press coverage of the Republican candidate for vice president, it's sometimes hard to decide whether Sarah Palin is incompetent, stupid, unqualified, corrupt, backward, or — well, all of the above."

If Griffin was willing to go to such lengths to smear a vice presidential candidate, ostensibly to influence an election, is it really a leap to consider that he would be willing to do the same with a man viewed as an "Islamophobe" by CAIR?

While discussing the report on-air with host Anderson Cooper, Griffin referred to claims made by Shoebat that *CNN* and CAIR had collaborated on the story and said they were "not true." At the end of Shoebat's rebuttal to Griffin's report, he again reasserted the claim:

> "We received an unsolicited email from an unimpeachable source that CAIR was fully involved and helped *CNN* with this smear. Obviously we cannot reveal the name as it would compromise him, which is frustrating for us."[76]

Griffin has a history that includes bearing false witness; he has yet to confess or apologize. Shoebat has a history that includes terrorizing Jews. Not only has he confessed and apologized but he was smeared by Griffin for doing so.

# ■ FORT HOOD MASSACRE

There are a select few events in history that are seared into our memories so permanently that not only do we remember the event itself but where we were and what we were doing when we heard the news.

On November 5, 2009 shortly after lunch, Texas talk show host Lynn Woolley and I were in the studio doing some post-production work after his show when we noticed a headline on the *Drudge Report* about a shooting at Fort Hood, TX. Woolley's 'Studio L' was located a short drive from Fort Hood, which made the news hit even closer to home than it otherwise would have.

As time passed and reports began coming in, it became known soon enough that the shooter, a one Nidal Malik Hasan was an Islamic Jihadist who shouted, "Allah-hu-Akbar" inside a Soldier Readiness Center before opening fire. There was massive carnage, in large part because soldiers were not permitted to carry weapons on-base and had to wait for police to arrive. Hasan wasn't allowed to carry a weapon either but that didn't prevent him from doing so – or using it. That's what criminals do; they break the law.

However, Hasan wasn't just a criminal. He was a major in the United States Army; he was a psychiatrist who also doubled as a soldier for his own God. As a Muslim, that made Hasan a 'Soldier of Allah' or an 'SOA' as stated on his business card.[77]

In the minutes and hours that passed after the shooting, the media appeared visibly uncomfortable with reporting the facts about Hasan; he was an Islamic Jihadist and wanted to kill people – infidels – who didn't share his religion. This reality was demonstrated perfectly in an exchange between *Fox News* Channel's Shepard Smith, who referred to Hasan as being "deceased" and US Senator from Texas, Kay Bailey Hutchison (R). It was like watching two people pass a hot potato back and forth:

> **Smith:** Other news organizations are identifying the shooter, the now deceased uh, uh, officer in the United States Army (cough), who, as you've reported to us here, was about to deploy to Iraq or Afghanistan, was upset about that and then today went on this shooting rampage. I've been given a name that's been reported elsewhere and uh, I, I, I'm not, I'm are.. Have you been given a name and what do you know about this suspect? How much are you able to tell us?
>
> **Hutchison:** Well, I have been given a name but I would not want to confirm that because I do not know if this person's family has been notified so I would not want to give the name. I do know that I have been given a name.[78]

Smith was comfortable reporting that the shooter had been killed but he was uncomfortable giving the shooter's name, presumably because it was Arabic. The irony is that Hasan had not been killed and it would have been more accurate if Smith had given Hasan's name and not reported that he was "deceased." Smith also seemed perfectly comfortable speculating on a possible motive by implying that Hasan was upset about an upcoming deployment.

Hutchison's response to Smith that she didn't want to reveal the shooter's name until the shooter's family had been notified only served to trump Smith's inexplicable omission of the name until getting it from the military.

On the following Sunday morning, Army Chief of Staff Gen. George Casey appeared on *ABC's This Week*, hosted by George Stephanopoulos. Shockingly, Casey stated that the murders of soldiers under his command would be dwarfed by "diversity" becoming a casualty:

"...what happened at Fort Hood was a tragedy, but I believe it would be an even greater tragedy if our diversity becomes a casualty here."[79]

The leader of the most powerful army in the world at the time of that interview seemed to imply that protecting diversity was more important than preventing the deaths of the men and women he was charged with leading. It was a breathtakingly shocking statement.

One year and a few days later, Shoebat would speak at a Fort Hood Memorial event near the scene of the massacre. Ultimately, the venue would be at the Killeen Civic Center which was barely more than a walk from the base. Shoebat would be one of several speakers at an event designed to honor the fallen with the truth. Other speakers included Robert Spencer, founder of *Jihad Watch*, and Ret. Delta Force General William Boykin.

The Lynn Woolley show would be a major factor in promoting the event and Lynn himself served as the memorial's Master of Ceremonies. The event was heavily promoted through radio and television commercials, billboards, prominent internet sites, local news stories, and media interviews. Titled *Diversity Starts with the Truth*, the message was a clear reference to the shocking words uttered by Casey one year earlier.

The speakers at the memorial event were all excellent, with Shoebat the last to speak. Though hundreds were in attendance, it was hoped that thousands would be on-hand. When Shoebat spoke, he was visibly angry that Americans had not realized the threat he had been warning of for so many years. He chastised the City of Killeen as well as a local pastor – by name – who decided not to attend; several weeks earlier, reports began to surface that the Chamber of Commerce was discouraging support for the memorial symposium.

A common theme ran through the entire event – America's leaders were not addressing a very dire threat to the nation; responsibility for doing so needed to shift toward her citizens. Shoebat did not shy away from identifying the problem as cowardice at nearly every level.

## ■ THE RISE OF TURKEY

In 2008, Shoebat released what he has called his "life's work," a book entitled *God's War on Terror: Islam, Prophecy, and the Bible*. A central theme in the book is the potential and even likelihood of a resurgent Ottoman Empire which, for centuries was based in what is modern day Turkey.

On the losing side in World War I, the Ottoman Empire was dismantled in 1924. Four years later, in 1928, a man named Hassan al-Banna founded the Muslim Brotherhood in Egypt based on Wahhabism. One year prior to the Brotherhood's founding, the Saudi royal family put down a Wahhabist revolt in response to the royal family's increased wealth and dealings with western civilizations.[80]

A prominent leader of the Brotherhood in 1928 was none other than Haj Amin al-Husseini, the same man who would later visit Shoebat's grandfather regularly due to the latter's status as 'Chieftain.'

The founders of the Brotherhood not only resented western civilization but they had developed a deep-seated hatred for the leadership in Saudi Arabia. In fact, the hatred for the royal family may have been greater than the hatred for the west.

The Muslim Brotherhood would loathe America even more after aligning with Hitler's Nazi Germany in World War II; it would be on the losing side again. Not only had they suffered a defeat very similar to what the Turks suffered in World War I but beginning in 1948, they had to deal with a new reality – a Jewish state. The Islamist Turks and the Brotherhood also had a common goal – the reinstatement of the Ottoman Empire and the Islamic caliphate.

Mustafa Kemal Atatürk founded the Republic of Turkey in 1923 and based the new Kemalist form of government on secularist principles. For decades, Turkey would be a strong ally of the west, bridging gaps between the Middle East and western civilizations.[81] However, the Muslim Brotherhood's birth just five years after the inception of Turkey's secularist government would begin a movement that would aim for the Ottoman Empire's reinstatement courtesy of a one hundred year plan.

Seventy years later – in 2003 – a man named Recep Tayyip Erdoğan would become Turkey's Prime Minister. As leader of the Justice and Development Party (AKP), Erdoğan was at the head of a party seeking Islamist resurgence in that nation.[82]

In fact, Turkey had taken its insistence on secularism so seriously; it had laws on the books that required individuals or groups who called for reinstatement of the Ottoman Empire to be dealt with seriously. Erdoğan found himself on the wrong side of such laws when he publicly recited a poem in 1998 that read, in part, as follows:

"The mosques are our barracks, the domes our helmets, the minarets our bayonets and the faithful our soldiers..."[83]

As a result of speaking those words in public in 1998, Erdoğan was convicted of inciting racial hatred and prevented from assuming the job of Prime Minister after his party was voted into power in November of 2002. The rules were subsequently changed so that he could in fact become Prime Minister.[84] Then in 2007 another member of the Islamist AK party – Abdullah Gül – was elected president of Turkey. Gül's ties to Erdoğan were known to be very close, with the former stepping down as Prime Minister when Erdoğan was cleared. Gül subsequently assumed the role of Foreign Minister before becoming president.[85]

Prior to the rise of the AK Party, the Kemalist military had been an extremely effective check against Islamist regimes. That all changed in 2010, when several Military leaders were arrested and charged with planning to overthrow the government. Turkey would soon be in the hands of the Islamists.

Shoebat's reasons for wanting to warn people about Turkey has much more to do with what such a scenario could mean globally than what it would mean inside Turkey's borders. There is an aspect to it geopolitically, says Shoebat, that westerners just don't seem to grasp. The Islamic culture doesn't believe in individual nation states. It believes in one Islamic caliphate, where Islamic law or Sharia dictates how everyone should be ruled.

He understands the Wahhabist influence behind the Muslim Brotherhood. When in Chicago, he was a Muslim Brotherhood activist – in addition to being a member of the PLO. All of the indicators available – when factoring in Shoebat's history – are that he is more than qualified to make these claims. It's hard to refute him when he puts it in the following terms.

> "Erdoğan is saying 1.5 billion Muslims are waiting for the Turkish government to arise. This is pretty scary. Turkey rules only 70 million people so why are they talking about 1.5 billion Muslims?"[86]

Shoebat's history, family tree, and conversion to Christianity should cause westerners to take heed of what he says. His assertions were further bolstered in November of 2010 when a website known as Wikileaks released confidential cables that showed American diplomats' extreme concern over the rising Islamist influence inside the Turkish government.[87]

## ■ BATTLE ASSESSMENT

A common theme of Shoebat's message is that Muslim males often marry non-Muslim females and raise their children as Muslim. What a touch of irony it must be for him – and for anyone in the west who is willing to look at the truth – that he himself was one of those children; his mother's prayers and soft, nuanced guidance helped to birth her son again, years later in 1993. One of western civilization's greatest warriors against Islamic fundamentalism was a product of the strategy used by Muslim fundamentalists – the use of non-Muslim women as mothers for Muslim children. In the case of Walid Shoebat, that strategy not only failed but it backfired in a major way.

During one of his many speaking engagements, Shoebat spoke at The Worldwide Christian Center in Pompano Beach, FL in 2011. The Pastor of the church – O'Neal Dozier – is the subject of another chapter in this book **[See Chapter 7, p. 191]**. Moments prior to his one hour presentation, it was brought to Shoebat's attention that the Executive Director for CAIR–South Florida – Nezar Hamze[88] – was in attendance.

A main point of Shoebat's message that day was that Islam is an evil religion that doesn't honor its women. He went even further, saying that the anti-Christ would be Islamic and that Islam is the religion of the anti-Christ. At one point, Shoebat pointed to the following passage of the Bible in Daniel 11:37-39 to rebuke the arguments that the anti-Christ would be an atheist who does not desire women. The passage reads as follows:

[37]He shall regard neither the God[a] of his fathers **nor the desire of women**, nor regard any god; for he shall exalt himself above them all.

[38]But in their place **he shall honor a god of fortresses**; and **a god which his fathers did not know** he shall honor with gold and silver, with precious stones and pleasant things.

[39]Thus **he shall act against the strongest fortresses with a foreign god**, which he shall acknowledge, and advance its glory; and he shall cause them to rule over many, and divide the land for gain.[89]

Shoebat's argument was that the anti-Christ will honor a god of war and that he will not honor the *desire* of women. Both assertions refute the claims of those who insist the anti-Christ will be atheist and homosexual. Shoebat maintained that Biblical scholars have misinterpreted that verse to mean the anti-Christ will not desire women. Shoebat then pointed to the treatment of Muslim women in the Islamic world, saying they are treated as second class citizens and that their wishes, wants, and desires are not honored in Islam.

After Shoebat was finished, Hamze confronted him near the front of the church for debate. At one point, the CAIR official told Shoebat he was wrong about Muslim women. Hamze admitted to Shoebat – and to the circle of observers which had formed – that he too was the son of a Christian mother and a Muslim father. Hamze objected to Shoebat's claims about how women in Islam are treated and insisted that in Islam, women are actually honored more than men.

Shoebat's response was a knockout punch:

"If that's true, why didn't you honor your mother and become a Christian?"

As I watched the exchange that was taking place between a former Muslim terrorist and a member of CAIR inside a Christian church, I wondered about the likelihood of something similar being permitted in a mosque.[90]

In the story of David and Goliath, the underdog David was thrust into duty because the much more qualified – and supposedly more courageous – warriors cowered in the face of such an imposing enemy. Goliath was huge; he dwarfed those who dwarfed David. But David had a much stronger faith; it gave him the edge he needed. In that regard, he carried a stronger weapon than did any of his brothers.

Coincidentally or not, it is Shoebat who is standing up to the Islamic Goliath, armed with little more than the truth and a committed faith while US political and military leaders cower like David's brothers as they defend the worst secularism has to offer – political correctness, multiculturalism, and diversity.

As a former Muslim, Shoebat is considered an apostate. As such, he is a greater target for Islamists than is someone like the Chief of Staff of the US Army, Gen. George Casey for example. Yet, it is Shoebat who is speaking out while the leaders of the west practically admit – by refusing to state what a majority of Americans already instinctively know – that Goliath wants a fight and continues to be met with appeasement.

Encountering cowardice is a frustrating reality for Shoebat. It has caused pastors who agree with his message to back away at the moment of truth. Secretly, many pastors have told him they stand with him but can offer no more than prayers as their support. Should that really be considered standing with someone?

Like many of the other Davids in this book, Walid Shoebat's battle with Goliath is still being waged but a look at history may provide some insight into where his journey might lead. Perhaps by looking at the path of a man Shoebat's great-grandfather considered a personal friend would demonstrate some parallels.

From 1929 – 1939 Winston Churchill had fallen out of favor with his countrymen. His pleas about the threat of Hitler's Nazism not only fell on deaf ears; they fell on offended ones – ears not willing to listen for fear of what it would mean if Churchill was right. Wishing evil away did not work. It brought World War II.

Then, in 1940, after Prime Minister Neville Chamberlain had been unabashedly ashamed by his attempts to appease Adolf Hitler, he relinquished his position to Churchill, who would eventually lead the British in the Allies' defeat of Nazi Germany.[91]

Churchill was vindicated but at great expense to his nation and the world. It was a price he would rather not have paid. Had Churchill been listened to sooner, perhaps Hitler could have been stopped; we'll never know how that alternate scenario would have played out but it is beyond dispute that Churchill was right about Nazism.

Shoebat, unlike Churchill, was a member of the enemy he later attempted to warn his fellow countrymen about. However, both men shared similar views about Islamic fundamentalism. In 1899, Churchill wrote the following about Islam:

"How dreadful are the curses which Mohammedanism lays on its votaries! Besides the fanatical frenzy, which is as dangerous in a man as hydrophobia in a dog, there is this fearful fatalistic apathy. The effects are apparent in many countries. Improvident habits, slovenly systems of agriculture, sluggish methods of commerce, and insecurity of property exist wherever the followers of the Prophet rule or live. A degraded sensualism deprives this life of its grace and refinement; the next of its dignity and sanctity.

The fact that in Mohammedan law every woman must belong to some man as his absolute property, either as a child, a wife, or a concubine, must delay the final extinction of slavery until the faith of Islam has ceased to be a great power among men. Individual Moslems may show splendid qualities – but the influence of the religion paralyses the social development of those who follow it. No stronger retrograde force exists in the world. Far from being moribund, Mohammedanism is a militant and proselytizing faith. It has already spread throughout Central Africa, raising fearless warriors at every step; and were it not that Christianity is sheltered in the strong arms of science, the science against which it had vainly struggled, the civilization of modern Europe might fall, as fell the civilization of ancient Rome."[92]

In addition to both Churchill and Shoebat having a familial connection, both would hold similar views on the motives of the enemy western civilization refuses to identify. In many ways, Shoebat is fighting a battle that mirrors the one Churchill fought – domestic opposition coupled with a very real threat that fellow countrymen would rather wish away.

However, as it did with Churchill, the tide began to slowly turn for Shoebat as events unfolded slowly, over time.

Shoebat's mother sowed the seeds for his re-birth; his wife helped to deliver him; now the former Muslim terrorist understands the meaning of the Biblical metaphor that likens the Messiah's followers to a bride which must prepare for His second coming. The symbolism is not lost on Shoebat who maintains that standing up to Islamic fundamentalism is part of that preparation as women are reviled in Islam and revered in Christianity.

Once again, the woman's role in defeating evil is a central one.

*Author's Note:* As this book was going to press, it was learned that five sitting US Congressmen – led by 2012 former Presidential candidate Rep. Michele Bachmann (R-MN) – sent a letter to the office of the Inspector General at the State Department (cc: Hillary Clinton). The letter was intended to spur an investigation into concerns about

"Department of State policies and activities" resulting from Muslim Brotherhood influence.

The letter cited an example that stemmed from information that Shoebat had uncovered one year earlier. Specifically, the letter addressed a report that:

> "...the Department's Deputy Chief of Staff, Huma Abedin, has three family members – her late father, her mother and her brother – connected to Muslim Brotherhood operatives and/or organizations. Her position affords her routine access to the Secretary and to policy-making."[93]

This information was the direct result of Shoebat's findings. Consider, a man who became an American patriot after leaving the world of the Muslim Brotherhood not only remains largely unsung but continues to have his American patriotism impugned and questioned by those who have labeled him a fraud.

The case against such *accusers* being patriots would seem to be easier to prove.

# EPILOGUE

In the story of David and Goliath, a young shepherd boy, armed with nothing more than a sling and five smooth stones, faced an enormous, evil giant. David was the least likely candidate to do so. Stronger earthly men, who were obliged to take up the fight, took a pass instead. The ominous task of battle fell to David by default. No one else was willing to stand up to the giant who threatened their nation.

When David hit the beast between the eyes, the Philistine fell dead to the ground. David would become king as a result but not before he had to fight another battle with the sitting king – Saul. Before Goliath was slain, Saul was willing to grant David anything, as long as it was on contingency and subject to enmity. Saul didn't just find his courage when there was nothing left to fear; he strapped it on in order to confront a hero. Why was Saul averse to confronting a beast who sought to enslave his people but eager to confront an honorable man who freed them from certain bondage? It was something worse than cowardice masquerading as courage; vindictiveness toward the man who eliminated the source of such cowardice seemed to rise. It is also a phenomenon each David in this book faced as well, to varying degrees.

After thousands of years have passed, David is still viewed as a man of God. He was someone whose faith was so strong; it trumped fear of any earthly consequences. His colleagues refused to fight Goliath for one simple reason; they allowed fear to rise and faith to fall. After thousands of years, their legacy is one of cowardice and faithlessness. If you could transport yourself thousands of years into the future, what would you want your legacy to be?

What if the stone from David's sling had only weakened Goliath? What if it didn't kill him? Suppose it had dazed him to the point that all it would take was for David's fellow countrymen to pounce on the giant and finish him off. Would they do it? If one is inclined to give them the benefit of the doubt, the answer would be in the affirmative. Is it not more shameful to avoid finishing off a weakened nemesis than to avoid taking him on at full strength? Would not the legacy ascribed to people who ignore an evil and wounded adversary out of fear be far worse than David's brethren, who never had the opportunity?

This book was not solely about ten heroic men who fought in the spirit of David, nor was it only about the ten opponents they sent reeling. It was also about the men who refused to seize upon a vulnerable Goliath, an evil beast that had been weakened by ten underdogs. Each one of these unsung Davids seriously wounded his adversary. However, far more often than not, no one who wielded earthly power of consequence joined them, even when the corrupt, deceitful, and wicked entity was badly wounded, dazed, and wobbly in the knees. Reinforcements didn't come, even when there was blood in the water.

None of these ten heroes will have a legacy on par with David but what about the legacies of the men who did not come to their aid? Will they not carry more disgrace because they stood down even when victory was at hand? Even David's countrymen didn't do that.

Short of an intervention that includes the actual hand of God, the only hope good men have is to acquire a faith in Him that commands we offer assistance to such Davids, without fear or reservation.

In the words of Edmund Burke, *"When bad men combine, the good must associate; else they will fall, one by one, an unpitied sacrifice in a contemptible struggle."*[1]

# APPENDIX

## Chapter 1

APPENDIX A

| | | | | | |
|---|---|---|---|---|---|
| | | | BH 316 276 2251 | | |
| 6.52 | | | | | |
| 9·02 | Malcolm Cassell | 447980726 | Pacific Center Cypherworks | Network Admin | |
| 9·22 | Alan Meyer | On 310788 2850 | Urgent | | X |
| 10·11 | Alex Chairman Rendell − | 202 863 7114 | Emergency | | X |
| 11·03 | Lloyd Grove | 202-439-0319 | | | |
| | | | | | |

PPB2 0775

# APPENDIX B

August 13, 2000

Aug. 13, 2000
agreement
between Stan
Lee Media and
Venture Soft

Venture Soft Co., Ltd.
Imperial Tower 14th Floor
1-1-1 Uchisaiwaicho
Chiyoda Ku, Tokyo 100-0011
Japan

Gentlemen:

This letter agreement sets forth the principal terms of an agreement
between Stan Lee Media, Inc. ("SLM") and Venture Soft Co., Ltd. ("VS"),
regarding the creation of a joint venture to become the premiere distributor of
original and co-created branded content in Japan and Korea (the "Territory") by
capitalizing on the strengths of VS as the dominant anime and manga creator and
distributor in the Territory and SLM as a dominant creator of globally branded
super-hero franchises in the U.S. The joint venture to be created hereby is
tentatively named "Stan Lee Japan."

The purpose of this joint venture is intended to result in the creation of
a company that is expected to become a publicly traded company in Japan that is
dedicated to:

## APPENDIX C, Page 1

**HILLARY RODHAM CLINTON**
**FOR U.S. SENATE COMMITTEE, INC.**
**450 7TH AVE., SUITE 804**
**NEW YORK, NY 10123**

**www.hillary2000.org**

**FACSIMILE TRANSMITTAL SHEET**

| TO | FROM |
|---|---|
| Steve Gordon | David Rosen, National Finance Director |
| **COMPANY:** Stan Lee Media | **DATE** 8/24/00 |
| **FAX NUMBER:** 818.205.1180 | **TOTAL NO. OF PAGES INCLUDING COVER:** 2 |
| **PHONE NUMBER:** | **SENDER'S TELEPHONE NUMBER:** (212) 239-2000 |
| **RE** Stock Transfer | **SENDER'S FACSIMILE NUMBER:** (212) 967-1392 |

☐ URGENT  ☒ FOR REVIEW  ☐ PLEASE COMMENT  ☐ PLEASE REPLY  ☐ PLEASE RECYCLE

**NOTES/COMMENTS:**

## APPENDIX C, Page 2

**HILLARY RODHAM CLINTON FOR U.S. SENATE COMMITTEE, INC.**
450 7TH AVENUE, SUITE 804
NEW YORK, NY 10123

www.hillary2000.org

**MEMORANDUM**

TO: STEVE GORDON
FROM: DAVID ROSEN
SUBJECT: STOCK TRANSFERS
DATE: 8/3/00

Following is the most current information regarding the stock transfer. Please call with any questions.

### WORKING FAMILIES PARTY

$100,000

Brokerage Account: Morgan Stanley / Dean Wittier
Account Name: WFP
Account #: 770-033236-329
Account Rep: Mike Bracla
Administrative Assistant: Tara Caso
Ph: 718-370-4610

*DONE*

Morgan Stanley/Dean Wittier
900 South Ave.
Suite 101
Staten Island, New York 10314

Paid for by Hillary Rodham Clinton for U.S. Senate Committee, Inc.
Contributions are not tax deductible for federal income tax purposes.

# APPENDIX D

# Chapter 2

APPENDIX A

Ing. Joseph Doriel
Management & Development Consulting Eng.

אינג' יוסף דוריאל
מהנדס יועץ לניהול ופיתוח

## ANALYSIS OF THE TV RECORD

### FROM THE NETZARIM JUNCTION TRAGEDY ON SEP. 30, 2000

DESCRIPTION OF THE SPACE HIDDEN FROM POSSIBLE IDF SHOOTING –

BEHIND THE CONCRETE BARREL.

IN THE SCHEMATIC DRAWING (IN ORIGINAL SCALE OF 1:25) THE
CONCRETE BARREL IS SUGGESTED TO BE OF 70 cm DIAMETER.
IN CASE OF A LARGER DIAMETER THE SPACE HIDDEN FROM POSSIBLE

IDF SHOOTING INCREASES.

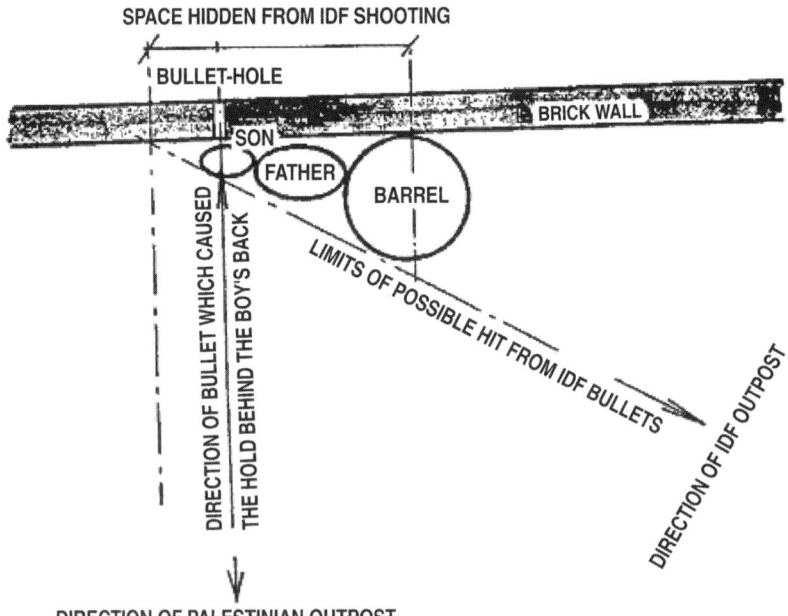

# Chapter 4

APPENDIX A

**Form 990-PF**

Department of the Treasury
Internal Revenue Service

## Return of Private I

or Section 4947(a)(1) Nonexem
Treated as a Private F

Note: The organization may be able to use a copy of this r

For calendar year 1998, or tax year beginning _____ , 199

| Use the IRS label. Otherwise, please print or type. See Specific Instructions. | Name of organization<br>CHICAGO ANNENBERG CHALLENGE |
| --- | --- |
| | Number and street (or P.O. box number if mail is not delivered to street address)<br>115 SOUTH SANGAMON |
| | City or town, state, and ZIP + 4<br>CHICAGO, IL 60607 |

## APPENDIX B

**CONTACT PERSON:**  Mike Klonsky, Co-Director
Small School Workshop/University of Illinois at Chicago
115 S. Sangamon Street, 3rd Floor
Chicago, IL 60607
312-413-8066

## APPENDIX C

### WUO "Pine Street Bomb Factory"

California. He stated that during April, 1970, one
CLINTON EVERETT WILLARD rented the apartment for a year
period ending March, 1971. At the time he claimed to be
employed by Mr. EZRA HENDON, an attorney in Berkeley,
California. When          arrived at the building in mid-April,
1971, he discovered the apartment apparently abandoned.
On inspection he discovered bombing paraphernalia which
led him to contact the FBI.

          viewed photographs of various WUO members
and identified photographs on California drivers licenses
in the names CLINTON EVERETT WILLARD and ROBERT PEARSON
WHITE as being identical to the man who rented the apartment.
(Both the WILLARD and WHITE drivers licenses had come to the
attention of the FBI in previous investigation insofar as
both individuals in whose names these licenses were issued
died as infants.)          also identified a photograph of WUO
member CLAYTON VAN LIDEGRAF as being identical to the
older man who helped to move "WILLARD" into the apartment.
(On May 20, 1971
Kent State University, Kent, Ohio, was shown the WILLARD
and WHITE drivers licenses and advised that both bore the
photograph of MARK JOSEPH REAL, whom he knew to have been
the WUO leader in the Kent area in late 1969.)

          Inspection of the apartment yielded an amount of
explosives and bomb making paraphernalia. Fingerprints were
subsequently lifted from articles in the apartment by
Special Agents of the FBI. Fingerprints of the following
WUO members were found in this apartment:

| | |
|---|---|
| KAREN LYNN ASHLEY | HOWARD NORTON MACHTINGER |
| ➤ WILLIAM CHARLES AYERS | JULIE NICHAMIN |
| KATHIE BOUDIN | JEFFREY DAVID POWELL |
| PETER WALES CLAPP | SHELDON ROSENBAUM |
| JOHN WILLARD DAVIS | MARK WILLIAM RUDD |
| DAVID JOSEPH GILBERT | MICHAEL LOUIS SPIEGEL |
| NAOMI ESTHER JAFFE | LAWRENCE MICHAEL WEISS |
| MICHAEL THOMAS JUSTESEN | CATHLYN PLATT WILKERSON |

384

TOP SECRET

# Chapter 5

## AMENDED IN SENATE AUGUST 19, 1976
## AMENDED IN ASSEMBLY APRIL 21, 1976

### CALIFORNIA LEGISLATURE—1975–76 REGULAR SESSION

# ASSEMBLY BILL      No. 3154

## Introduced by Assemblyman Brown
## February 19, 1976

### REFERRED TO COMMITTEE ON LOCAL GOVERNMENT

An act to add Section 34270.1 to the Health and Safety Code, relating to housing authorities.

### LEGISLATIVE COUNSEL'S DIGEST

AB 3154, as amended, Brown (L.Gov.), Housing authorities: commissioners: San Francisco.

(1) Under existing law, when the governing body of a city and county so determines, the mayor is required to appoint either 5 or 7 members as commissioners of a housing authority, subject to governing body confirmation. If 7 commissioners are appointed, the extra 2 are required to be tenants of the authority and 1 must be a tenant over 62 years of age.

This bill would require the appointment of 5 members by the mayor and require the mayor to appoint 2 additional tenants of the authority; if the authority has tenants or within 1 year of when the authority first does have tenants. One of the tenant commissioners appointed would be required to be over 62 years of age if the authority has tenants over 62.

(2) Under existing law there is no requirement that members of a housing authority in a city and county be residents of the city and county.

This bill would require all commissioners appointed on and

## AB 3154                    — 2 —

and after January 1, 1977, to the housing authority in a city and county to be residents of the city and county at the time of their appointment and during the term thereof.
Vote: majority. Appropriation: no. Fiscal committee: no. State-mandated local program: no.

*The people of the State of California do enact as follows:*

1    SECTION 1. Section 34270.1 is added to the Health
2  and Safety Code, to read:
3    34270.1: When the governing body of a city and
4  county adopts a resolution pursuant to Section 34270, the
5    *34270.1   The provisions of this section apply to an*
6  *authority in a city and county.*
7    *Notwithstanding any other provision of law to the*
8  *contrary; including Section 34272, the*  mayor shall
9  appoint five persons as commissioners of the authority *in*
10  *a city and county.* The mayor shall appoint two
11  additional commissioners who are tenants of the
12  authority if the authority has tenants, or within one year
13  after the authority first does have tenants. One such
14  tenant commissioner shall be over 62 years of age if the
15  authority has tenants of such age. *Appointments shall not*
16  *be subject to confirmation by the governing body of the*
17  *city and county.* All commissioners appointed on an d
18  after January 1, 1977, shall be residents of the city and
19  county, at the time of their appointment and during their
20  term of office. A failure to maintain residence in the city
21  and county shall cause the office to be vacant. *Vacancies*
22  *in office for whatever reason, including but not limited*
23  *to, the expiration of a term, shall be filled by the mayor*
24  *as provided for in this section.*

# APPENDIX A, Page 3

**Collateral References:**
Cal Jur 3d Public Housing § 13.
*Law Review Articles:*
Review of Selected 1972 Code Legislation. 4 Pacific LJ 625.

## § 34270.1. Appointment of commissioners in City and County of San Francisco

The provisions of this section apply to an authority in a city and county.

Notwithstanding any other provision of law to the contrary, including Section 34272, the mayor shall appoint five persons as commissioners of the authority in a city and county. The mayor shall appoint two additional commissioners who are tenants of the authority. One such tenant commissioner shall be over 62 years of age if the authority has tenants of such age. Appointments shall not be subject to confirmation by the governing body of the city and county. All commissioners appoinnted on and after January 1, 1977, shall be residents of the city and county, at the time of their appointment and during their term of office. A failure to maintain residence in the city and county shall cause the office to be vacant. Vacancies in the office for whatever reason, including but not limited to, the expiration of a term, shall be filled by the mayor as provided for in this section.

Added Stats 1976 ch 1400 § 1.
**Cross References:**
County seat of San Francisco City and County: Gov C § 23638.

### NOTES OF DECISIONS

City and County of San Francisco is both city and county and has powers of both. Blum v San    Francisco (1962) 200 CA 2d 639, 19 Cal Rptr 574.

## § 34271. Appointment of commissioners by governing city of county

When the governing body of a county adopts such a resolution it shall appoint five persons as commissioners of the authority. The governing body shall appoint two additional commissioners who are tenants of the authority if the authority has tenants, or within one year after the authority first does have tenants. One such tenant commissioner shall be over 62 years of age if the authority has tenants of such age.

The amentments to this section enacted by the Legislature at the 1975–76 Regular Session shall not affect the office of any commissioner of a housing authority, which on January 1, 1976, has seven commissioners, but the successors to the two additional commissioners appointed pursuant to the changes in this section which were

475

APPENDIX B

# The City and County of San Francisco
### STATE OF CALIFORNIA

To all to whom these presents shall come; Greeting:

Reposing special confidence in the fidelity and ability of

## Reverend James Jones

I do, by these presents, by virtue of the authority vested in me by the Housing Authorities Law of the State of California, appoint him a member of the Housing Authority in and for the City and County of San Francisco he to hold said office for the term ending April 27, 1980 from and after the thirtieth day of November 1976 vice Stephen Walter, term expired

In Testimony Whereof, I have signed my name and have caused the seal of my office to be affixed hereto this thirtieth day of November, 1976.

Attest

Executive Deputy to the Mayor

Mayor

BB-17-X

# APPENDIX C

(d. ... ... number)
17357

ANDRE MENNET

SWISS BANK CORPORATION    P.O. BOX 3370-PANAMA 4, PANAMA
... S.A.    TELEPHONE: 24-3359
... BUILDING 6th FLOOR    CABLE: SWISBANK
CALLE ... No. 47    TELEX: 171 ...

11/9/82    1643    b7c

November 18, 1978

Mr. Fedor Timofeyev, Consul
48 Chandra Nagar Street
Prashad Nagar
Georgetown, Guyana

Dear Comrade Timofeyev,

The following is a letter of instructions regarding all our assets which we want to leave to the Communist Party of the Union of Soviet Socialist Republics. Enclosed in this letter are letters which instruct the banks to send the cashiers checks to you. I am doing this on behalf of Peoples Temple because we, as Communists, want our money to be of benefit for help to oppressed peoples all over the world, or in any way that your decision-making body sees fit.

There are two basic accounts which are in fixed time deposits. One is located in Swiss Bank Corporation, P.O. Box 3370, Panama 4, Panama. In this account are two deposits. One is for $557,000.00 and it is on a thirty day rotation so it can be withdrawn almost immediately which the letter of instruction so instructs. The other is for $1,486,000.00 and it matures on July 6, 1978 so at that time you could receive a cashiers check for that amount. The other account is located in the Union Bank of Switzerland, P.O. Box 6792, Panama 5, Panama. In this account are seven fixed time deposits. The following is a list of amounts and dates due (not including interest earned):

| | |
|---|---|
| $300,000 | May 31, 1979 |
| $200,000 | July 5, 1979 |
| $1,623,000 | July 25, 1979 |
| $1,000,000 | Aug. 21, 1979 |
| $82,536 | Aug. 29, 1979 |
| $1,036,000 | Sept. 21, 1979 |
| $1,000,000 | July 20, 1979 |

The account number for the account at Union Bank of Switzerland is 121-00-191A. The account number for the account at Swiss Bank Corporation is #3357.

With the enclosed letters you should have no difficulty in receiving the checks upon the above mentioned maturity dates.

Account # 121-00-191A

RUDOLF KELLER
Assistant Vice President
UNION BANK OF SWITZERLAND (PANAMA) INC.

CALLE MANUEL MARIA ICAZA No. 41    APTDO. POSTAL 6792
TEL. 64-9444    PANAMA 5, R.P.
    TELEX: 991 PANUBS

Cooperatively yours,

Annie J. McSwain

# Chapter 7

APPENDIX A

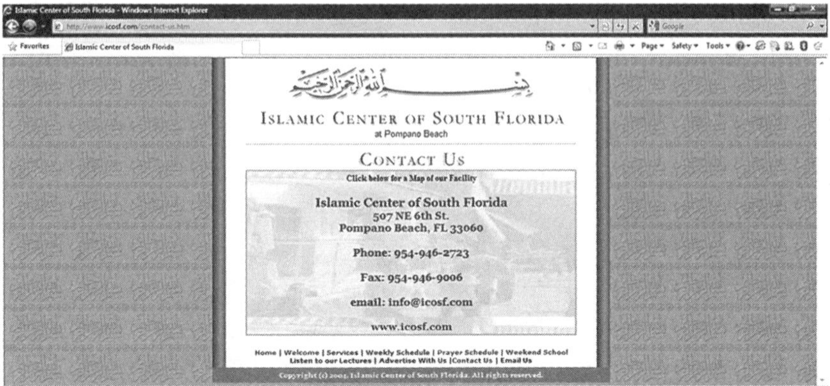

ISLAMIC CENTER OF SOUTH FLORIDA
at Pompano Beach

CONTACT US
Click below for a Map of our Facility

**Islamic Center of South Florida**
507 NE 6th St.
Pompano Beach, FL 33060

Phone: 954-946-2723

Fax: 954-946-9006

email: info@icosf.com

www.icosf.com

Home | Welcome | Services | Weekly Schedule | Prayer Schedule | Weekend School
Listen to our Lectures | Advertise With Us |Contact Us | Email Us
Copyright (c) 2005, Islamic Center of South Florida. All rights reserved.

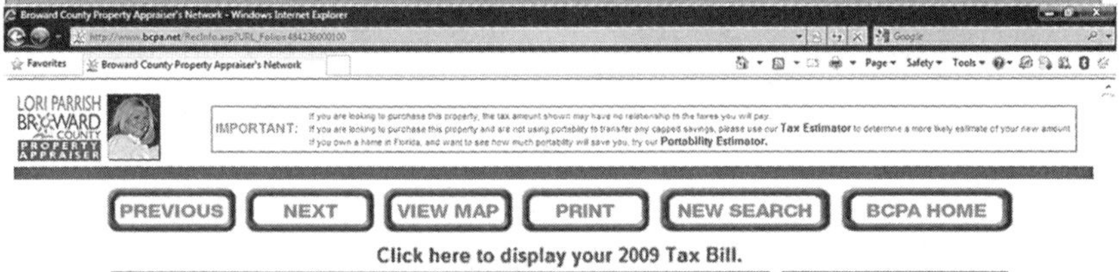

LORI PARRISH
BROWARD
COUNTY
PROPERTY
APPRAISER

IMPORTANT: If you are looking to purchase this property, the tax amount shown may have no relationship to the taxes you will pay.
If you are looking to purchase this property and are not using portability to transfer any capped savings, please use our **Tax Estimator** to determine a more likely estimate of your new amount.
If you own a home in Florida, and want to see how much portability will save you, try our **Portability Estimator**.

| PREVIOUS | NEXT | VIEW MAP | PRINT | NEW SEARCH | BCPA HOME |

Click here to display your 2009 Tax Bill.

| Site Address | 507 NE 6 STREET , POMPANO BEACH | | ID # | 4842 36 00 0100 |
|---|---|---|---|---|
| Property Owner | NORTH AMERICAN ISLAMIC TRUST | | Millage | 1511 |
| Mailing Address | 507 NE 6TH ST POMPANO BEACH FL 33060 | | Use | 71 |

| Legal Description | 36-48-42 BEG 430 W & 25 S OF NE COR OF S1/2 OF NW1/4 OF NW1/4 OF SW1/4,W 206.6,S 275.13,E 206.11, N 275.8 TO POB LOT N |
|---|---|

| Property Assessment Values | | | | | |
|---|---|---|---|---|---|
| Year | Land | Building | Just Value | Assessed / SOH Value | Tax |
| 2010 | $623,080 | $863,170 | $1,486,250 | $1,486,250 | |
| 2009 | $623,080 | $863,170 | $1,486,250 | $1,486,250 | |
| 2008 | $623,080 | $861,160 | $1,484,240 | $1,484,240 | |

# Chapter 8

APPENDIX A, Page 1

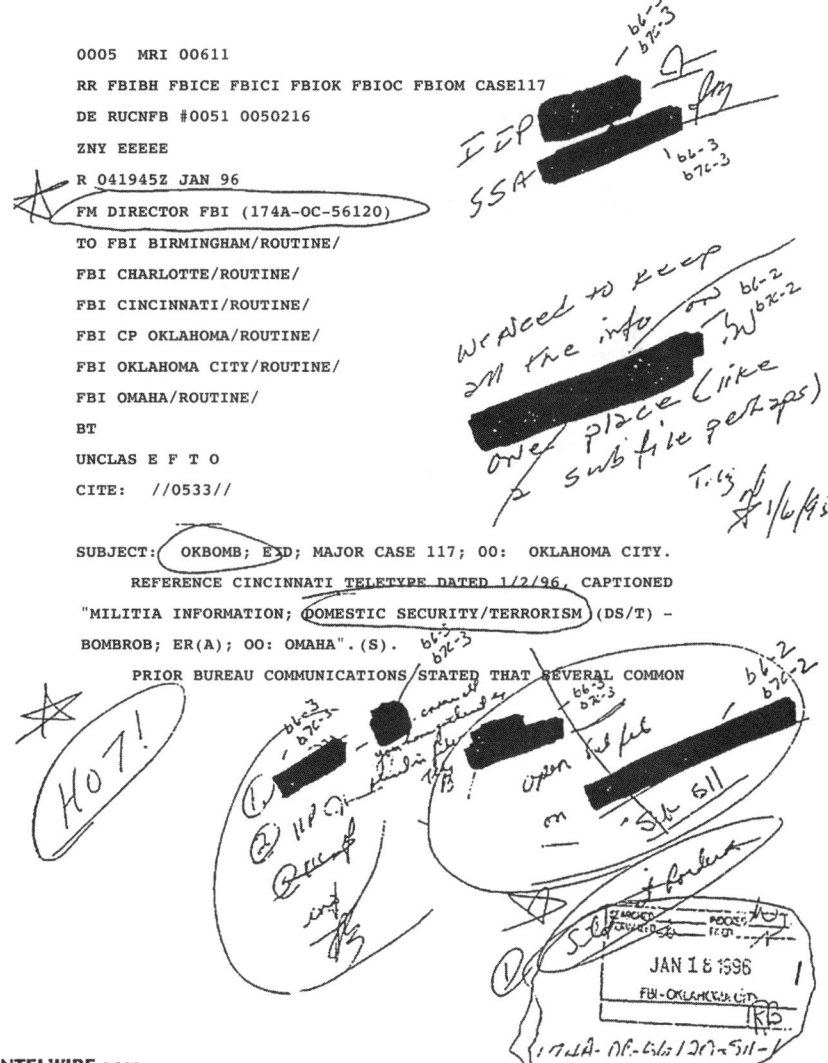

```
0005  MRI 00611

RR FBIBH FBICE FBICI FBIOK FBIOC FBIOM CASE117

DE RUCNFB #0051 0050216

ZNY EEEEE

R 041945Z JAN 96

FM DIRECTOR FBI (174A-OC-56120)

TO FBI BIRMINGHAM/ROUTINE/

FBI CHARLOTTE/ROUTINE/

FBI CINCINNATI/ROUTINE/

FBI CP OKLAHOMA/ROUTINE/

FBI OKLAHOMA CITY/ROUTINE/

FBI OMAHA/ROUTINE/

BT

UNCLAS E F T O

CITE: //0533//

   SUBJECT:  OKBOMB;  ESD;  MAJOR CASE 117;  OO:  OKLAHOMA CITY.

      REFERENCE CINCINNATI TELETYPE DATED 1/2/96, CAPTIONED

   "MILITIA INFORMATION; DOMESTIC SECURITY/TERRORISM (DS/T) –

   BOMBROB; ER(A); OO: OMAHA".(S).

      PRIOR BUREAU COMMUNICATIONS STATED THAT SEVERAL COMMON
```

# APPENDIX A, Page 2

PAGE TWO DE RUCMFB 0051 UNCLAS E F T O

CHARACTERISTICS UTILIZED BY THE ROBBERS IN THE BOMBROB
INVESTIGATION INCLUDED THE USE OF SPANISH TERMINOLOGY AND THE
RENTING OF GETAWAY VEHICLES IN THE NAMES OF PROMINENT FBI
OFFICIALS.  ALSO POINTED OUT WAS THE POSSIBILITY THAT ONE OF THE
ROBBERS MAY HAVE HAD PRIOR MILITARY LAW ENFORCEMENT OR EXPLOSIVES
TRAINING.

    IN REFERENCED TELETYPE, A CINCINNATI CW WHO KNOWS ▓▓▓▓
▓▓▓▓▓▓▓ TO THE ARYAN NATIONS (AN), CHURCH OF JESUS
CHRIST CHRISTIAN, HAYDEN LAKE, ID (100A-SU-9595), STATED THAT
▓▓▓ WAS A ▓▓▓▓▓▓▓▓▓▓▓▓▓▓▓▓▓▓▓▓▓▓ WHO IN
ADDITION TO ▓▓▓▓▓▓▓▓▓▓▓▓▓▓▓▓ EXPERTISE, ALSO POSSESSED
KNOWLEDGE OF ▓▓▓▓▓▓ AND ▓▓▓▓▓▓▓ IS KNOWN TO PROVIDE
SUCH TRAINING TO AN MEMBERS DURING ANNUAL AN CONGRESS SESSIONS
HELD IN HAYDEN LAKE.

    CW RECALLED THAT, APPROXIMATELY THREE YEARS AGO WHILE HE WAS
IN THE HOME OF ONE ▓▓▓▓▓, ▓▓▓▓▓▓▓, ▓, ▓▓▓▓ RECEIVED
A TELEPHONE CALL FROM ▓▓▓ WHO INFORMED THAT HE WAS, AT THAT
TIME, IN THE STATE OF VERMONT AND HAD JUST COMPLETED COMPILING A
LIST OF NAMES OF ▓▓▓▓▓▓▓ CW CONTINUED THAT THIS
INFORMATION WAS CONFIRMED BY AN HEAD PASTOR RICHARD BUTLER
APPROXIMATELY 13 MONTHS AGO. ▓▓▓▓ IS KNOWN TO THE FBI AS AN

# APPENDIX A, Page 3

PAGE THREE DE RUCNFB 0051 UNCLAS E F T O

ATTONEY WHO REPRESENTS RADICALLY CONSERVATIVE INDIVIDUALS/ *b70-1*

MOVEMENTS AND IS THE ▓▓▓▓▓▓ OF ▓▓▓▓▓▓▓ WHO REPRESENTS *b6-1*

THE C.A.U.S.E. FOUNDATION, WHICH HAS AN AFFILIATION. *b7c 1*

    IN EARLY 1995, CW ▓▓▓▓▓▓▓▓▓ AND ▓▓▓▓▓▓▓ AT THEIR

▓▓▓▓▓▓ ▓▓ PROPERTY AND SAW SEVERAL PLASTIC FOLDERS

CONTAINING AUDIO TAPES LABELED "LEARNING SPANISH". ▓▓▓TOLD CW

THAT HE WAS LEARNING SPANISH AND THAT IT WAS IMPORTANT TO KNOW

OTHER LANGUAGES.

    WHILE THERE IS NO EVIDENCE TO DIRECTLY LINK ▓▓▓▓▓ TO

THE BOMBROB INCIDENTS, IT WOULD APPEAR POSSIBLE THAT ▓▓ COULD

HAVE KNOWLEDGE AND/OR CONSPIRATORIAL INPUT INTO SUCH CRIMINAL

ACTIVITY.

    INFORMATION HAS ALSO BEEN RECEIVED THROUGH THE SOUTHERN

POVERTY LAW CENTER (SPLC) THAT ONE ▓▓▓▓▓▓▓▓▓▓, AKA *b6-2*

▓▓▓▓▓▓▓▓▓ ▓▓▓▓▓▓▓▓▓ TELEPHONE CALL FROM *b7c-2*

TIMOTHY MCVEIGH, ON OR ABOUT 4/17/95, TWO DAYS PRIOR TO THE

OKBOMB ATTACK, WHEN ▓▓▓▓▓▓, PER A SOURCE OF THE SPLC, WAS IN

THE WHITE SUPREMACIST COMPOUND AT ▓▓▓▓▓▓, OK. ▓▓▓▓▓▓

ALLEGEDLY HAS HAD A LENGTHY RELATIONSHIP WITH TIMOTHY MCVEIGH,

ONE OF TWO INDICTED OKBOMB DEFENDANTS. THE SOURCE OF THE SPLC

3

## APPENDIX A, Page 4

PAGE FOUR DE RUCNFB 0051 UNCLAS E F T O

6-2  ADVISED THAT ██████████ IS CURRENTLY RESIDING WITH ██████████ IN b6-1

76-2  ██████████ NC, AND PLANS TO LEAVE THE U.S. VIA MEXICO, IN  b7c-1

THE NEAR FUTURE.  THE SOURCE FURTHER ADVISED THAT HE/SHE HAS

LEARNED THAT ████████████████████ FOR AN UNKNOWN REASON.

PRIOR OKBOMB INVESTIGATION DETERMINED THAT MCVEIGH HAD

PLACED A TELEPHONE CALL TO ELOHIM CITY ON 4/5/95, A DAY THAT HE

WAS BELIEVED TO HAVE BEEN ATTEMPTING TO RECRUIT A SECOND

CONSPIRATOR TO ASSIST IN THE OKBOMB ATTACK.  THE OKBOMB COMMAND

POST IS ATTEMPTING TO VERIFY THE VERSION OF EVENTS AS SET FORTH

BY THE SOURCE AND TO DEVELOP FURTHER INFORMATION.

THE ABOVE IS PROVIDED FOR INFORMATIONAL PURPOSES.

BT

#0051


NNNN


4

## APPENDIX B

Date: 10/01/1997  07:41 pm  (Wednesday)
From: Juliette N. Kayyem
To: orange.of21.SM001!WINSTON
Subject: Trentadue mission

This is like coordinating the invasion of Normandy.  We are on for
Monday; the declination memo is done.  Is this ok with Eric's schedule (I
can call whoever does that.)  I talked to Faith and she is going to think
about the best way to approach Hatch, and possibly Dorgan, and I will
get back to you.  Also, we will be contacting the FBI and Jesse Trentadue
at the same time (about 2 hours before the press release.)  Thanks, jnk

USA010 0244

# Chapter 9

## APPENDIX A, Page 1

[b](6) Mr, DoD OGC

From: [b](6) Mr, DoD OGC
Sent: Friday, February 01, 2002 10:40 AM
To: [b](6) Ms, DoD OGC
Subject: RE: Luncheon Speaker - Islam and Middle Eastern politics and culture - February 5th - RESPONSE DATE - 1/31

[b](6)

Is it too late to sign up?

[b](6)

> -----Original Message-----
>From: [b](6) Ms, DoD OGC
>Sent: Thursday, January 24, 2002 12:33 PM
>To: [b](6) Mr, DoD OGC; Allen, Charles, Mr, DoD OGC; [b](6)
[b](6) Mr, DoD OGC; [b](6) Maj, DoD OGC; [b](6)
Ms, DoD OGC; [b](6) Ms, DoD OGC; [b](6) Mr, DoD OGC;
[b](6) Mr, DoD OGC; [b](6) , Mr, DoD OGC; [b](6)
[b](6) Mr, DoD OGC; [b](6) Mr, DoD OGC; [b](6)
Mr, DoD OGC; [b](6) Mr, DoD OGC; [b](6) Ms, DoD OGC;
[b](6) Mr, DoD OGC; [b](6) Mr, DoD OGC; [b](6)
Ms, DoD OGC; [b](6) Ms, DoD OGC; [b](6) Mr, DoD
OGC; [b](6) Mr, DoD OGC; [b](6) Mr, DoD OGC; [b](6)
[b](6) Mr, DoD OGC; [b](6) Mr, DoD OGC; Cobb, Whit, Mr, DoD
OGC; [b](6) Mr, DoD OGC; [b](6) Mr, DoD OGC; [b](6)
[b](6) Mr, DoD OGC; [b](6) Ms, DoD OGC; Dell'Orto, Dan, Mr,
DoD OGC; [b](6) Mr, DoD OGC; [b](6) , Mr, DoD OGC;
[b](6) Mr, DoD OGC; [b](6) Mr, DoD OGC; [b](6)
[b](6) Mr, DoD OGC; [b](6) Mr, DoD OGC; [b](6) Ms, DoD
OGC; [b](6) COL, DoD OGC; [b](6) LTC, DoD OGC;
[b](6) Ms, DoD OGC; [b](6) Mr, DoD OGC; [b](6)
[b](6) Mr, DoD OGC; [b](6) Maj, DoD OGC; [b](6) ,
Mrs, DoD OGC; [b](6) Mr, DoD OGC; [b](6) LTC, DoD OGC;
Haynes, WJ, Mr, DoD OGC; [b](6) Ms, DoD OGC; [b](6)
[b](6) Maj, DoD OGC; [b](6) Ms, DoD OGC; Koffsky, Paul, Mr, DoD
OGC; Larsen, Douglas, Mr, DoD OGC; [b](6) COL, DoD OGC;
[b](6) LtCol, DoD OGC; [b](6) COL, DoD OGC; [b](6)
[b](6) Ms, DoD OGC; [b](6) Ms, DoD OGC; [b](6) Ms,
DoD OGC; [b](6) Ms, DoD OGC; [b](6) Ms, DoD OGC;
[b](6) Mr, DoD OGC; [b](6) Ms, DoD OGC; [b](6)
[b](6) COL, DoD OGC; [b](6) Mr, DoD OGC; [b](6) Mr,

1

## APPENDIX A, Page 2

DoD OGC; [(b)(6)] Mr, DoD OGC; [(b)(6)], Mr, DoD OGC; [(b)(6)], [(b)(6)] Ms, DoD OGC; [(b)(6)], Mr, DoD OGC; [(b)(6)] Ms, DoD OGC; [(b)(6)] Mr, DoD OGC; [(b)(6)] Ms, DoD OGC; [(b)(6)] Mr, DoD OGC; [(b)(6)] Mr, DoD OGC; [(b)(6)] Mr, DoD OGC; [(b)(6)], Mr, DoD OGC; [(b)(6)] [(b)(6)] Dr, DoD OGC; [(b)(6)] Mr, DoD OGC; [(b)(6)] Mr, DoD OGC; [(b)(6)], Mr, DoD OGC; [(b)(6)], Ms, DoD OGC; [(b)(6)] Maj, DoD OGC; [(b)(6)] Mr, DoD OGC; [(b)(6)] [(b)(6)] COL, DoD OGC; [(b)(6)] LCDR, DoD OGC; [(b)(6)] Ms, DoD OGC; [(b)(6)] Mr, DoD OGC

>Subject: Luncheon Speaker - Islam and Middle Eastern politics and culture - February 5th - RESPONSE DATE - 1/31
>Importance: High
>
>Hi everyone,
>
>    Remember our luncheon series? Although this luncheon is not part of that series, I have been able to obtain a speaker who can talk to us on whichever of the above topics we would like, or give us a taste of each, and to take questions. Mr. Haynes has no objections to our going forward with this project, but his schedule is too hectic to commit at this time. We probably need to narrow the topic to allow for the short time at a luncheon.
>
>Anwar Awlaki is the Imam at Dar Al-Hijrah in Falls Church, Va, which is one of the largest Islamic Centers in the United States. He is currently working on his PhD in Human Resource Development at George Washington University, received a Master of Education Leadership from San Diego State University and his BS in Civil Engineering from Colorado State University. He completed Islamic Studies in Yemen. He has been doing extensive public speaking on the above topics, especially since the events on September 11. Mr. Nihad Awad, President of the Counsel of American-Islamic Relations has also expressed interest in attending. Mr. Amr Moussa, the Secretary General of the Arab League, will be in D.C. on February 4th and 5th, although I don't think that our luncheon will have the clout to get his attendance!
>
>I had the privilege of hearing one of Mr. Awlaki's presentations in November and was impressed both by the extent of his knowledge and by how he communicated that information and handled a hostile element in the audience. I particularly liked how he addressed how the average

2

## APPENDIX A, Page 3

Middle Eastern person perceives the United States and his views on the
international media.
>
>I have reserved one of the executive dining rooms for February 5th,
which is the date he preferred, from 12:00 to 1:30. He will be
leaving for an extensive period of time on February 11th. We will
need a minimum attendance of 15 to get those rooms. Unfortunately, we
all have to eat the same thing and the food has to be served to get
one of those rooms. Assuming that sandwiches will be the easiest
thing to get consensus on, here are the selections:
>
>Smoked turkey
>Roast Beef
>Smoked Ham
>East side West side (beef, turkey and bacon on marbled rye)
Vegetarian
>- the chef will create something special for vegetarians
>
>It will come with a salad and beverage. The cost will range between
$14 to $15, depending on how many attend. If you are interested in
attending, please let me know the following ASAP:
>
>1. Your sandwich choice (remember majority rules) - if I am wrong
about a sandwich and you want to try for consensus on a hot chicken,
beef, pasta, seafood or salad, please let me know. Most of the others
will have additional expense.
>2. The time, if 12-1:30 is not the best
>
>I need a firm number and money by 1/31. My room is 3D941. Sorry for
the short notice, but we had several delays along the way!
>
>Thanks for your consideration - I think you'll enjoy it if you come.
He is very informative and this is certainly a hot topic that we would
all like to learn a little more about.
>

>

Chapter 10

APPENDIX A

# Churchill, Noted British Statesman
_Sep 9th 1929   Humboldt Standard_

Churchill and his party, including his brother, Major John Churchill, the latter's son John Churchill, Jr., and his son Randolph, were met at Grants Pass Saturday by Gerald Campbell. The party continued to Crescent City, where they stayed Saturday night, continuing to Eureka yesterday morning. They were met at the Eureka Inn by F. W. Georgeson, publisher of the Humboldt Standard, upon their arrival here.

# An impressive guest list

Eureka was a planned overnight stopover for Churchill since he had made arrangments to meet with old friend, Frederick Georgeson, editor of The Humboldt Standard. Arryving on Sept 8, 1929, Churchill was treated in grand manner by high society members of British and Scot descent. That evening a banquet and reception was given at the Inn in Churchill's honor.

## APPENDIX B

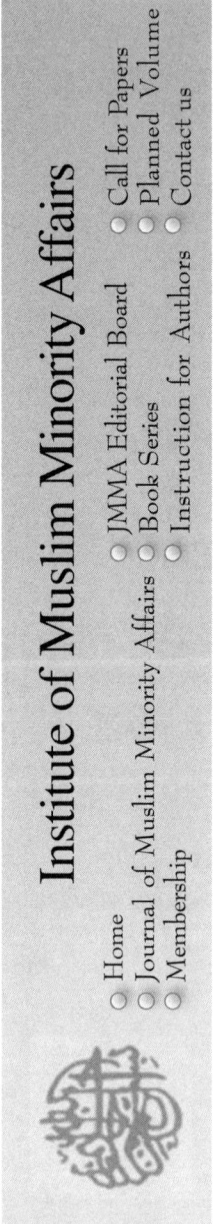

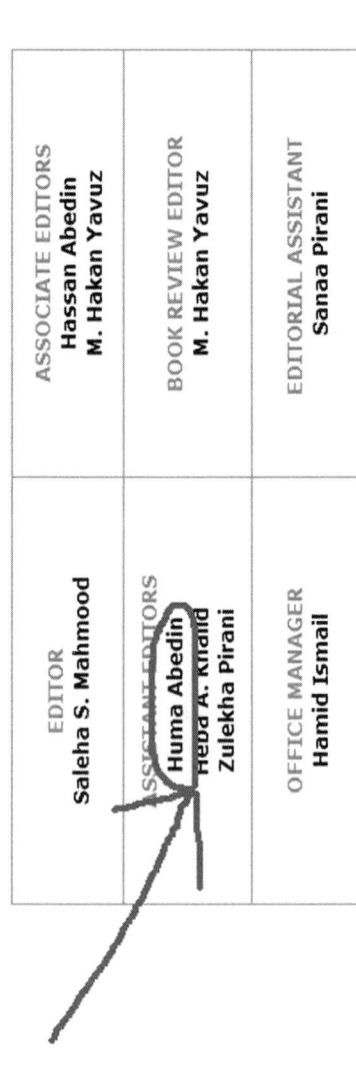

Institute of Muslim Minority Affairs

○ Home
○ Journal of Muslim Minority Affairs
○ Membership

○ JMMA Editorial Board
○ Book Series
○ Instruction for Authors

○ Call for Papers
○ Planned Volume
○ Contact us

*JMMA* Editorial Board

EDITOR
**Saleha S. Mahmood**

ASSISTANT EDITORS
**Huma Abedin**
**Heba A. Khalid**
**Zulekha Pirani**

OFFICE MANAGER
**Hamid Ismail**

ASSOCIATE EDITORS
**Hassan Abedin**
**M. Hakan Yavuz**

BOOK REVIEW EDITOR
**M. Hakan Yavuz**

EDITORIAL ASSISTANT
**Sanaa Pirani**

ADVISORY EDITORIAL BOARD
**Baha Abu-Laban**     University of Alberta, Canada
**Imtiaz Ahmad**     University of Dhaka, Bangladesh
**Munir D.Ahmed**     Deutches Orient-Institute, Germany
**Ameer Ali**     Murdoch University, Western Australia
**Zafar Ishaq Ansari**     International Islamic University, Pakistan

## Chapter 1

1. Art Moore, "'Smoking gun' tape of Hillary previewed," *World Net Daily*, April 25, 2007; link is http://www.wnd.com/news/article.asp? ARTICLE_ID = 55389

2. Hillary Clinton Senior Thesis at Wellesley College, 1969; link is http://rakesprogress.files.wordpress.com/2007/08/hillaryclinton thesis.pdf

3. Art Moore, "Full Hillary 'smoking gun' video released: Filed as Evidence against New York Senator, husband; link is http://www. wnd.com/?pageId = 42205

4. Tom Blumer, "AP's Fouhy, In Analysis of 2010 Congressional Land-scape, Calls GOP Base 'Confused' on ObamaCare; link is http://news busters.org/blogs/tom-blumer/2009/09/14/aps-fouhy-analysis-2010-congressional-landscape-calls-gop-base-confused

5. *YouTube*, "Hillary Uncensored": http://www.youtube.com/watch? v = xq8aopATYyw

6. Peter Paul, *Hillary Truth blog*; link is http://hillarytruth.blogspot.com/

7. "The Cuban Coffee Caper," TIME Magazine, February 12, 1979; link is http://www.time.com/time/magazine/article/0,9171,920092,00.html

8. Doug Cogan, "Peter Paul and Hillary: A Timeline," Against Hillary Clinton, July 27, 2007; link is http://www.againsthillary.com/2007/ 07/29/peter-paul-and-hillary-a-timeline/ embedded link to call log is http://i7.tinypic.com/24fjig7.jpg

9. "Stan Lee to Invade Asia," *Anime News Network*, August, 30, 2000; link is http://www.animenewsnetwork.com/news/2000-08-30/stan-lee-to-invade-asia

10. Agreement between SLM and Venture Soft, August 13, 2000 http://i5.tinypic.com/3ywz0c0.png

11. Lloyd Grove, "This Just In…" *Washington Post*, August 15, 2000; link is http://www.paulvclinton.com/This_Just_In

12. Lloyd Grove, "Hillary Returns Bucks to Ex-Felon," *Washington Post*, August 17, 2000; link is http://www.paulvclinton.com/Hillary_Returns_Bucks

13. Art Moore, "Fraud Lawsuit Targets Hillary," *World Net Daily*, August 22, 2005; link is http://www.wnd.com/?pageId = 31906

14. Katherine Skiba, "Desiree Rogers Leaving White House Post," *Chicago Tribune*, February 26, 2010; link is http://articles.chicago tribune.com/2010-02-26/news/ct-met-desiree-rogers-out-0227-20100226_1_desiree-rogers-social-secretary-white-house

15. Doug Cogan, Ibid; link to image is http://i11.tinypic.com/2edch 9g.jpg

16. Doug Cogan, Ibid; link to image is http://i5.tinypic.com/3ywz 0c0.png

17. Accuser, *Hillary Truth blog*; link is http://hillarytruth.blogspot.com/

18. Accuser, *Hillary Truth blog*; link to image is http://photos1.blogger. com/img/223/7990/640/rosen % 20fax % 20cover % 20clean.jpg

19. Accuser, *Hillary Truth blog*; link to image is http://photos1.blogger. com/img/223/7990/640/rosen % 20fax % 20p % 202.jpg

20. Discover the Networks, Bertha Lewis; link is http://www.discover thenetworks.org/individualProfile.asp?indid = 2459

21. Richard Poe, "Working Families Party: Activities, Agendas, and Alliances," Discover the Networks, 2005; link is http://www.discover thenetworks.org/Articles/wfpparty.html

22. John R. Emshwiller, "For Clinton, 2000 Fund-Raising Controversy Lingers," *Wall Street Journal*, September 14, 2007; link is http://online.wsj.com/article/NA_WSJ_PUB:SB118973400928827314.html

23. *Google* Image; link is http://lh6.ggpht.com/scuzzler/RRlIInDKABI/AAAAAAAAAVc/-bbkEqzVD1U/s512/pp + bill + c + air + force + 1 + best.jpg

24. Brian Ross, *ABC's 20/20* program, aired on July 13, 2001; link is http://video.google.com/videoplay?docid = 1098759488588186036#

25. John O. Edwards, "Peter Paul Promises Blockbuster Hillary Revelations," *Newsmax*, September 29, 2003; link is http://archive.news max.com/archives/articles/2003/9/28/124252.shtml

26. Bill Alpert, "The Rage Offstage at Marvel," *Barrons*, June 30, 2008; link is http://online.barrons.com/article/SB121461369005812701. html?mod = article-outset-boxon#articleTabs_panel_article%3D1

27. Federal Bureau of Prisons / Prison locator; link is http://www.bop. gov/iloc2/InmateFinderServlet?Transaction = IDSearch&needing-MoreList = false&IDType = IRN&IDNumber = 78802-012&x = 71&y = 16

28. *Newsmax*, "New York Times Trashes Hillary Accuser," February 9, 2005; link is http://archive.newsmax.com/archives/ic/2005/2/9/115634.shtml

29. *Newsmax*, "Prosecutor: Hillary a Victim," May 12, 2005; link is http://archive.newsmax.com/archives/ic/2005/5/12/11351.shtml

30. *Newsmax*, "Bush Prosecutor Nixes Rosen Bombshell tape," May 18, 2005; link is http://archive.newsmax.com/archives/ic/2005/5/18/94801.shtml

31. Leslie Eaton, "Clinton Link to Fund-Raiser Adds Spice to Mundane Trial," May 11, 2005, *New York Times*; link is http://www.nytimes. com/2005/05/11/nyregion/11clintons.html

32. Josh Gerstein, "A Clinton Fund-Raising Group Is Fined for Under-stating Gifts," *New York Sun*, January 5, 2006; link is http://www.ny sun.com/national/clinton-fund-raising-group-is-fined/25343/

33. New York Senate 2000, Amended FEC Report, January 30, 2006, p. 34; link is http://www.paulvclinton.com/amended_fec_report_jan_ 30_2006.pdf

34. *YouTube* Video, Stan Lee Deposition, February 23, 2005; link is http://www.youtube.com/watch?v = z8jkqGKK_0U

35. Colette Wilson, FEC Complaint, December 29, 2007; link is http:// www.paulvclinton.com/FEC_complaint_123107.pdf

36. Adam Liptak, "Justices, 5-4, Reject Corporate Spending Limit," January 21, 2010, New York Times; link is http://www.nytimes. com/2010/01/22/us/politics/22scotus.html

37. Citizens United, *Hillary The Movie* website; link is http://hillarythe movie.com/index.htm

38. *Associated Press*, "Alito Shakes Head as Obama Slams Citizens United," January 28, 2010; link is http://www.firstamendment center.org/news.aspx?id = 22551

39. Josh Gerstein, "After 4 years, Clintons' accuser sentenced to 10," July 22, 2009, *POLITICO*; link is http://www.politico.com/blogs/ joshgerstein/0709/After_4_years_Clintons_accuser_sentenced_to_ 10.html

40. Ibid

41. Patrick Healy, "Obama Meets Party Donors in New York," December 5, 2006, *New York Times*; link is http://www.nytimes.com/2006/ 12/05/us/politics/05obama.html?pagewanted = print

42. "Obama Declares he's Running for President," February 10, 2007, *CNN*; link is http://articles.cnn.com/2007-02-10/politics/obama. president_1_obama-amount-of-american-lives-first-african-ameri can-president?_s = PM:POLITICS

43. "Hillary's Oval Office Dreams 'Truth Boated' by Paul v. Clinton," June 13, 2008; link is http://paulvclinton.com/

44. "2008 Democratic Popular Vote," Real Clear Politics; link is http://www.realclearpolitics.com/epolls/2008/president/democratic_vote_count.html

## Chapter 2

1. Judea Pearl, "The Daniel Pearl Standard," *Wall Street Journal*, January 30, 2008; link is http://online.wsj.com/article/SB12016 5176905126961.html

2. Jerry Gordon, "Phillipe Karsenty: 'al Dura worst blood libel in a century,' Israpundit, October 9, 2007; link is http://www.israpundit.com/2007/?p = 6070

3. James Fallows, "Who Shot Mohammed al-Dura?" the *Atlantic Magazine*, June 2003; link is http://www.theatlantic.com/magazine/archive/2003/06/who-shot-mohammed-al-dura/2735/

4. "Al-Durah – The Birth of an Icon," *The Israel Situation*, January 27, 2008; *YouTube* with link is http://www.israelsituation.com/2008/01/al-durah-the-birth-of-an-icon/

5. Jerry Gordon, Ibid

6. Joseph Doriel, "Summary of a Professional Investigation Regarding the Killing of a 12 Year Old Boy at Nezarim Junction," October 23, 2000; link is http://www.palestinefacts.org/dura_report.html and http://208.84.118.121/dura_report.html

7. Bob Simon, "To Be Continued: An End To The Violence Seems A Long Way Away," *CBS: 60 Minutes*, October 24, 2000; link is http://www.cbsnews.com/stories/2000/10/24/60II/main243723.shtml

8. David Kupelian, "Probe: Famous 'martyrdom' of Palestinian boy 'staged,' Shooting of intifada's 12-year-old poster-child called 'street theater,' *World Net Daily*, April 26, 2003; link is http://www.wnd.com/news/article.asp?ARTICLE_ID = 32137

9. "Israel 'sorry' for killing boy," *BBC*, October 3, 2000; link is http://news.bbc.co.uk/2/hi/middle_east/954703.stm

10. Lisa Goldman, "A child is dead: Charles Enderlin on the 'Al-Durrah incident,' 10 years later, +972, October 11, 2010; link is http://972mag.com/a-child-is-dead-charles-enderlin-on-the-al-durrah-incident-10-years-later/

11. Richard Landes and Manfred Gerstenfeld, "The Muhammad Al-Dura Blood Libel: A Case Analysis," Scholars For Peace in the Middle East, Institute for Global Jewish Affairs – Post-Holocaust and Anti-Semitism No. 74: November 2, 2008; link is http://www.spme.net/cgi-bin/articles.cgi?ID = 4603

12. James Fallows, "Who Shot Mohammed al-Dura?" *Atlantic Monthly*, June, 2003; link is http://www.theatlantic.com/past/issues/2003/06/fallows.htm

13. Richard Landes and Manfred Gerstenfeld, "The Muhammad Al-Dura Blood Libel."

14. Ibid

15. Ben Barrack Show, Interview with Richard Landes, *KTEM* 1400 Radio, September 2, 2007

16. Richard Landes and Manfred Gerstenfeld, "The Muhammad Al-Dura Blood Libel."

17. James Fallows, "Who Shot Mohammed al-Dura?"

18. Jamie Glazov, "Israel-Hate: France's National Sport," *FrontPage Magazine*, May 16, 2006; link is http://archive.frontpagemag.com/readArticle.aspx?ARTID = 4413

19. Media-Ratings, "France 2: Arlette Chabot et Charles Enderlin doivent être démis de leurs fonctions immédiatement," November 22, 2004; link is http://m-r.fr/actualite.php?id = 1064

20. Cinnamon Shenker, "Will France denounce a Muslim icon?" *World Net Daily*, May 24, 2006; link is http://www.wnd.com/news/article.asp?ARTICLE_ID = 50348

21. David Solway, "Hero of Our Time," *FrontPage Magazine*, October 21, 2010; link is http://frontpagemag.com/2010/10/21/a-hero-of-our-time/

22. Richard Landes and Manfred Gerstenfeld, "The Muhammad Al-Dura Blood Libel."

23. Richard Landes, "Pallywood, According to Palestinian Sources..." Documentary, Second Draft website, September 15, 2005; link is http://seconddraft.org/index.php?option = com_content&view = article&id = 522:pallywood-qaccording-to-palestinian-sourcesq &catid = 58:according-to-palestinians-sources&Itemid = 159

24. Ibid

25. Richard Landes and Manfred Gerstenfeld, "The Muhammad Al-Dura Blood Libel."

26. Esther Schapira, "Three Bullets and a Dead Child," 2002 Documentary film; link is http://www.liveleak.com/view?i = 2b9_123 8254655

27. Richard Landes, "Al-Dura, According to Palestinian Sources II...Birth of an Icon," Documentary, Second Draft website, December 20, 2005; link is http://seconddraft.org/index.php?option = com_content&view = article&id = 55:the-birth-of-an-icon& catid = 58:according-to-palestinians-sources&Itemid = 159

28. Ibid

29. Ibid

30. Ibid

31. Esther Schapira, "Three Bullets and a Dead Child"

32. Ibid

33. "Lynch mob's brutal attack," *BBC*, October 13, 2000; link is http://news.bbc.co.uk/2/hi/middle_east/969778.stm

34. Raymond Whitaker, "A strange voice said: I just killed your husband," UK Independent, October 14, 2000; link is http://www.in dependent.co.uk/news/world/middle-east/a-strange-voice-said-i-just-killed-your-husband-635341.html

35. "Lynch mob's brutal attack," *BBC*

36. Mark Seager, "I'll have nightmares for the rest of my life," *The Daily Telegraph*, October 15, 2005; link is http://rotter.net/israel/mark.htm

37. Ibid

38. Esther Schapira, "Three Bullets and a Dead Child"

39. Richard Landes, "According to Palestinian Sources III... Icon of Hatred," Documentary, Second Draft website, June 13, 2007; link is http://seconddraft.org/index.php?option = com_content&view = arti cle&id = 54:icon-of-hatred&catid = 58:according-to-palestinians-sources&Itemid = 159

40. Mark Seager, "I'll have nightmares for the rest of my life"

41. John Rosenthal, "France: The Al-Dura Defamation Case and the End of Free Speech," *World Politics Review*, November 3, 2006; link is http://www.worldpoliticsreview.com/articles/312/france-the-al-dura-defamation-case-and-the-end-of-free-speech

42. Court's Decision on Karsenty, 17th Chamber, Case No. 0433823049, October 19, 2006; link is http://www.theaugeanstables.com/al-durah-affair-the-dossier/courts-decision-in-the-karsenty-case/

43. Palestinian Centre for Human Rights, Statement under oath by a photographer of France 2, signed by Talal Hassan Abu Rahma, October 3, 2000; link is http://www.pchrgaza.org/special/tv2.htm

44. John Rosenthal, "France: The Al-Dura Defamation Case and the End of Free Speech"

45. Ibid

46. Esther Schapira, "Three Bullets and a Dead Child"

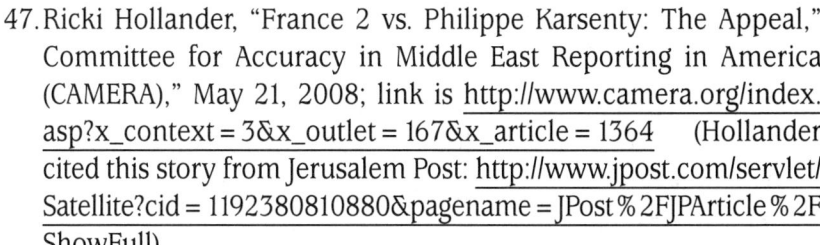

47. Ricki Hollander, "France 2 vs. Philippe Karsenty: The Appeal," Committee for Accuracy in Middle East Reporting in America (CAMERA)," May 21, 2008; link is http://www.camera.org/index.asp?x_context = 3&x_outlet = 167&x_article = 1364 (Hollander cited this story from Jerusalem Post: http://www.jpost.com/servlet/Satellite?cid = 1192380810880&pagename = JPost%2FJPArticle%2FShowFull)

48. Ben Barrack Show, Interview with Richard Landes, *KTEM* 1400 Radio, November 25, 2007

49. Richard Landes and Manfred Gerstenfeld, "The Muhammad Al-Dura Blood Libel."

50. Henri Astier, "Gaza media battle in French court," *BBC News*, November 13, 2007; link is http://news.bbc.co.uk/2/hi/europe/709 2262.stm

51. Email received from Landes on April 5, 2011

52. Nidra Poller, "Out Damn Spot," *Front Page Magazine*, April 9, 2008; link is http://archive.frontpagemag.com/readArticle.aspx?ARTID = 30542

53. Ben Barrack Show, Interview with Richard Landes, *KTEM* 1400 Radio, March 23, 2008

54. Ibid

55. Nidra Poller, "Out Damn Spot"

56. Ibid

57. Ben Barrack Show, March 23, 2008

58. Ben Barrack Show, November 25, 2007

59. Karsenty Court of Appeals Decision (English), The Augean Stables, May 21, 2008; link is http://www.theaugeanstables.com/al-durah-affair-the-dossier/karsenty-court-of-appeals-decision-english/

60. Ibid

61. Ben Barrack Show, Interview with Richard Landes, *KTEM* 1400 Radio, May 25, 2008

62. Philippe Karsenty, "French Court Vindicates Al-Dura Hoax Critic," Pajamas Media, May 21, 2008; link is http://pajamasmedia.com/blog/french-court-vindicates-al-dura-hoax-critic/

63. "Al-Durra Case Revisited," *Wall Street Journal Europe*, May 27, 2008; link is http://online.wsj.com/article/SB121183757337520921.html and http://blog.camera.org/archives/2008/05/wall_street_journal_weighs_in.html

64. Ben Barrack Show, November 25, 2007

65. Nidra Poller, "A Hoax?" Wall Street Journal Europe, May 27, 2008; link is http://online.wsj.com/article/SB121183795208620963.html and http://blog.camera.org/archives/2008/05/wall_street_journal_weighs_in.html

66. Anne-Elisabeth Moutet, "L'Affaire Enderlin: Being a French journalist means never having to say you're sorry," *The Weekly Standard*, July 7, 2008, Vol. 13, No. 41; link is http://www.weeklystandard.com/Content/Public/Articles/000/000/015/284xawsb.asp?page = 3

67. Tom Gross, "Amazement as Sarkozy Gives Propagator of Al-Dura Myth an Award," Mideast Media Analysis, September 1, 2009; link is http://www.tomgrossmedia.com/mideastdispatches/archives/001051.html

68. Ibid

69. Sun Tzu, "The Art of War," Translated by Gary Gagliardi, p. 41, Clearbridge Publishing, Seattle, WA

70. Annette Young, "Interview with Charles Enderlin," France 24, July 10, 2010; link is http://www.france24.com/en/20101006-young-charles-enderlin-journalism-israeli-palestinian-conflict

71. Ibid

72. Yaakov Lappin, "Reuters admits altering Beirut photo," *Ynet News*, August 6, 2006; link is http://www.ynetnews.com/articles/0,7340, L-3286966,00.html

73. Jim Miklaszewski and Mike Viqueira, "Lawmaker: Marines killed Iraqis 'in cold blod,'" *MSNBC*, May 17, 2006; link is http://www. msnbc.msn.com/id/12838343/

74. North County Times, June 15, 2011; link is http://www.nctimes. com/news/local/military/article_4d980698-b22a-5373-b615-d0 f1abe38673.html

75. Howard Kurtz, "Newsweek Apologizes," *The Washington Post*, May 16, 2005; link is http://www.washingtonpost.com/wp-dyn/content/ article/2005/05/15/AR2005051500605_pf.html

## Chapter 3

1. Will Weisser and Freddy Cuevas, "Honduran president deposed, exiled in coup," *Associated Press*, June 29, 2009; link is http://www. boston.com/news/world/latinamerica/articles/2009/06/29/honduran _president_deposed_exiled_in_coup/

2. "Obama: Honduras Coup 'Not Legal,'" *Associated Press / CBS News*, June 29, 2009; link is http://www.cbsnews.com/stories/2009/06/29/ politics/main5122779.shtml

3. Ben Smith, "Obama: Cambridge police acted 'stupidly'," *POLITICO*, July 22, 2009; link is http://www.politico.com/blogs/bensmith/0709/ Obama_Cambridge_police_acted_stupidly.html

4. Matthew Walter and Andres R. Martinez, "Zelaya Seeks Support as OAS Seeks Return Back to Honduras," Bloomberg, July 3, 2009; link is http://www.bloomberg.com/apps/news?pid = newsarchive&sid = aOSQNfG9EKoc

5. Miguel Estrada, "Honduras' non-coup," *Los Angeles Times*, July 10, 2009; link is http://articles.latimes.com/2009/jul/10/opinion/oe-estrada10

6. Zhang Xiang, "Honduran interim gov't announces to quit OAS," Xinhuanet, July 4, 2009; link is http://news.xinhuanet.com/english/2009-07/04/content_11651090.htm

7. Organization of American States website, September 9, 2010; link is http://www.oas.org/en/member_states/authorities.asp#Cuba

8. Mary Anastasia O'Grady, "Honduras at the Tipping Point," *Wall Street Journal*, July 6, 2009; link is http://online.wsj.com/article/SB124683595220397927.html

9. Richard Landes, "Pallywood: According to Palestinian Sources," The Second Draft, 2006; link is http://www.seconddraft.org/index.php?option = com_content&view = article&id = 522:pallywood-qaccording-to-palestinian-sourcesq&catid = 58:according-to-palestinians-sources&Itemid = 159

10. Janine Zacharia, "Hamas retains deadly reach in West Bank," *Washington Post*, September 4, 2010; link is http://www.washingtonpost.com/wp-dyn/content/article/2010/09/03/AR2010090305869.html

11. Karl Penhaul, "Zelaya Landing Blocked," *CNN News* report, July 6, 2009; link is http://edition.cnn.com/video/#/video/world/2009/07/06/penhaul.honduras.airport.clashes.cnn?iref = videosearch

12. William A. Jacobson, "CNN Falls for the Honduran Fauxtester," Legal Insurrection, July 8, 2009; link is http://legalinsurrection.blogspot.com/2009/07/cnn-falls-for-honduran-fauxtester.html

13. Juan Forero, "In Honduras, One-Sided News of Crisis," *Washington Post*, July 9, 2009; link is http://www.washingtonpost.com/wp-dyn/content/article/2009/07/09/AR2009070902820.html

14. Daniel Greenfield, "Zelaya's Chief Propagandist Endorses Hitler and the Holocaust," Canada Free Press, October 1, 2009; link is http://www.canadafreepress.com/index.php/article/15313

15. U.N. Press Release, June 30, 2009; link is http://www.un.org/News/Press/docs/2009/ga10842.doc.htm

16. Foreign Staff, "Honduran President Manuel Zelaya vows to enter country as new regime faces isolation," *UK Telegraph*, July 6, 2009; link is http://www.telegraph.co.uk/news/worldnews/centralamerica andthecaribbean/honduras/5758056/Honduran-President-Manuel-Zelaya-vows-to-enter-country-as-new-regime-faces-isolation.html

17. U.N. Press Release, July 3, 2006; link is http://www.un.org/News/Press/docs/2006/org1469.doc.htm

18. Andres R. Martinez and Helen Murphy, "Micheletti, Vowing Zelaya Prosecution, Open to Talks," Bloomberg, July 1, 2009; link is http://www.bloomberg.com/apps/news?pid = newsarchive&sid = avXhLRfCzdIY

19. "Ousted Honduran Leader Arrives at Border, Steps Across," *Associated Press*, July 24, 2009; link is http://www.foxnews.com/story/0,2933,534763,00.html?test = latestnews

20. Ibid

21. Global Security, "Revolutionary Armed Forces of Colombia Fuerzas Armadas Revolucionarias de Colombia – FARC,"; link is http://www.globalsecurity.org/military/world/para/farc.htm

22. Fausta La Mysterieuse, "Honduras claims that FARC is financing Zelaya," Fausta's Blog, July 27, 2009; link is http://faustasblog.com/?p = 14378

23. Roberto Micheletti, "The Path Forward for Honduras," *Wall Street Journal*, July 27, 2009; link is http://online.wsj.com/article/SB1000 142405297020488630457431108317158174.html?mod = google news_wsj

24. Sara A. Carter, "Ousted Honduran leader accused of theft," *Washington Times*, July 22, 2009; link is http://www.washington times.com/news/2009/jul/22/zelaya-accused-of-cash-withdrawal/?page = 1

25. Gustavo Palencia and Edgar Garrido, "Ousted president Zelaya returns to Honduras," *Reuters*, September 21, 2009; link is http://www.reuters.com/article/worldNews/idUSTRE58K3JY2 0090921

26. Jose de Cordoba and John Lyons, "Protests Erupt Following Zelaya's Return," *Wall Street Journal*, September 23, 2009: link is http://online.wsj.com/article/SB125363138908430889.html

27. Ibid

28. Frances Robles, "They're torturing me, Honduras' Manuel Zelaya claims," *Miami Herald*, September 24, 2009; link is http://www.miamiherald.com/2009/09/23/v-fullstory/1248828/theyre-torturing-me-honduras-manuel.html

29. Ibid

30. "Ousted Honduran Leader Arrives at Border, Steps Across," *Associated Press*, July 24, 2009; link is http://www.foxnews.com/story/0,2933,534763,00.html?test = latestnews

31. "US Revokes Visas for Honduran Officials," *Associated Press*, July 28, 2009; link is http://www.breitbart.com/article.php?id = D99 NJ8R80&show_article = 1

32. Simon Gardner and Marco Aquino, "Honduras Talks Postponed," *Reuters*, July 22, 2009; link is http://www.montrealgazette.com/news/Honduras + talks + postponed/1815631/story.html

33. Daily Press Briefing, U.S. Department of State, Transcript from July 28, 2009 with Department Spokesman Ian Kelly; link is http://www.state.gov/r/pa/prs/dpb/2009/july/126589.htm

34. Fausta La Mysterieuse, "Is Obama doing Zelaya's bidding?" *Fausta's Blog*, July 29, 2009; link is http://faustasblog.com/?p = 14431 *The actual Hill article not available on-line at the time of this writing. Fausta posted relevant quotes.*

35. Ibid

36. Ibid

37. Susan Cornwell, "Senator asks Clinton to explain Honduran Policy," *Reuters*, July 30, 2009; link is http://www.reuters.com/article/idUSTRE56T7DM20090730

38. Mary Beth Sheridan, "Kerry's Attempt to Block DeMint's Honduras Trip Reveals Policy Feud," *Washington Post*, October 2, 2009; link is http://www.washingtonpost.com/wp-dyn/content/article/2009/10/01/AR2009100105015.html

39. Jim DeMint, "What I Heard in Honduras," *Wall Street Journal*, October 10, 2009; link is http://online.wsj.com/article/SB10001424052748703298004574459762462353766.html?mod=WSJ_hpp_sections_opinion#articleTabs%3Darticle

40. Ibid

41. Susan Cornwell, "U.S. appears to soften support for Hounduras' Zelaya," *Reuters*, August 6, 2009; link is http://www.reuters.com/article/worldNews/idUSTRE5746J720090805

42. "Honduran president makes offer to end political standoff," *Washington Times*, August 28, 2009; link is http://www.washingtontimes.com/news/2009/aug/28/honduran-president-makes-new-offer-to-end-politica/

43. Ibid

44. "Honduras leader's nephew killed," *BBC*, October 24, 2009; link is http://news.bbc.co.uk/2/hi/americas/8327196.stm

45. "Honduras de facto leader's nephew murdered," *The Times of India*, October 27, 2009; link is http://timesofindia.indiatimes.com/world/rest-of-world/Honduras-de-facto-leaders-nephew-murdered/articleshow/5168177.cms

46. "Kidnapping puts crisis-bound Honduras on edge," France 24 / AFP, October 28, 2009; link is http://www.france24.com/en/node/4911425

47. "Honduran abuses rampant after coup – rights groups," *Reuters*, October 12, 2009; link is http://www.reuters.com/article/idUSN12151282

48. Nicholas Casey, "Hondurans Pick a Leader to End Limbo," *Wall Street Journal*, November 30, 2009; link is http://online.wsj.com/article/SB125952888258868607.html?mod = WSJ_hpp_MIDDL TopStories

49. David Gollust, "US Calls Honduras Election Significant but Insufficient Step to End Political Crisis," *VOA News*, November 30, 2009; link is http://www.voanews.com/english/news/US-Calls-Honduras-Election-Significant-but-Insufficient-Step-to-End-Political-Crisis-78184422.html

50. Ibid

51. "Honduras swears in Porfirio Lobo as President," *BBC*, January27, 2010; link is http://news.bbc.co.uk/2/hi/8482707.stm

52. Ibid

53. Patrick Goodenough, "Obama on Wrong Side of Honduras Dispute, GOP Lawmaker Warns," *CNS News*, May 24, 2011; link is http://www.cnsnews.com/news/article/obama-wrong-side-honduras-dispute-gop-la

54. Mary Anastasia O'Grady, "WikiLeaks, Honduras and the U.S. Released cables make it clear that the U.S. knew Manuel Zelaya was a threat to democracy in Honduras," *Wall Street Journal*, December 20, 2010; link is http://online.wsj.com/article/SB10001424052748 703395204576023843828913256.html

## Chapter 4

1. Larry Grathwohl as told to Frank Reagan, "Bringing Down America: An FBI Informer with the Weathermen," Arlington House Pub - lishers, New Rochelle, NY, 1976, pp. 129-130

2. Ibid, p. 159

3. Ibid, p. 178

4. G. Edward Griffin, "No Place to Hide: The Strategy and Tactics of Terrorism," Documentary film, 1982; link is http://www.archive. org/details/NoPlaceToHide-TerrorismDocumentary

5. Stanley Kurtz, "Chicago Annenberg Challenge Shutdown? A cover-up in the making?" *National Review*, August 18, 2008; link is http://www.nationalreview.com/articles/225348/chicago-annen berg-challenge-shutdown/stanley-kurtz?page = 1

6. "Crossing Paths Daily: Obama and Ayers Shared an Office," *Verum Serum*, October 16, 2008; link is http://www.verumserum.com/ ?p = 2907

7. Ibid

8. "Transcript: Obama and Clinton Debate," *ABC News* / Politics, April 16, 2008; link is http://abcnews.go.com/Politics/DemocraticDebate/ story?id = 4670271&page = 2

9. "Bringing Down America: An FBI Informer with the Weathermen," p. 178

10. Bob Owens, "Eyewitness to the Ayers Revolution: An interview with Weathermen insider/FBI informant Larry Grathwohl on whether to believe Obama when it comes to Bill Ayers," *Pajamas Media*, October 28, 2008; link is http://pajamasmedia.com/blog/eye witness-to-the-ayers-revolution/?singlepage = true

11. O'Reilly Factor, "Former FBI Informant Details Spying on Radical William Ayers," *Fox News*, October 30, 2008; link to transcript is http://www.foxnews.com/story/0,2933,445684,00.html

12. Dinitia Smith, "No Regrets for a Love Of Explosives; In a Memoir of Sorts, a War Protester Talks of Life With the Weathermen," *New York Times*, September 11, 2001; link is http://query.nytimes.com/ gst/fullpage.html?res = 9F02E1DE1438F932A2575AC0A9679C8B63 &pagewanted = all

13. Ibid

14. "Bringing Down America: An FBI Informer with the Weathermen," p. 169

15. Ibid, p. 143, 152

16. Ibid, p. 138

17. Michelle Malkin, "What's on Bill Ayers' door," via the *Chicago Tribune*, October 15, 2008; link is http://michellemalkin.com/2008/10/15/whats-on-bill-ayers-door/

18. "Van Jones: A Radical, Anti-War Record Producer As Well?" *Verum Serum*, September 4, 2009; link is http://www.verumserum.com/?p=8166

19. Charles Cooper, "Van Jones Resigns as White House Advisor," *CBS News*, September 6, 2009; link is http://www.cbsnews.com/8301-503544_162-5290642-503544.html

20. "Obama: Police who arrested professor 'acted stupidly,' *CNN*, July 22, 2009; link is http://articles.cnn.com/2009-07-22/us/harvard.gates.interview_1_cambridge-police-gates-james-crowley?_s=PM:US

21. Aaron Klein, "Obama's 'green jobs czar' worked with terror founder: Van Jones served on board of activist group where ex-Weatherman serves as top director," *World Net Daily*, August 13, 2009; link is http://www.wnd.com/?pageId=106653

22. Andrew Ramonas, "Civil Rights Panel Releases Disparaging Black Panthers Report," *Main Justice*, November 24, 2010; link is http://www.mainjustice.com/2010/11/24/civil-rights-panel-releases-disparaging-black-panthers-report/

23. "Bringing Down America: An FBI Informer with the Weathermen," p. 92

24. Dinitia Smith, "No Regrets for a Love Of Explosives; In a Memoir of Sorts, a War Protester Talks of Life With the Weathermen," *New York Times*, September 11, 2001; link is http://query.nytimes.com/gst/fullpage.html?res = 9F02E1DE1438F932A2575AC0A9679C8B63&pagewanted = all

25. Jack Cashill, "Who Wrote Dreams From My Father?" *American Thinker*, October 9, 2008; link is http://www.americanthinker.com/2008/10/who_wrote_dreams_from_my_fathe_1.html

26. Cliff Kincaid, "Obama's 'Sex Rebel' Communist Mentor: The 'Naked Truth' About Frank Marshall Davis," *USA Survival*, 2008; link is http://www.usasurvival.org/docs/Rpt_Davis_Sex.pdf

27. Toby Harnden, "Frank Marshall Davis, alleged Communist, was early influence on Barack Obama," *The Telegraph*, August 22, 2008; link is http://www.telegraph.co.uk/news/worldnews/northamerica/usa/barackobama/2601914/Frank-Marshall-Davis-alleged-Communist-was-early-influence-on-Barack-Obama.html

28. Norimitsu Onishi, "Obama Visits a Nation That Knew Him as Barry," *New York Times*, November 9, 2010; link is http://www.nytimes.com/2010/11/09/world/asia/09indo.html?_r = 1

29. Peter Jamison, "Time Bomb: Weather Underground leaders claimed their bombings were devised to avoid bloodshed. But FBI agents suspect the radical '70's group killed an S.F. cop in the name of revolution," *San Francisco Weekly*, September 16, 2009; link is http://www.sfweekly.com/content/printVersion/1671173/

30. Ben Barrack (guest host), Matthew Hill Show, *IRN USA Radio*, September 18, 2009; link is mms://archives.inforadionet.com/irn/mhs/mhs091809.mp3

31. Peter Jamison, "Time Bomb," *San Francisco Weekly*, September 16, 2009

32. "Bringing Down America: An FBI Informer with the Weathermen," p. 182

33. Ibid, p. 63

34. Peter Jamison, "Time Bomb," *San Francisco Weekly*, September 16, 2009

35. Ibid

36. Ibid

37. Jamie Kilstein, Citizen Radio, Interview with Bill Ayers, December 1, 2010; link is http://citizenradio.lyndseybrown.co.uk/?p = 160

38. Cliff Kincaid, "Revolutionary Violence and Terrorism in America: The Legacy of the Weather Underground and the Search for Justice," Interview with Larry Grathwohl and Max Noel, part 4 of 7, America's Survival, September 11, 2010; link is http://www.youtube.com/watch?v = JSCtB3nCDVs&feature = player_embedded#!

39. "Bringing Down America: An FBI Informer with the Weathermen," p. 93.

40. Demian Bulwa, "S.F. police union accuses Ayers in 1970 bombing," *San Francisco Chronicle*, March 12, 2009; link is http://www.sfgate.com/cgi-bin/article.cgi?f = /c/a/2009/03/12/BATK16DHA4.DTL& type = printable

41. Phillip Matier and Andrew Ross, "Police officers to ld to zip lips on bombing," *San Francisco Chronicle*, March 18, 2009; link is http://articles.sfgate.com/2009-03-18/bay-area/17214231_1_jailhouse-death-mental-health-gary-delagnes

42. "Confirming Fears," *National Review*, November 19, 2008; link is http://www.nationalreview.com/articles/226347/confirming-fears/editors

43. Mark Rudd, "Mark Goes to the Darkside: My Talk to the FBI Training Academy, Quantico, VA." *Mark Rudd blog*, 2009; link is http://www.markrudd.com/?about-mark-rudd/mark-goes-to-the-darkside-my-talk-to-the-fbi-training-academy-quantico-va-.html

44. Cliff Kincaid, "Revolutionary Violence and Terrorism in America," Interview with Larry Grathwohl and Max Noel, part 6 of 7; link is http://www.youtube.com/watch?v = xlgsYNhDvKo&feature = player _embedded#!

45. Paul M. Barrett, "Years of Rage," *New York Times*, May 1, 2009; link is http://www.nytimes.com/2009/05/03/books/review/Barrett-t.html

46. Cliff Kincaid, "Justice for Victims of the Weather Underground," *Accuracy In Media*, March 3, 2009; link is http://www.aim.org/aim-column/justice-for-victims-of-the-weather-underground/

47. "Bringing Down America: An FBI Informer with the Weathermen," p. 159

48. Peter Jamison, "Time Bomb," *San Francisco Weekly*, September 16, 2009

49. Ibid

50. TIME Magazine, "Radicals: California's Underground," October 6 1975; link is http://www.time.com/time/printout/0,8816,913516, 00.html

51. Ibid

52. Ibid

53. "Bringing Down America: An FBI Informer with the Weathermen," pp. 118-122

54. Cliff Kincaid, "Terrorists on Tour," *Accuracy in Media*, April 23, 2009; link is http://www.aim.org/aim-column/terrorists-on-tour/

55. Ibid

56. Ibid

57. Ben Barrack Show, "Interview with Larry Grathwohl," *KTEM* 1400, Temple, TX, June 20, 2010

58. "Bringing Down America: An FBI Informer with the Weathermen," p. 37

59. Ibid, p. 171

60. Barbara Hollingsworth, "Ayers, Dohrn helped organize flotilla group," *Washington Examiner*, June 1, 2010; link is http://washing tonexaminer.com/blogs/beltway-confidential/ayers-dohrn-helped-organize-flotilla-group

61. Phone interview on January 24, 2011

## Chapter 5

1. Larry Lee Litke, "The Downfall of Jim Jones," February 27, 1980; link is http://truthsleuth.net/truthsleuthhome/downfallofjimjones.html

2. Ben Barrack Show, "Interview with David Conn," *KTEM* 1400, Temple, TX, October 2, 2009

3. George Klineman, Sherman Butler, and David Conn, "The Cult that Died: The Tragedy of Jim Jones and the People's Temple," p. 65, G.P. Putnam's Sons, New York, 1980

4. Phone conversation with David Conn, February 14, 2011

5. Ben Barrack Show, October 2, 2009

6. George Klineman, "The Cult that Died," p. 45

7. Larry Lee Litke, "The Downfall of Jim Jones."

8. Kyle-Anne Shiver, "Obama's Alinsky Jujitsu," American Thinker, January 8, 2008; link is http://www.americanthinker.com/2008/01/obamas_alinsky_jujitsu.html

9. In a February 14, 2011 interview, Conn confided in me that Putnam changed the title of Klineman's book from "Marxist God" to "The Cult That Died" before print.

10. George Klineman, "The Cult that Died," pp. 101-102

11. Ben Barrack Show, "Interview with David Conn," *KTEM* 1400, Temple, TX, December 13, 2009

12. Ibid

13. The Jonestown Institute, Jonestown Audiotape Primary Project: Transcripts, Prepared by Fielding M. McGehee, Tape Number: Q134; link is http://jonestown.sdsu.edu/AboutJonestown/Tapes/Tapes/Tape Transcripts/Q134.html

14. George Klineman, "The Cult that Died," p. 134

15. Lester Kinsolving, "Part 1: The Prophet Who Raises the Dead," *San Francisco Examiner*, September 17, 1972, page 1; link is http://jones townapologistsarticlearchive.blogspot.com/2007/11/part-1- prophet-who-raises-dead.html

16. Ibid

17. Lester Kinsolving, "Part 2: 'Healing' Prophet Hailed as God at S.F. Revival," *San Francisco Examiner*, September 18, 1972; link is http://jonestownapologistsarticlearchive.blogspot.com/2007/11/part -2-healing-prophet-hailed-as-god-at.html

18. Lester Kinsolving, "Part 3: D.A. Aide Officiates for Minor Bride," *San Francisco Examiner*, September 19, 1972; link is http://jonestow- napologistsarticlearchive.blogspot.com/2007/11/part-3-da-aide- officiates-for-minor.html

19. Lester Kinsolving, "Part 4: Probe Asked of People's Temple," *San Francisco Examiner*, September 20, 1972; link is http://jonestown apologistsarticlearchive.blogspot.com/2007/11/part-4-probe-asked- of-peoples-temple.html

20. Ibid

21. Ben Barrack Show, "Interview with Lester Kinsolving," *KTEM* 1400, Temple, TX, May 7, 2010

22. Ibid

23. Ibid

24. Ibid

25. Lester Kinsolving, "Part 5: The People's Temple and Maxine Harpe," *San Francisco Examiner* (never published), September, 1972; link is http://jonestownapologistsarticlearchive.blogspot.com/2007/11/part -5-peoples-temple-and-maxine-harpe.html

26. Lester Kinsolving, "Part 6: The Reincarnation of Jesus Christ – In Ukiah," *San Francisco Examiner* (never published), September 1972; link is http://jonestownapologistsarticlearchive.blogspot.com/2007/ 11/part-6-reincarnation-of-jesus-christ-in.html

27. Ibid

28. Lester Kinsolving, "Part 7: Jim Jones Defames a Black Pastor," *San Francisco Examiner* (never published), September 1972; link is http://jonestownapologistsarticlearchive.blogspot.com/2007/11/part -7-jim-jones-defames-black-pastor.html

29. Lester Kinsolving, "Part 8 / Final: Sex, Socialism, and Child Torture With Rev. Jim Jones," San Francisco Examiner (never published), September 1972; link is http://jonestownapologistsarticlearchive. blogspot.com/2007/11/part-8final-sex-socialism-and-child.html

30. George Klineman, "The Cult that Died," p. 232

31. Ben Barrack Show, "Interview with Lester Kinsolving," May 7, 2010

32. James Faulk, "Stoen says sorry over People's Temple," *The Eureka Times-Standard / Religion News Blog*, March 3, 2005; link is http://www.religionnewsblog.com/10445/stoen-says-sorry-over-peoples-temple

33. George Klineman, "The Cult that Died," p. 147

34. Ibid

35. Ibid, p. 159

36. Ibid

37. Ibid, p. 149

38. Ibid, pp. 149-150

39. John M. Crewdson, "Followers Say Jim Jones Directed Voting Frauds," *New York Times*, December 17, 1978

40. Ben Barrack Show, December 13, 2009

41. Jones Appointment to San Francisco Housing Authority; link is http://jonestown.sdsu.edu/AboutJonestown/PrimarySources/SF Housing.html

42. George Klineman, "The Cult that Died," p. 153

43. Ibid, p. 152

44. Ibid

45. Ibid, p. 153

46. Ibid

47. Marshall Kilduff and Phil Tracy, "Inside Peoples Temple," *New West Magazine*, August 1, 1977, pp. 30-38; link is http://jonestown.sdsu.edu/AboutJonestown/PrimarySources/newWestart.htm

48. Ben Barrack Show, October 2, 2009

49. Katy Grimes, "Frank Luntz and Willie Brown debate or entertain?" Cal Watchdog, February 5, 2010; link is http://www.calwatch dog.com/2010/02/05/frank-luntz-and-willie-brown-debate-or-entertain/

50. Email from David Conn to Ben Barrack, February 28, 2011

51. Ibid

52. Ibid

53. Academy of Achievement, "A Museum of Living History," Willie L. Brown, Jr. Biography; link is http://www.achievement.org/auto doc/page/bro0bio-1

54. Larry Lee Litke, "The Downfall of Jim Jones."

55. Ibid

56. Jeannie Mills, "Six Years with God," pp. 50-51, A&W Publishing, Inc. New York, NY, 1979

57. U.S. House of Representatives, "The Assassination of Representative Leo J. Ryan and the Jonestown, Guyana Tragedy: Report of a Staff Investigative Group to the Committee on oreign Affairs," May 15, 1979; link is http://jonestown.sdsu.edu/AboutJonestown/Pri marySources/HouseReportText.html

58. Larry Lee Litke, "The Downfall of Jim Jones."

59. Ben Barrack Show Interview, May 7, 2010

60. Ibid

61. Jerry Brown for Governor 2010 Campaign Website; link is http:// www.jerrybrown.org/about

62. Darryl Fears and Carol D. Leonnig, "Duo in ACORN Videos Say Effort Was Independent," *Washington Post*, September 18, 2009; link is http://www.washingtonpost.com/wp-dyn/content/article/ 2009/09/17/AR2009091704805.html?sid = ST2011020203536

63. R. Stickney, "ACORN Docs Pulled from Dumpster," *NBC San Diego*, November 24, 2009; link is http://www.nbcsandiego.com/news/ politics/ACORN-Documents-Pulled-from-Dumpster.html

64. Derrick Roach, "San Diego ACORN Document Dump Scandal," Big Government, November 23, 2009; link is http://biggovernment. com/droach/2009/11/23/breaking-san-diego-acorn-document-dump-scandal/

65. Larry O'Connor, "Calif. Attorney General Offers Incoherent, Troubling Answers When Asked About ACORD Doc Dump," Big Government, November 27, 2009; link is http://biggovernment.com/sright/ 2009/11/27/calif-attorney-general-offers-incoherent-troubling-answers-when-asked-about-acorn-doc-dump/#more-37458

66. Ben Barrack Show, December 13, 2009

67. U.S. Marshals Service, "History – Incident at Wounded Knee," 1973; link is http://www.usmarshals.gov/history/wounded-knee/

68. Charles Nichols, "Jerry Brown's finest hour," *LA Anti-Establishment Examiner*, June 19, 2010; link is http://www.examiner.com/la-in-los-angeles/jerry-brown-s-finest-hour?render = print

69. Larry Lee Litke, "The Downfall of Jim Jones."

70. Phone conversation with David Conn, March 6, 2011

71. George Klineman, "The Cult that Died," p. 259

72. Ibid

73. Marshall Kilduff and Phil Tracy, "Inside Peoples Temple," *New West Magazine*, August 1, 1977

74. Larry Lee Litke, "The Downfall of Jim Jones."

75. Ibid

76. Ben Barrack Show, October 2, 2009

77. Larry Litke, "The Downfall of Jim Jones."

78. Ibid

79. Jonestown Audiotape Primary Project: Transcripts by Fielding M. McGhee, III, The Jonestown Institute, Tape Number: Q 352; link is http://jonestown.sdsu.edu/AboutJonestown/Tapes/Tapes/TapeTranscripts/Q352.html

80. Ibid

81. Ibid

82. Financial Letters of November 18, Jonestown Institute; link is http://jonestown.sdsu.edu/AboutJonestown/PrimarySources/FinancialLetters_Nov18.html

83. Jared Loughner YouTube page; link is http://www.youtube.com/user/Classitup10

# Chapter 6

1. Rev. Wayne Perryman, "UNVEILING the Whole Truth: What the Media Failed to Tell American Voters," p. 146, Book Publishers Network, 2008

2. Peter Kirsanow, "Blacks, Democrats, and Republicans," National Review, March 15, 2011; link is http://www.nationalreview.com/corner/262180/blacks-democrats-and-republicans-peter-kirsanow

3. Holy Bible, Genesis 9:18-27, Bible Gateway; link is http://www.bible gateway.com/passage/?search = genesis%209:18-29&version = AMP

4. Phone conversation with Wayne Perryman, April 26, 2011.

5. Wayne Perryman, "The 1993 Trial on the Curse of Ham, Introduction," People of Color Training Center; link is http://www.peopleof color1.com/curse_of_ham.htm

6. Letter from Encyclopedia Britannica to Wayne Perryman, November 11, 1994, Unfounded Loyalty: An In-Depth Look into the Blind Love Affair Between Blacks and Democrats, p. 267, Hara Publishing, 2003.

7. Letter from Zondervan Publishing House to Wayne Perryman, January 20, 1995, Unfounded Loyalty, p. 264

8. Letter from Thomas Nelson Publishers to Wayne Perryman, October 26, 1994, Unfounded Loyalty, p. 266

9. The American Presidency Project, Political Party Platforms, Democratic Party Platform of 1844; May 27, 1844; link is http://www.pres idency.ucsb.edu/ws/index.php?pid = 29573#axzz1KlK4lmDZ

10. Republican Party founded, This Day in History, March 20, 1854; link is http://www.history.com/this-day-in-history/republican-party-founded

11. Rev. Wayne Perryman, "Whites, Blacks & Racist Democrats: The Untold History of Race & Politics Within the Democratic Party From 1792-2009," 2010, p. 9, Book Publishers Network

12. John Fund, "More Acorn Voter Fraud Comes to Light," *Wall Street Journal*, May 9, 2009; link is http://online.wsj.com/article/SB12418 2750646102435.html

13. Rev. Wayne Perryman, "Whites, Blacks & Racist Democrats," pp. 22-24

14. Michelle Malkin, "What's missing from the New York Times coverage of ACORN," September 16, 2009; link is http://michelle malkin.com/2009/09/16/whats-missing-from-the-new-york-times-coverage-of-acorn/

15. David Postman, "Doubts linger as Gregoire win certified," *The Seattle Times*, December 31, 2004; link is http://seattletimes.nw source.com/html/localnews/2002136418_recount31m.html

16. Peter Roff, "Al Franken May Have Won His Senate Seat Through Voter Fraud," *U.S. News and World Report*, July 20, 2010; link is http://www.usnews.com/opinion/blogs/peter-roff/2010/07/20/Al-Franken-May-Have-Won-His-Senate-Seat-Through-Voter-Fraud

17. "Thousands of protesters surround Wis. Capitol," *Associated Press*, February 19, 2011; link is http://www.msnbc.msn.com/id/41664858/ ns/us_news-life/

18. Wayne Perryman, "Whites, Blacks & Racist Democrats," pp. 9-10.

19. Spartacus Educational, Preston Brooks; link is http://www.spar tacus.schoolnet.co.uk/USAbrooksP.htm

20. Spartacus Educational, Charles Sumner; link is http://www.spar tacus.schoolnet.co.uk/USASsumner.htm

21. "How the senators voted on impeachment," CNN, February 12, 1999; link is http://www.cnn.com/ALLPOLITICS/stories/1999/02/12/ senate.vote/

22. Wayne Perryman, "Whites, Blacks & Racist Democrats," pp. 20-21

23. Spartacus Educational, Andrew Johnson; link is http://www.spar tacus.schoolnet.co.uk/USAjohnsonA.htm

24. Wayne Perryman, "Whites, Blacks & Racist Democrats," pp. 16-17

25. Al Sharpton's Speech at the Democratic National Convention, 2004; link is http://www.americanrhetoric.com/speeches/convention 2004/alsharpton2004dnc.htm

26. Famous American Trials, "The Andrew Johnson Impeachment Trial," 1868, A Trial Account by Douglas O. Linder; link is http://law2.umkc.edu/faculty/projects/ftrials/impeach/impeachmt.htm

27. "Amendment XV to the U.S. Constitution, Answers.com; link is http://www.answers.com/topic/amendment-xv-to-the-u-s-constitution

28. Wayne Perryman, "Unfounded Loyalty," p. 100, Hara Publishing, 2003

29. Ibid

30. Michelle Malkin, "Crash course: Your illustrated guide to the Tea Party saboteurs," April 12, 2010; link is http://michellemalkin.com/2010/04/12/crash-course-your-illustrated-guide-to-the-tea-party-saboteurs/

31. "Political activist pleads guilty in windo-smashing," *The Denver Post*, December 22, 2009; link is http://www.denverpost.com/ci_14045675

32. "Black Man Pleads Guilty to Posing as Obama-Hating White Supremacist on Facebook," *Fox News / Associated Press*, August 14, 2009; link is http://www.foxnews.com/story/0,2933,539445,00.html

33. Saul Alinsky, "Rules for Radicals," p. 29; link is http://www.crossroad.to/Quotes/communism/alinsky.htm

34. Wayne Perryman, "Unfounded Loyalty," pp. 102-103

35. Ibid

36. Steven Ertelt, "Pro-Life Billboard on Black Abortions Causes Outrage in NYC," *LifeNews*, February 23, 2011; link is http://www.lifenews.com/2011/02/23/pro-life-billboard-on-black-abortions-causes-outrage-in-nyc/

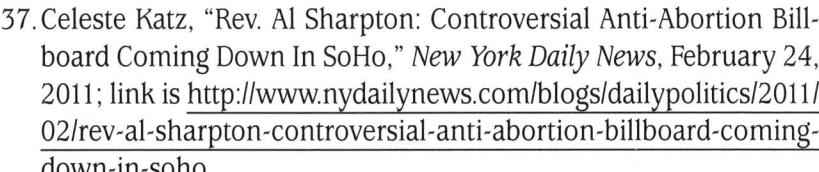

37. Celeste Katz, "Rev. Al Sharpton: Controversial Anti-Abortion Billboard Coming Down In SoHo," *New York Daily News*, February 24, 2011; link is http://www.nydailynews.com/blogs/dailypolitics/2011/02/rev-al-sharpton-controversial-anti-abortion-billboard-coming-down-in-soho

38. Dave Chappelle, Chappelle's Show, *Comedy Central*, January, 2003; link is http://www.comedycentral.com/videos/index.jhtml?title = frontline-clayton-bigsby&videoId = 24400

39. Christopher John Farley, "On the Beach with Dave Chappelle," *Time Magazine*, May 15, 2005; link is http://www.time.com/time/arts/article/0,8599,1061415,00.html

40. Stephen Brown, "Libyan Rebels Terrorize Black Africans," *Front Page Magazine*, April 22, 2011; link is http://frontpagemag.com/2011/04/22/libyan-rebels-terrorize-black-africans/

41. The Ku Klux Klan, The Burning Question, August 2010, News Releases; link is http://kukluxklan.bz/release.html

42. Wayne Perryman, "Whites, Blacks & Racist Democrats," pp. 22-23

43. Mike Romain, "Official Document Says Black Panther Was 'Representing the Democratic Party,'" *Election Journal*, May 30, 2009; link is http://www.electionjournal.org/2009/05/30/official-document-says-black-panther-was-representing-the-democratic-party/

44. Michelle Malkin, "Whitewashing Black Racism," *Frontpage Magazine*, July 14, 2010; link is http://frontpagemag.com/2010/07/14/whitewashing-black-racism/

45. "Voting Rights Official Calls Dismissal of Black Panther Case a 'Travesty of Justice,'" *Fox News*, September 24, 2010; link is http://www.foxnews.com/politics/2010/09/24/voting-rights-official-calls-black-panther-dismissal-travesty-justice/

46. Chelsea Schilling, "'Want freedom? Kill some crackers!' New Black Panther Obama DOJ refused to prosecute: 'I hate white people – all of them!'" July 7, 2010; link is http://www.wnd.com/?pageId = 175817

47. Wayne Perryman, "Unfounded Loyalty," p. 197

48. Cloward-Piven Strategy, Discover the Networks; link is http://www.discoverthenetworks.org/groupProfile.asp?grpid = 7522

49. Hannity Interview Archive, "Ayers Audio Could Detail What Obama Knew," *Fox News*, October 22, 2008; link is http://www.foxnews.com/story/0,2933,443241,00.html

50. Wayne Perryman, "Unfounded Loyalty," p. 199

51. Wayne Perryman, "Whites, Blacks & Racist Democrats," p. 145

52. Ibid, p. 54

53. Ben Barrack Show, Interview with Wayne Perryman, April 13, 2008

54. Jon Meacham, "We Are All Socialists Now," *Newsweek*, February 7, 2009; link is http://www.newsweek.com/2009/02/06/we-are-all-socialists-now.html

55. The Disputed Presidential Election of 1876, Digital History; link is http://www.digitalhistory.uh.edu/database/article_display.cfm?HHID = 139

56. United States History, Compromise of 1877; link is http://www.u-s-history.com/pages/h396.html

57. "The Compromise of 1877," The Black House, March 8, 2011; link is http://bhonline.org/blog2/2011/03/08/the-compromise-of-1877/

58. Wayne Perryman, "Unfounded Loyalty," pp. 231-234

59. Tom Zeller Jr., "Holocaust Denial – Crime or Free Speech?" *New York Times*, February 15, 2007; link is http://thelede.blogs.nytimes.com/2007/02/15/holocaust-denial-crime-or-free-speech/

60. "Combating Holocaust Denial: Origins of Holocaust Denial," *Holocaust Encyclopedia*, January 6, 2011; link is http://www.ushmm.org/wlc/en/article.php?ModuleId = 10007273

61. Middle Tennessee State University, The Holocaust\Shoah Page: Kristallnacht; link is http://frank.mtsu.edu/ ~ baustin/knacht.html

62. Ibid

63. Rev. Wayne Perryman, "Whites, Blacks & Racist Democrats," p. 54

64. Thomas D. Clark, "Introduction to re-release of The Clansman by Thomas Dixon," The University Press of Kentucky, 1970, pp. xi-xii; link is http://books.google.com/books?id = R5UdDoaQHr8C&pg = PR17&lpg = PR17&dq = thomas + dixon + democrat + clansman& source = bl&ots = OqKSarYdXD&sig = Qcb7Pma8M8IqSfRAw2QY jixL2i0&hl = en&ei = z-bJTfn6CIfb0QHgr9jcCA&sa = X&oi = book_ result&ct = result&resnum = 1&sqi = 2&ved = 0CBoQ6AEwAA#v = onepage&q = democrat&f = false

65. Rev. Wayne Perryman, Whites, Blacks & Racist Democrats, p. 51

66. Ibid, p. 54

67. David Barton, American Heritage-KKK Lynching (killing) Republicans D9-P2-10:00; nvsvictor, July 15, 200k; link is http://www.you tube.com/watch?v = VVzJ2RIlUwE&feature = player_embedded

68. Thomas D. Clark, "Introduction to re-release of The Clansman by Thomas Dixon," pp. xvii-xviii

69. Father James E. Coyle Memorial Project; link is http://www.father coyle.org/index.htm

70. Religious violence – American style, Albert J. Menendez, Instituted for First Amendment Studies, 1998; link is http://www.publiceye. org/ifas/fw/9606/violence.html

71. Hilmar Von Campe, "Defeating the Totalitarian Lie: A Former Hitler Youth Warns America," HighWay Publishing, 2008, p. 50

72. Ibid, pp. 50-51

73. Armenian Genocide, *New World Encyclopedia*; link is http://www. newworldencyclopedia.org/entry/Armenian_Genocide

74. David Hardaker, "Facing up to the Past," Foreign Correspondent, February 28, 2006, Series 15, Episode 22; link is http://www.abc. net.au/foreign/content/2006/s1576063.htm

75. Armenian Genocide, Armenian National Institute; http://www. armenian-genocide.org/genocide.html

76. Armenian Genocide, *New World Encyclopedia*

77. Michael Zak, "Republican Roots of the 1964 Civil Rights Act," Big Government, May 31, 2010; link is http://biggovernment.com/mzak/2010/05/31/republican-roots-of-the-1964-civil-rights-act/

78. Mike Riggs and Amanda Carey, "Sen. Robert Byrd not only was a KKK member but led his local Klan chapter," *The Daily Caller*, June 28, 2010; link is http://dailycaller.com/2010/06/28/sen-robert-byrd-not-only-was-a-kkk-member-but-led-his-local-klan-chapter/

79. Bill Clinton, "Bill Clinton recalls Byrd warmly," *Washington Post*, July 2, 2010; link is http://voices.washingtonpost.com/44/2010/07/bill-clinton-recalls-byrd-warm.html?wprss = 44

80. King's Last March, American Radio Works, American Public Media; link is http://americanradioworks.publicradio.org/features/king/c1.html

81. Robert Byrd, Memphis Riots and the Coming March on Washington, Speech of Senator Robert C. Byrd, Appendix Two, March 29, 1968

82. Wayne Perryman, Unfounded Loyalty, p. 128

83. Lyndon Baines Johnson Library and Museum, President Lyndon B. Johnson's Address to the Nation, March 31, 1968, National Archives and Records Administration; http://www.lbjlib.utexas.edu/johnson/archives.hom/speeches.hom/680331.asp

84. William R. Mann, "Jared Loughner: Modern Liberalism's Natural Consequence," *Canada Free Press*, January 11, 2011; link is http://www.canadafreepress.com/index.php/article/32038

85. Wayne Perryman, Unveiling the Whole Truth, p. 155

86. Ibid, p. 156

87. Perkins Coie; link is http://www.perkinscoie.com/seattle-united-states-of-america/

88. Wayne Perryman, Unveiling the Whole Truth, p. 249

89. Ibid, p. 251

90. Ibid, pp. 255-256

91. Ibid, p. 257

92. Ibid, p. 262

93. Ibid, p. 270

94. Africans in America, Resource Bank, Dred Scott's fight for freedom, PBS; link is http://www.pbs.org/wgbh/aia/part4/4p2932.html

95. Wayne Perryman, Unveiling the Whole Truth, p. 303

96. Ibid, p. 283

97. Ibid, p. 304

98. Ibid, p. 315

99. Ibid, p. 318

## Chapter 7

1. Photo taken at TWCC on March 13, 2011

2. Author's first-hand account, March 13, 2011

3. The Worldwide Christian Center website, Our Pastor page; link is http://www.twwcc.org/about/pastors-corner/

4. Ibid

5. Harris Meyer and Julie Kay, "Judicial Nominating Questions out of Line?" Law.com, January 16, 2004; link is http://www.law.com/jsp/law/LawArticleFriendly.jsp?id = 900005537724

6. Ibid

7. Cornell University Law School, United States Constitution, Article VI; link is http://topics.law.cornell.edu/constitution/articlevi

8. Ibid, "Judicial Nominating Questions out of Line?"

9. Leviticus 18:22, Holy Bible, New King James Version; link is http://www.biblegateway.com/passage/?search = leviticus % 2018:22& version = NKJV

10. Ibid, "Judicial Nominating Questions out of Line?"

11. Ibid

12. Brendan Farrington, "Pastor: Lord revealed next Florida governor," Sacramento Bee via JewsOnFirst, May 22, 2006; link is http://www.jewsonfirst.org/06bprint/back020p.html

13. Ibid

14. Darran Simon, "Jeb Bush ally slams Islam," The Miami Herald, July 8, 2006; link is http://www.archives2006.ghazali.net/html/mosque_protest.html

15. Mohamed Akram, "An Explanatory Memorandum on the General Strategic Goal for the Brotherhood in North America," Investigative Project on Terrorism, 1991; link is http://www.investigativeproject.org/document/id/20

16. Americans Against Hate, Pompano Mosque; link is http://www.americansagainsthate.org/Pompano_Mosque_NAIT.html

17. Joe Kaufman, "Islamist Center of South Florida," *Front Page Magazine*, July 11, 2006; link is http://archive.frontpagemag.com/read Article.aspx?ARTID = 3625

18. Ibid, "Jeb Bush ally slams Islam."

19. Bob Norman, "Bush Appointee: We're at War With 'Evil' Islam," *Broward New Times*, July 7, 2006; link is http://blogs.browardpalm beach.com/pulp/2006/07/bush_appointee_were_at_war_wit.php

20. O'Neal Dozier on family values, religion, and Islam, *Shalom Show TV* Part 2, April 11, 2011; link is http://www.youtube.com/watch? v = Z9A50j1wa-g&NR = 1

21. Dr. O'Neal Dozier, Who's On The Lord's Side Politically: A Faith-based guide to the democratic process, p. 99, Armour of Light Publishing, 2008

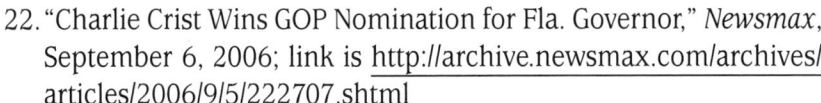

22. "Charlie Crist Wins GOP Nomination for Fla. Governor," *Newsmax*, September 6, 2006; link is http://archive.newsmax.com/archives/articles/2006/9/5/222707.shtml

23. Gregory Lewis, "Crist camp drops controversial Pompano minister," *Fort Lauderdale Sun-Sentinel*, September 23, 2006, via Democratic Underground; link is http://www.democraticunderground.com/discuss/duboard.php?az = view_all&address = 102x2527508

24. CBS Miami via Independent Conservative; link is http://www.independentconservative.com/2006/09/24/

25. Ibid, Shalom Show TV Part 2

26. Dozier, Who's On The Lord's Side Politically, p. 98

27. Joe Kaufman, "Islamist Center of South Florida."

28. Steve Emerson, "Evil Exposed: Holy Land Trial Shows Charity's Hamas Ties," *New York Post*, October 29, 2007; link is http://www.investigativeproject.org/534/evil-exposed

29. Discover the Networks, Nihad Awad; link is http://www.discoverthenetworks.org/individualProfile.asp?indid = 755

30. "Bush: U.S. Muslims should feel safe," *CNN*, September 17, 2001; link is http://articles.cnn.com/2001-09-17/us/gen.bush.muslim.trans _1_muslims-islamic-quran?_s = PM:US

31. Kari Huus and Tom Curry, "The day the enemy became 'Islamic fascists,' *MSNBC*, August 11, 2006; link is http://www.msnbc.msn.com/id/14304397/ns/politics/t/day-enemy-became-islamic-fascists/

32. Dozier, Who's On The Lord's Side Politically, p. 109

33. Holy Bible, Luke 12:48; link is http://www.biblegateway.com/passage/?search = luke % 2012:48&version = NKJV

34. Robert Spencer, "Jeb Bush sends letter of support to CAIR," Jihad Watch via Americans Against Hate, June 5, 2005; link is http://www.jihadwatch.org/2005/06/jeb-bush-sends-letter-of-support-to-cair.html

35. Letter from Florida Attorney General Charlie Crist to CAIR Americans Against Hate; link is http://www.americansagainsthate.org/OrlandoLettersCAIR.htm

36. Daniel Pipes, "CAIR Accepted as 'Mainstream,'" *Daniel Pipes Blog*, January 21, 2004; http://www.danielpipes.org/blog/2004/01/cair-accepted-as-mainstream

37. "U.S. Muslim Religious Council Issues Fatwa Against Terrorism," Fiqh Council of North America Memorandum, July, 2005; link is http://www.discoverislam.com/fatwajuly2005.pdf

38. Discover the Networks, George Galloway; link is http://www.discoverthenetworks.org/individualProfile.asp?indid = 1102

39. Patrick S. Poole, "Key Charlie Crist Ally Hosted Hamas Fundraiser in Florida Mosque," Big Peace, August 30, 2010; link http://bigpeace.com/pspoole/2010/08/30/patrick-poole-key-charlie-crist-ally-hosted-hamas-fundraiser-in-florida-mosque/

40. Ibid, Shalom Show TV Part 2

41. Bill Whittle, Turncoat Nation, May 26, 2011; link is http://www.youtube.com/watch?v = xRYXGIi5340

42. Scent of Woman, http://www.imdb.com/title/tt0105323/

43. O'Neal Dozier, "A Giant in the land," Sermon, October 2006

44. Ibid

45. Ibid

46. Ibid

47. Aaron Klein, "Obama church published Hamas terror manifesto," World Net Dailey, March 20, 2008; link is http://www.wnd.com/?pageId = 59456

48. "2008 Jewish Vote for Obama Exceeds All Expectations," National Jewish Democratic Council, November 5, 2008; link is http://www.njdc.org/site/page/jewish_vote_for_obama_exceeds_all_expectations

49. Peter Wallsten, "Allies of Palestinians see a friend in Obama," *Los Angeles Times*, April 10, 2008; link is http://articles.latimes.com/2008/apr/10/nation/na-obamamideast10

50. "Hamas unveils memorial to activists killed in last year's Israeli raid on Gaza-bound flotilla," *Washington Post*, May 31, 2011; link is http://www.washingtonpost.com/world/hamas-unveils-memorial-to-activists-killed-in-last-years-israeli-raid-on-gaza-bound-flotilla/2011/05/31/AGXnTNFH_story.html?wprss = rss_world

51. "Obama Friends Bill Ayers, Code Pink Top Activists Behind Gaza Flotilla," *Fox Nation*, June 1, 2010; link is http://nation.foxnews.com/gaza-flotilla-raid/2010/06/01/obama-friends-bill-ayers-code-pink-top-activists-behind-gaza-flotilla

52. O'Neal Dozier, "A Giant in the land," Sermon, 2006

53. Ibid

54. Ibid

55. "Christian Racism Rampant in Dearborn, MI," The United West, *YouTube Video*; link is http://www.youtube.com/watch?v = nswT9XS5v5g&feature = player_embedded

56. "Mosque lawsuit seeks source of CAIR funding: Dispute over planned construction targets controversial group's financial records," *World Net Daily*, December 7, 2007; link is http://www.wnd.com/?pageId = 44939

57. Joseph Puder, "Why CAIR Dropped its Lawsuit Against Andrew Whitehead," *Front Page Magazine*, April 26, 2007; link is http://archive.frontpagemag.com/readArticle.aspx?ARTID = 26296

58. Interview with O'Neal Dozier, Ben Barrack Show, March 30, 2008

59. Bob Unruh, "Pastor stages own protest against CAIR," *World Net Daily*, January 16, 2010; link is http://www.wnd.com/?pageId = 122088

60. Ibid

61. Phone interview with Dozier, June 13, 2011

62. "Pastor stages own protest against CAIR," *World Net Daily*

63. Interview with O'Neal Dozier, *Ben Barrack Show*, July 17, 2006

64. "Pastor stages own protest against CAIR," *World Net Daily*

65. Interview with O'Neal Dozier, Ben Barrack Show, July 17, 2006

66. Interview with O'Neal Dozier, Ben Barrack Show, November 23, 2006

67. Michael Bloomberg, "Speech after Ground Zero Mosque cleared for construction," *Wall Street Journal*, August 3, 2010; link is http://online.wsj.com/article/SB10001424052748703545604575407673221908474.html

68. Celeste Katz and Adam Lisberg, "Mayor Bloomberg's office: Inviting imam linked to 1993 WTC bombing to City Hall was mistake," *New York Daily News*, November 12, 2009; link is http://www.nydailynews.com/news/2009/11/12/2009-11-12_mayor_bloombergs_office_inviting_imam_linked_to_1993_wtc_bombing_was_mistake.html

69. Stop Shariah Now, "Introduction: Tenets of Shariah Law,"; link is http://www.stopshariahnow.org/index.php?option=com_content&view=article&id=328&Itemid=149

70. First Amendment of U.S. Constitution; link is http://topics.law.cornell.edu/constitution/first_amendment

71. Shariah: The Threat to America (An Exercise in Competitive Analysis – Report of Team 'B' II), The Center for Security Policy, Center for Security Policy Press, 2010; link is http://www.worldsecuritynetwork.com/documents/Shariah_The_Threat_to_America_(Team_B_II_Report)_9-14-10.pdf

72. Fred Grimm, "Fear-mongering's at its bigoted peak for primaries," *Miami Herald*, August 16, 2010; link is http://www.miamiherald.com/2010/08/16/1778992/fear-mongerings-at-its-bigoted.html

73. Paula Zahn Now, Transcript, *CNN*, May 8, 2007; link is http://transcripts.cnn.com/TRANSCRIPTS/0705/08/pzn.01.html

74. Frank Walker, "West must act to end jihad: Imam," *Australian Sun-Herald*, March 21, 2004; link is http://www.smh.com.au/articles/2004/03/21/1079789939987.html

75. Ibid

76. Ben Barrack Show, November 23, 2006

77. We The People Press, *YouTube* video of Dozier speaking; http://www.youtube.com/watch?v = 8SOQMwbMhwU

78. Anthony Man and David Fleshler, "Allen West defeats Ron Klein," *Fort Lauderdale Sun-Sentinel*, November 3, 2010; link is http://articles.sun-sentinel.com/2010-11-03/news/fl-election-us-congress-20101102_1_ron-klein-republican-allen-west-tea-party-activists

79. Shalom Show TV, Part 1

80. Sylvester Stallone, Rambo: First Blood Part II, 1985; link is http://www.imdb.com/title/tt0089880/

## Chapter 8

1. Jayna Davis, "The Third Terrorist: The Middle East Connection to the Oklahoma City Bombing," WND Books, 2004; link to website is http://jaynadavis.com/

2. Photos and Meeting Minutes from WWII, Tell the Children the Truth; link is http://tellthechildrenthetruth.com/gallery/index.html

3. "Reporter J.D. Cash Dead At 55," *The McCarville Report*, May 6, 2007; link is http://wwwtmrcom.blogspot.com/search/label/J.%20D.%20Cash

4. Phone conversation between author and Bruce Willingham on September 23, 2010; link to *McCurtain Gazette* website is http://mccurtain.com/aboutus.shtml

5. Ibid

6. Ambrose Evans-Pritchard, "Bomb squad seen before blast," *World Net Daily*, May 30, 2001; link is http://www.wnd.com/index.php?fa = PAGE.printable&pageId = 9424

7. "McCurtain County, Oklahomoa," The U.S. Census Bureau website; link is http://quickfacts.census.gov/qfd/states/40/40089.html

8. John Stadtmiller, "The Intel Report," Guest host Scott Horton, *Republic Radio*, July 22, 2005; link is http://weekendinterviewshow.com/InterviewDisplay.aspx?i = 115

9. Ibid

10. Ambrose Evans-Pritchard, 'Glenn and Kathy Wilburn,' *World Net Daily*, May 29, 2001; link is http://www.wnd.com/?pageId = 9419

11. Ibid

12. Ibid

13. Ibid

14. Ibid

15. Ambrose Evans-Pritchard, "Bomb squad seen before blast," *World Net Daily*, May 30, 2001; link is http://www.wnd.com/news/article.asp?ARTICLE_ID = 23016

16. Ibid

17. Ibid

18. Ambrose Evans-Pricthard, "John Doe 2: Evans-Pritchard: FBI 'had no intention' of finding accomplices," *World Net Daily*, May 31, 2001; link is http://www.wnd.com/?pageId = 9440

19. Jon Dougherty, "Accomplices known to FBI," World Net Daily, June 1, 2001; link is http://www.wnd.com/?pageId = 9458

20. Ibid

21. Ibid

22. Ibid

23. Ibid

24. Ibid

25. *Associated Press*, "FBI Files: McVeigh May Have Had Help," February 25, 2004; link is http://www.foxnews.com/story/0,2933,112426,00.html

26. Scott Horton, "Weekend Interview Show," Interview with J.D. Cash, November 26, 2005; link is http://weekendinterviewshow.com/InterviewDisplay.aspx?i = 147

27. Ibid

28. Jayna Davis, "The Third Terrorist: The Middle East Connection to the Oklahoma City Bobming," WND Books, 2004; link to website is http://jaynadavis.com/

29. Photos and Meeting Minutes from WWII, Tell the Children the Truth; link is http://tellthechildrenthetruth.com/gallery/index.html

30. Jon Dougherty, "Accomplices known to FBI," *World Net Daily*, June 1, 2001; link is http://www.wnd.com/?pageId = 9458

31. Ambrose Evans-Pritchard, "Bomb squad seen before blast," *World Net Daily*, May 30, 2001; link is http://www.wnd.com/news/article.asp?ARTICLE_ID = 23016

32. J.D. Cash, "The Spy Who Came in from the Cold," McCurtain Daily Gazette via John Doe Times, February 11, 1997; link is http://www.constitution.org/okc/jdt03-16.htm

33. Jon Dougherty, "Judge never read ATF informant file," *World Net Daily*, June 19, 2001; link is http://www.wnd.com/?pageId = 9696

34. Ibid

35. Scott Horton, "Weekend Interview Show," Interview with J.D. Cash, November 26, 2005; link is http://weekendinterviewshow.com/InterviewDisplay.aspx?i = 147

36. J.D. Cash and Lt. Col. Roger Charles, "Ex-Green Beret involved in attack?" *McCurtain Daily Gazette* / Re-print on WND, July 21, 2005; link is http://www.wnd.com/?pageId = 31403

37. Ibid

38. Ambrose Evans-Pritchard, "The Secret Life of Bill Clinton," *World Net Daily*, December 9, 1999; link is http://www.wnd.com/news/article.asp?ARTICLE_ID = 14869

39. J.D. Cash and Lt. Col. Roger Charles, "Ex-Green Beret involved in attack?" *McCurtain Daily Gazette* / Re-print on WND, July 21, 2005; link is http://www.wnd.com/?pageId = 31403

40. University of Missouri-Kansas City School of Law; link is http://www.law.umkc.edu/faculty/projects/ftrials/mcveigh/more conspirators.html

41. "Declassified FBI memo reveals twists in probe," *World Net Daily,* January 6, 2004; link is http://www.wnd.com/?pageId = 22643

42. Southern Poverty Law Center website, bio for Morris Dees; link is http://www.splcenter.org/who-we-are/leadership/morris-dees

43. Scott Horton, "Weekend Interview Show," Interview with J.D. Cash, November 26, 2005; link is http://weekendinterviewshow.com/Inter viewDisplay.aspx?i = 147

44. Ibid

45. "Declassified FBI memo reveals twists in probe," *World Net Daily,* January 6, 2004; link is http://www.wnd.com/?pageId = 22643

46. Ibid

47. John Stadtmiller, "The Intel Report," Guest host Scott Horton, *Republic Radio,* July 22, 2005; link is http://weekendinterview show.com/InterviewDisplay.aspx?i = 115

48. Lloyd de Vries, "FBI Tries To Limit Info Searches," *CBS News,* January 21, 2005; link is http://www.cbsnews.com/stories/2005/01/21/ national/main668365.shtml

49. J.D. Cash, "FBI surrenders documents that judge ordered," *McCurtain Daily Gazette,* October 21, 2005; link is http://www.mccurtain. com/cgi-bin/okcscript.cgi?record = 1346

50. "Did Oklahoma City Bombers Have Help?" *Fox News,* April 17, 2005; link is http://www.foxnews.com/story/0,2933,153635,00.html

51. Jon Dougherty, "Accomplices known to FBI," *World Net Daily,* June 1, 2001; link is http://www.wnd.com/?pageId = 9458

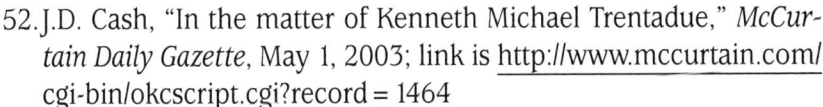 

52. J.D. Cash, "In the matter of Kenneth Michael Trentadue," *McCurtain Daily Gazette*, May 1, 2003; link is http://www.mccurtain.com/cgi-bin/okcscript.cgi?record = 1464

53. Ibid

54. Ibid

55. J.D. Cash, "In the matter of Kenneth Michael Trentadue – Part Two," *McCurtain Daily Gazette*, May 10, 2003; link is http://www.mccurtain.com/cgi-bin/okcscript.cgi?record = 1463

56. Ibid

57. OIG Report, "A REVIEW OF THE JUSTICE DEPARTMENT'S HANDLING OF THE DEATH OF KENNETH MICHAEL TRENTADUE AT THE BUREAU OF PRISONS' FEDERAL TRANSFER CENTER IN OKLAHOMA CITY," December, 1999; link is http://www.justice.gov/oig/special/9912.htm

58. "Interview with Dr. Fred Jordan," *Fox 25 KOKH*, 1997; link is http://www.youtube.com/user/hillbillyjihad32

59. J.D. Cash, "In the matter of Kenneth Michael Trentadue – Part Three," *McCurtain Daily Gazette*, May 15, 2003; link is http://www.mccurtain.com/cgi-bin/okcscript.cgi?record = 1462

60. Ibid

61. Ibid

62. Ibid

63. J.D. Cash, "In the matter of Kenneth Michael Trentadue – Part Four," *McCurtain Daily Gazette*, May 20, 2003; link is http://www.mccurtain.com/cgi-bin/okcscript.cgi?record = 1461

64. Ibid

65. Ibid

66. J.D. Cash, "In the matter o Kenneth Michael Trentadue – Part Five," *McCurtain Daily Gazette*, May 30, 2003

67. Ibid

68. Ibid

69. *YouTube* video of Orrin Hatch interview from October 10, 1997; link is http://www.youtube.com/user/hillbillyjihad32#p/a/u/1/LG fEkvpsKAs

70. U.S. Senate website; link is http://senate.gov/legislative/LIS/roll_call_ lists/roll_call_vote_cfm.cfm?congress = 111&session = 1&vote = 000 32#position

71. Mike McCarville, "Reporter J.D. Cash Dead at 55," *The McCarville Report Online*, May 6, 2007; link is http://wwwtmrcom.blogspot. com/2007/05/reporter-j-d-cash-dead-at-55.html

## Chapter 9

1. Lt. Col. Anthony Shaffer, Operation Dark Heart, Thomas Dunn Books / St. Martin's Press, New York, NY, 2010, p. 16

2. Ibid, pp. 16-17

3. Ibid, p. 166

4. Ibid, p. 169

5. Lt. Col. Shaffer's written testimony, Before the House Armed Service Committee (HASC), Congress of the United States, February 15, 2006; link is http://www.abledangerblog.com/2006/ 02/lt-col-shaffers-written-testimony.html

6. Operation Dark Heart, p. 170

7. Ed Morrissey, "Who Is Dr. Preisser?' Captain's Quarters, September 24, 2005; link is http://www.captainsquartersblog.com/mt/ archives/005505.php

8. Operation Dark Heart, p. 170

9. F. Michael Maloof, "If we only had acted," *The Washington Times*, October 8, 2005; link is http://www.washingtontimes.com/news/ 2005/oct/8/20051008-101924-8719r/?page = all#pagebreak

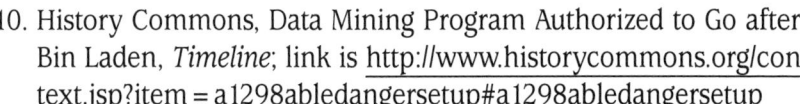 

10. History Commons, Data Mining Program Authorized to Go after Bin Laden, *Timeline*; link is http://www.historycommons.org/con text.jsp?item = a1298abledangersetup#a1298abledangersetup

11. Charles R. Smith, "The Chinese Army Spy and Condoleezza Rice," *Newsmax*, January 24, 2001; link is http://archive.newsmax.com/archives/articles/2001/1/23/203153.shtml

12. Shane Harris, "Army project illustrates promise, shortcomings of data mining," *National Journal* / Government Executive, December 7, 2005; link is http://www.govexec.com/dailyfed/1205/120705 nj1.htm

13. Shane Harris, The Watchers: The Rise of America's Surveillance State, Penguin Press, HC, 2010, p. 112

14. AJStrata, "Able Danger, China, Cohen, AQ Data Purge = 9-11," The Strata-Sphere: high-flying political debate," December 7, 2005; link is http://strata-sphere.com/blog/index.php/archives/1042

15. Testimony of Erik Kleinsmith, House Armed Services Committee, February 15, 2006; link is http://www.abledangerblog.com/hear ing.pdf

16. AJStrata, "Able Danger Hearings Part IV," The Strata-Sphere, February 18, 2006; link is http://strata-sphere.com/blog/index. php/archives/1354

17. Lt. Col. Shaffer's written testimony, Before the House Armed Service Committee (HASC), Congress of the United States, February 15, 2006; link is http://www.abledangerblog.com/2006/02/lt-col-shaffers-written-testimony.html

18. Operation Dark Heart (un-redacted chapter), pp. 171-172; link is http://www.abledangerblog.com/chapter14.pdf

19. Transcript, House Armed Services Committee, February 15, 2006; link is http://www.abledangerblog.com/hearing.pdf

20. Operation Dark Heart, p. 175

21. Lt. Col. Shaffer's written testimony

22. Douglas Jehl, "Senators Accuse Pentagon of Obstructing Inquiry on Sept. 11 Plot," *New York Times*, September 22, 2005; link is http://www.nytimes.com/2005/09/22/politics/22intel.html?ex = 1285041600&en = be75f65b369fa799&ei = 5090&partner = rssuserland&emc = rss

23. Lt. Col. Shaffer's written testimony

24. "Able Danger Officer Disciplined," CBS News / AP, February 26, 2010; link is http://www.cbsnews.com/stories/2005/09/30/terror/main892266.shtml

25. Operation Dark Heart, pp. 172-173

26. Brian Ross and Vic Walter, "FBI Informant Says Agents Missed Chance to Stop 9/11 Ringleader Mohammed Atta," *ABC News Nightline*, September 10, 2009; link is http://abcnews.go.com/Blotter/Whistleblowers/911-ringleader-mohammed-atta-stopped-fbi-informant/Story?id = 8540605

27. House Armed Services Committee Hearing, February 16, 2006

28. Lt. Col. Shaffer's written testimony

29. Email exchange between Philip Zelikow and Philip Shenon, 2007; link is http://www.philipshenon.com/pdf/zelikowemail.pdf

30. Chris Strohm, "Groups call for the resignation of Sept. 11 commission director," Government Executive, March 22, 2004; link is http://www.govexec.com/dailyfed/0304/032204c1.htm

31. Lt. Col. Shaffer's written testimony

32. Operation Dark Heart, p. 175

33. Lt. Col. Shaffer's written testimony

34. Douglas Jehl, "9/11 Panel Explains Move on Intelligence Unit," *New York Times*, August 13, 2005; link is http://www.nytimes.com/2005/08/13/politics/13intel.html

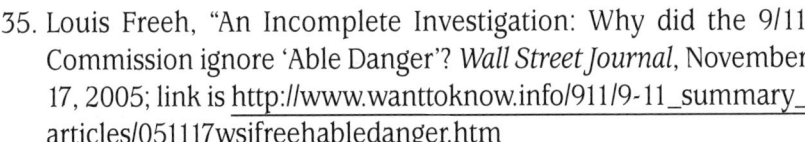

35. Louis Freeh, "An Incomplete Investigation: Why did the 9/11 Commission ignore 'Able Danger'? *Wall Street Journal*, November 17, 2005; link is http://www.wanttoknow.info/911/9-11_summary_articles/051117wsjfreehabledanger.htm

36. Rep. Curt Weldon Speech on Able Danger, Congressional Record / *Newsmax*, October 21, 2005; link is http://archive.newsmax.com/archives/articles/2005/10/21/143949.shtml

37. Jack Cashill, "Oklahoma City, TWA Flight 800, and the Gorelick connection," *World Net Daily*, April 16, 2004; link is http://www.wnd.com/news/article.asp?ARTICLE_ID = 38068

38. "Jamie Gorelick's wall," *The Washington Times*, April 15, 2004; link is http://www.washingtontimes.com/news/2004/apr/15/20040415-094758-5267r/

39. The National Archives; link is http://media.nara.gov/9-11/MFR/t-0148-911MFR-00934.pdf

40. *YouTube* video of Curt Weldon, Informedru's Channel; link is http://www.youtube.com/user/Informedru#p/search/1/tpGBdxm_P3s

41. House Armed Services Committee Hearing, February 16, 2006

42. Lt. Col. Shaffer's written testimony

43. Operation Dark Heart, p. 244

44. Ibid, p. 263

45. Lt. Col. Shaffer's written testimony

46. Rep. Curt Weldon Speech on Able Danger, Congressional Record / Newsmax, October 21, 2005; link is http://archive.newsmax.com/archives/articles/2005/10/21/143949.shtml

47. "Feds probe Clinton aide over missing papers," *CNN*, July 21, 2004; link is http://articles.cnn.com/2004-07-20/politics/berger.probe_1_documents-lanny-breuer-samuel-sandy-berger?_s = PM: ALLPOLITICS

48. John F. Harris and Allan Lengel, "Berger Will Plead Guilty To Taking Clssified Paper," *Washington Post*, April 1, 2005; link is http://www.washingtonpost.com/wp-dyn/articles/A16706-2005Mar31.html

49. Operation Dark Heart, p. 274

50. Curt Weldon speech on Able Danger, October 21, 2005

51. Ibid

52. Jack Cashill, "Part 3: How Sandy Berger Paid Back the GOP," *World Net Daily*, January 30, 2007; link is http://www.cashill.com/twa800/how_sandy_berger_paid.htm

53. Lt. Col. Shaffer's written testimony

54. Ibid

55. Curt Weldon speech on Able Danger, October 21, 2005

56. "The White House Fires a Watchdog: The curious case of the inspector general and a Presidential ally," *Wall Street Journal*, June 17, 2009; link is http://online.wsj.com/article/SB124511811033017539.html

57. Department of Defense Office of the Inspector General, "report of Investigation," Case Number H05L97905217, September 18, 2006; link is http://www.abledangerblog.com/ig-abledanger-alt.pdf

58. Curt Weldon speech on Able Danger, October 21, 2005

59. Department of Defense Office of the Inspector General report

60. Doug Stanton, Horse Soldiers: The Extraordinary Story of a Band of US Soldiers Who Rode to Victory in Afghanistan, Scribner Press, 2009, p. 27.

61. "The Able Danger Whitewash," *Flopping Aces*, September 22, 2006; link is http://floppingaces.net/2006/09/22/the-able-danger-whitewash/

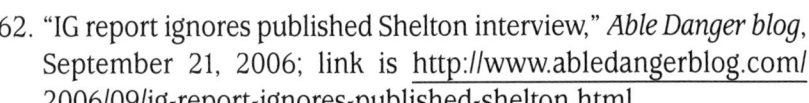

62. "IG report ignores published Shelton interview," *Able Danger blog*, September 21, 2006; link is http://www.abledangerblog.com/2006/09/ig-report-ignores-published-shelton.html

63. Curt Weldon speech on Able Danger, October 21, 2005

64. "The Able Danger Whitewash," *Flopping aces*; link is http://floppingaces.net/2006/09/22/the-able-danger-whitewash/

65. DoD OIG Report, p. 60; link is http://www.abledangerblog.com/ig-abledanger-alt.pdf

66. DoD OIG Report, p. 13; link is http://www.abledangerblog.com/ig-abledanger-alt.pdf

67. DoD OIG Report, p. 65

68. Ibid

69. Ibid, p. 87

70. Ibid, p. 90

71. Ibid, p. 57

72. Ibid, p. 89

73. Ibid, p. 90

74. Peter Pry bio, Reference.com; link is http://www.reference.com/browse/curt + weldon

75. Pry, Peter, "Rebuttal of the Department of Defense Office of the Inspector General Report on the Able Danger Program," link is http://www.abledangerblog.com/rebuttal.pdf

76. Ibid

77. Ibid, p. 6

78. Ibid, p. 8

79. Ibid, p. 14

80. Curt Weldon, "Weldon Rejects DoD Report on Able Danger & Harassment of Military Officer," September 21, 2006; link is http://www.abledangerblog.com/2006/09/weldon-blasts-back-at-deceptive-ig.html

81. Ibid

82. Shira Toeplitz, "Democrats: Joe Sestak must explain job offer," *POLITICO*, May 27, 2010; link is http://www.politico.com/news/stories/0510/37840.html

83. "Weldon Questions Timing of FBI Raid at Daughter's Home," *Fox News Channel*, October 16, 2006; link is http://www.foxnews.com/story/0,2933,221439,00.html

84. Phone interview with Curt Weldon, June 29, 2011

85. Letter from Rep. Chris Shays to Maj. General Elbert N. Perkins, October 10, 2006; link is http://www.abledangerblog.com/shays letter.pdf

86. Operation Dark Heart, pp. 144-145

87. Ibid, p. 159

88. Ibid, p. 187

89. Ibid, p. 188

90. Ibid, p. 189

91. Ibid, p. 264

92. Caroline Gammell, "Osama bin Laden dead: killed yards from Pakistan's 'Sandhurst," *The Telegraph*, May 2, 2011; link is http://www.telegraph.co.uk/news/worldnews/asia/pakistan/8487772/Osama-bin-Laden-dead-killed-yards-from-Pakistans-Sandhurst.html

93. Peter Lance, "The Private War of Anthony Shaffer," *Playboy Magazine*, January, 2011, p. 50, 146; link is http://www.peterlance.com/Private_War_Anthony%20Shaffer_12.15.10.pdf

94. Catherine Herridge, "Al Qaeda Leader Dined at the Pentagon Just Months After 9/11," *Fox News*, October 20, 2010; link is http://www.foxnews.com/us/2010/10/20/al-qaeda-terror-leader-dined-pentagon-months/

95. The United States Army, Secretary of the Army, The Honorable Thomas E. White; link is http://www.11thcavnam.com/white/white4.htm

96. Catherine Herridge, "Al Qaeda Leader Dined at the Pentagon Just Months After 9/11."

97. Ibid

98. Karen E. Crummy, "Warrant withdrawn in 2002 for radical cleric who praised Fort Hood suspect," *The Denver Post*, December 1, 2009; link is http://www.denverpost.com/technology/ci_13897548

99. Catherine Herridge, "New Documents in Fort Hood Shooting Case Raise Concerns About Prosecution's Handling of Evidence," *Fox News*, July 18, 2011; link is http://www.foxnews.com/us/2011/07/18/new-documents-in-fort-hood-shooting-case-raise-concerns-about-prosecutions/

100. Paul A. Romer, "Galligan out as Hasan's defense attorney," *Temple Daily Telegram*, July 20, 2011; link is http://www.tdtnews.com/index/news/show/75865

101. Catherine Herridge, Pamela Browne, Cyd Upson & Gregory Johnson, "New Details Emerge of Radical Imam's Lunch at the Pentagon," *Fox News*, May 20, 2011; link is http://www.foxnews.com/politics/2011/05/19/exclusive-new-details-emerge-al-qaeda-terror-chiefs-lunch-pentagon/

102. Public Intelligence, "DoD Email Discussing Anwar al-Awlaki's 2002 Presentation at the Pentagon," May 21, 2011; link is http://publicintelligence.net/dod-email-discussing-anwar-al-awlakis-2002-presentation-at-the-pentagon/

103. "Dar al-Hijrah Mosque," Investigative Project on Terrorism; link is http://www.investigativeproject.org/case/417

104. Pierre Thomas, Martha Raddatz, Rhonda Schwartz and Jason Ryan, "Fort Hood Suspect Yells Nidal Hasan's Name in Court," *ABC News*, July 29, 2011; link is http://abcnews.go.com/Blotter/fort-hood-suspect-nabbed-al-qaeda-inspire-magazine/story?id = 14187568

105. Stephen C. Webster, "Peace group tried to scrub involvement with soldier linked to Ft. Hood plot," The Raw Story, July 28, 2011; link is http://www.rawstory.com/rs/2011/07/28/exclusive-peace-group-tried-to-scrub-involvement-with-soldier-linked-to-ft-hood-plot/

106. "Fort Hood Suspect Yells Nidal Hasan's Name in Court," Ibid

107. Interview with Alex Jones, "Anthony Shaffer: Awlaki a US double agent before 9/11," Armies of Liberation, March 7, 2012; link is http://armiesofliberation.com/archives/2012/03/07/anthony-shaffer-awlaki-a-us-triple-agent-before-911/

108. Catherine Herridge, "Mueller grilled on FBI's release of al-Awlaki in 2002," Fox News, March 8, 2012; link is http://www.foxnews.com/politics/2012/03/07/mueller-grilled-on-fbis-release-al-awlaki-in-2002/

109. Catherine Herridge, "EXCLUSIVE: Pentagon Attempts to Block Book on Afghan War," *Fox News*, September 10, 2010; link is http://www.foxnews.com/politics/2010/09/09/military-intelligence-attempts-block-book-afghan-war/

110. Operation Dark Heart, p. 2

111. The 9/11 Commission Report: Final Report of the National Commission on Terrorist Attacks Upon the United States, January 26, 2004; link is http://www.9-11commission.gov/report/911Report.pdf

112. BBC, "Pakistan 'backed Haqqani attack on Kabul' – Mike Mullen, September 22, 2011; link is http://www.bbc.co.uk/news/world-us-canada-15024344

## Chapter 10

1. Documents on German Foreign Policy 1918-1945, Series D, Vol XIII, London, 1964, p.881 ff; link is http://tellthechildrenthetruth.com/gallery/index.html

2. "Trip to Big Trees Wins High Praise," *The Humboldt Standard*, September 9, 1929

3. Kathy Dillon, "An impressive guest list," *The Humboldt Times-Standard*, Sunday, November 7th (year unknown)

4. "Why I Left Jihad: The Root of Terrorism and the Return of Radical Islam," Walid Shoebat, Top Executive Media Publishing, 2005, p. 15

5. Ibid, p. 17

6. Raffi Berg, "Palestinian militant turned peacemaker," *BBC News*, January 26, 2004; link is http://news.bbc.co.uk/2/hi/middle_east/3430077.stm

7. The Right Scoop website, *YouTube* video; link is http://www.therightscoop.com/walid-shoebat-fired-up-at-six-flags

8. Quotations website; link is http://quotations.about.com/cs/winston churchill/a/bls_churchill.htm

9. "Why I Left Jihad: The Root of Terrorism and the Return of Radical Islam," Walid Shoebat, Top Executive Media Publishing, 2005, p. 21

10. The Right Scoop website, *YouTube* video; link is http://www.therightscoop.com/walid-shoebat-fired-up-at-six-flags

11. "Obsession: Radical Islam's War Against the West," 2006; link is http://obsessionthemovie.com/index.html

12. Ben Barrack Show, "Let's Talk About Something Important," Interview with Walid Shoebat on March 18, 2007.

13. President George W. Bush, White House archives, September 17, 2001; link is http://georgewbush-whitehouse.archives.gov/news/releases/2001/09/20010917-11.html

14. Josh Gerstein, "Islamic Groups Named in Hamas Funding Case," *New York Sun*, June 4, 2007; link is http://www.nysun.com/national/islamic-groups-named-in-hamas-funding-case/55778/

15. Daniel Pipes, "Here's what CAIR doesn't say about me – or its record," *Orange County Register*, December 22, 2002; link is http://www.campus-watch.org/article/id/417

16. IPT News, "Surprisingly Candid Answers From the Muslim Brotherhood," Investigative Project on Terrorism, August 27, 2008; link is http://www.investigativeproject.org/756/surprisingly-candid-answers-from-the-muslim-brotherhood

17. Amin al-Husseini, Tell the Children the Truth; link is http://tellthechildrenthetruth.com/gallery/index.html

18. Discover the Networks, "The Muslim Brotherhood's Project for Israel and America," link is http://www.discoverthenetworks.org/viewSubCategory.asp?id = 853

19. Investigative Project on Terrorism, "Individual Terrorists: Abdullah Azzam," link is http://www.investigativeproject.org/profile/103

20. Discover the Networks, "Abdullah Azzam," link is http://www.discoverthenetworks.org/individualProfile.asp?indid = 844

21. Ben Barrack Show, "Let's Talk About Something Important," Interview with Walid Shoebat on March 18, 2007

22. Official Bio of Ahmed Rehab, Executive Director of CAIR Chicago; link is http://www.cairchicago.org/ahmedrehab.php

23. IPT News, "Spinning the Asbahi Resignation," Investigative Project on Terrorism, August 7, 2008; link is http://www.investigativeproject.org/744/spinning-the-asbahi-resignation

24. Ben Barrack Show, "Let's Talk About Something Important," Interview with Walid Shoebat on March 18, 2007

25. Ibid

26. Discover The Networks, "Nihad Awad," 1994; link is http://www.discoverthenetworks.org/individualProfile.asp?indid = 755

27. Ben Barrack Show, "Let's Talk About Something Important," Interview with Rich Ward on December 24, 2006

28. Adam Barndt, "Former terrorist Shoebat polarizes UWM audience," *The UWM Post*, December 10, 2007; link is http://www.uwm post.com/2007/12/10/former-terrorist-shoebat-polarizes-uwm-audience/

29. UWM Conservatives, "Walid Shoebat," *YouTube* Video, December 5, 2007; link is http://www.youtube.com/watch?v = VPAVsUkuHTA

30. Adam Barndt, "Former terrorist Shoebat polarizes UWM audience," The UWM Post, December 10, 2007; link is http://www.uwm post.com/2007/12/10/former-terrorist-shoebat-polarizes-uwm-audience/

31. Walid Shoebat, "From Terror to Truth," Speech at the University of Wisconsin-Milwaukee, Vimeo, December 4, 2007; link is http://vimeo.com/4154910

32. Ben Barrack Show, "Let's Talk About Something Important," Interview with Walid Shoebat on December 12, 2007

33. Discover the Networks, "Muslim Students Association," 2010; link is http://www.discoverthenetworks.org/printgroupProfile.asp?gr pid = 6175

34. Interview with Zakaryia Ezzat on November 3, 2010

35. Joshua Banta, "Walib Shoebat vs. Humboldt State University," *North Coast*, February 20, 2009; link is http://www.indybay.org/newsite ms/2009/02/20/18572106.php

36. Ben Barrack Show, "Let's Talk About Something Important," Interview with Walid Shoebat on February 22, 2009

37. Ibid

38. Christopher Hedges, "The War Against Tolerance," Truthdig, February 11, 2008; link is http://www.truthdig.com/report/item/ 20080211_the_war_against_tolerance/#Richard

39. Ben Barrack Show, "Let's Talk About Something Important," February 22, 2009

40. Christopher Hedges, "The War Against Tolerance," Ibid

41. Jorg Luyken, "The Palestinian 'terrorist' turned Zionist," *Jerusalem Post*, March 30, 2008; link is http://www.jpost.com/Home/Article. aspx?id = 96502

42. Arabic web page dedicated to Mahmoud al-Mughrabi; link is http://www.moghrabi-jerusalem.com/shohdaaa/mahmoud.htm

43. Arabic website carrying video news report from Al-Jazeera; link is http://rachedarfaoui.over-blog.com/article-36803579.html

44. "Operation 'Wooden leg,'" *Israeli Air Force* website; link is http://www.iaf.org.il/4694-33087-en/IAF.aspx

45. United Nations General Assembly, Thirty-second session, "Question of Palestine," page 26, July 5, 1977; link is http://unispal.un.org/pdfs/A32132.pdf

46. Edward Said and Christopher Hitchens, "Blaming the Victims,"p. 100, Verso Publisher, September 13, 2001

47. Quote from Shoebat via email correspondence, September 24, 2010

48. Jorg Luyken, "The Palestinian 'terrorist' turned Zionist," Ibid

49. Ibid

50. United Nations General Assembly, "Report of the Special Committee to Investigate Israel Practices Affecting the Human Rights of the Population of the Occupied Territories," A/33/356, Thirty-third session, Agenda item 55, November 13, 1978; link is http://unispal.un.org/UNISPAL.NSF/0/1751DB3DFEC8CA06052565AE006EEBEC

51. Religions, "Muslim Spain (711-1492)," BBC, Last updated on 2009-09-04; link is http://www.bbc.co.uk/religion/religions/islam/history/spain_1.shtml

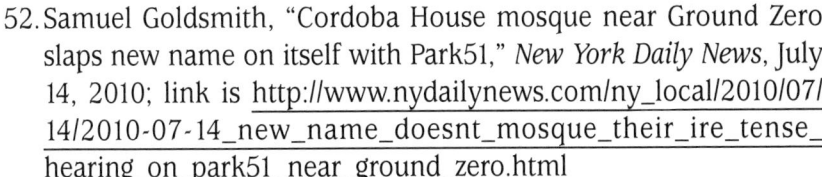
52. Samuel Goldsmith, "Cordoba House mosque near Ground Zero slaps new name on itself with Park51," *New York Daily News*, July 14, 2010; link is http://www.nydailynews.com/ny_local/2010/07/14/2010-07-14_new_name_doesnt_mosque_their_ire_tense_hearing_on_park51_near_ground_zero.html

53. "Ground Zero Imam Rauf's shocking statement made after 9/11 attacks (translated from Arabic)," *Web Today*, August, 2010; link is http://888webtoday.com/articles/viewnews.cgi?id = EklEZpVAFFUpDupZpE

54. "9/11 Mosque Imam Wrote Much of the Guts of Obama's Historic Cairo Speech!" *Web Today*, August 24, 2010; link is http://888webtoday.com/articles/viewnews.cgi?id = EklkyAFAFVxHELEDIJ

55. Fox & Friends, *Fox News Channel*, Interview with Dana Perrino and Brian Kilmeade, August 23, 2010; link is http://video.foxnews.com/v/4318040/imams-taxpayer-funded-mideast-tour/

56. O'Reilly Factor, *Fox News Channel*, Laura Ingraham guest host of debate between Walid Shoebat and Barry Lynn, August 27, 2010; link is http://www.youtube.com/watch?v = 9458_udInSk&feature = player_embedded#!

57. Brent Baker, "CBS Uses Opposition to Ground Zero Mosque to Lecture About 'America Becoming Islamophobic,'" Media Research Center, August 26, 2010: link is http://www.mrc.org/biasalert/2010/20100826090731.aspx

58. Paul Vitello, "Amid Rift, Imam's Role in Islam Center Is Sharply Cut," *New York Times*, January 14, 2011; link is http://www.nytimes.com/2011/01/15/nyregion/15mosque.html

59. Aaron Klein, "Ground Zero imam: 'Apostates against Islam must be jailed,'" *World Net Daily*, January 23, 2011; link is http://www.wnd.com/index.php?fa = PAGE.view&pageId = 254789

60. Walid Shoebat, "The Mosab Yousef Saga: Did Hamas 'Defector' Dupe All of Us?" *Pajamas Media*, May 5, 2011; link is http://pajamas media.com/blog/the-mosab-yousef-saga-did-hamas-'defector'-dupe-all-of-us/?singlepage = true

61. Ibid

62. Ibid

63. Timothy Stenovec, "Huma Abedin: Biography of Anthony Weiner's Wife," *The Huffington Post*, June 7, 2011; link is http://www.huffin gtonpost.com/2011/06/07/huma-abedin-pictures_n_872537. html#s288677

64. "The 'Sisterhood' List and It's Defined Goals," June 13, 2011; link is http://www.shoebat.com/blog/archives/1202

65. Oxford Centre for Islamic Studies, Director and Fellows; link is http://www.oxcis.ac.uk/fellows.html

66. Jorgen S. Nielsen, "Contemporary Discussions on Minorities in Islam," Brigham Young University Law Review, June 6, 2002, p. 366; link is http://lawreview.byu.edu/archives/2002/2/Nie8.pdf

67. Cliff Kincaid, "Is the FBI Investigating Obama?" Accuracy in Media, June 22, 2011; lin is http://www.aim.org/aim-column/is-the-fbi-investigating-obama/

68. Institute of Muslim Minority Affairs, Editorial Board; link is http://www.imma.org.uk/editorialboard.htm

69. Jennifer Gould Keil, "Huma Abedin taking time off from Weiner, job," *New York Post*, June 30, 2011; link is http://www.nypost.com/p/news/local/brooklyn/premature_evacuation_SvQwcvAcIT2eSF5 eg4htIN

70. Josh Margolin, Brigitte Stelzer, and Dan Mangan, "Weiner in therapy; says hard part will be convincing Hillary Clinton he's recovered," *New York Post*, July 22, 2011; link is http://www.ny post.com/p/news/local/brooklyn/weiner_is_facing_hilluva_dilemma _fARecuQmlbXsVpzca6ruDK

71. Drew Griffin and Kathleen Johnston, "'Ex-terrorist' rakes in homeland security bucks," *CNN U.S.*, July 13, 2011; link is http://articles.cnn.com/2011-07-11/us/terrorism.expert_1_walid-shoebat-israeli-police-homeland-security?_s = PM:US

72. Walid Shoebat website, "CNN Smear Campaign – the Missing Facts: What Anderson Cooper did not know," July 14, 2011; link is http://www.shoebat.com/documents/cnn_smear2.htm

73. Ibid

74. Tony Perry, "Marine gets no jail time in killing of 24 Iraqi civilians," Los Angeles Times, January 25, 2012; link is http://articles.latimes.com/2012/jan/25/local/la-me-haditha-20120125

75. "CNN Anchor Distorts National Review Quote in Interview With Sarah Palin," *Fox News*, October 23, 2008; link is http://www.foxnews.com/story/0,2933,443801,00.html

76. Walid Shoebat website, "CNN Smear Campaign," Ibid

77. Michelle Malkin, "Nidal Hasan's calling card explained," November 9, 2009; link is http://michellemalkin.com/2009/11/09/nidal-hasans-calling-card-explained/

78. *Fox News Channel*, Exchange between anchor Shepard Smith and U.S. Senator Kay Bailey Hutchison, November 5, 2009.

79. George Stephanopoulos, "Ft. Hood: Gen. Casey Doesn't Rule Out Terrorism," *ABC News*, November 8, 2009; link is http://blogs.abcnews.com/george/2009/11/ft-hood-gen-casey-doesnt-rule-out-terrorism.html

80. Muslim Brotherhood, Tell the Children the Truth; link is http://tellthechildrenthetruth.com/mbhood_en.html#part1

81. Mustafa Kemal Atatürk, "The founder of the Turkish Republic and its first President," 1881-1938; link is http://www.ataturk.com/content/view/12/26/

82. "Does Prime Minister Erdoğan Accept Turkish Secularism?" *Middle East Quarterly*, Spring 2007, pp. 89-90; link is http://www.meforum. org/1672/does-prime-minister-erdogan-accept-turkish-secularism

83. "Profile: Recep Tayyip Erdoğan," *BBC*, July 18, 2007; link is http:// news.bbc.co.uk/2/hi/europe/6900616.stm

84. "Turkey's charismatic pro-Islamic leader," *BBC*, November 4, 2002; link is http://news.bbc.co.uk/2/hi/europe/2270642.stm

85. "Profile: Abdullah Gul," *BBC*, August 28, 2007, link is http://news. bbc.co.uk/2/hi/europe/6595511.stm

86. Michael Carl, "Surprise! Guess who's biggest Islamic threat: Terror experts's warning cites this NATO member," *World Net Daily*, March 12, 2010; link is http://www.wnd.com/?pageId = 127521

87. "Diplomatic Cables Reveal US Doubts about Turkey's Government," *Der Spiegel*, November 28, 2010; link is http://www.spiegel.de/international/world/0,1518,731590,00.html

88. CAIR-South Florida hires new Executive Director, CAIR Florida, Press Release, December 6, 2010; link is http://fl.cair.com/sfl/Articles.aspx?cid = 4&aid = 3454

89. New King James Bible, Daniel 11:36-39; link is http://www.bible gateway.com/passage/?search = Daniel % 2011:36-39&version = NKJV

90. The Worldwide Christian Center, Sunday Worship Service, Guest Speaker: Walid Shoebat, March 13, 2011; link is http://www.twwcc.org/

91. "Historic Figures: Winston Churchill (1874 – 1965), *BBC*, Undated; link is http://www.bbc.co.uk/history/historic_figures/churchill_winston.shtml

92. Winston Churchill, "The River War," First edition, Vol. II, pp. 248-250, London: Longmans, Green 1899

93. Letter from Michelel Bachmann, Louie Gohmert, Lynn Westmore-
land, Trend Franks, and Thomas Rooney to Ambassador Harold W.
Geisel, Deputy Inspector General, Department of State, June 13,
2012; http://bachmann.house.gov/uploadedfiles/ig_letter_dept_of_
state.pdf

## Epilogue

1. Edmund Burke, "Thoughts on the Cause of the Present Discon-
tents," London, Printed for J. Dodsley in Pall-Mall, 1770, p. 106; link
is  http://books.google.co.uk/books?id = kbouAAAAMAAJ&pg = PA
106#v = onepage&q&f = false

# INDEX